Richard Ingrams

Also by Harry Thompson

Tintin
The Man in the Iron Mask

Richard Ingrams
Lord of the Gnomes

HARRY THOMPSON

HEINEMANN : LONDON

First published in Great Britain 1994
by William Heinemann Ltd
an imprint of Reed Consumer Books Ltd
Michelin House, 81 Fulham Road, London SW3 6RB
and Auckland, Melbourne, Singapore and Toronto

A CIP catalogue record for this book
is available at the British Library
ISBN 0 434 77828 1

Typeset by Falcon Graphic Art Ltd
Wallington, Surrey
Printed and bound in Great Britain
by Clays Ltd., St Ives Plc.

Contents

Acknowledgements

As I am unable to master a typewriter, let alone a word processor, many, many thanks must go to Michele Kimber and Eva Jensen for typing the manuscript of this saga. Thanks must go too to my father Gordon Thompson, for all his help with the research. It would be ungracious of me not to make special mention of Patrick Marnham, whose official history of *Private Eye*'s first two decades was quite invaluable as source material.

I would also like to thank the following for their kind assistance: Naim Attallah; Norman Balon; Vincent Beasley; Alec Binney; Deborah Bosley; David Cash; Jonathan Cecil; Michael Charlesworth; Peter Cook; Alan Coren; Nigel Dempster; Fiona Douglas-Home; Jack Duncan; Liz Elliot; John Ellis; Jane Ellison; Barry Fantoni; Tessa Fantoni; Paul Foot; David Ford; Jubby Ford; Paul Halloran; Bill Hamilton; Sarah Hannigan; Ian Hislop; R.C. Ingram; Fred Ingrams; Leonard Ingrams; Sarah-Jane Ingrams; Victoria Ingrams; Lawrence LeQuesne; Diane Lester; Christopher Logue; Hilary Lowinger; Maggie Lunn; Candida Lycett Green; Peter McKay; Sheila Molnar; Andrew Osmond; Sir Alexander Reid; John Richards; Tony Rushton; Willie Rushton; Christopher Silvester; Bill Tidy; Barry Took; Peter Usborne; Auberon Waugh; John Wells; my wife Fiona and, of course, Richard Ingrams himself.

Both Mary Ingrams and Christopher Booker preferred not to be involved in this book. Their stories have had to be told largely by other people; if they feel that they have been under-represented as a result, I can only apologise.

One of Ingrams' great heroes, Hesketh Pearson, said that 'The majority of reliable biographies are unreadable and the majority of readable biographies are unreliable'. It is my fervent hope, therefore, that this book will be unreadable in the first instance and unreliable in the second.

Prologue

I first met Richard Ingrams in 1980, when I was a student journalist. An errant clergyman at one of the Oxford colleges had managed the extraordinary triple feat of molesting a number of small choirboys, raking off the proceeds from souvenir sales, and disguising a German Nazi as a visiting cleric in order to pursue a homosexual affair with him in a room off the cloisters. Mindful of possible scandal, the college authorities proposed to do nothing. 'I know it's true and you know it's true,' hissed the Dean down the telephone at our news editor, 'and if you print one word of it, you'll be finished at this university, all of you.' Ah, the good old British sense of truth and justice. Burning with outrage, we contacted the national press.

The Dean soon made short work of the reporter from the *People*, who emerged from their little chat bathed in sweat, with the air of a man who's just gone twelve rounds with Mrs Thatcher in a Turkish bath. 'Don't touch it, sonny,' he gasped. 'They've got it sewn up. You haven't got the proof to make it stand up in court.' Richard Ingrams needed no such assurances. He knew it was true. He didn't even need to hear the evidence. He could just feel it in his bones. *Private Eye* went ahead and printed the story, and in due course the clergyman and his Teutonic plaything were put gloriously to flight.

A few weeks later, I was summoned to London for an audience with the great man. I made my way to Soho, climbed the rickety stairs to his office, was ushered into his presence, and

1

Richard Ingrams

jumped – as did all first-time visitors – on catching sight of the life-sized cardboard cut-out of Sir James Goldsmith behind the door. Ingrams leaned forward and spoke, picking his words with care. He had enjoyed my piece, he explained. Most entertaining. Obviously I would be leaving Oxford soon, and looking for some sort of employment. Did I have anything in mind? *Good heavens*, I thought, *he's offering me a job.* I fingered my tie nervously. Yes, I was keen to get into journalism, I ventured, but nothing too serious . . . perhaps a job on some sort of satirical publication, if one would have me . . . ? His granite visage failed noticeably to flicker. Had I received any firm offers to date? Yes, I said, from the BBC and the *Daily Mirror*. Good, he said. Whichever one of those you decide to accept, do keep sending in stories, won't you? He leaned back. That was it. The audience was over. Brief though our meeting had been, I sensed, somehow, that I had been in the presence of a remarkable man. A powerful man. A man who had just completely wasted a second-class rail fare from Oxford.

A few years later, while working as a producer at BBC Radio Comedy, I was given charge of *The News Quiz*, a topical panel game on which Alan Coren sparkled along with very few others, and persuaded Ingrams to join up as regular opposing team captain to give Coren a run for his money. Subsequently, a curious thing happened. The more I saw of Ingrams, the less I seemed to know of him, the less there was to grasp. As I saw more of his friends and colleagues, I realised that I was not alone in this perception. One who worked alongside him for many years told me:

'You know how certain people have a charisma which so fascinates others, that they endlessly discuss the minutiae of that person's behaviour? Richard was like that. If he wasn't there, and *Private Eye* people gathered, nobody would talk about anything else except Richard. Why was he like he was? What were his parents like? What was his marriage really like? Would he ever leave his wife? The speculation was endless, but he never revealed an inch.' An enigma, then, yet one who managed to command a remarkable degree of loyalty from his troops.

This was a man who launched a ferocious assault on the

2

political establishment not from behind a beard or a banner but a
Berkshire church organ; who admits to personal cowardice, and
yet who stood alone against Goldsmith and Maxwell, and whose
magazine brought down the likes of Profumo and Thorpe; who
has been described as 'a saint' by Candida Lycett Green, and 'evil'
by Desmond Wilcox; who for many years attacked others from
a position of unassailable personal morality, yet whose marriage
collapsed and who now, by his own wry admission, lives happily
'in sin'; who edits a magazine for oldies, but who is invariably
surrounded by younger fans and followers. I attended an Ingrams
party that was gatecrashed by the lead singer of Pink Floyd,
Dave Gilmour. Ingrams had never heard of Pink Floyd. 'Are you
by any chance related to Sir Ian Gilmour?' he pondered, as the
singer joined in a typically sausage-fingered Ingrams rendering of
'Jerusalem' at the piano. It was an extraordinary sight.

His life, it would seem, has more than its fair share of
contradictions. After all these years, his friends still regard him
as a mystery. 'You'll never get to the bottom of Ingrams,' said
Coren, taking me to one side. 'There isn't a bottom to get to,'
smiled Ingrams. Well, we shall see.

1 The Flying Banker

If any individual's character could be said to derive in equal measure from his mother and his father, then that individual is Richard Ingrams. Leonard St Clair Ingrams OBE made his name as a brilliant financier. He was one of those commanding pre-war figures who combined breeding, good looks, intelligence and sporting prowess in abundance, the kind of chap that would periodically have been offered the throne of Albania. He was one of Britain's foremost long-jumpers, and made the squad for the *Chariots of Fire* Olympics in 1924. On family holidays by the seaside he showed no inclination to run in slow motion through the shallows, but his athleticism did take the form of spectacular double somersaults and backflips into the sea, to the mild embarrassment of his loved ones.

At work Leonard was nicknamed 'the flying banker' because he travelled everywhere on business in his private plane, especially between Britain and Germany; as a young man, he flew between the towers of Munich cathedral. More than once he barely escaped with his life from a tangle of canvas and wire. Leonard was urbane, witty and charming, and women found him irresistible. Jean Cocteau, who met him at Oxford, was similarly impressed, and inserted him, thinly disguised, into one of his novels. Young and old were captivated. He proffered his twelve-year-old nephew Sandy – now Sir Alexander Reid – his first gin and lime, with the hint of a smile and the tongue-in-cheek confidence, 'Now let's have a secret drink, shall we?'; and Sandy went away feeling terribly grand and grown-up. That's the effect Leonard had on people.

His brother Harold Ingrams was, perhaps, an even more exciting figure; a latter-day Lawrence of Arabia, he lived for fifteen years among the Bedouin of the Hadramaut, finally bringing 1500 tribes together in 1937 to the sign the 'Ingrams Peace', which ensured long-term stability in the area. He later settled down with his wife Doreen in Stoke, where they dressed as Bedouin, conversed daily in fluent Arabic, and brought long-term instability to their neighbourhood, before eventually splitting up.

Yet for all his panache, Leonard was not the life and soul of every party. His wit was quiet and sardonic rather than cheerful, concealing a melancholy side to his character. He came from a long line of strongly protestant schoolmasters and orthodox clergymen, and he shared their Victorian formality. This made him a remote, intolerant parent who kept an emotional distance from his family. Meanwhile, he transferred his captivating affections from woman to woman rather too easily; his first marriage, to a budding Hollywood starlet named June Dunham, had disintegrated in mutual rancour. He was a combative man, who liked to win, be it in his professional or his personal life.

In the banking world, this attitude had won Leonard Ingrams his fortune. Possessed, according to one anonymous newspaper columnist, of 'a perfect poker face, a salty wit and a shrewd financial brain', he had quickly abandoned a fledgling accounting career with Cooper's to go and work for the Chemical Bank in Germany, leaving his family behind in Blighty with few qualms. Then, with the advent of war in 1939, Leonard took a clever gamble. A number of the London banks were owed huge sums of money by their counterparts in the newly-occupied German territories, debts which now might never be paid off. Leonard offered to buy these debts for 10 per cent of their value, payable not in cash but in the form of shares in his company, an issue which was apparently limitless. In 1945 it was officially decreed that all such pre-war debts were to be paid back in full. Thus was the value of Leonard's company multiplied by ten at the stroke of a pen.

After the war it was Leonard who was employing Cooper's

6

and not the other way round. Their auditor, coincidentally named Ingram, remembers Leonard's brief visits to London as nerve-racking affairs. 'Ingrams was an imposing figure; physically, much taller than my six foot and with a massive head. Less visible but more worrying was a powerful intellect and incredible speed of thought. He must have considered me a total idiot . . . His financial transactions were ingenious. Shake the dust off any list and lurking beneath would be a highly complex transaction.'

There is a fine line between confidence and arrogance which Leonard Ingrams strode alongside, without crossing. Richard, who has inherited his father's wit and intelligence, walks the same path. He also inherited his father's good looks and charm, his capacity for inscrutable silences, his melancholy interior and some of his emotional reticence.

The shiny contours of Leonard Ingrams' glittering career took something of a dent in recent years, when a biography of Kim Philby appeared containing a snapshot taken at an Anglo-German Fellowship dinner in the 1930s. This was an organisation at which Anglos such as Unity Mitford practised fellowship with Germans of the Ribbentrop variety, at tables bedecked with little swastikas. Kim Philby, as a member of two separate intelligence services, had an excellent excuse for being among the throng. Leonard and his wife Victoria, it has been suggested, might have struggled to find as good a reason for being pictured next to him.

For Victoria, the visit to the Fellowship was mystifying. 'London was swarming with Germans just before the war and we had an awful lot of Germans in the house and a lot of German friends. Leonard made me go with him to the Anglo-German Fellowship meeting where Ribbentrop spoke – he seemed all for it. Once the war broke, he was completely the other way. Quite extraordinary. I never could understand the man at all. But of course, I couldn't express my opinions either. For my part, directly Hitler had gone and murdered Ernst Roehm, I couldn't even bear to think of him any more.'

Leonard, of course, never discussed his politics with his family. Confusing, then, that he should turn up once again in connection with the Nazis, only this time in a rather different capacity – as part of Hitler's personal death list of his least favourite Britons. Richard Ingrams fondly hopes that his father was working for British Intelligence all along. Certainly, he was working for them once the war got under way; turned down as a fighter pilot on grounds of age, he masterminded black propaganda at the Ministry of Economic Warfare, where he enjoyed close links with the SOE and SIS. Leonard worked alongside another old Berlin hand, his great friend Sefton Delmer, head of the Political Warfare Executive. Delmer's patriotic credentials are unimpeachable, and yet he too had been thick with the most unpleasant National Socialists; the first man into the Reichstag after the fire and an acquaintance of Adolf Hitler, Delmer could pop round and visit the Fuehrer at any time he wanted, and address him on jovial first-name terms ('Adolf?' 'Ah, Sefton.' There could be no odder three-word conversation). Delmer later paid tribute to Leonard Ingrams' work for British Intelligence: 'He looked the part of the mysterious Mr X to perfection. He was tall and athletic . . . and his eyes and mouth had just the right expression of drawling sardonic pity for the world around him.'[1]

It is doubtful whether anybody will ever unravel the labyrinthine logic behind Leonard's wartime schemes – poison pen letters in old ladies' handwriting, written in violet ink and smuggled across the Pyrenees from Lisbon; seditious new year cards posted to Germany from Stockholm; bogus bank account details supplied for a dead Hungarian financier. Less obscurely, he did set up a radio station broadcasting a convincing mixture of news and lies to Germany. There already was such a station, run by future Labour government minister Richard Crossman, but Crossman's effort contented itself with half-wittedly pumping out knee-jerk political propaganda. 'Ingrams expressed his complete contempt for Crossman's station, with its appeals to the workers to shake off the fascist yoke and all that stuff,' wrote his colleague Ellic Howe.[2] Leonard mixed his lies with real secrets, daringly culled from his other work, to lend an air of plausibility to station GS(E)-1. 'But what did those cabalistic initials signify?' asked Howe. 'Geheimsender 1 (Secret transmitter 1)? or perhaps Generalstaß 1 (General Staff 1)? Ingrams sardonically suggested that Gurkensalat 1 (Cucumber Salad 1) was the probable answer.'[3]

Leonard's family knew nothing of his work, as they knew so little of his life away from home. All they knew were the domestic radio broadcasts and *Listener* articles, bravely reassuring the populace that Germany only had three months' supply of linseed oil left, and so forth. They never knew, for instance, that Leonard had been sent by the Foreign Office to Nuremburg, to interrogate Goering and the other members of the Nazi hierarchy prior to the warcrimes trials there (Ribbentrop, he told friends contemptuously, was 'a cringer').

In retrospect, it is unlikely that Leonard Ingrams could have been unpatriotic enough to have been an out-and-out Nazi. Equally, it is unlikely that he was involved in intelligence work before the war – some evidence of it would surely have emerged. Leonard's banking work depended on the goodwill of the German government, of whatever hue, so it seems probable that he was merely doing his best to keep them sweet. A word to his wife would have helped, though. The young Richard may have wondered, for instance, why Hitler's former foreign press chief Dr Ernst F. Hänfstängel was sending him birthday cards, addressed to 'wild-eyed Richard'.

Leonard Ingrams, so used to taking on the world and winning, failed completely to subjugate only one major adversary in life – his wife. Victoria Reid came from a more obviously patrician background than he. Whereas Leonard's upbringing was Victorian in the moral sense, in her case it was literal: her father Sir James Reid had been Queen Victoria's personal physician and confidant, and her mother Susan a Royal Maid of Honour. Their family home, at Ellon in Aberdeenshire, was a trinket-filled mausoleum to the late Queen, every horizontal surface a thicket of engraved crests, silver photo-frames, brooches containing lockets of hair, horses' hoof inkstands, anything that might tenuously be linked to the royal personage. Long after her death, the old Queen seemed to reach down and hold the Reid family in her antiquated thrall.

With the exception of Prince Albert and her beloved ghillie John Brown, Sir James Reid had been the most important man in Queen Victoria's life, a friend to whom she unburdened her heart. 'I am told Gladstone's voice is nearly gone,' she informed him with feeling. 'I only hope it will go altogether.' Yet despite her devotion to this faithful ally, the snob in her did not approve of his marriage to Susan Baring (whose brother was a Lord), particularly as James, at fifty, was many years Susan's senior. When Victoria heard the news that they were engaged to be married, she summoned James to give him a stern dressing-down. He ensured her that it wouldn't happen again – quite a brave joke to make in the circumstances. The Queen retaliated by interrupting their honeymoon at frequent intervals, with bulletins concerning her bowel movements: 'BOWELS ARE WORKING FULLY STOP'. Susan later described how the Queen had 'died in my Jamie's arms, and her last words were that she would do anything he liked'; while her relative the Kaiser watched from the other side of the bed, no doubt dreaming of an unprotected Belgium. It was, incredibly, only in death that the royal doctor saw his patient undressed for the first time, so prudish had the old lady been. At her request, he put a picture of John Brown and a lock of Brown's hair into her coffin.

Sir James went on to name his only daughter Victoria Susan Beatrice, after his Queen, his wife and his mother, in that order of importance. To Victoria, her father seemed a distant figure, old, whiskery and remote, stern-faced behind a bushy moustache and pince-nez. His handkerchief was usually dirty and his flies often undone, she noticed, a tendency to ignore the sartorial that his grandson has directly inherited. Other figures were to become more influential in Victoria's life than her elderly father: her mother's brother, the writer Maurice Baring, and Tatiana, her own brother Ned's glamorous Russian émigrée wife. Her two brothers dutifully followed their father into establishment pillarhood – Sir Edward Reid becoming a banker and Sir Peter a Third Sea Lord – but a wayward, rebellious streak soon revealed itself behind Victoria's quiet, well-bred exterior. She was still only a child when her bedroom door mysteriously painted itself bright red in the night.

Victoria was the sort to pitch in and do things regardless of the social consequences, and upon reaching adulthood she

offended her family's sense of propriety by signing up as a
nurse – following the example of Tatiana, when she had first
come to Britain. During the Blitz Victoria donned a tin helmet
and got stuck into the rubble with relish. 'The daylight raids were
quite fun. When they came into your own street and polished off
people you knew it was tremendously exciting,' she recalls with
vestigial bright-eyed pluck. Above all she had no time for the sacred
dust-gathering memory of Queen Victoria; it was music that moved
her, more than anything else. At St Paul's School for girls she had
been taught by Gustav Holst, who had fired her emotions in a way
that her father never could.

What rankled with her family most of all, however, was
her decision – taken as a young nurse in 1932 – to convert
to Catholicism. In part she was acting under the influence of
Maurice Baring, himself a convert, in part she was struck by
the added fortitude with which Catholic patients withstood pain
in the dreadful conditions at St Thomas' Hospital, and in part
she was consciously rebelling at the complacent Protestantism
of her brothers Ned and Peter. Victoria embraced Catholicism
with characteristically fervent enthusiasm, becoming a determined
religious terrorist working to undermine the stolidly Presbyterian
bulwarks of Reid family life. One victim was the garage, from
which all cars were evicted so that it could be consecrated as
a Roman Catholic chapel. 'They were very cross *indeed* about
that garage,' recalls Ned's son Sandy. Ned and Peter wanted her
out, and drove their cars up the aisle. Susan, who got on well
with her daughter and thought cars rather modern and frightful,
let the chapel stay. When Susan finally died, and Ned inherited
the garage, Victoria gave him £500 to go away. The garage was
recently the subject of a learned academic pamphlet, written by
Victoria sixty years on.

In 1934, Leonard Ingrams, dashing, brilliant, athletic, charming
and strong-willed, and Victoria Reid, clever, sweet-looking, fiercely independent and equally strong-willed, swam into each other's
orbit. Each was instantly captivated. Each brought down the full
weight of family hostility on the other. Victoria's Catholicism horrified his devoutly Protestant father the Reverend William Ingrams;

11

and Leonard was divorced with a son to his name, which didn't go down a bundle with the Reids. Each family looked down on the other's representative. It only made Victoria and Leonard more determined to go ahead with their union, and they wed in May 1935.

It was a marriage made in heaven – but whose heaven? She was a Catholic, and a fighting one at that; he detested Catholicism with a hardened prejudice that probably owed its origins to the Glorious Revolution. On paper, the match should have been an unhappy one; but like many pairings that appear unhappy on paper, the reality was different. It was far worse. 'I was absolutely besotted by him,' remembers Victoria. 'He was a man who cast a spell. There are such men; and it happened to every woman he looked at. I saw it again and again, if it didn't happen I wondered what was wrong. He would cast such a spell you'd give up everything to go after him. I was such a retarded fool.' She did indeed give up a lot for him. For marrying a divorced man she was excommunicated by the church, an indignity she stoutly ignored.

Even before the end of their honeymoon, they were throwing books at each other. The constant separations, in peacetime and in war, made matters worse. 'He never spoke about anything he did – his work was hush-hush. It has a bad effect on you if you're working out evil all the time. You become a bit evil yourself. He was never the same after the war.' As relations deteriorated swiftly from those first heady months, Leonard abused and ridiculed Victoria and her beliefs. He bragged about having any and every woman he wanted. He may have been an extraordinary man, but in truth, sadly, he was not much of a husband.

Victoria resisted him impassively. From her, Richard has inherited his stubbornness, his rebelliousness, his refusal to conform or give in, his love of music, his dislike of marital infidelity, and – although not a Catholic himself – his affection for Catholicism and its traditions. He admits: 'I've always had the feeling, because of my mother's influence, that Catholicism was sort of the "proper" religion, and other people were just playing at it.' His own religion, his father's Protestantism, has

12

drifted further away from his heart.

Leonard Ingrams made the mistake of confusing his wife's acceptance of his dictates with acquiescence; but it was nothing of the sort. Victoria it was who won the battle for the hearts and minds of her sons, a battle they didn't even know was taking place. When Leonard died of a heart attack, eight years after the war, he died an emotional stranger to his own children.

2 Four Brothers

Leonard and Victoria's eldest child was Peter John – P J for short – born in February 1936, precisely nine months after the wedding. P J was cool, confident, unquestionably a leader. He also had a wild streak, which invariably lent that essential dash of risk to the escapades he led his brothers into. When Victoria took her four boys to visit Lady Fisher, who lived on the fifth floor at Hampton Court, their polite conversation was interrupted by the blasts of police whistles from the gardens outside. There, strung out in mountaineering formation across the sloping roof of the palace, were four small Ingramses, with P J in the lead. P J liked his mountaineering, and royal security, it seems, was operating at its usual level. He was a strong boy, a good athlete, academically determined, with a wilful, dominating, reckless personality; 'All his life, he thought he could do things that nobody else could do,' recalls Victoria. There was a lot of his father about P J.

Richard – Ditch – came next, in August 1937; Ditch, because that was the closest P J could get to pronouncing his name when he was born. Ditch was the most well-behaved and obliging of the Ingrams boys, the one who always stopped to help his mother with the washing-up while the others disappeared. His infant school teacher described him as 'One of the nicest pupils I have ever had in my class . . . so willing and so eager to do his very best in everything.' Victims of the satirical scourge of British society may care to know that as a small child he wore a dress, and possessed a white teddy bear called Fluffy. Like his brothers, Richard inherited his mother's musical abilities; indeed, according to Victoria, he could sing long before he could speak, a skill he did not pick up until he was three. Of course, a mother's judgement of what actually constitutes singing may differ from that of others. Frederick Sharp, who lived next door, wrote to her when Richard was two:

Dear Madam,
I should be extremely obliged if you could do something to quieten your crying baby. I have suffered from it for considerably over a year now and it is driving me distracted. Today for example it cried almost incessantly from 4 p.m. till after 6 p.m.

Once he'd got the hang of speaking rather than singing, Ditch grew up into a large, kind, amusing, and consistently scruffy boy with a talent for impressions. His ambition was to be a pilot like his father, but of all the brothers he was the one whose character most resembled his mother's. Perhaps – subconsciously – because of this, he was Leonard's favourite son.

Third was Rupert, who could charm his way out of the tightest corner. Hopeless with cash, lazy at school, the only one of the four not to go to university, it didn't matter with good looks like his. A frail, semi-invalid child with a weak heart, Rupert grew up into a dashing, handsome young man, with dark curls, a feminine mouth and a classic fondness for cars and girls. Instinctively debonair and polished, he had a definite touch of P J's irresponsibility in his make-up. Rupert was born in 1939, and Michael Ingrams – Leonard's son from his first marriage – wrote to his father from school to discuss what to call the new arrival: 'I cannot think of a name excep (*sic*) Theodorick and things like that. Why not call him Leonard?'

Adding the PS: 'I'm glad you think there will be no war. Our French master – like a lot of Frenchmen – is a downright pessimist and says there will be war inside two months.'

No doubt Leonard Ingrams had mistaken the air raid sirens being tested for Richard's singing.

Michael's suggestion was saved for the last of the brothers, who was born in 1941 after the now customary two-year interval. As the smallest of the four, Leonard junior enjoyed the youngest brother's usual combination of protection (in public) and persecution (in private) from his elders. He was usually the one tied to the totem pole by P J, while Richard was the one most likely to come and release him. 'He was very kind to me,' recalls Leonard, 'and he was the most amusing too.' Little Leonard was a jolly child who laughed loudly at Richard's jokes. As he grew older and found his own sunlight away from his brothers' shadow, he mellowed into a quiet, serious student of considerable academic brilliance, outstripping even Richard and P J in this respect; although he still retained his youthful high-pitched giggle. Crucially for his fortunes, he was the only one of the four to inherit his father's mastery of financial matters.

Home during wartime was 'The Chesnuts' in Ellon, some fifteen miles north of Aberdeen, the formerly tranquil Reid household, where the ghost of Sir James, were he to have walked the corridors, would probably have been bowled over by a gang of small boys charging round the corner in formation. In the walled garden they played bumble-puppy (whacking a tennis ball tied by a string to a tall pole). They played tenni-quoits (chucking a rubber quoit over a high net). They played with bows and arrows (almost fatally). P J led them all on hair-raising climbs up the nearby crags. Cricket was essential of course, which P J always won. Tree houses were built, and then there was the tree which accidentally burnt to the ground. All 'tremendous adventures', according to the younger Leonard's fond memory. There were brawls too. 'Any two of them got on very well,' says Victoria, 'but if there was a third then that was hopeless. It was a great misfortune not to have had a girl in the family.' On one occasion, in the course of being chased around the house by P J, Richard tripped and impaled himself on a large brass curtain hook. Doctor Wardrop, who lived next door, did the honours and eased his body off the offending projection; even in a wounded state Richard had his brothers in stitches with a perfect impression of the doctor's Aberdeen accent.

As if Ellon was not one long vacation already, the Easter holidays usually saw this mayhem visited on other hapless families.

Delia Peel, a relative with a large house in Norfolk, felt that her great-nephew Robert would benefit from having the Ingrams boys to stay, and so invited them for a holiday on the Broads. 'The Peels were a very high-hat family,' says Victoria, who likes to play down her own patrician background. 'Guns in the umbrella stand, that sort of thing.' Alas, the invitation was not repeated after Rupert appropriated one such mislaid air rifle and shot Robert Peel in the bottom.

Victoria had to learn to be severe over her boys' misdemeanours; it was no good saying 'wait until your father gets home', as in his case it would usually have taken several months. For the most part, however, her attitude was that of the fondly indulgent mother hen. She cooked, cleaned, washed-up after them and darned any curtain-hook rips in their clothes; unusually for the period, she let them sleep until lunchtime every day if they wanted; and she turned a blind eye at mealtimes to the volleys of flying foodstuffs that would never have been tolerated by her husband. Her only restriction was that radio Test match commentaries were banned from the dining-room table, a source of crushing regret to all the boys – Richard especially, who as a Middlesex supporter always hoped that Denis Compton would be among the runs.

Her loyalty to her brood was absolute, and remains so to this day. Those who attack Richard in print are still liable to receive fiercely protective letters from the old lady: 'Do not forget, when you abuse my son, that there is a mother tigress lurking in the background ready to pounce,' for example. Richard's love for his mother is as huge as his embarrassment at this correspondence is terminal. After Sandy Reid's wife wrote a biography of Sir James Reid,[1] drawing on the Doctor's diaries to show the full extent of the Queen's relationship with John Brown, Sandy found himself sitting at a lunch next to Princess Margaret, who subjected him to a tirade of vulgar abuse. Victoria promptly despatched a scorching letter to the impertinent Princess, demanding to know how she dare have the effrontery to be rude to a member of the Reid family.

Such actions, of course, are born not just from personal

self-belief, but from utter confidence in one's status and social standing. Victoria brought up her children to detest snobbery, and to stand outside class distinctions wherever possible, but patrician confidence radiates out from every member of her family in all their dealings. They have a keen sense of tradition, and an emotional need to defend their country against commercialism, corruption and ignorance. The Rt. Hon. Alan Clark would doubtless be reassured to discover that they have never once had to contemplate buying their own furniture.

The Chesnuts was not a big house, but it rambled in an acceptably capacious sort of way, large enough to hide small boys and their wrongdoings: 'a pleasant capacity for rough and tumble', as the younger Leonard puts it. When Victoria was not in London, falling bricks bouncing off her tin hat, she and her mother Susan would hold Red Cross parties, filling the drawing room with old ladies knitting socks for the troops on the Russian front. P J and Richard would hide behind the sofa for hours, so as to erupt into the room at precisely the most heart-stopping moment; whilst out in the wheatfields of the Ukraine, Russian soldiers died lonely deaths in the freezing mud, wearing bright woollen Scottish socks.

Everyone in the house bar the four boys was female: Susan, Victoria, the cook, two maids, and Madé, the French governess, who had previously been governess to the Queen Mother. Susan saw to supplementing the education the boys received at the local school, drumming the intricacies of classical music and French literature into their souls. French was often spoken at mealtimes when Susan was present. Victoria's brother Ned had bought Ellon Castle in 1925 and moved his family up there, but his son Sandy Reid would come down to the Chesnuts to be schooled *en français* with the Ingrams children. 'They were an extraordinary family,' he says. 'Rather exclusive. Rather unruly. But always so intelligent and aware.' Susan would sit and sing at the piano, surrounded by her heavy silver mementoes and her photographs of Sir James, who stared gloomily out at her from behind posed whiskers. It was a nineteenth-century upbringing, a slice of Victoriana frozen in the 1940s, almost as if the entire Ingrams family was one generation in arrears.

18

Then came 1945, and the collapse of the German nation in the face of manpower shortages, the overwhelming might of the allied armies and who knows what combination of financial skulduggery and poison-pen Christmas cards prepared by Leonard Ingrams. The love of his sons – or perhaps the regard of his sons – was extremely important to Leonard, and his absences during the war had lost him valuable ground. It was time to resume battle with Victoria, a battle he could never hope to win. The principal battleground chosen was, inevitably, religion. Victoria wanted her boys to be Catholics like her, Leonard wanted them to be Protestant. Many hurled and damaged books later, they came up with a bizarre compromise: the boys' religion would alternate, P J and Rupert to be Catholic, Richard and young Leonard Protestant.

Even once the deal had been struck, however, serious problems remained. With the exception of Victoria and Father Ronald Knox, who had taught him at school, Leonard wouldn't allow Catholics into the house. On this basis he actually proposed that P J be sent overseas until his education was complete, a suggestion which makes it easy to understand why he found the hearts and minds of his sons so elusive. A second problem was that Victoria cheated on the agreement from the word go, whipping the two Protestant boys off to be baptised as Catholics the moment his back was turned. Richard didn't find this out until 1989: 'The funny thing was, when reminded of it, I could very dimly remember it. I must have been about three or four at the time.'

Nevertheless, whenever Leonard was in London, he would troop off with Richard and Leonard junior to the Royal Hospital Church in Chelsea each Sunday, where they would respectfully observe the pensioners parading before an NCO with a feathered helmet, before filing in for the 11 a.m. service. Victoria, P J and Rupert, meanwhile, would set off in the other direction for mass – the one service a week allowed to them by Leonard. If there were any other services to be attended, then, says Victoria, 'we slipped quietly out of the back door and nothing was ever mentioned'. It was never a happy compromise, but the need to keep all arguments hidden from the children kept it alive. 'He

19

didn't hammer at me when the boys were there,' adds Victoria, 'because they would have stuck up for me.'

Although his parents presented this apparently convincing united front, Richard was already rather nervous of his father and sympathetic to his mother, whom he had intuitively identified as the underdog. Despite this, almost intangibly, he and his Protestant brother Leonard developed into slightly more level-headed adults than their two Catholic siblings, perhaps out of a subconscious feeling of conformity which P J and Rupert were able to eschew. 'We two were slightly more feet-on-the-ground,' says Leonard junior. Their father's influence certainly seems to have encompassed a degree of financial awareness: Victoria still keeps a bill from 1947 for weed-clearing, presented by 'R.R. and L.V. Ingrams'. R.R. claims 4d for two hundred weeds, L.V. claims 2d for one hundred, and both are prepared to negotiate a further unspecified sum for clearing the terrace.

Home in London was two elegant medium-sized Georgian terraced houses in Cheyne Row, with connecting doors knocked through on two floors. Leonard *père* had first leased, then purchased the original property (he expanded it himself) from the Baring family. Now, he found himself cast adrift in the Baring family milieu. Victoria and the boys sometimes spoke to each other in mysterious Baring family slang, using words like sixcloisters (nostalgic), Brahms (highbrow), gorgeriser (literally, something that made your gorge rise), Antrim boat (putting yourself out needlessly for someone, after a fishing trip once organised for the fish-hating Lord Antrim), and many others too obscure to define: lubie, floatface, entamer, shroudhouse and so on. Furthermore, Catholics seemed to abound in the area: Ronald Knox, who had become Victoria's confessor, was a frequent visitor, and the gloomy and oddly-named parish priest Father de Zulueta lived opposite. With his fiercely anti-Roman point of view, poor Leonard must have felt like a healthy man in a leper colony.

Unable or unwilling to spend much time in London getting to know his sons, he resorted instead to exporting his family *en bloc* to Germany for the holidays, to Chiemsee, Bad Homburg and Lake Constanz; but emotionally, they might as well have stayed at home. The lifestyle of the mainly American occupation forces merely opened their eyes to the luxuries they'd been missing, like Coca-Cola, television and the motor car. 'We never had a car,' explains Richard. 'My father was very old-fashioned. We never had a telly either – he was an ultra-traditionalist. He thought the telly was in some way *infra dig*, rather like the Sky dish is considered now.'

Holidays at home with Muv (as Victoria was known) were much more fun. There were outings to see Alastair Sim in *Peter Pan* at the Scala, Bertram Mills' circus, and *Hey Presto!* at the Westminster Theatre. There were always musical evenings too, Victoria and her boys forming a quintet, with Richard on cello. Ralph Vaughan Williams, who was known to the family, popped round once or twice. When Leonard did come home, everything was different. Life was sterner, tempers were shorter, there were rules to be observed. He tried to be popular with the boys, he tried so hard, but charm, wit, dazzling intelligence, such things are wasted on a man's own sons, who want someone to wrestle with and play cricket with for hours in the garden on long summer evenings.

Perhaps, when the Ingrams gang were stampeding through the corridors or roaming the crags at Ellon, it didn't matter too much that they barely had a father, what with Victoria and Susan there to wash their socks, get their meals ready on time, and to call the doctor when P J claimed another victim; but now, this cushy life was coming to an end. The gang was about to be broken up.

3 Onions and Chipped Enamel

'It seemed a very nice school,' says Victoria. 'They presented a very nice face to you . . . then they closed the door.' This was West Downs, in Winchester, chosen as a 'suitable' prep school for the Ingrams boys. It was the personal fiefdom of its headmaster Kenneth Tindall, a large, beetle-browed, dome-headed tyrant with a stooping neck whose heavily measured tread as he stalked the corridors, cane in hand, brought fear to any boy who heard it. 'He was rather too free with that cane,' recalled Lord Sherfield, a frequent victim.[1] When his cane was out of commission, he resorted to a size 13 slipper, administered over the side of a bath: 'The chipped enamel of the baths bears witness over forty years of where his enthusiasm had overstretched his aim,' wrote Mark Hichens, another alumnus.[2] 'He was an awful man,' decided Victoria, 'a great hulking type who was subject to furious book-throwing rages.' Must have reminded her of someone she knew.

Tindall was a devout classicist, who refused point-blank to allow any science whatsoever to be taught in the school, and hardly any literature or history either. Latin terminology was compulsory when describing the various parts of the school building; permission had to be sought to go to the *foricas*, for instance, where strict silence was to be observed when urinating. Tindall, nicknamed Guzzer – a corruption of geyser, as his foul temper was always blowing up – was Victorian to the core, and banned all modern fripperies such as sweets, the wireless and visits to

22

the cinema. All reading matter was censored, and no thrillers or comics were allowed, save of course the virtuous *Eagle*. Instead, school life was based around scouting and strict military discipline. Boys were organised into scout patrols (Owls, Eagles and so forth) and spent their lives saluting, parading, knot-tying, signalling, bandaging, basket-making, book-binding and running the animal ambulance, to the dismay of local animals.

The importance of obeying orders unquestioningly was drummed into every boy from his first day at school; West Downs boys educated by Tindall between the wars were killed in droves in World War Two, at a rate far exceeding those killed in World War One who had been educated under the previous headmaster. Several generals and admirals, even a field marshal and an Admiral of the Fleet, went to West Downs. The school also had a long tradition of turning out fascists – Sir Oswald Mosley went there, as did Julian Amery's brother, John, who was executed for treason after the war. Sir Peter Scott was another famous old boy; the dying Captain Scott had entered a paragraph in his polar diary imploring his sculptress wife Kathleen to send their son to a good school. Duped in much the same way as Mrs Ingrams, she had sent not only her son but a statue for the front garden of a naked boy, arm upraised, bearing the words 'Here am I, Send me'. Peter Scott always denied ferociously to his fellow pupils that the statue was meant to be him. Well he would, wouldn't he.

Tindall was obsessed with sporting prowess, promoting large, athletic boys within the hierarchy of the school and sparing little time for the weedier specimens. Older, bigger boys were given a virtual free hand in imposing discipline on their smaller juniors, by way of the 'Patrol Leaders' meeting', a sort of officially-sanctioned kangaroo court. Boxing was encouraged as another way of settling differences. Boys had to stand up for themselves in this intimidating atmosphere, and parental visits were frowned upon. Fraternisation with anyone outside the school was forbidden altogether – the local youths were referred to scornfully as 'guttergrubs'. Entertainment was negligible, and almost the only things to look forward to were the regular executions at Winchester prison just down the road, when the black flag flew and the other prisoners banged cans and cutlery as one of their number went to his death.

Clucking and fussing in the midst of this all-male Victorian preserve was Theodora, Tindall's wife, known as Tumty on account of her initials T.M.T. Well-intentioned, tireless, resourceful and a bit of a twit, she was the epitome of the jolly-hockey-sticks type, indeed she had even gone so far as to secure a hockey blue at Cambridge. Theodora wrote soothing and optimistic letters to parents even as their beloved little ones were being tortured with wet towels several floors below. During staff shortages, she had been known to wash-up the entire school's dinner plates in one go. Twice a day she took every boy's temperature and inspected every boy's head, before forcing malt and virol (whatever that was) down their throats. Theodora was frequently gripped by health fads. Following a lecture at the school by a famous Antarctic explorer who had outlined the bracing benefits of the polar climate, she became obsessed with the virtues of cold air, and insisted that all school windows were left wide open in the depths of winter. This was known to the boys as The Little Ice Age. She also took to hanging bags of raw onions about the school to ward off disease, following further expert advice. Visits to her sanatorium subsequently increased dramatically, as she spent much of her time treating high-velocity onion injuries.

Try to imagine Joyce Grenfell married to the Graham Sutherland portrait of Winston Churchill, and you will have a fairly accurate picture of Mr and Mrs Tindall and their bedside manner. By and large, their staff were not a great deal better. There was 'Griffin', the head of scouting, as described by Mark Hichens: 'With little time for airy-fairy notions and tortuous modern theories, "Griffin" believed in hard work, a well-ordered routine and a firm discipline.'[3] Now there's a surprise. Then there was W.J. Tremellen, the French master, a First World War fighter pilot with a wooden leg, who wore a beret and Royal Flying Corps tie. He had a novel way with linguistics, teaching boys the French word for 'never', for instance, by throttling them until they shouted *jamais!* Despite the beret, he was actually Scottish.

In short, West Downs was the very worst possible type

of prep school, remembered – as are all such places – with misleadingly rosy nostalgia by most of those who went there. Most, but not all.

P J, of course, adored it. He jumped right in at the deep end and quickly swam to the surface. 'He never really left, in a way,' remembers Richard. Which is not to say that Tindall adored P J, who was a little too cocky for his liking. 'Critical and aggressive, with annoying habits. I doubt if he bothers his head much about the good of the body corporate,' grumbled Tindall in his school report. P J was just coasting, though, and having a good time. When he finally left in 1949, he eased up a gear and passed the Shrewsbury scholarship exam without breaking stride, to the mixed chagrin and pleasure of Kenneth Tindall. 'We shall miss Peter John *tremendously*,' gushed Theodora.

Richard, by contrast, loathed and detested every brutal minute. When he arrived to join his elder brother in 1946, the school had recently returned home from its wartime evacuation at Blair Castle. The buildings were cold, empty and vandalised by the soldiers that had been billeted there, and the whole place smelled of paint. Only the chapel wasn't carved with initials and smeared with chalk, so Richard often found himself drifting there for comfort and solace, reinforcing the religious faith his mother had instilled in him. 'He is still rather solemn and quiet,' fretted Theodora just after his arrival, in a rare display of unease.

What Theodora had failed to spot, as indeed had Victoria, was that Richard had suffered a major shock to the system. For P J, the trustworthy brother whose lead and example he had always followed, and under whose wing he had been placed at the school, had changed utterly the moment they had been left alone together. As soon as the big West Downs doors had closed behind them, P J had begun to treat Richard like dirt. 'You see,' explains Richard, 'you were only supposed to have friends in your own age group, and he was in the year above me, so it was *infra dig* for him to associate with me. He was very nasty,' Richard adds softly, 'because I was sort of blubbing and letting him down, and he was ashamed of me.'

Victoria didn't realise what was happening until many years

25

later, when all four boys were at West Downs. 'One term they were going back, and I was running around like a demented hen with four trunks, and I suddenly saw Richard sitting in the corner with tears running down his face. I was told then. And Peter John was hitting him, and telling him to shut up.' In fact Richard was not P J's only victim. Leonard too was bullied, P J calling him 'the wort'. Tindall noticed, but preferred to apply his 'fend-for-yourself' policy. 'I can't say that Peter John was much use as a pater to his younger brother,' he scoffed later, when P J left the school.

Curiously, Tindall rather liked Richard where he had not cared for P J. Richard had decided to buckle down and do his time like a model prisoner; he was physically solid and good at cricket; and he appeared to be keen on Latin (in fact he was nothing of the sort – he was just scared to step out of line. 'I remember thinking, aged about nine, what was this language we were all learning? Nobody had said what it was. I looked up this atlas and saw a country called Latvia, and I decided it must be from there'). Richard's school reports positively glowed. 'He has intelligence and a keen desire to do well. He has a more even temperament than Peter John. In the Shakespeare play he spoke his two dull lines clearly and unselfconsciously.' To Tindall, this latter achievement displayed many virtues indeed. Richard was becoming a model ant in the nest.

'He is a sensible, straightforward and useful member of the community. One can rely on him to do his best in any department of school life,' glowed Tindall later. 'He is seldom ruffled and goes about things in a cheerful and confident manner.' If only Tindall had guessed – had been capable of guessing – what miseries were being quietly suppressed behind this pleasant façade. Theodora, meanwhile, fussed around him aimlessly as she did all her charges. 'Dear Mrs Ingrams . . . I wondered whether you wanted Richard to continue his flat feet exercises? And we imagine you would like Rupert to continue with his iron tonic', etc. etc. Who knows what damage the pair of them were doing, with their stupid inability to see beyond the empty certainties of their own limited lives? As George Melly said, 'Scratch almost any ex-public schoolboy in

26

permanent revolt and you will find a festering hatred for some long-dead pedagogue.'

Rupert, with his physical infirmities, was the special target of Tindall's scorn and contempt. 'He has had to be regarded as a semi-invalid and has therefore come to think too much about himself . . . [he is] deliberately idle. He has little idea of obedience or of helping-on the general life of the community. The fact that he was spoilt by his nurse is very illuminating and probably accounts largely for the fact that he is so self-centred . . . He should make a good socialist minister.' (One assumes that Kenneth Tindall had not voted for Mr Attlee.) Rupert, like Richard, was enduring a difficult start at West Downs. 'Oh nanny,' Tindall had written on his first report. Richard stuck up for him though, and Rupert fluttered his eyelashes at Mrs Tindall and managed to charm her round to his side.

The Ingrams boys concealed their emotional ups and downs from their mother at home with the traditional, non-committal, Foreign Office diplomacy of the English prep school boy. Fans of Geoffrey Willans and Ronald Searle's superb comic creation Nigel Molesworth will instantly recognise Molesworth's letters home from St Custard's in Richard's letters from West Downs. Where Nigel had scrawled:

Dearest Mummy (and Daddy)
We played against porridge court on Saturday. We lost
9–0. The film was a western. Will you send me a bakterial
gun. They are 6/6 at grabbers.

With love from
Nigel[4]

Richard scrawled:

Dear Muv
We have left off vests. On Friday there was a match
against twyford; the first eleven lost and the second eleven
drew. The dress rehearsal for the play is on Tuesday. There
is a full rehearsal today.

With love from
R.R. Ingrams.

27

A whole churned life lay between those ridiculous lines. Mrs Molesworth, at least, was party to her son's Christian name.

One insurmountable problem Richard and his brothers faced was the single-barrelled nature of the Ingrams name. West Downs was simply crammed with double-barrels. In Richard's form alone were Wingfield-Digby, Tennyson-d'Eyncourt, Beresford-Pierse, Browne-Swinburn, Cottrell-Dormer, Harvey-Watt and Crichton-Stuart. To Richard and his then best friend Scott it was made clear that they were second-class citizens. Confidence, however, came gradually, and with it the first signs of journalistic endeavour. In 1949 Rupert reported home that 'Dich has inventer (*sic*) a newspaper for his form called the S.D.II weekly newspaper'.

Other future interests stirred quietly amid the grim dormitories and form-rooms. A love of the theatre was one; Tindall's sole redeeming feature was a weakness for drama, and he wrote and starred in many of the school plays himself. Every year, as a laborious joke, he pretended that there would be no play, then 'surprised' the school by mounting a rather good one at the last minute. Tindall always sternly joined in the discouragement of friendships between boys of different ages, lest they lead to homosexual relationships, and a strict 'no-looking' policy was operated in the changing-rooms for the same reason; but when it came to the theatre he was more than happy to pile boys into girls' dresses in considerable numbers. P J took the lead as Rosalind in the 1949 production of *As You Like It*, while Richard had to be content with Amiens, lord in exile. By 1950 Richard had graduated to Orsino in *Twelfth Night*. Although most of his West Downs dramatic career consisted of dull lines spoken clearly and unselfconsciously, he had been irrevocably bitten by the acting bug.

Literature was another interest, discreetly engendered by the sympathetic Mr Turner, an organ-playing English master who was the only member of the common room manifestly under eighty years of age. He would read his class extracts from A.G. McDonnell's *England, Their England*, which certainly didn't fit the Tindall scheme of things. Turner was to become a family friend and an occasional guest at Cheyne Row. The music teacher Dorothy Lunn was another gifted maverick, who consolidated Richard's affection for the piano, although she criticised him relentlessly: 'I fancy he thinks he can succeed musically without much drudgery . . . a rather casual spirit and not much determination.' 'As will be seen from the report on his music lessons,' snorted Tindall, 'he is inclined to think himself a better musician than he really is.' Of course, there was cricket too. Admits Richard: 'My finest hour was when I became the wicketkeeper of the West Downs team. I was very good. It's the only sporting thing I've ever been any good at.' Finally, there was gardening. The impressive school gardens at West Downs inspired Richard and his brothers to go to work on the garden at Cheyne Row in the holidays, creating a camomile lawn and other botanical specialities. 'When we had finished,' says Leonard, 'I remember Richard walking round putting bogus Latin names on all the plants. On one rose he wrote *Crapula vercingetorix.*'

Leonard had arrived at West Downs in 1949, and was promptly condemned by Tindall as 'lifeless and lethargic'; but he too, like Richard, kept his head down, avoided any hint of subversion and played the orthodox model pupil role well. For one brief spell that year, all four boys found themselves reunited at West Downs – in body if not in spirit – as Ingrams Maximus, Major, Minor and Minimus. Then P J was away to Shrewsbury, with Richard hard on his heels in 1950. Richard went one better than his elder brother, winning an exhibition to the famous public school.

Leonard Ingrams senior had been a pupil at Shrewsbury, and his father, the even crustier Reverend William Ingrams, had been a housemaster there, so there was never really any doubt that Richard would follow P J's footsteps to the West Midlands; but it was a daunting prospect, to start all over again, at a new school, alone, with a rampant P J once more in the ascendant. In the long run, however, Shrewsbury was to prove an entirely different proposition from West Downs.

4 Rushton to the Rescue

From Victorian times, Shrewsbury School had been housed in a large Georgian military edifice outside the town, solidly earthed on a bank above the River Severn. Half the windows looked out over the river, a spectacular view that took in the Quarry – a large public park – and three churches over to the far side, a panorama seemingly placed there to torment classroom-bound pupils on summer afternoons. To compensate those stuck inside, the school boasted an impressive library with one or two good Turners; boys educated beneath its groaning shelves invariably went on to greater scholastic glories. So much for the prospectus. For all these attractions, to the young Richard Ingrams, arriving as the nights darkened in the autumn of 1950, it might as well have been Colditz.

Like West Downs, Shrewsbury held all things Latin and Greek dear to its never-changing heart. All new boys were designated as 'douls', from the Greek word *doulos* meaning slave, part of a rich classical tradition that enabled the little mites to be thrashed within an inch of their lives whenever circumstances (or older boys) dictated. Anyone who didn't exclusively study the classics was considered inferior. Other subjects were frowned upon: 'I still know virtually nothing about history,' Richard told the *Observer* in 1990, 'my knowledge of literature hasn't been gained from school, I know a little French but no other (modern) language, and I know nothing about science. I am therefore very ignorant.'

To anyone coming directly from West Downs, life had a

30

familiar, spartan quality. For most of the year the school woke up
to mornings so cold they would have thrilled Theodora Tindall; icy
baths were compulsory at dawn. Living conditions were primitive,
and Churchill House – the late Victorian brick building where
Richard was billeted – was falling to bits. The headmaster, Jack
Peterson, was a keen sports lover; sportiness, of course, was
next to godliness, and members of the school rowing eights and
football elevens were venerated. The remaining poor unfortunates
were forced into cross-country runs in driving rain. 'Sometimes
there was an awful run that the whole school went on and there
were men with whips at the back – it was all done as if it were
a hunt,' recalls Richard. 'Now I think about why I *really* didn't
enjoy school, it all comes back to those cold muddy afternoons.
I was hopeless. I always finished last.'

Shrewsbury's pupils were an odd mix – patricians like the
Ingrams boys, 'oiks' from the Lancashire mill towns whose
fathers were something in commerce, and day boys from the
town, petty bourgeoisie whose parents were generally assumed
to be unable to stump up the full fees and thus were treated
like unwelcome bacteria. First-years were known as one-year-olds,
second-years as two-year-olds and so on, in a system apparently
derived from the one used to regulate race horses. Over the
years, though, a more elaborate hierarchy had emerged among
the boys, based upon various detailed gradations of age, class,
authority and sporting prowess. One's status in this hierarchy
was expressed by a convoluted dress code – what colour scarf
you were allowed to wrap around your neck, what kind of tie or
waistcoat you were permitted to display, whether the coat could
be worn closed or open, precisely how many buttons might be
done up or undone – and of course the vital question of whether
or not you were allowed to walk on the lawn, and if so which bit.
Tony Rushton, cousin of the comedian Willie, kindly attempted
to help me by listing the rules from his own days at Shroozie,
as it was known. 'If you were in one of the school teams, you
were awarded what was known as a school first. If you got two
school firsts, then you got to wear a certain tie. If you were
an upper sixth Praepostor you automatically qualified for that

31

one too, I think . . .' He tailed off, having completely lost the plot. It was all utterly absurd of course; but like all successful schools, Shrewsbury had recognised its pupils' need to compete, and had given them something worthless and cheap to compete over, elevating an insubstantial facet of school life to a position of desirable status.

One day, Richard too would walk those lawns, coat flapping at precisely 45° from the third button at a constant tangent to the square of the hypotenuse; but the winter of 1950 found him cold, unhappy, frightened and alone. 'Silent . . . sober . . . still a child in many ways,' his house master put in his report. As an academic school, Shrewsbury allocated its boys into forms according to ability, not age, so in class he found himself sitting next to large, unfriendly boys who were good at rowing. The classics master, Street, was incredibly old and fierce and exerted control through fear. One day, Street announced that he had discovered certain boys in the form were using cribs in their translations, and that he had a list of all the culprits' names. If they were to put their cribs through the letterbox of his house that evening, he would say no more about the matter; if they failed to do so, however, their fate would be unspeakable and horrific.

There was no list, of course; Street was engaging in time-honoured schoolmaster's bluff, knowing full well that everyone in the form was using a crib. When you are thirteen years of age though, and two hundred miles from home, you don't stop to consider such things. So afraid was Richard, that his feet refused to drag him anywhere near Street's letterbox. That night, Street broke into Richard's dreams, stalking him, hunting for the crib. In his nightmare, Richard resolved to post the offending object through Street's letterbox there and then. If he walked out of the dormitory through the main door though, he would surely be caught; that left only the window.

Because he was fast asleep and therefore physically relaxed, Richard wasn't killed when he hit the ground. He merely broke his arm and did enough minor damage to the rest of his body to end up temporarily in a wheelchair. Not unnaturally surprised to find himself on wet gravel in the middle of the night, he then had to spend a further ten minutes banging on the front door, trying to persuade somebody to come and let him in. Alec Binney, his housemaster, telephoned Victoria in the small hours to tell her that Richard had broken his arm. 'Was it his bow arm?' was her first question.

Shortly afterwards, Binney wrote a letter to Victoria suggesting a solution. 'I propose to have him tethered to his bed each night . . . a monitor will do it for him.' So it was that Richard found himself every evening having to be strapped firmly to his bedstead by a sixth-former; it is amusing but entirely unproductive to speculate whether this had any lasting effect. In the short term, Richard was in danger of becoming a local celebrity, but he was soon upstaged by another boy, who jumped from a fourth floor window into a flowerbed, got up and walked away unhurt, leaving behind a pair of comically deep footprints in the soil.

Meanwhile Richard's own letters to his mother were beginning to open up, as he discovered the delights of the cinema. 'There was a film on saturday called *The Red Shoes* – ballet, but very good in its little way. The house is all over holly and decorations – it's quite like Christmas' (probably because it was Christmas – the 15th of December, anyway). The next instalment: 'I went to a western last night called *Stagecoach* – it was rather wet, except when the Apaches attacked it, and then it was most odd that none of the six horses were injured although the coach was plastered with arrows. I have found my bathing trunks, you will be pleased to hear. Yours, Richard. PS. What are bloomers?'

News began to flow from Shrewsbury to Cheyne Row. Mr Justice Pritchard, an Old Salopian, addressed the school on speech day on 'The need for a sense of responsibility in modern youth'. A Maharajah's son joined the school, who Richard claimed had to be addressed as 'Your Highness'. The Bishop of Lobombo came to preach, and the school reached the semi-final of the Arthur Dung cup (almost certainly a misprint for the Arthur Dunn cup). The sheltered political atmosphere of Shrewsbury began to shape Richard's budding opinions too. 'There was a debate last night about whether kindness can cure crime. I got up and said that stocks were a good idea – which met with universal acclamation,' he wrote. In 1951, Richard improved on the exhibition he had won the previous year by winning a scholarship. 'I hope we may claim some of the share in this success,' wrote Kenneth Tindall in a wheedling letter to Victoria. Some share in the state of nervousness that had led to his fall from the dormitory window would have been more appropriate.

Things could almost be said to have been looking up as the summer of 1951 approached, bringing with it the chance to keep wicket for one of the Churchill House cricket elevens. Then, a cloud loomed across the horizon. Churchill's, it transpired, had a better wicketkeeper of Richard's generation. His name was William Rushton. Yet, this rivalry aside, Willie was ultimately to be the saving of Richard Ingrams at Shrewsbury. The two became inseparable. Willie was worldly, dapper and confident, and always tremendously entertaining – an 'all purpose buffoon' as one master put it – and Richard wrapped himself in his friend's company like a comforting blanket (not, I hasten to add, a reference to the impressive statesmanlike bulk Rushton later achieved, which had not at this stage manifested itself).

'I thought of Willie as being very sophisticated, really. He'd always been to the latest musicals. He knew all the tunes, like *South Pacific*, long before I did, and used to sing them all. His father was a publisher, a very nice quiet man who had all these records by Jack Buchanan and Jack Hulbert, which Willie used to play.' It was Willie who introduced Richard to one of the great loves of his life, and his most important humorous influence, the Beachcomber column in the *Daily Express*. The two boys were very different, but in a complementary way: Willie filled the social hole in Richard's life, while Richard plugged the academic gap in Willie's, for Willie was neither classicist nor scholar. 'We gave each other confidence,' explains Richard. Conveniently, they both lived in South-West London and their birthdays were just one day apart.

Willie didn't share Richard's spiritual side. 'When we were all confirmed, aged around about fifteen, I remember desperately trying to whip up some religious fervour,' he recollects. 'You had to have a chat with the chaplain, and I couldn't think of what to ask. Then someone suggested asking whether you should keep your eyes shut when you pray – I thought, "That's good, that'll use up five minutes".' Nor did Richard's musicality interest him. 'Good heavens no, I was spared that. Although he did sometimes unpack his cello in the railway carriage on the way up to Shrewsbury, to empty the compartment. There's nothing better than unzipping a cello to keep people out of a railway compartment.' They did, however, share an interest in acting, and together they went to every audition going. The school magazine's reviewer clearly enjoyed *The Admirable Crichton*, in which Rushton starred as Lord Loam: 'His treatment of the most comic portions of the part was a real joy, in its lightness and sureness of touch . . . of the others, Ingrams as the Hon. Ernest Woolley was measurably the best – his sublime egotism and flow of fatuous epigrams were handled as to the manner born, in a most witty and delightful performance.'

Willie claims not to remember much about their time together at school. 'I understand why the Sixties should be a blur, we'd discovered drink by then, but why the Fifties should be a blur I don't know. I just remember it was beautiful in that part of Shropshire – Blandings country. The sort of place you go to die, not to be educated. But Shrewsbury was isolated from the outside world – it tended to go along with whatever the *Daily Telegraph* was saying.' Shrewsbury was to become proud of Willie Rushton. He was recently invited back to his old school, to give a speech opening a new science block. 'The bugger's open', ran the speech in its entirety, whereupon he sat down again.

Richard's friendship with Willie set a pattern that was to be repeated throughout his life; since that first comforting discovery of a vastly amusing friend who could take his mind off everyday horrors, Richard has always surrounded himself with entertainers. In conversation, he likes to sit back and soak up the jokes and anecdotes of others, and his eyes quickly glaze over if the performance begins to falter. It's one of the reasons he's such a good editor, and why strangers find him such a difficult man to talk to. Richard never bared his soul to Willie; he never does, to those whose main function is to entertain him. Willie still thinks that Richard enjoyed his time at Shrewsbury. He didn't; he enjoyed his time with Willie.

Willie performed one other vital function for Richard. Gradually, without realising it, he formed an opposite pole for Richard to pull himself away from P J. His older brother of course, revelled in Shrewsbury. In fact, when he finally left, such a wrench was it that he continued to send letters to the school magazine saying that it had gone downhill. P J ruled the roost at Shrewsbury, and the masters liked him. 'He was lively and rebellious, but very able and a close friend,' recalls Alec Binney. Michael Charlesworth, who also taught Peter John, agrees. 'He was a very attractive, intelligent boy with lots to say. Bolshy in a nice way, likeable, smart, very musical, a keen Catholic. I wouldn't say he was reckless, but he did do things on the spur of the moment, without adequate preparation.'

For Richard and his friends, this picture was inevitably tempered by their junior perspective. P J was one person who stuck in the mind of Willie Rushton. 'He was extraordinary. A very terrifying person, very very sarcastic, he could put you down like a shot. He was a very well-known character, a friend of Michael Heseltine's, very talented, very bright, he had a lot going for him. But he could be an absolute bastard. I was terrified of him.' For some years, Richard's relationship with his elder brother had been queasily ambivalent; he was P J's friend in the holidays as a member of the Ingrams gang, his victim in term time as an unwanted, blubbing embarrassment. Now Willie began to supplant the gang altogether, as Richard spent more and more of the holidays in his company. Further and further from his brothers he drifted, a widening gap that was never to close.

Willie and Richard spent endless hours at the Classic Cinema in the King's Road, at the Gaumont and at the Essoldo, later fictionally relocated to Neasden in the pages of *Private Eye*. On long afternoons they completed their humorous education with Ealing comedies, Marx Brothers and Danny Kaye films, and Jacques Tati double bills. Their favourite was *Monsieur Hulot's Holiday* which they enjoyed so much they watched it three times in a row starting one lunchtime. 'We didn't move,' says Willie.

'We thought it was the best thing ever. In fact, there are still elements of Monsieur Hulot in Ingrams, like the walk. Certainly, for a long while afterwards, he had that strange bouncing walk of Hulot's.' 'It was the golden age of cinema,' stresses Richard, as everyone does about the films of their youth.

Most days, Willie would bicycle over to Cheyne Row, where Victoria held court in her kitchen, in the absence of her husband. 'I can't remember his mother ever being out of the kitchen. There was this massive poodle in there called Toby (purchased to keep her company while the boys were away at school). She always called me Sir Harry, for reasons I never fully understood and didn't like to ask. She'd suddenly make a steak, without having asked you to lunch – suddenly put this wonderful plate in front of you. But it was a very holy kitchen – it practically smelled of incense. It was very odd not being Catholic in it. I remember a very strange man, Father Zulueta, constantly popping in for cups of tea. Actually, I felt a little uncomfortable in there, but then I've always felt going to Westminster Cathedral is a bit like entering Dracula's castle.'

When Leonard was back from Germany, the incense, the priests, the sense of kitchen-as-shrine, all discreetly melted away. Willie never visited the house when Leonard was there. He only observed him from afar on parents' day at Shrewsbury. 'I remember this tremendously elegant creature. I always think of him in a white suit, floating about in the distance wearing a panama. His entire family were terrified of him, this distant figure.' On other rare visits he'd be dressed in black, always in a big hat, like the ghost of a slender G.K. Chesterton. Always distant, in every sense.

On 30 August 1953, Leonard Ingrams died suddenly of a heart attack at Feldafing, Bavaria, at the cruelly young age of fifty-three. The next morning, his auditor R.C. Ingram called at his office in Bishopsgate to find the place in disarray. The secrets of Leonard's brilliant labyrinthine business deals, it seems, had died with him. 'I seem to remember the word "brainstorm" being offered in explanation,' says Ingram. 'That may have been accurate. Like the man in the song whose "brain was so loaded

37

it nearly exploded", Leonard Ingrams possibly was one of those machines designed to work at such a pace that they incorporate the seeds of their own destruction.'

For Richard, as indeed it must have been for his brothers, the blow was shattering – perhaps even more so than if his father had been conventionally close to him. He had not just lost a father, but any forlorn chance of ever forging a proper paternal relationship. That tiny flame of hope on the backburner flickered and died, but the darkness it left behind was as absolute as if his father had been his best friend. That winter, at school, he clung to P J as a new paternal role model, a candidate as unsuited to the task as his real father had been. His academic work went off the rails. 'Downright carelessness,' huffed his form master. His Greek master was more pained: 'It is hard to tell if the outward attitude of – to say the least – *indifference* to his work is just an attitude or not. He has too much ability, surely, to play at cynicism.'

His housemaster Alec Binney was more measured and understanding in his comments. 'He is in the process of emerging from his shell, and there will be a certain amount of diversionary activity, some of it probably ill-judged; but I do not doubt that the outcome in the long run will be good; for he has a core of solid good sense.' Binney was right, of course. Nonetheless, all his life since then, Richard has cultivated the friendship of older men, frequently of an avuncular cast: Malcolm Muggeridge, Sefton Delmer, John Piper and so on. Perhaps it is a little glib to dismiss them simply as father substitutes – they represent a deeper personal affection for a type of disappearing Englishman than that; but Richard Ingrams himself wryly acknowledges the obvious connection between his father and his 'old men'.

The turmoil within his family was not just emotional but physical. No sooner had Leonard been buried than Victoria arranged for Rupert, who had just arrived at Shrewsbury, to be transferred to Stonyhurst, the Roman Catholic boarding school. Leonard junior, who was still at West Downs (where he had become Head of School), was immediately converted to Catholicism and entered for Stonyhurst as well. The Tindalls were hopping mad. 'There was an awful hoot about that,' says Victoria. 'Mr Tindall, Mrs Tindall, they had me on the mat – they thought it was a dreadful thing to do. "Are you prepared to risk Leonard's career?" Tindall shouted. They thought all Catholics were terrible people and that Stonyhurst was an awful place.' Certainly Victoria hadn't wasted any time. 'Rupert was off like a shot,' recalls Willie Rushton. P J laughed and told Rupert that Stonyhurst was a 'bloody hotel'. Yet his brother was pleased to be going.

Soon afterwards, two events occurred which along with his father's death marked a significant turning point in Richard's life. In 1954, P J won a classical scholarship to Hertford College, Oxford, and departed Shrewsbury in a blaze of glory. For the first time in his life, Richard was at school without a single one of his brothers. His response was to flourish. Alec Binney's reports noted the change. 'At times last year I felt he was behaving a little out of character – emulating his brother, perhaps, as a "figure". This term he seems more natural, more himself – and on the whole the better for it.' Then the following term: 'I am more than ever convinced . . . that the removal of that powerful personality, his brother, has left him free to develop his own, which is by no means cast in the same mould.'

Around the same time, Willie Rushton too lost his father. Naturally, this double blow brought the two boys closer together than ever. For the first time, with all the strings to Cheyne Row cut, Shrewsbury began to exert a discernible emotional pull; the school ceased to be something to endure, and became something to exploit. Away from his lessons, Richard began to gather around him the nucleus of that group which would go on to produce *Private Eye*, and make such a momentous contribution to the comic, journalistic and political life of the nation over the next thirty years.

5 A Pseud is Born

The Salopian was one of those dreadful school magazines that had disappeared so far up the rear of the authorities as to be almost unreadably boring. 'A dull and pompous periodical given over in the main to long accounts of sporting fixtures' was how Richard described it in *The Life and Times of Private Eye*. A typical letter, contributed by one M.A. Hill, ran as follows: 'Dear Sir, I would like to take this opportunity of thanking all those masters who have umpired in house matches this term.' God rot the soul of M.A. Hill, wherever he may be now.

P J had contributed occasionally, and at the age of sixteen Richard too tried his luck, with what he fondly imagined to be a humorous poem:

> I wanted some money,
> I wrote them a verse;
> I thought it was funny,
> I wanted some money.
> It was excellent, honey*;
> To line my silk purse.
>
> *Honey: an imaginary female.

(The lines continued in the same vein for some time, but that's quite enough rhymes on the word 'money' – Ed.)

The poem was signed 'Otis', after Groucho Marx's Otis P. Driftwood, a *nom de plume* Richard had first used in letters home. This disaffection with their names was common among the Ingrams boys – Leonard had started signing his letters 'Dancy'. By now too Richard had ceased to address Victoria as 'Muv', and she had become known instead as 'Dear old trout'.

'Otis' soon began to develop a genuine talent for words, usually illustrated by Willie Rushton, who conveniently turned out to be a first-rate cartoonist. Burgeoning with confidence, the pair set about attacking broad types of their schoolfellows whom they disapproved of. Their principal target was the 'Pseud', short for pseudo-intellectual, an Ingrams word that *Private Eye* has since used so often that it has officially entered the English language.

> There is a tribe that in the world exists
> Who might be called the pseudo-culturists.
> Who think they can to heavenly realms aspire
> By warbling Handel in the concert choir;
> He who acclaims as masterpieces all
> The tawdry paintings of the mad Chagall.
> Who quotes from Blake or from Professor Freud,
> This man I label with the title 'Pseud'.

Ignoring the fact that this last rhyme would have us pronounce 'Pseud' as 'Psyoid', and the substitution of 'pseudo-culturists' for 'pseudo-intellectuals' because very little rhymed with the latter, a Shrewsbury craze was born. A Pseuds' Psociety was formed, and special black ties with β– embroidered on them were ordered. Even some of the masters were persuaded to join. There was a leaving breakfast at the end of every term, and on one memorable occasion, a pseudo-intellectual cricket match was played in deep snow, on the school playing field, in midwinter after dark.

Gradually, Richard and Willie began to take over *The Salopian*, ousting dreary reports of house matches in favour of their comic sallies. That they were allowed to do so at all is a tribute to the far-sightedness of the master in charge, a young maverick called Lawrence LeQuesne. LeQuesne was a brilliant history teacher, the radical young man of the Common Room, whose constant criticism of Shrewsbury's traditional absurdities was found rather trying by his colleagues. Relaxed and informal with his charges, he quietly tempered the *Daily Telegraph* world of Shrewsbury by encouraging boys to read the *New Statesman* as well. He also laughed like a drain at Richard and Willie's jokes. 'He was the reason I pursued comedy,' explains Willie. '*The Salopian* was very mild, you'd never have seen our satirical future in it. But LeQuesne laughed at every joke, with the loudest laugh you'd ever heard. It used to echo across the common.'

LeQuesne remembers the first *Salopian* that Richard and Willie really got hold of. 'It was an entirely mock issue dated 1554 – we had just been celebrating the school's fourth centenary, with considerable pomp, so it was apposite – printed by William Caxton and consisting of take-offs of various well-established features of the magazine: Old Boy News – "no entries, since we don't have any old boys yet" – numerous sporting events, including, I regret to say, the Bloody Mary Skulls instead of the Victoria Sculls, which was a major event of the school's rowing year. Only two competitors appeared in any of the events, P. Sidney and F. Greville, the two great men of the school's early days, of whom everybody had been hearing rather too much. It was great fun, and it was very typical of Richard: slightly deflating, without being really unkind enough to be called satirical. So far as I remember, it didn't even get us into trouble with the authorities, as *The Salopian* quite often did. The authorities were aware from time to time that they were being very gently ribbed, and they weren't used to it. In fact after the 1554 issue, Richard was very keen to follow it up with a mock *Eton College Chronicle*, to take the mickey out of Eton, and was rather upset when, eventually, I for once put my foot down and said no: I could see too much trouble coming. Jack Peterson, the headmaster, had been an Eton housemaster and was devoted to the place, and I didn't think he would find it funny.'

LeQuesne remembers the Pseud as the most characteristic of Richard's creations: 'The influence of Richard's elder brother, Peter John, may have counted for something here. They were both very blasé, consciously world-weary, and dissociated themselves utterly from all forms of strenuousness officially approved by the school. The Pseud was half admired and half derided: somewhere at the heart of this, I think, was the dread of the vulnerability incurred by revealing that something mattered

42

very much to you.'

The Caxtonian issue was unsigned, but full of giveaway phrases: 'thou aunchent troute' made an appearance, as did 'ye pfeuds, ye yobbes and ye hackes'. This latter reference marked the start of a new channel of attack, on those dull, stodgy, unexciting members of the community who followed the rules slavishly and enjoyed no life outside their schoolwork; a group which would later be viciously satirised at Oxford as 'The Grey Men'. In his first editorial after being formally appointed to the editorship in December 1954, Richard wrote: 'The enemy is stodge. The new boys do not know this; for the first few days of the happiest of their life, they hop happily along singing sweet songs; but then the stodge, with a green spotlight lighting up its yellow face, rears its ugly foot and brings it down with a squelch on the inno-cent victims. Down they sink into the mud and begin to become the leaders of the future.' For 1954, this was radical stuff indeed, albeit disguised in a passage of politely meaningless slapstick.

As in the *Private Eye* of the future, the opinionated material was tempered with humour for its own sake. 'Dear Sir – I am deeply in love with my House Matron. What can I do?' begged a bogus reader's letter. 'Uncle Otis' replied: 'I can only suggest that you try to stop loving her; it ought not to be very difficult.' Just a joke, but the peremptorily expressed moral standpoint embodied in the answer will be familiar to readers of the Ingrams *Eye*.

This takeover of *The Salopian* had not, of course, been achieved single-handedly. A Shrewsbury schoolboy's friends tended to be found within his own house – in Richard's case this meant 'Sir Harry' (Willie Rushton) of course, 'The Bloat' (T.J. Lewis, who went on to be Head of School and later managing director of Blackwells in Oxford) and 'The Coot' (an American pupil so nicknamed because of his fiercely short haircut); but it was in the world of *The Salopian* and the school debating society, also presided over by Lawrence LeQuesne, that Richard found writers and humorists of comparable ability. No more than colleagues at this stage, and a year younger, Paul Foot and Christopher Booker looked up to Richard and Willie as figures to be emulated.

'At Shrewsbury I was on Ingrams' coat tails,' says Foot.

'I worshipped him and wanted to be near him. In our last year we sat next to each other in the Classical Upper Sixth. I was in a position of *total* hero-worship to him.' Foot was a dark-haired, honest-featured, earnest young man, eager to please and 'widely suspected of taking things too seriously' as Ingrams put it.[1] Although he came from the famous Foot family of mainly socialist politicians (Michael Foot was his uncle), he unwisely set his stall out in the debating society before his own political views had coalesced into anything coherent. 'We had a debate about the landed gentry,' recalls Foot, 'and of course I spoke against the landed gentry, but I didn't actually know what the landed gentry was.' Richard tore him to pieces. 'He delivered the most ferocious attack on me, saying that the world was full of weeds and wets, and that I was one of them, and the only thing that *mattered* was the landed gentry. It was partly done out of his sense of the satirical.' Richard was obviously sufficiently impressed with the weed and wet Foot to recruit him for *The Salopian*. Although no humorist, Foot's burning obsessions at the time were Beethoven, about whom he was learning from Richard, and Olivier's *Richard III*, a film he went to see nineteen times, knew off by heart, and which inspired him to contribute a long and desperately boring article to the magazine.

Christopher Booker was a very different type. Witty and full of good ideas but also formal and difficult to get to know, the young Booker has been variously described by Ingrams as 'a tousle-haired intellectual' in his more charitable moments, and as 'Fotherington-Thomas' when charity palled.[2] 'He had spectacles and golden curls and he was very keen on butterflies and fossils. He used to go out on his bicycle and look for fossils on a Sunday afternoon.' Booker's parents were teachers, his mother the strong-willed head of her own girls' public school, his father a quiet old-fashioned liberal schoolmaster who could do the *Times* crossword in five minutes. It was he who had taught his son all about wild flowers, the stars, paleontology, the kings and queens of England, and so on. 'Booker is the only man I know who can instantly tell you things like who the prime minister was in 1931, marvels Richard.

This disparate bunch, who went on to form the creative heart of *Private Eye*, were drawn together by their talents, rather than by the unifying pull of friendship, starting as they meant to continue. Foot and Booker, who edited *The Salopian* after Richard left, never got on particularly well. 'I didn't really know Booker then,' says Foot, 'and I still don't.' Nonetheless, the group struck outsiders as imposing and admirable. Willie's younger cousin Tony Rushton, whose academic career was lagging behind somewhat, felt 'rather in awe of these superior intellectual beings – they did seem an impressive bunch. Richard was an elitist, definitely. He was very superior; although not in an unpleasant way – he was never a bully.'

That none of the four actually became friends at school (with the exception of Richard and Willie) was partly because of the system, which as at West Downs actively discouraged friendships between boys of different ages to prevent homosexual relationships forming. It seems to have worked. 'Everyone was pretty innocent. There were a lot of what you'd call romantic friendships between boys,' remembers Richard, 'but in an entirely innocent way. I suppose I had my share.' 'There was a low wash of sexual interest,' explains Michael Charlesworth, 'but that was about it.'

For a large boarding school, the staff room seems to have been remarkably free of dubious characters. One possible exception to this was Foot's original housemaster in School House, Anthony Chenevix-Trench. Chenevix-Trench had been a prisoner of war at the hands of the Japanese, an experience he made reference to when beating boys with what seemed like unncessary regularity. Ironically, when he moved on to become Headmaster of Eton, one or two of his pupils complained to the *Eye*, unaware of the Shrewsbury connection, and Paul Foot wrote a whole page attacking him. Chenevix-Trench was recently the subject of critical references in a history of Eton written by a former colleague, which had old Salopians and Etonians scurrying out of the woodwork to support and condemn him in equal measure.

Friendship aside, Lawrence LeQuesne feels that the pattern of the Ingrams-Rushton-Foot-Booker working relationship was set for life at Shrewsbury. 'My strong impression is that none of them has changed very much. They did of course find plenty of common ground to meet on; but at heart Paul was already the crusader, William the humorist, Christopher the ideas man, and Richard the satirist, whose basic inspiration was a deep-rooted hostility to taking things seriously.' Also, of course, Richard was the natural editor of the four. The school hierarchy provided him with the built-in seniority to achieve this post almost unopposed; the question of seniority at *Private Eye* would one day become a much more vexed affair.

In 1955 a more direct forerunner of the *Eye* than *The Salopian* was published, in the form of *The Wollopian*, a one-off attack by the editors on their own magazine. Gentle subversion from the inside had been surpassed by slightly less gentle subversion from the outside. The letters, all of them entirely fictitious, must have made familiar reading to M.A. Hill:

> Dear Sir,
>   I trust that the *Wollopian* will fulfil its obligation to Wollopians old and new by printing a photograph of the Fives Courts as they were before the ivy was blown down.
>
> Yours sincerely,
J.B. Blowlamp

The overall subject matter was a notional school rebellion of the *If . . .* variety. There were caricatures of English masters, heavily influenced by Ronald Searle, plenty of blunt advice from 'Uncle Otis', and the prophetic notice: 'WANTED: the editor of this rag, on charges of libel'. '*The Wollopian* was wonderful,' enthuses Foot, one of its authors. 'An entirely satirical paper based on the school – a schoolboy *Private Eye*, and it was damned good. It really laughed at the masters and the school hierarchy. It was exceedingly subversive.' Four decades later, the number of in-jokes (an obsession with the word phlegm, for one) and old jokes (cod horoscopes and agony columns) makes *The Wollopian* a slightly tiresome read to the outsider, but it is to the eternal credit of LeQuesne and the school authorities that it was allowed to be published uncensored.

46

A major row was in the offing, however, over the content of the supposedly more august *Salopian*. Sir John Wolfenden, a past Shrewsbury headmaster, had chaired a report into the proposed relaxation of the laws regarding homosexual intercourse, and his findings had been serialised in a Sunday newspaper. Richard got up in the debating society and encouraged boys to discuss the matter, saying that no one should be afraid to speak out of turn, as even past headmasters were writing articles about homosexuality in the press. Then, with the amusing conceit of the talented seventeen-year-old, he reported his own remarks prominently in *The Salopian*.

The reaction was immediate. Bemused old boys, who had taken it like men when 'Otis' had filled their magazine with inexplicable jokes about phlegm, could stand aside no longer. The mere mention of sodomy alongside the cricket results had them complaining in droves, purple with rage. Richard received a summons to visit the headmaster. He was to write at once to Sir John Wolfenden and apologise for his rudeness, explained Peterson. Wolfenden replied to Richard, mustering all the pomposity he could manage, saying that he was not so concerned about his own reputation, more about the reputation of the school (yawn). Richard prepared a leader column about the matter, but all further mention of the issue was then banned from the pages of *The Salopian*. Peterson wrote his errant editor a letter, man to man, explaining his decision.

> My dear Ingrams,
> I know that you are quite sincere in the views that you hold
> . . . and that you have the interests of the school at heart, and I
> must beg you to believe that the line you proposed to take would
> in fact have caused a great deal of distress and acrimony. The
> columns of *The Salopian* are not the proper place to ventilate
> large issues of this sort.

'We got our own back the following issue,' says Richard. 'As an act of rebellion we had a huge leader about tiddlywinks and what a good game it was. I actually started a tiddlywinks club. That was our pathetic response.' Sarcastic rather than pathetic,

47

and of course entirely lost on Peterson, who saw the subsequent outbreak of tiddlywinks as evidence that his strictures had been taken solemnly to heart.

By now the reader will probably have formed a mental picture of Ingrams, Rushton and co. sporting goatee beards, standing behind blazing barricades on the school parade ground, waving home-made placards and hurling Molotov cocktails at the staff. In fact, nothing could have been further from reality. Richard didn't want to destroy the system, he never has done, merely to laugh at it and if possible bring it into line with his own set of values. The same could be said in varying degrees for his accomplices at the time, including Foot, who was still a long way from becoming the hard left smash-the-state firebrand of the 1960s. They may have attacked the establishment on paper, but away from that paper, they *were* the establishment.

'It's important to emphasise,' says Lawrence LeQuesne, 'that although Richard Ingrams was a very unusual Salopian, he was not at all actually subversive. Well, by implication perhaps; but in no other way. He kept the rules, and in some of the externals did conform to the established model of the successful Salopian. His occasional clashes with authority were never *serious*: it was all for the fun of the thing, for seeing just how far you could put your toe over the line and get away with it. Things weren't evil, they were absurd, and their absurdity was to be enjoyed.'

By the time he left, Richard was head boy of Churchill House (Rushton was his No.2), a Praepostor (prefect), the possessor of a full complement of three 'A' and five 'O' levels, winner of the headmaster's drawing prize, president of the Halifax Society, leader of the school orchestra, senior editor of *The Salopian*, a member of the School Forum (an elite current affairs debating group), house platoon commander, band sergeant and drummer in the school corps. Flapping waistcoats, open buttons, walking at odd angles across the lawn, he was eligible for the lot. 'The harsh authoritarian air of public school life did *not* nurture the first seeds of savage indignation in the breasts of the young satirists,' he confirmed later.[3]

Rushton, Foot and Booker all held responsible positions too.

'We certainly weren't disassociated intellectuals,' stresses Foot. 'By the time we got into the sixth form it wasn't at all the ruthless, disciplinarian, corporal punishment-inclined school that it had seemed in our first few years. Even though Shrewsbury ran counter to everything that's in my character, we were very successful there, Richard and I.' Foot was school captain of boxing and head of School House, where the new master in charge, Michael Charlesworth, remembers him as an immensely popular figure, who could keep control without ever resorting to the use of the stick. When Foot left, he wrote to Charlesworth saying, 'I'm sorry I was so quiet when I said goodbye, but I just could not bear to leave.' He continued to write emotionally-charged letters to Charlesworth for years afterwards.

Lawrence LeQuesne feels that if Richard and co. had a weakness, it was their constant, deep-rooted hostility to taking things seriously, at least in public, and their dedication to taking the mickey out of those who did. 'It's been a long-standing criticism of *Private Eye*, hasn't it, that it's rootless, that it lacks all real edge because it's not *for* anything, only against everything around at the moment; and in that Richard was a faithful member of his generation, and I think still is.' On this point, however, LeQuesne is incorrect: Richard, and *Private Eye* with him, stood for Old England, the status quo, and the values of his upbringing. He mocked the establishment not to bring it down but to keep it in line, and rid it of humbug, hypocrisy, pomposity, cruelty, and bland attention to the rulebook. His mother had warned him off snobbery; but for a seventeen-year-old boy there's a fine dividing line between looking down on some graceless corrupt parvenu for his moral emptiness, and sneering at him merely because of his background. On occasion, 'Otis' overstepped that line.

> Alas! Alas! for all those gay Huzzars
> The men who line the pages of Debrett . . .
> Ousted by this much more ignoble set
> Forced to forsake their castles and to beg
> From men they would not otherwise have met.

Like a Tory Grandee bemoaning the appointment of Geoffrey

Dickens MP to a junior ministerial post, he went on to describe the offending animals:

> Now stuffed with food they waddle to their cars
> With shirts bedewed with gravy and with sweat
> Dim eyes look up and cannot see the stars –
> Oh! Base usurper of the baronet
> Unworthy of the ancestral coronet.

The army was to knock this Dempsterish stuff out of him with a size 12 military boot.

Headmaster Jack Peterson's retrospective view of the Ingrams years was typically decent but lacking in perception: 'Ingrams was a very able boy, a classical scholar, no trouble at all, a model boy. Booker was an extraordinarily staid young man, reserved and studious. Paul Foot had all the makings of an angry young man, but he was not in fact a difficult boy. These people were quite unnoticed when they were at Shrewsbury.' Unnoticed by Peterson, perhaps, who was more concerned with whether fifteen-stone Binns Major would be fit to play at centre-forward in the vital Repton game. Not unnoticed by the more talented members of his staff, however, who deserve enormous credit for promoting intelligent boys over dull sportsmen, and encouraging Ingrams and co. on their idiosyncratic path.

LeQuesne, of course, was influential, and Michael Charlesworth; but the guiding hand of Richard's housemaster Alec Binney (incidentally the journalist Victoria Mather's uncle) should also not be underestimated. Binney was a tolerant, sensible, ruminative, pipe-smoking type, rather pedantic, straight as a die and very popular with his boys, partly on account of having a very glamorous young wife called Heather. He was also extremely short-sighted, and entertained his pupils with the story of how this defect had put paid to his recruitment as an SOE agent during the war. Asked as an exercise to run down a corridor, burst into a room and shoot six sandbags with just six bullets, Binney couldn't actually make out any sandbags at all, and so discharged all six shots into the ceiling. He failed the test and settled for schoolmastering instead. Willie Rushton remembers him as 'a very worldly man, conscious of the ups and downs of the real world and the need to be prepared for it – much more so than some of the other teachers, who saw the school as a soap opera, a little island. He wasn't a Salopian himself, which made a lot of difference.'

Rushton reckons that there is a lot of Alec Binney in Richard Ingrams, whether he knows it or not. 'He has the same air as Binney – all those long silences. Richard is like a pipesmoker who doesn't actually smoke a pipe – deliberate, reflective, lighting his mental pipe while waiting for the words to form in his mind. I tried to be like Binney myself but I couldn't do it, because of my teeth. The pipe whistled across them, causing immense pain and suffering, and ended up on the other side where I sucked up wet nicotine, which was absolutely disgusting.'

Yet of all the masters at Shrewsbury, the most influential on Richard's education was an individual not encountered yet, for he was a small, bald-headed, gnome-like man who rarely ventured into the world outside his classroom. This was the compelling figure of Frank McEachran, 'Kek' to his charges, teacher of English literature, and the sixth form's only respite from the classics. For forty years, Kek riveted all who came into contact with him; his trick was to break works of poetry and literature down into 'spells', short, memorable gobbets that encapsulated the beauty of the spoken word. 'He was amazing, outstanding,' says Richard. 'I don't know how he got away with it, but his classes were nothing to do with "A" Levels.' These spells included T.S. Eliot, foreign translations of *Hamlet*, even bits of Hitler's speeches that were powerfully written. Pupils had to learn them by heart and get up on a chair and recite them. In the case of the head of school, addressed by Kek as 'The Grand Nipper', this caused much amusement.

'At that time, none of us had ever heard of T.S. Eliot,' says Richard. 'Auden was the same, Kek taught us lots of Auden, and made us read books about D.H. Lawrence. It was a highly subversive thing to do then, at that school – if you read poetry at all at Shrewsbury, it was usually Wordsworth. I spent most of my time translating Housman into Latin verse – that was

51

the sort of thing you did. So for this man to come along with
W.B. Yeats and so on was very subversive indeed. Sometimes
he would get the whole form reciting the spells in unison. He
didn't seem like he was part of the staff at all, he was a complete
outsider. In fact, the staff thought he was a crank. I can still
recite all this stuff now. Booker and Footie say the same – when
we meet, we still exchange spells.'

Foot agrees. 'We're still muttering it. People stop us in the
street and say, "You're talking to yourself", and what we're doing
is, we're reciting some Kek spell. He shoved into our heads the
sound of poetry, the music of poetry, he forced it into your
head just at the time when it needed to be forced into your head.'
When Foot left, he wrote to Michael Charlesworth recounting
how he and Richard 'still spend hours with a tape recorder,
delving into the works of Dylan Thomas, Yeats, D.H. Lawrence,
Spender, MacNeice etc. – appreciation for which we both owe to
the enthusiasm and genius of one great man, Frank McEachran.'

Dr Johnson said, unkindly, that 'A fellow shall have strange
credit given to him, if he can but recollect striking passages from
a few books, keep the authors separate in his head, and bring
his stock of knowledge artfully into play'. Today McEachran's
published volume of spells seems dry and faded, suffused with
Thirties modernity, and hard to appreciate for those who were
not present when the little man dazzled his classroom. The shining
pebbles chosen on the beach are never the same when you get
them home. The title 'spells', coined by the pupils, coincidentally emphasised McEachran's interest in the 'incantatory' use of
poetry, chanting it in order to understand the intertwining of
sound and sense; but seeing them on the page, bereft of context,
it is hard to enthuse as old Salopians do. Undoubtedly, you had
to have been there, hearing aloud the sound of 'the poets exploding like bombs'. Idiosyncratic, self-possessed, thoughtful, a bit
of a showman but quietly and deeply religious, McEachran may
very well have been the first of Richard Ingrams' paternal 'old
men'.

The school reports of McEachran, Binney, LeQuesne and
others provide an insightful commentary upon Richard's final years

at Shrewsbury – by turns providing ammunition and confounding those who wish their theories about the long-term editor of *Private Eye* to be confirmed. Detractors will be amused by one long-running theme, spelt out most clearly at the end of 1954: 'He has all the imagination that a scholar requires; it is his impatience with facts that prevents him at present from rising to the top flight.' Again, in 1955: 'He still neglects the letter unduly in favour of the spirit.' Or, from his music teacher: 'It is a crying shame that a lad of his ability and intelligence should be so easily satisfied with himself . . . everything does *not* work out all right as a result of playing "straight through" sticky patches.' Conversely, those who contend that the *Eye*'s cult of the Pseud is evidence of anti-intellectualism will be confounded to discover that it began here, amid fevered discussions as to the respective merits of Yeats, Spender, Eliot and Dylan Thomas.

Richard's casual tendency to rely too heavily on his instincts led him to fail the scholarship exam to Brasenose College, Oxford, but the following year he tried again and was accepted as a commoner by University College. Poor Willie had to stay on, graduating to head of Churchill House, as he desperately tried to find a university prepared to accept the innumerate; he had taken 'O' level maths twice a year since the age of sixteen, and failed every time. He abandoned the game after the seventh attempt, by which time he had become the oldest boy in the school. He never did find a university place.

Although he had never really enjoyed being young, Richard had at least found a *modus vivendi* at Shrewsbury, and a measure of cheerfulness. His path was now clear: on to Oxford to exploit and polish the academic, journalistic, musical, comedic and theatrical skills brought out by his teachers. But this being the mid-1950s, the state had other plans. Oxford had to be postponed. It was time for National Service and the joys of army life – cold showers, icy wakenings at dawn, crumbling barracks, petty regulations, bullying, and compulsory runs through freezing mud. He would be all alone once again. It all sounded horribly, depressingly familiar; only this time, it was to be much, much worse than ever before.

Richard Ingrams

A final word on Shrewsbury, meanwhile, from Tony Rushton: 'I'll tell you an odd thing. Me, Booker, Willie, Richard, Foot, we all grew up, got married, and had sons. And do you know, not one of them was sent to Shrewsbury School.'

6 The Blunt End

It was at least a consolation to Richard that he would enter the army as an officer, and maintain some of the praeposterous privileges of the Shrewsbury sixth form; the USB (Unit Selection Board) was supposed to be a formality. This turned out to be a lie, however. Three menacing majors sat behind a desk to confront the reassuringly burly but disturbingly gentle and scruffy looking youth that shuffled in before them.

'You play soccer, of course. Shrewsbury's a soccer school.'

Richard slowly shook his head. 'No, Sir'.

'Well what the devil *did* you play, then?'

'The cello.'

That was it. 23286687 Ingrams R.R., Sergeant, Royal Army Education Corps. Says Paul Foot: 'All you had to do was say you'd been to public school and you were automatically marked out for being an officer. But he would have gone in with that satirical and contemptuous attitude to the officers interviewing him, and would have been demoted for that reason.'

'I think my mother was deeply appalled,' says Richard, 'because it was automatically assumed that people like me would become officers. *I* was appalled. The propaganda of being told "You are leaders" at school led you to assume that you wouldn't have to mix with all those others for too long. When it didn't happen there was just this . . . deep shock.' To make matters worse, P J, who had been allowed to delay his National Service until after three enjoyable years at Oxford, had his selection board interview a few days later. Taking careful note of Richard's débâcle, he hired an expensive suit, borrowed a bowler and an umbrella, and told the board a lot of lies about his exploits on the rugger field. They thought P J was wonderful, and offered him a commission in the Coldstream Guards. He spent two years in Kenya, being waited on by servants and sitting in cane chairs with James Fox, later that most pukka of actors.

Richard had filled in the dead time before joining the army with a variety of holiday jobs, working at Selfridges and tutoring Sefton Delmer's son Felix at their farmhouse in Suffolk. There was also a family holiday to Scotland. Since Leonard's death, family holidays had tended to be low-budget affairs; the previous few summers had been spent on domestic walking trips. What had made the last holiday or two different, however, was the presence of a family friend, Mary Morgan. The Morgan family was of Welsh descent, but had lived in Dublin, where Mary's uncle owned the Russell and Hibernian hotels. Mary's father had been killed in Malta during the war, so her mother Pauline had eventually packed her bags, bundled up Mary and her younger sister Selina, and decamped to a roving existence in London. With patrician thriftiness, Victoria Ingrams was taking in lodgers following Leonard's death, while his bequest was sorted out; so Pauline and Mary (Selina having drifted off) moved in to Cheyne Row as paying guests.

Victoria quickly decided that Mary would be a good match for Richard. 'I thought she was nice. Quite amusing, and she worked in interior decoration,' she says briskly. A reliable, thickset girl with strong features, Mary seemed to Victoria to possess those vital domestic qualities that would enable her to take on the mantle of looking after her beloved Richard. Victoria liked to select her boys' future wives. 'Mary was over here being a débutante – lots of Hermès scarves and black handbags,' remembers John Wells, who later became friends with Richard at Oxford. 'She was being produced by Victoria as "suitable" – brought up to occupy the next slot. That was definitely the arrangement.' The grooming would take some time; first Mary had to be converted to Catholicism. 'She did the flowers in the church or something,' says Willie Rushton. 'I remember her down in the kitchen at Cheyne Row, she was always there.'

Throughout that summer, Mary waited patiently, while Richard hung about with her in a cautious, non-committal way. 'It's very likely my mother thought she was suitable, because Mary rather latched on to her,' says Richard. 'She'd never got on with her own mother.' Pauline Morgan was an unreliable manic depressive and the victim of Mary's dark celtic temper. 'Mary could be pretty alarming,' recalls one Cheyne Row visitor. 'I remember being in the room when the telephone rang, and she picked up the receiver, and just said "Bitch!" and slammed it down. I said, "Who was that?" and she said simply, "My mother".' To Richard and Victoria, however, Mary seemed quiet, jolly, charming and patient. She'd have to be. She had two whole years to wait.

In the autumn of 1956 Richard reported to the army at Aldershot, where he promptly caught pneumonia and almost died. Just in case he was shirking, he was made to parade in full kit with his temperature running well over the 100° mark. How he longed to take a rest cure on a Kenyan verandah, like P J. Instead, he got the toughest posting of the lot: Korea. Although the Korean war was technically over, Korea was a country blasted back to the Stone Age in some places by battle, with little skirmishes still constantly breaking out all over. It was bleak, primitive and desperately poor. In the basic wooden huts that served as the troops' barracks, there was no sanitation and the temperature often dropped to minus 40°. There was nothing whatsoever to do and everyone had to be in by nine o'clock. In short, it was not unlike a British boarding school.

On account of his lack of maths, Willie Rushton had suffered a similar fate to Richard's, failing even to make the Education Corps, and he now found himself in the lower ranks of a tank regiment. He acknowledges: 'Shrewsbury gave us the ability to survive in the army – like the old planters who survived Changi jail better than the troops out from England. To us, a hut on the moors at Catterick full of sheep wasn't that different from a dorm at Shroozie. It just never occurred to us to rebel. Nowadays nobody would do National Service, they'd all just sit down on the ground and say "Bollocks"; but it was only ten years after the end of the war, and all our fathers had gone off and worn steel helmets. It was what we were raised to do.'

Korea, though, was an extreme. Temperatures were so harsh that the sea froze over and the ink solidified in the wells. Each soldier was only allowed to spend one winter there before going for a spot of R&R in Kowloon. Military service was split roughly into two areas – the sharp end and the blunt end. John Wells, coincidentally, was up at the sharp end with the 1st Battalion Royal Sussex, near Imjin where the Gloucesters had taken such terrible casualties. A mile or two across the Demilitarised Zone were hundreds of thousands of Chinese communist troops; every night an 'active patrol' of terrified schoolboys would be sent out to probe the DMZ or blow up a Chinese ammunition dump. One night Wells's patrol ran into a patrol of their Chinese counterparts; both groups ran off into the night in opposite directions, in utter brown-trousered terror.

Richard was mercifully stationed at the blunt end, a hundred miles to the south-west at Inchon by the Yellow Sea, where boredom replaced fear as the prime motivating force in soldiers' lives. Shivering in borrowed American kit (British army clothing being utterly insubstantial), he wrote sarcastically to his mother: 'Phlegm will prevail, I think . . . for all the groans and moans, this place has done me a grey deal of good' (*sic*). His letters to Michael Charlesworth, however, reveal an eager schoolboy clinging unhappily to his past: 'I've been corresponding with chips off the old block from all corners of the globe . . . I'm waiting on tiptoe for the new history of Shrewsbury School . . . Things here are a good deal more strenuous than the Classical Remove . . . My regards to the Matron.'

Richard Ingrams has all but blotted his time in Korea from his memory. He keeps only three reminders: a typed programme from an army Mozart recital, one letter from 'Sir Harry' and a tattered photograph of the parade ground. It was the unhappiest time of his life. Homesickness gripped him like a vice. 'I remember gazing at pictures of English trees and green fields with an intensity as powerful as any pin-up might inspire,' he says.[1] Socially, he had to learn fast – how to swear, how to skive (it was the end of the eager boy who helped his mother with the washing-up), how to smoke like a chimney and how to drink: 'There was a tremendous amount of boozing. There was no social life at all and you couldn't go out in the evenings, so everybody used to get pissed every night. We all used to smoke first thing in the morning, because it was such a shock to be woken by someone shouting at you. I used to leave half-empty fags by my pillow to steady myself. There were wild scenes in the mess, men taking their clothes off and what have you.' Because it was a UN force, the rickety bar was packed with all nationalities: maudlin, homesick Americans; boozed-up, aggressive Australians; impassive Gurkhas; all of them – loudly or quietly – getting smashed out of their heads in their own particular way. Richard sang the Eton Boating Song in a Noël Coward voice at the piano. The British contingent laughed at the joke. The other nationalities wondered what on earth had been delivered into their midst.

As well as putting his internal organs through a crash course, Sergeant Ingrams was learning about life on the other side of the tracks. 'The army changed my attitude towards the class system. Before I went in, I'd been a bit of a snob. Now I became much more on the side of the lower orders, partly because of the way in which the army was run. The officers didn't have to do anything except strut around wearing these Sam Brownes, and it was left to everybody else to do all the work, all the real organisation of the army.' 'I realised that the officers weren't really fit to be in charge and that it was the NCOs who knew how to run things. The discovery made me more of a bolshevik.'[2]

Thousands of miles away on the Rhine, Willie Rushton was undergoing a similar awakening, that was to inform the opinions of *Private Eye*: 'In 1956 we knew bugger all about life, but the army taught us fast. It was like the *Reader's Digest*, all human life was there. I became deeply conscious of all these uneducated troopers of sixteen learning bar-room German much faster than I could, in order to pick up girls. I thought, what a tremendous waste of all this intelligence and native wit. Whereas the officers . . . being an officer was like going into the Law, where you're still eating rice pudding and brussel sprouts, and being cuffed round the ear by matron; they were totally isolated from the real world at all stages of life. Being in the lower ranks was a very good antidote to Shrewsbury.' The school, of course, had been kind enough to promote Ingrams, Rushton and co. to positions of power. Unlike boys from most public schools, they did not know what it was to be ordered about by halfwitted contemporaries. As a result, Richard retains to this day a dislike of any kind of formal system of authority and any kind of uniform.

In Korea, the Ingrams version of bolshevism was as low-key as his subversion at Shrewsbury. 'I became a rebel, not in a courageous but in a cowardly way, but rebellious nevertheless.'[3] His job as a 'Schoolie' was to run the library, and teach English to illiterate soldiers. 'I remember a very stroppy man who refused to co-operate in any way; I always tried to get them write something to begin with, but this chap refused to write anything, so in the end I said, "Just write about what you think of the army". That inspired him, and he scribbled away, mostly "fuck" and "cunt", and I was put on a charge for allowing him to write it. But I regarded it as a major triumph, because I'd actually got this man to put pen to paper, which he'd never done before.'

Richard began to make one or two friends among his illiterate charges, but he was still desperately in need of someone like Rushton who could entertain him. He eventually found his entertainer in the shape of John Ellis, a self-educated Liverpudlian regular NCO working in Intelligence and Field Security, who'd laughed at the Eton Boating Song. Ellis was a lot older than Richard – he'd been in the Palestine Police in the 1940s – and was such an optimist he'd actually volunteered for Korea. A delightful man, Ellis never stopped talking in his characteristic Liverpudlian accent; he never stopped laughing either, and he enjoyed every second of his military life. By his own description, he was '5 foot 8½, dark with large ears, a red nose, thin as a skeleton staff, with curly hair like barbed wire. Oh, we had some fun, Richard and me. I thoroughly enjoyed it. Volunteered for everything that was going. It was an adventure!' But surely, Richard didn't enjoy himself at all? 'Well, maybe . . .' laughs Ellis, 'but by heck, we had some fun.'

Like Willie Rushton at Shrewsbury, John Ellis imagined that Richard had enjoyed the army, when of course he'd detested every minute; what he'd enjoyed was the company of John Ellis. Richard submerged his natural melancholy under a big wave of cheerfulness, and the two of them knocked aimlessly around Inchon, Richard providing a literary commentary. Ellis had an affair with a WRVS girl. 'Ellis,' said Ingrams, 'it's right out of a Somerset Maugham short story.' He gave his friend a copy of Chesterton's *Life of Shaw*, as part of the educative process. The hills around the base were full of children, thousands of them, refugees who'd fled the north and were now freezing to death in the open. Ellis and Ingrams spent most of their days feeding these orphans with sweets and snacks, and bringing them newspapers to wrap themselves in at night, while the piano tinkled in the bar and the Brits, Gurkhas, Americans and Aussies drank themselves into oblivion. 'I shall be famous one day, Ellis,' confessed Richard, in a moment of ambitious resentment at their plight.

As winter turned briefly into spring, and the thermometer prepared its great leap into the scorching extremes of the Korean summer, Ellis came to the end of his tour of duty and left. Down in the dumps again, Richard turned to the company of Captain Ambrose, his scholarly CO in the Education Corps. Although a regular, Ambrose was not himself a military-minded man, and saw Richard's dilemma. The answer, he suggested, might lie in the shape of the vastly witty John Wells, a highly amusing young lieutenant up at the sharp end. Wells takes up the story: 'Ambrose was the Education Officer, so he used to come up from base camp to the sharp end every week, and he always used to say to me that there was a very funny man down at the base. The first time I actually saw Ingrams was in the small wooden garrison chapel at Inchon, where he was playing the harmonium at matins. Of course, I didn't connect the immensely amusing Old Salopian sergeant I'd been told about with the incongruous, baboon-like figure at the harmonium. His big, sausage-like fingers moved across the keys with a sovereign disregard for any minor

61

musical infelicities that might have detracted from the overall design. It is, on reflection, this businesslike simplicity of approach to whatever he is doing that is his most striking quality. I was put in mind of a mild-mannered orang-utan, and the resemblance has ripened with the year.'[4]

Wells would have to wait three more years to be introduced to Ingrams, for Richard was released from the horrors of Inchon before they could meet, and sent to Kowloon for his R&R. Not that he enjoyed it, as the army had managed to put him off the East for life, although he'd liked the Korean people a great deal. As luck would have it, while in Kowloon, he bumped into John Ellis, and the two of them spent their break together, laughing and joking, and rowing out to the floating restaurant in Aberdeen Bay. 'Oh, we had some fun,' says Ellis. The young sergeant kept trying to warn his older friend off the hearty types who served as regulars in the army. 'Ellis,' he would say, 'a strong handshake is a sure sign of a weak character.'

Richard's next posting was to Kuala Lumpur in Malaya, in August 1957, the middle of the rainy season. The Education Officer took an immediate dislike to him and shunted him on up-country to Seremban, where the communist terrorists of Chin Peng were making life unpleasant for the British Army. John Richards, a career soldier who was a corporal in Signals, describes the place: 'Seremban was a small market town full of Gurkhas with one cinema and plenty of snackfood stalls. We lived in bashas – straw huts with a two foot gap between the wall and the floor, mosquito nets and electric fans turning slowly in the roof, like in an old film.' As in Korea, there was a blunt bit and a sharp bit. 'They were good times for us at the base,' says Richards, 'but it was a lot tougher in the *ulu* – the jungle. A lot of the airborne guys didn't come out.'

Who should Richard bump into in his first few days but John Ellis. Fate was being very kind. 'Seremban was damned hot,' says Ellis, 'but not too bad. I mean, there was a football team!' Ellis and Ingrams blagged a ride to the seaside on a three-tonner. On the way back it overturned, injuring Ellis and crushing his leg. 'Richard made all these jokes about me limping and that,' he says. 'But oh, we had some fun.' The man was irrepressible. As in Korea, Richard continued to play the piano, only this time he restricted himself to Russian-language 'Volga Boatmen'-type songs. Of course, as many of his fellow soldiers suspected, he couldn't speak a word of Russian, but no one ever managed to prove it. 'He was full of fun,' says John Richards, unaware that Richard was still hating every minute.

Richard also continued to display an overt antipathy towards the officer class: 'I remember one day these Gurkha officers came into the library wearing silly shorts and leather Sam Browne belts. And I remember this officer strutting about in these shorts looking very arrogant, and I thought, "There goes a real shit".' The officer's name was Andrew Osmond. 'We had to go up to this godforsaken, sweaty, jungly outpost, just tents and corrugated iron,' remembers Osmond. 'There were about half a dozen young officers of the Gurkha regiment, who had all come to take a language exam in order to qualify for a higher salary, dressed up to the eyebrows, starched olive puttees, lords of the earth. I was one of them and I was the last to go. And I was watching this utterly hopeless-looking sergeant sorting out books with a Chinese girl. He was spotty and totally miserable. He didn't speak – he just gave me a look of utter, malevolent hatred. I've never forgotten it.'

On 19 January 1958, Richard's boat was due to leave for England, but he had a parting shot lined up for the officers in his life. With Ellis, John Richards and others, he formed a concert party – the Seremban Sidekicks – and put on a New Year show, *Rock Around Rasah*, at the British Army Children's School. 'It was a hilarious show about red-faced brigadiers,' says Ellis. 'Richard didn't have a very high opinion of them.' The audience, by all accounts, was full of them. Ingrams and Ellis did a stand-up double act, with sketches like 'A General Impression' (geddit?) and 'The Rasah Assizes', in which Richard put John Richards on a charge for having abbreviated shorts. Ellis was the straight man, who also did the Aussie accents. Richard did the impressions. 'He was a great mimic,' remembers Ellis. 'It was just like *It Ain't 'Alf 'Ot Mum*. Oh, we had some fun.'

'It was *very* like *It Ain't 'Alf Hot Mum,*' agrees John Richards. 'The opening number was called "Meet The Chorus", with the chorus "girls" dressed in crepe paper skirts, bra and boots D.M S. There was a professional singer on National Service, H.R.P. Hague, who sang in a sort of turbo-vibrato warble with Richard backing him on elephant's teeth. For the finale, I played the snare drum in Neville Trickett's skiffle group, with Brian Pike on tea chest and Richard on piano; "Cumberland Gap" will never ring the same.' On the second night of the show, unknown to Ingrams, John Richards blacked out his front teeth and grinned as Richard began the Rasah Assizes sketch; 'We were determined to phase him, and it worked.'

To anyone who knows Richard Ingrams now, the idea of him getting involved with a skiffle group is hard to credit, but it happened. In fact many have convinced themselves that this unusual period in his life helped form his celebrated distaste for the homosexual act – suggesting that he might have been assaulted by some over enthusiastic would-be Bombardier Beaumont. Tony Rushton, for one, is sure this is the case. Sadly, for those eager to rout out a little scandal, it just didn't happen; for if it had, somebody, somewhere, in Malaya or Korea, would have heard about it. Says John Wells: 'The whole time we were in Korea, there was only one instance of a homosexual attack, when a US Sergeant grabbed an enlisted man in the night. And that was a *big* case.'

'I don't believe it at all,' Willie Rushton confirms. 'I think it was just Tone firing a long shot, that's all. It starts off as one of life's questions: most people who interview me, like Lynn Barber, start off with "Why does Ingrams hate gays?" So I reply, "I don't think he does". But it's not a very interesting answer, so now people have started trying to provide their own answers. They feel, "Ah well, this question has now gained substance, I'd better think of an answer". So where you might once have been asked, "When was Ingrams on the moon?" and answered, "He never was on the moon", now people say, "But he could have been there, actually, in late 1957, when I didn't see him for three months".'

So the celebrated rumours of a homosexual attack on Ingrams

in the army are all, happily or sadly depending on your point of view, a load of nonsense. Besides, now his National Service was over, the 'suitable' girl who'd been groomed to become his wife was waiting for him, down in Victoria's kitchen. At least, that was the plan.

7 A Present from Africa

Richard's boat left Malaya in January, and arrived back in England in May, which was impressively slow even for 1958. As a parting shot, the army left him with a nasty tropical skin disease, which pitted his babyfaced features. It looked, according to his brother Leonard, like terrible eczema. 'He went on suffering from that skin complaint for some time,' says Paul Foot, 'and he had to have a lot of baths and sun-ray treatment.' 'He always looked underage before,' adds Willie Rushton, 'but he came back looking fifteen years older than when I saw him. He needed it actually. He was such a pink-faced cheerful boy when he set off.' Indeed, Richard need not have worried. Women seemed to find the new, rugged-faced, Mark II Ingrams strangely irresistible.

It was not long before this new attractiveness to the opposite sex was road-tested successfully. 'We had a marvellous party to celebrate his homecoming at Cheyne Row,' remembers Leonard vividly. No one in the family has forgotten that party. 'It was terrific,' says Victoria. 'It was all over the garden and the studio. Next morning when I got up there were still people drinking in the garden.' Mary was there, but the party would always be remembered as the night that Richard met Fiona Douglas-Home. 'Do you remember Ditch at Cheyne Row, falling for Fiona the night they met?' Victoria's cousin Susan gushed romantically, in a letter to Victoria.

Fiona Douglas-Home was a blood relative of Richard's – their mothers were first cousins on the Baring side. She had two brothers, the journalist Charles, who became editor of *The Times*, and the pianist Robin, Princess Margaret's lover, who sadly killed himself. Her mother Margaret was Princess Diana's great aunt, another musician and by all accounts a formidable figure indeed; her uncle was Sir Alec Douglas-Home, soon to become Conservative prime minister. 'In fact she had a face rather reminiscent of a female Alec Douglas-Home,' remembers Leonard, who was a nosy teenager at the time. Before the imagination runs riot, conjuring mental pictures of the young Richard Ingrams whirling some skeletal cabinet minister in a dress round the dance floor, it should be stressed that what Leonard means is that she had an upturned nose and a delicate bone structure. She also had a soft voice and attractive red hair, by the way.

'Fiona was a great character,' enthuses Leonard, who was rather jealous, 'a considerable person. She was subtle, well-educated, completely different from Mary. It was a long and very serious relationship.' The party was not in fact their first encounter; they'd met a week or two previously, when their mothers had taken them to a concert at the Festival Hall. Fiona had taken a shine to Richard then, damaged skin and all. 'Actually, I thought the skin was just adolescence,' she admits. 'Besides, it was his mind that attracted me. Although he *was* very good-looking and attractive, and he didn't care about it. He didn't try to make an impression on women, which some women of course find attractive.'

Richard and Fiona fell in love, and began a relationship. His way of impressing her was to take her to the Essoldo, to see constant Marx Brothers and Monsieur Hulot films. 'I enjoyed those,' she says dutifully. Lest it seem that she was little more than an *ersatz*-Rushton, there was also some rather more highbrow fare. 'We went to various concerts, theatres, films. He opened my eyes. He was the first person to take me to an Ingmar Bergman film. He wanted me to come with him to see Casals play at Prades. He was obsessed with the cello, so that was a great pilgrimage for him, but sadly I couldn't get the time off from the National Gallery, where I worked, so he had to go alone. But I am everlastingly grateful to Richard for the enhancement he contributed to my life, the widening of my horizons.' Like many of his family Richard was a natural teacher, as had been shown at Shrewsbury, where he had increased Paul Foot's stock of knowledge about Beethoven, and in Korea, where he had taught his illiterate protégé to spell all those rude words.

More glamorous dates than these had their drawbacks; at the Blue Angel nightclub in Berkeley Square, Richard had walked slap bang into Andrew Osmond, the strutting young Gurkha lieutenant with the silly shorts, out for the evening with a group of officer friends. Anyway, scruffy flannels and an old jacket didn't go down well in nightclubs. Rather more appropriately, Fiona and Richard attended church services together, at Westminster Abbey. They chose a pre-Reformation church, you'll note; 'He and I both shared the feeling that it was the sort of thing we wanted from the C of E at that time.'

Fiona also went to stay with Richard at Ellon, as Mary had, and they bicycled for miles about the surrounding countryside. He painted watercolours of the landscape, or took photographs, as his father used to do; but he never painted or photographed Fiona. There was always a faint sense of keeping her at arm's length, partly out of gentility, and partly out of the difficulty Richard still felt in committing himself emotionally. 'There was an unspoken, wistful melancholia about Richard. None of his family ever really discussed how they felt. I think he found solace in all things artistic. Also, I think the army had been agony for him – he'd found it very difficult to conform to military discipline.' The absence of his father still weighed heavy. 'Even then, the people he went around with were on the whole much older than him – family friends like Paul Dehn the writer and Roger Furse, Lord Olivier's costume and set designer. He didn't find it all that easy to communicate with his contemporaries, except for buffooning.' Speaking of which, was Willie Rushton much in evidence in their relationship? 'Oh, *yes*! Very much so. Terrific!' Her face broadens into a delightful smile, even at this distance in time.

There was, however, a very large fly in the romantic ointment. For the night of Richard's homecoming party was not only the night that Richard fell for Fiona, it was the night that P J fell for

Fiona too. 'I saw quite a lot of P J,' she admits. 'I found him very good company. We used to go to films and things together. He was intelligent, interesting and academic. He was a much more restrained character than Richard.' P J, more restrained? The boy must have been soft-soaping for all he was worth. 'He never behaved badly in my company. I was very charmed by him. I don't know how P J really felt about me, but Richard was always first for me. I didn't think Richard minded.'

Richard did mind, very much. Victoria recollects: 'In the end the whole thing came out, and they had a blazing row; and P J stepped down.' Victoria was furious with Fiona at the time, for what she saw as playing her two boys off against each other, and upsetting her plans for Richard and Mary. She had a powerful ally in the shape of Fiona's mother Margaret, whom Richard and Fiona nicknamed 'Hatchet'. Victoria and Margaret did not want such close relatives as their children to marry; 'We were both so afraid they might get engaged,' says Victoria. 'That was an awful time from my point of view, and her mother's. We both saw it was hopeless, and wanted to stitch it up.'

Then of course, there was another reason for opposing the match. *That* reason. Fiona explains: 'I wasn't sure whether I was acceptable in Victoria's eyes, because I was not a Catholic. She didn't welcome me as Mary was there too, as the "official" maternal candidate. She was a very nice girl, very good-looking indeed,' Fiona adds diplomatically. Says Leonard: 'There was a period when it was either Mary or Fiona – we didn't know which it would turn out to be. Occasionally, Mary would go off in a huff, because she'd found Richard had landed up spending the evening with Fiona.' To swing the contest in Mary's favour, Victoria even tried to recruit Willie Rushton to bring the relationship to an end, but Willie insisted on staying well clear of the whole tangle. Eventually, Mary Morgan drifted back to Ireland in defeat.

Ironically, later in life, Fiona Douglas-Home actually converted to Roman Catholicism, but it was not religion that ended the affair. Fiona's father, who lived in Scotland, was abandoned by his second wife and left alone to bring up their little son. Fiona had to go north to look after him. With this unselfish willingness to keep house for a helpless man, and a tendency towards Roman Catholicism, who knows, in another life, Victoria might have felt that Fiona Douglas-Home would have made Richard an ideal wife. As it was, Fiona went to see him sometimes in Oxford during his first year, but the affair was ultimately killed by distance.

This was not the only marital battle that Victoria had to fight as she strove to get a good deal for her eligible sons. Rupert left the army and quickly got into debt. 'He was hopeless with money,' says Victoria, 'on the verge of bankruptcy. He never went to university and he hadn't found his niche, but he was finding it, he would have been a motor mechanic, and a brilliant one, but he'd got all these debts.' Then Rupert met the famously beautiful Baroness Davina Darcy de Knayth, Britain's youngest peeress in her own right, a descendant of Clive of India, and mind-bogglingly rich. The baroness's mother was less than pleased when her daughter brought home a beautiful young man with dark curly hair, a winning smile, a single-barrelled name and absolutely no cash whatsoever. Leonard Ingrams recalls: 'My mother fought a long and serious battle with Davina's mother and stepfather; she was very pro-Davina, who's a splendid person. There was a lot of opposition to Davina marrying Rupert – they were young, he was un-monied, he was unlike her – and my mother became their ally.'

'They thought that he was after her money, but he didn't even know about it,' spits Victoria disdainfully. Victoria won her battle; in the end, she always won. Not only did the marriage go ahead, but Davina converted to Catholicism. Leonard eventually got married too, to the elegant, independent Rosalind; and, yes, she became a Catholic as well. 'It's extraordinary how my mother converts people to Catholicism,' says Richard. 'All her daughters-in-law have become Catholics.'[1]

While Richard, Rupert and Leonard grappled with the niceties of completing their education and settling down, P J . . . well, P J did an extraordinary thing. He'd returned from his tour of duty with the Guards in Kenya just before Richard came home, and while out there, he'd taken pity on a deaf Kikuyu boy called Thieri Njine. Thieri's family had thrown him out of their hut because he couldn't speak properly, and had sent him to the local witch doctor. In an effort to cure him, the witch doctor had branded him on the tongue, hands and backside. The local District Commissioner and representative of the Colonial Office, John Nottingham, had rather embraced political correctness ahead of its time, and put the blame for Thieri's plight at the door of the white man in general. Seeking to atone for the failures of his race, he made indeterminate promises to Thieri's family that he would be taken care of. At this point P J stepped in, in his breezy, cavalier manner: 'My mother will take care of the boy.' After all, couldn't Victoria handle anyone, anything and everything?

So it was that P J and Thieri flew back from Kenya together, Thieri shouting all the way at the top of his voice in the aeroplane. P J dumped the lad in the kitchen at Cheyne Row and explained to his mum that she'd have to look after him for ten days. Victoria didn't bat an eyelid. Her eyelids might perhaps have done a little gentle batting had she known that P J had not the faintest idea what was going to happen to the boy when the ten days were up, or that Thieri was not so much deaf as mad as a hatter. In fact P J rather forgot about Thieri and got onto a trainee teacher's course at the Stone House prep school in Broadstairs; the boy was left in Victoria's kitchen for a number of years. Oh, the British Empire.

'You couldn't leave him in the room for one minute without something awful happening,' sighs Victoria. 'If I went to the loo I had to take him with me. We took him up to Scotland and he put live coals on the piano. Then he ran into all the other cottages in the village and cut all the buttons off all the coats that were hanging up. You could never second-guess him; for instance, when he put black coaly handprints all over the high ceiling – I've never found out how he did that. I got so fed up with him going all over the house unravelling toilet paper and sprinkling Ajax everywhere, I thought I would lock him in his bedroom; but he just climbed out of the window into the next house and did the same thing there'; and they'd thought Richard singing as a baby had been bad.

'He had this obsession with water. He'd frequently turn on every tap in the house and flood the place. He always put his pyjamas down the loo at night. Not that he was good with clothes. I got him some shoes and socks. He let me put them on, tie them up, pull them up nicely, and when I'd finished, he gently took them all off again. So when I went out in the street with him, people would shout, "Can't you give him some shoes and socks?" He wouldn't eat any English food. When we went into the greengrocer's, he'd make for the bananas and steal them all. It was very difficult. He slept on the lino, did war dances in Cheyne Walk, and tried to kill every passing cat. Luckily I had an awfully nice daily, Mrs Livett, who'd keep hold of him while I went out and did whatever I had to do.'

By this time, Thieri was madly in love with Victoria and wouldn't leave her side. 'I took him to see a specialist in Harley Street,' she said. 'It was very funny. You can imagine the scene, deep pile carpets and a receptionist, and Thieri kept climbing up me as if I were a tree. The man, whoever he was, couldn't get anywhere near him. The authorities were terribly worried about how old he was – I think he was about eleven – and had I got his date of birth? On and on they went – and was I the mother? So I said yes.

'Then, through the County Council, I heard there was a local deaf school at Parson's Green, and they said that he could go there. He climbed up the headmistress, who was very tall and thin, as if she was a pole, and damaged her back. So instead we drove him up to a big Catholic deaf school at Boston Spa; there was a Monsignor Kelly there who looked after the deaf, and it was he who first said that there was a lot of hearing in him. That was the first time we realised that Thieri could hear. Of course it was a school for intelligent girls, and the nuns didn't want him around assaulting the girls and that sort of thing, so that was a failure too.

'Eventually it was Rupert who tackled the headmistress of the school, and through her, got the Rudolph Steiner people near Aberdeen to take him in term time, while I had him in the holidays. They never refuse anyone. They're absolutely dotty.' Gradually, reports filtered back from the Rudolph Steiner school, indicating that they were beginning to realise just what

72

they'd taken on. 'He is rather restless, and at any opportunity he will try to perform a kind of war dance.' 'Whenever he gets the chance to be near a tap unattended by an adult, he will at once create a flood all over the floor.' 'At times he can sit for almost half an hour, completely motionless and with a strange expression on his face. On the other hand, after meals he is hyperactive, hopping on one leg or swinging to and fro rhythmically from his elbows, continuously shouting his only word, "Awake!".'

As Thieri grew up and become something of a physical and sexual handful, the Rudolf Steiner school managed to get him transferred to an institution for mentally handicapped men in Chorley, which he attempted to demolish in the night. So they sent him for two weeks of tests at Lancaster Mental Hospital, and when the fortnight was up, refused to take him back. 'The doctor at Lancaster was absolutely furious,' says Victoria. 'Awfully nice, but furious, as well he might be. Thieri's been there ever since. Just the other day I got a letter from them, saying that some Kenyan students from his district had visited Lancaster, and that they'd located his family. But nothing will come of that. They won't have him back. They're pulling down that place now, so I don't know what's going to happen.'

Richard, like the rest of his family, was completely devoted to Thieri, and played with him for hours. He added a certain *je ne sais quoi* to the social life at Cheyne Row – musical evenings with Richard on cello, Victoria on violin, Rupert on viola, P J on flute, and live coals on the piano. There were also raucous Sunday lunches, attended by the whole family, which Fiona Douglas-Home remembers as being something of an intellectual assault course. 'Sunday lunch was always huge, with guests joining in the cut and thrust. There was a lot of challenging, taunting conversation, you had to be on your guard all the time. Victoria was the main teaser, although she was the one person who didn't get teased back.'

Michael Ingrams, Leonard's son from his first marriage, was a frequent visitor at these lunches. He was now an actor, and had got himself a part in *Sweeney Todd* at the Regent Theatre, Hayes. 'He was quite different from the others,' says Fiona. 'He

73

was genial, and hadn't got the same kind of edge to his conversation that Victoria's sons had.' Michael Ingrams later moved to France. Another regular guest was a quiet, intelligent friend of P J's, a student called Tim Aldred, and then of course there was Willie Rushton. Occasionally John Ellis came to stay, and he and Richard would go pub crawling, or visit the Tate Gallery. Ellis was very taken with Fiona, and when she and Richard split up after the summer of 1959 he sent her a poem, 'To a Lady in Distress'.

For a while, in that summer of 1958, the whole brood was back together again, a brief second flowering of the Ingrams clan as a family group, rumbustious once more in the familiar surroundings of Cheyne Row. John Wells describes the setting: 'I remember they had that William Morris willow-patterned wallpaper against unpainted oak panelling, and there were a lot of bits of musical instruments about the place. It was really elegant and old-fashioned, but at the same time very, very comfortable. It was almost Bloomsbury – there was a very great respect for music, painting and furniture, but at the same time everything was extremely relaxed and slightly run down. In the garden, which was walled, there was a studio on which Richard and Willie Rushton had copied various impressionist paintings, including one of the Bridge at Arles.' It was not the sort of place anyone really wanted to leave in a hurry; but soon, it would be time for all the boys to take their leave once more, this time for good.

As an inevitable concession to the departures of her sons along their various paths, Victoria split the property back into its two constituent parts, and put part of No. 16 Cheyne Row up for rent. Not surprisingly there were many prospective takers, one of whom was the broadcaster Robert Robinson and his fiancée. Victoria seemed a reluctant guide as she showed them round, particularly as they had come to view without an appointment. Then the future Mrs Robinson, who was completely smitten with the house, noticed the Catholic collecting box on the hall table. She informed Victoria that they were thinking of getting married in the Catholic church up the street, which was not true. It worked. The Robinsons were instantly bumped to the top of the queue, moved in, and later bought the whole house. Robert Robinson still remembers looking out of the window into the walled garden, where Rupert canoodled in the twilight with Davina, entranced by her beauty. 'They were like courtly lovers . . . the most beautiful couple you could imagine.'

Ever the doting mother, Victoria smoothed her boys' paths with generous financial assistance as they went their separate ways. 'My husband left a lot of money in his company, but we didn't see any of it for several years, then it all came in at once. I thought, very stupidly, that all the boys were growing up and were just getting to that age where they needed it.' She split a large proportion of the inheritance four ways. 'Rupert wasted all his. He was *hopeless* about money.' Rupert had been working for a publishing house in Bloomsbury and had promised to try and publish a comic novel about National Service that Richard and Willie had written, entitled *Shredded Wheat For The Generals*, but as his company mainly published religious books it is hardly surprising that he failed to do so. He used his inheritance to start a coachworks, which failed completely; he then settled in the country with Davina and their three children.

Leonard was the only one to follow his father's example and turn his money into more money. He won a scholarship to Corpus Christi, Oxford, where he obtained a First in Greek and Latin Literature, and toyed with the idea of becoming a don. Thereafter he decided to rebel against Victoria's plans for his professional life. Victoria's mother came from the Baring family, they of the famous Baring's Bank, with whom it would have been easy for someone of Leonard's financial acumen and family background to obtain a lucrative position. Indeed, this is precisely what Leonard intended to do, whereas Victoria could think of nothing worse than her son joining the stuffy old family bank. Against her will he joined Baring's and was posted to Saudi Arabia, where he became the leading light in the choral and orchestral life of Riyadh and Jeddah. Described in the local press as 'a precise man of quiet wit', he joined the board of Baring's and was made an OBE. He is now a straight-laced banker, a director of Robert Fleming's and owner of the famous Garsington Manor, at which he stages the

Richard Ingrams

Garsington Opera Festival each year; he and Rosalind have four children, a house in Siena, and pots of money.

P J was not so fortunate. After teacher training in Birmingham, he used his inheritance to buy Lime House, a private school in Dalston near Carlisle, of which he appointed himself headmaster. 'Again, he had the teaching thing, it was very strong in them,' says Fiona Douglas-Home. 'He was brilliant at being a prep school headmaster,' adds Richard. 'He had a sort of rapport with boys – partly I suppose, because he was still one himself.' An unconventional establishment, Lime House combined regular schoolwork with exciting climbs along the cliffs and up mountains, invariably led by P J. When not bounding up the rocks, he did his best to look the part of a headmaster, affecting rimless glasses which sat authoritatively below his domed forehead.

Even at a distance, he continued to taunt his younger brother. When Richard became famous, he told the papers: 'Richard is a socialist, he would not send his children to my school. Richard is, of course, one of the richest men in England.' He went on to heap exaggerated praise on Sir Alec Douglas-Home, by now *Private Eye*'s chief target, purely to annoy Richard. Which is not to say that P J was not genuinely true blue; during a postal strike, he organised the boys of Lime House into a blackleg 'Cumberland Postal Service', and told a union delegation that came protesting to 'push off'. P J remained eccentric, independent, and cricket-mad; he refused to turn up to his brother's wedding because the Test match was on television. He was also something of a womaniser. He had several girlfriends, and although he married a girl named Kate Binchy, it all quickly collapsed. She left him after he managed to sire an illegitimate daughter in Norfolk. Fiona Douglas-Home thinks that behind the dash and bravado, P J was even more melancholy than Richard. 'It was much more evident with him,' she says, 'he was more tormented. He had a very unhappy life.' Richard agrees. 'He was terrifically buttoned-up, much more than me.'[2]

In the late 1960s, P J rescued two more unfortunate waifs from the Third world, but this time he had somewhere to keep them; he put the Paaradekh brothers through Lime House school at his own expense. Sadly, these two Indian boys were not robust, sturdy creatures like Thieri, and in March 1968 one of them collapsed and died of exposure on an expedition led by P J through a Cumbrian blizzard. Then, in October 1972, he took a thirteen-strong party of pupils on a tough climb above Hawes Water near Penrith. A fourteen-year-old boy was killed and three others injured by a landslip. A Mountain Rescue spokesman condemned the choice of route as 'dangerous'. P J's luck, which had stayed with him on the rooftops of Hampton Court and the crags of Ellon, had finally run out. His life was ruined by the deaths of the two boys. Racked with guilt, he never recovered.

Of all the Ingrams boys, the only one to keep his inheritance sitting idly in the bank was Richard. This was because he was saving his share for a particular purpose; something specific, that he would not be able to put into practice for another three years.

8 A Lot of Men in Duffle Coats

In October 1958 Richard hitched a lift with a neighbour up to Oxford, where the great grey façade of University College stands to attention over the High Street, concealing an unexpectedly dainty front quad. He deposited his bags in his room and went and sat in the College Hall. Another freshman walked in after him. By an amazing coincidence, it was Paul Foot. 'It wasn't until I walked nervously in that day, into this huge hall, and I heard this voice saying "Foot" and I looked up and there was Richard, that either of us knew the other was going to Univ. We immediately clung together from the nervousness of being in this new place, we were delighted to see each other, and very, very quickly became close friends – much closer than we'd been at school.' Richard couldn't have been more surprised if John Ellis had walked round the corner and suggested they have a bit of fun.

After Richard had left Shrewsbury Foot and Booker had taken over *The Salopian*, Booker had managed to wriggle out of military service on medical grounds, and had gone to work for Arnold Goodman and others as a solicitor's clerk, before taking up a place at Cambridge. Foot, meanwhile, had entered the army, and through the blatantly ill-concealed influence of his father – who was governor of Jamaica – had secured a cushy posting in the West Indies as a second lieutenant, before moving on to Oxford. 'Richard and I were absolutely inseparable at university,' he says. 'We were really deep friends, and spent hours and hours

together talking, and playing tapes, and reading poetry.' Foot
needed Richard as a friend that first term. Word had got out that
his father had sent him a telegram at the college, reading: 'GET
A FIRST STOP BE PRESIDENT OF THE UNION STOP.' Foot senior,
like three of his brothers, had been president of the Union, and
saw nothing wrong in applying a little overt parental pressure.

Fate had not finished larking about with Richard. Soon afterwards, he was invited to tea by a girl from St Hilda's College
named Diana Rose, who told him that among her *very* exciting
guests was someone that he would *adore*, that he just *had* to
meet. The guest in question turned out to be Andrew Osmond, the
strutting Gurkha officer from Seremban. 'He looked at me,' says
Osmond, 'and I looked at him, and he said, "I've seen you before
– bloody officer!"' And that's how it began, we became firm pals
after that. Until then I was what was called a "deb's delight". I just
went to parties in London with pals from the army. But after that I
became good friends with Richard, Paul Foot, all that gang.' Says
Richard: 'Osmond always had an off-putting appearance. Smart,
crinkly hair, always very well dressed in cavalry twills, with quite
a lot of money, and like Footy, he had a car. People saw him as
I had in the army.' Enviously, in other words, surrounded as he
was with the overt trappings of success. It seems, though, that
underneath it all Osmond was a thoroughly decent chap. He was
also, like Foot, the complete opposite of Richard. They were to
complement each other well over the next few years.

University College in 1958 was a relaxed institution, upmarket,
unacademic, where nobody was too worried if you slacked. An
article in a university magazine just before Richard came up
described the place: 'Univ. men's absorbing devotion to fun
shows as clearly in the bedsteads they sometimes hurl into
the High on bump-supper nights as in the ballast they provide
so regularly in the bottom half of the class lists. The true Univ.
man, the genuine article, does not belong to the Christian Union
cell which holds fuggy prayer-meetings in its beige bed-sit, or to
the lean and dedicated cyclists' troupe lurching its well-oiled way
on some oft-renewed pilgrimage to the nearer Cotswolds, nor
will he join in the tragi-comic indefatigability of the polo-necks

79

who struggle to keep a debating society alive . . . The visible emblems of the really "good college man" are the sleek Volkswagens outside the gates, the gnawed, coverless *Tatler*s in the Junior Common Room, the worn rugger boots, broken hockey sticks skulking in improbable corners, the rank beer mugs, prolific, *passim.*'

There was also a strong element of hard-drinking northerners at the college, one of whom was Jack Duncan, a working-class Geordie, who encountered the ecstatically reunited Ingrams and Foot on their first day: 'My first recollection was that we saw these two ridiculous figures, very pleased with themselves, in daft hats and silly costumes, swanning around the quad, and immediately identified them as a couple of real prats. I really didn't like the look of them at all, and was horrified at the thought that Oxford might be comprised of types like that.' Needless to say, Jack Duncan and Richard Ingrams soon became the best of friends.

Reassuring as it was to collect a new (and highly eclectic) gang together so soon, in other respects Richard found Oxford disappointing. In an article for *Oxford Opinion* magazine at the start of his second term, he outlined the types of people he had hoped to see at the university: 'Strange men waving prayer-wheels ambling slowly past the shops; men in cloaks and kilts, shorts and sandals, beards and bowler hats. Occasionally there emerged from the schools the man who wore a toga throughout the year and carried a large Old Etonian golfing umbrella. They were unselfconsciously peculiar and I looked forward to them.'[1] Explains Richard: 'One had the idea of Oxford being a very glamorous place. Full of eccentrics and aesthetes and witty people. But when I got there, there were just a lot of men in duffle coats wandering up and down the High Street.'[2] (Although, as he went on to concede, a duffle coat was cheap, kept the bowels warm and reminded the bearer of the aunt who had purchased it.) Particularly galling was the lack of fellow humorists: 'I had expected Oxford to be full of very funny people who would all be wanting to do the kind of things that I wanted to do, but in the end there were only five of us.' There wasn't even a decent cartoonist, so Rushton was persuaded to visit at weekends, as a sort of honorary undergraduate. 'There are very few people who can make jokes,' explains Richard.[3]

Witty and amusing it might not have been, but in fact the generation that passed through Oxford in the years 1958–61 was a high-flying one, and full of future stars. Peter Jay, David Dimbleby, Melvyn Bragg, Alan Coren, Brian Walden, Julian Mitchell, Sheridan Morley, John Wells, Esther Rantzen, the young Winston Churchill, Lord Gowrie, Ferdinand Mount, Auberon Waugh, Piers Plowright, Gordon Honeycombe, Glyn Worsnip, Ken Loach, Dennis Potter, Ken Trodd all made their name there. Sir Robin Butler, later the Cabinet Secretary who made an idiot of himself in front of the Scott Inquiry into the arms-to-Iraq affair, was president of Richard's Junior Common Room. It is true that each Oxford generation is judged rather spuriously on the relative size of a tiny clutch of celebrities of the future, but in this instance the healthy incidence of big names is symptomatic of a genuinely flourishing atmosphere of achievement.

The reason, if one can be found besides mere genetic coincidence, lay in the pattern of National Service recruitment and the political reactions of those who had been put through it. Alan Coren, who hadn't gone through the army, explains: 'The National Service generation was far more adult, inevitably, because the majority of students were two years older. We were also the first full-blooded generation that had come through the grammar schools, which had really taken off post-Beveridge in 1948. The cultural tide was with us – *Lucky Jim* had come out, *Look Back In Anger*, and Suez had shaken people's faith in the establishment. Oxford seemed to be a place of quiet grown-up men who were holding political opinions because they'd actually tested them out there, who had a strong social sense because they'd experienced life outside. They'd encountered the working classes in the army. Socialism still appeared to be a principle which when put in place would change the country, so they took it seriously, they were less anarchic than kids are now. It was more committedly left-wing, more grown-up.'

The most confident Oxbridge generations are generally those which believe they will be personally instrumental in supplanting an older order. Explains Coren: 'Traditional areas like the Foreign Office and the civil service were being deconstructed with the end of empire; while broadcasting was exploding, newspapers were expanding, and the media were hoovering up graduates. The charmed circle of government was clearly going to be threatened in due course. It felt like the engine room of social change – you knew these people were going to count. It was a very good time. I get depressed when I go there now.' More grown-up these students may have been in a social sense, but politically and philosophically they were embarrassingly naive and convinced of their own rectitude. It is ironic that Richard Ingrams and *Private Eye*, attacking from a primarily moral perspective (which took various political forms over the years), did more long-term damage to 'the charmed circle of government' than the ex-grammar school boys' front-on socialist assault.

At a British university at the turn of the 1960s, though, it was social death to be anything other than a socialist, and inverted snobbery had entirely supplanted snobbery itself. Continues Coren: 'You'd meet people who, for the first time, disclaimed their origins. My room-mate was from Eton and genuinely embarrassed about the fact.' These attitudes filtered into every area of university life, taking a firm hold not just in the political arena but in drama and journalism, areas that Richard Ingrams and his friends had come to conquer. The result was a collision.

Of course, Ingrams and co. had been politicised by National Service as well, but not in a humourless fashion. They regarded Etonians with fake cockney accents, and socialist re-interpretations of *King Lear*, with equal derision. They found it astonishing that anyone who'd seen the outside world for two years could continue to regard undergraduate politics as an important matter. Humour was definitely the dividing line; even an earnest liberal like Foot couldn't help but laugh at how incredibly seriously Dennis Potter and his circle took themselves and their work. A success story like David Dimbleby can chuckle now at the way he and his friends would sit up until 2 a.m., discussing aspects of politics and philosophy that they'd learnt that day as if they'd known them all their lives – 'We must have been insufferably arrogant,'

82

he says[4] – but at the time such mockery would inevitably have been regarded as a challenge. Ingrams and his group were seen therefore as cynical, anarchistic, too-clever-by-half troublemakers. They were also secretly envied by the men in duffle coats for their assured self-confidence.

Another effect of National Service, particularly on the Ingrams gang, was to lessen their regard for the sanctions of authority and consequently the amount of work they were prepared to do. 'National Service made them all very unserious about academe,' says Alan Coren, 'unlike straight-from-school types like me.' Says Richard: 'If you'd been out in the world for two or three years, it was a bit like going back to school. It didn't seem important. People like me, Foot and Osmond just wanted to fart around, put on plays and write magazines.' To non-National Service graduates like the actor Jonathan Cecil, this cavalier disregard for authority was slightly awe-inspiring: 'We felt very young and naive in comparison. They'd been through the army for two years, filthy songs and sex and swearing, and having to square up to actual violence and guns, things which we mere boys didn't know about at all. So yes, there was a gulf. Ex-National Servicemen tended to patronise us, although not Richard, I don't think he ever did.' The ex-army boys inevitably took the lead in the cultural and extra-curricular life of the university.

The vehicle selected by Ingrams and Foot for their initial satirical assault on the rest of Oxford was a small magazine called *Parson's Pleasure* (named after a stretch of river where dons tend to bathe in the nude; as the two main undergraduate publications are named *Isis* and *Cherwell*, most alternative titles tend to involve some fluvial reference). *Parson's Pleasure* was owned and edited by an undergraduate from Christ Church college called Adrian Berry, now the *Telegraph*'s science correspondent. It was filled mainly with gossip – meaningless to outsiders – about the Christ Church 'bloodies', the name then given to the chinless wonders who have traditionally visited their excesses on that unfortunate college. Despite this wilful obscurantism, *Parson's Pleasure* sold well enough to keep its head just above water, albeit with a little help from the Berry family. Richard was instantly struck by the fact that people were interested in reading about strangers. '*Parson's Pleasure* prefigured *Private Eye* in that sense, because it brought home to me that you don't have to know who people are to enjoy reading about them . . . in fact, people like reading about people they don't know anything about.'[5]

Berry was already bored with putting out the magazine single-handed, and was only too pleased to find two people eager to take it on. Their first issue nonetheless contained an article foisted on them by their erstwhile proprietor, which included the sentence: 'The relationship between – and – [two undergraduates' names] is becoming so scandalous as to merit the attention of the authorities.' Ingrams and Foot had provoked their first-ever libel action. Of course they made Berry pay for it, but as his parents actually owned the *Daily Telegraph* this was no great imposition. Soon, *Parson's Pleasure* had converted to the Ingrams/Foot model, with joke leader columns, parodies and a cast of regular characters, after the model of Beachcomber and Peter Simple. 'Between the turgid waters of *Isis* and *Cherwell* we will steer our jolly little barque,' wrote Ingrams. In due course, the 'jolly little barque' was banned by W.H. Smith. 'It was the true forerunner of *Private Eye*,' says Andrew Osmond.

The registered address of *Parson's Pleasure* was 'Univ 1:3', Foot's room on the University College front quad. Remembers Ingrams: 'He shared with a man called Tim Pugh, who was very long-suffering, because there was this constant tea party going on in these rooms, and magazines were being produced, and all these groupies were coming in and sitting around drinking tea and things. It was great fun.' As Foot and Ingrams had developed into handsome young men, there was a never-ending supply of young female undergraduates to help fold and staple their efforts; for the first time ever, Richard was really beginning to enjoy himself in an educational establishment. Sometimes his younger brother Leonard would come over from Corpus and laugh at everybody's jokes. Richard and Paul Foot were joint editors of the magazine, but Foot claims that Ingrams was the real editor. 'I've always been a rotten editor – he's the one who assessed the stuff, put it in, and ruthlessly spiked things,' says Foot modestly. 'He was plainly an editor from the beginning.'

First to be attacked were the Grey Men, library-dwellers who, according to Osmond, 'wore a tie and did their essays on time.' Generically, these were direct descendants of the 'Stodges' of Shrewsbury, in Ingrams' words, 'the splendid bleating sheep'. He wrote: 'It is only men with pathetic minds who have to immerse themselves in routine to avoid the boredom of living with their own personalities.' There was a quiz – 'Are you grey?' – and Ingrams scathingly attacked the officially-produced *Directory of Opportunities for Graduates*: 'This is a drab book; written by grey-flannelled minds for the increasing number of men who join commuters' clubs and the futile rat-race of financial success.' For the most part, the grey men tended to come from the ranks of non-military servicemen, and Ingrams was merely railing against their conformity, trying to drag them out of the libraries into the light; but to Potter, Loach and Trodd, custodians of *Isis* maga-zine and the Oxford left, Ingrams was an elitist to be attacked. In retaliation, the barrels of the *Parson's Pleasure* guns swung leftwards.

Dennis Potter had attacked a play in *Isis* for the cardinal sin of being 'uncommitted'. Ingrams responded with a cod-*Isis* review of the Marx Brothers' *A Night In Casablanca*: 'The basic failure of the film is due to the fact that it fails to assert the merits of a self-determinising stratocracy. The point is so often sacrificed to some very irrelevant frivolity, and consequently the nihilistic tendencies of the virtually self-appointed seneschal are constantly being overstressed.' Potter's over-elaborate vocabulary, his use of words such as 'posit' and 'purposive', was consistently scorned in *Parson's Pleasure*. He was told that he was 'inclined to burble', and that he 'can and must write matter of less bias and more art'. Foot joined in, with the claim that 'no one, except Brian Walden, ever takes Dennis Potter seriously'. 'I remember Dennis Potter coming round and giving a talk at Univ,' says Richard. 'He addressed the Liberal Club, and I remember him saying that whenever he saw a Rolls-Royce he spat at it, and everybody thought that this was tremendous.' Everybody else, that is.

Potter and his Labour Club mates from *Isis* were lambasted relentlessly for such intolerance. 'They cannot disagree without condemning. They rarely laugh. The proverbial fire in their bellies eats away any latent sense of humour.' Richard Ingrams complained that stories in *Isis* were 'all about cracked teapots and women with unwashed hair'. 'I deplore two things about *Isis*,' he summed up. 'The attempt to combine a rather negative undergraduate form of socialism with the arts, theatre, and criticism; and the inability to enjoy jovial events. This indicates a lack of genuine artistic versatility and enthusiasm (Julian Mitchell is an exception) and a lack of humour.' Added Jack Duncan, appropriately for him: '*Isis* is never stained with beer.' Ultimately *Private Eye*'s fight was not just with the old order, but with its former university adversaries grown up, in positions of influence, and seemingly just as pleased with themselves as they had been in 1959. The bad feeling between the two groups continues to this day; when Potter viciously attacked Ian Hislop on Radio 4's *Start The Week*, one could hear years of bottled-up resentment pouring out.

When Dennis Potter and Kenith Trodd (he was called Kenneth in those days) finally went down from Oxford, *Isis* printed a series of tributes to them. *Parson's Pleasure* responded with its own stinging memorial: 'The Trotters and Podds, staggering under the monumental chips on their shoulders and lacerated by their multi-sided complexes, have finally moved on to other hitherto normal pastures. Let's hope this year's freshmen aren't as embittered, depressing and fatuous as many of their recent axe-grinding predecessors.' Unexpectedly, however, Trodd changed his mind and decided to stay. 'God only knows why, after taking four years over his degree, he should continue to inflict us with his presence. Haven't we had enough of his sneering and snarling? I wish somebody would find him a cause – such as the improvement of the cultural activities of Eskimos – and that he would actually do something about it instead of pontificating to the ingenuous readers of *Isis* week after dreary week.' Ingrams could be utterly relentless in revenge. Jonathan Cecil, who was essentially a bystander, remembers: 'Even then I was puzzled by the almost venomous acerbity of Ingrams' pen, contrasting with his personal gentleness.' Gentle as he was, he never forgot an enemy.

In addition to attacking the grey men and the Potter–Trodd axis, *Parson's Pleasure* continued its traditional assault on the aimlessly monied 'bloodies' of Christ Church, a leading light among whom was Auberon Waugh. The eldest son of Evelyn Waugh, Auberon had been invalided out of National Service after trying to clean a sub-machine-gun which he was pointing at himself. The resulting hail of bullets removed his spleen, one lung, and several of his ribs. Lying wounded while waiting for an ambulance to arrive, he had remarked to his platoon sergeant, 'Kiss me, Chudleigh'. Sergeant Chudleigh had not recognised the allusion and had treated Waugh with great circumspection thereafter. Sufficiently recovered to take his place at Oxford, Waugh made an attempt to reacquire *Parson's Pleasure* as the bloodies' official organ. Upon being thwarted, he penned a thinly-veiled attack on Foot which somehow crept into *Isis*. It spoke of 'scruffy men in roll neck sweaters who lay about on the floor of their lodgings late at night talking left-wing politics, drinking cocoa and trying to seduce girls who were also wearing roll neck sweaters.'

The fact that Waugh's assault was humorous made him a worthy and admired adversary. The antics of his circle also provided almost endless opportunities for vengeful attack. Says Waugh: 'I do remember scenes of tremendous drunkenness. The Oxford myth I knew was very much my father's ideal – one sees it in a rather coarse, crude form nowadays – that myth of lotus-eating and champagne-drinking.' Waugh goes on to define the refined version of the myth, as enjoyed by himself: 'The Oxford Union was going through the Dimbleby days. [David] Dimbleby was "General King" and [Peter] Jay was "Intellectual King". As a kind of anti-Dimbleby movement, I founded a ghastly club of Christ Church hoorays . . . I remember a party in a room in Canterbury Quad, where the ceiling was almost as high as this one [at Waugh's home, in Combe Florey]. One of my friends was sick, but didn't vomit downwards, he stood up and leaned back and vomited upwards. He produced this remarkable column of vomit which hit the ceiling and left a deep stain, before, of course, coming down.'[6] One of Waugh's set, named Aubrey Bowden, was later apprehended for grabbing a woman outside the Bodleian Library. He got off, because it transpired he was so drunk that he thought she was a telephone box. Waugh himself was eventually thrown out of the university.

The Oxford Union brigade referred to was yet a fourth set of people – Jay, Walden and Dimbleby (who boasted a piano in his rooms) were the stars – to whom *Parson's Pleasure* had a more ambivalent attitude. This was partly because Foot himself was heading that way (he was eventually to fulfil his father's telegram and become Union president) and partly because Richard and he found them to be a nicer bunch on the whole. So there were attacks – Brian Walden was urged 'to retire gracefully from the public eye before he degenerated into a public bore' – but also a good deal of sympathy for Peter Jay, who was praised for his 'brilliant brain and natural ability for public-speaking'. Anyone who was anyone attended the ostentatious party celebrating Jay's engagement to Margaret Callaghan, including Richard, who by now had become a firm friend of Jay's too. Peter Jay was considered the one student of his generation most likely to go on and do remarkable things. The world still awaits.

None of the divisions between these various groups were particularly clear cut. Waugh was considered personally acceptable, and Richard also got on well with Ken Loach, who frequently acted in the same plays. *Parson's Pleasure* could even be downright complimentary to some people: a young Somerville student who sang a political song at the ETC (Experimental Theatre Club) cabaret, named Esther Rantzen, was described as 'scintillating'. Ms Rantzen, it seems, was a jolly girl, dark-haired and not noticeably ambitious.

As with *Private Eye* many years later, being one of Richard's friends was no defence against being attacked. Sometimes the mentions were nice ones: 'Outrageously handsome ex-Ghurka Andrew Osmond', or 'Farouche genius Jack "My sideburns are the mostest" Duncan'. At other times, Osmond was attacked for drunkenly fighting in a Rome fountain, while Richard annihilated Jack Duncan's production of Jacques' *Ionesco*: 'The play itself is downright bad; the script is utterly corny, the characters are colourless and superficial . . . the Producer must be blamed for an inability to anticipate the audience reaction . . . altogether a moderately ludicrous and wholly unsatisfactory evening.' It turned out that the ETC had leaned on Duncan to produce *Ionesco*, when he had wanted to do *The Dumb Waiter* instead, by the then little-known Harold Pinter. 'The play was crap,' he now admits, 'but my production of it was excellent.' In fact only one person's dramatic efforts seemed exempt from criticism. Reviewing Vanbrugh's *The Provok'd Wife*, starring Ken Loach, *Parson's Pleasure* explained that 'Richard Ingrams is absolutely brilliant'.

The magazine did not merely restrict itself to letting fly against the pretensions of others; like *Private Eye* after it, there were jokes too. Under the pseudonym 'Ian Phlegm', Richard wrote a parody adventure serial, whose central character was called Vuckoff. Garden gnomes joined phlegm as a constant reference; one copy advertised in large red letters on the front, 'Free Inside – New Plastic Gnome'. Inside was a pink slip headed 'Erratum': 'We apologise sincerely to all those who bought this week's copy under the impression that they would receive a New Plastic Gnome. We found after trial and error that the gnomes would not stay in the copies. This we had not foreseen. We are gravely sorry for any inconvenience our readers may have suffered.' On one memorable occasion, the university proctors became involved, after a cartoon appeared of a giraffe in a bar, saying 'The high balls are on me'.

In the absence of Adrian Berry's money, *Parson's Pleasure* was being kept afloat by a large ad for *Tribune*, the left-wing newspaper, which appeared in every issue. This was generously paid for by Paul's uncle, Michael Foot, out of his own pocket, but after ten issues one or two ructions were prompted in the impecunious *Tribune* offices as to where exactly such money should be spent. The ad was withdrawn, and *Parson's Pleasure* sadly folded. It was later resurrected by a wealthy undergraduate named Christopher Lennox-Boyd, with Noel Picarda (a friend of Foot's from the army) at the helm; but Ingrams and Foot had already moved on to other things. The name Picarda, incidentally, was later immortalised in the Dear Bill column in *Private Eye*. Picarda was 'a ripe swarthy character', according to Jack Duncan. Alan Coren knew him well: 'Picarda was a sort of grotesque Brian Howard figure, an aesthete, immensely talented, very funny. It was impossible to be in Picarda's company for two or three minutes without falling about. But he had no way of expressing that talent in a concrete fashion. He couldn't actually write.' Picarda later changed his name to Kemp in a failed attempt to become an MP, became a schoolteacher instead, and now lives in London with Jonathan Aitken's mother.

Richard's new project was *Mesopotamia*, an out-and-out comedy magazine designed to incorporate the best of both Oxford and Cambridge university humour. The reason for the title? 'Er . . . because it was supposed to be between two rivers.' *Mesopotamia* was the brainchild of Peter Usborne, a dynamic Old Etonian businessman-in-the-making from Balliol, who had resolved to recruit all the leading humorists at the university. Uz, as he was nicknamed, had been brought up on Belloc and Lear by his father, and on P.G. Wodehouse by his uncle (who had a complete collection), and dearly wished to emulate their work. In the summer of 1959 he had launched the magazine single-handed, billing it as 'a new magazine of dedicated lunacy', and freely admits that his solo efforts were 'pretty dreadful. One of the few people who came up and said well done was Richard Ingrams, who I knew through studying classics. About a year later, *Parson's Pleasure* collapsed and he had nothing to do, so he joined *Mespot*. Then it did become really good – he had a real talent for jokes. Foot was around a bit too – he came to the parties.'

Foot didn't stay long at *Mesopotamia*, as his Union career was taking off, but it was not long before Usborne recruited Andrew Osmond, while Willie Rushton, who'd found a job cartooning for the *Liberal News* in London, continued to come up at weekends and provide the illustrations. They met regularly in Usborne's rooms at Balliol, or in Osmond's room on Longwall Street, where, says Usborne, 'my chief role was melting with laughter'. One morning Usborne assembled the group to meet a potential new recruit – 'the funniest man in Oxford'. A boyish young man with floppy blond hair stood before them. It was John Wells, from the sharp end out in Korea, who instantly recognised the baboon-like organist of Inchon. Says Wells: 'I'd rather reluctantly done an audition for the ETC cabaret and Peter Usborne was there. The next morning he turned up at my digs in St Giles and told me I was the funniest man in Oxford, and I was to come round to Balliol. And I met Foot, Ingrams, Osmond, Rushton, the original *Private Eye* lot, all in one morning, just suddenly.'

The addition of Wells's wit and Usborne's capacity for original ideas made *Mesopotamia* funnier and more successful than *Parson's Pleasure*. It was a full colour glossy magazine, not a pamphlet, with more universally applicable humour and no personal attacks, on account of its supposed Cambridge connection. One of Usborne's first bright ideas was to make a flimsy plastic record and glue it to the cover, a device much used by the *Eye* in later years. Picarda and the future actor Roland MacLeod lent a hand. 'It sold like the clappers,' says Usborne. 'I remember just after it came out, walking across the quad in Balliol and hearing John Wells's voice coming out of every other window.'[7] Another brilliant idea, provided by Usborne's brother Julian, was to sell an issue in a cloth-bound cover, with a packet of mustard and cress seeds that could actually be grown on the magazine. Says Ingrams: 'Usborne was this hyperactive, balding, very enthusiastic man who was absolutely brilliant at getting things done. For an undergraduate to organise that thing with the mustard and cress was quite something.' Peter Usborne is now managing director of Usborne Books, and a millionaire.

The Cambridge connection never quite came off; there was only one Cambridge contributor, a man called Armitage. Usborne had the idea of going to Eights Week in Cambridge with a radio-controlled plane, trailing a banner saying 'Read Mespot', but sadly the wind was blowing in the wrong direction and the plane disappeared. Despite this setback, Ingrams and Wells had established a real talent for collaboration, and the content of the magazine was getting better and better. Says Osmond: 'I remember lying on the floor of Uz's rooms in Balliol, helpless, weak with laughter.'[8] Recalls Ingrams: 'A lot of our jokes were based on National Service, tough RSMs and ridiculous officers.

On the record, Wells did a sketch of an RSM growling "What's your name?" Answer: "Lady Violet Bonham-Carter".' As with *Parson's Pleasure*, the occasional dull slab of prose still made an appearance, but that weakness was usually alleviated by a sprinkling of Rushton cartoons.

There was a very funny bogus membership card, given away free, which outlined the term's activities of the OU Dental Club: for example, 'Sun. May 1st: *Pre-Molars and Their Uses* by W.F.T. Shed FRCAM, Keble Lecture Room.' There was a board game entitled 'The Arms Race', and an alleged advertisement for 'The London School of Beats', using photographs of Wells dressed as a beatnik. Beatniks were another obsession of Ingrams, who wrote a piece describing – amongst other things – the beatnik's morning shave with the jagged edge of a half-opened can of baked beans. Grey men, of course, were universal enough to come in for their regular share of stick too. In a memorable publicity stunt, Usborne rented the front window of the Isis Recording Studios in Broad Street, and persuaded Lady Rosemary Fitzgerald, a twenty-year-old from Lady Margaret Hall, to spend the entire day sitting there writing an essay on 'Protoplasm and its uses'. She was the grey woman, writing the archetypally grey essay.

Most of these stunts tended to devolve on Wells because of his performing skills. It was he who had to take over from Lady Rosemary when she got bored, and sit in the shop window picking his nose. He recalls: 'Ingrams had decided that the grey men were taking over, so we all obediently abused them; they usually appeared in drawings by Rushton, clumping along in baggy flannels and a duffle coat. Occasionally I impersonated them in photographs, with my trousers tucked in my socks beside a bicycle outside the library, creating havoc by mismanaging a punt on the river, or sitting in the shop window, hamster-like at my weekly essay, blind to the merry pageant of life.'[9]

Meanwhile, after the reign of Potter and Trodd, *Isis* itself had been put up for sale, and had been bought by David Dimbleby and a friend of his called John Spicer. They immediately made the magazine more liberal, and after a term, installed their Union friend Foot as editor. Foot promptly recruited Ingrams to divide his comic efforts between *Isis* and *Mesopotamia*. The great bastion of serious undergraduate publishing had fallen. A novel scheme was immediately hatched; *Isis* would sponsor a record-breaking pub crawl around Oxford, partly to review the pubs in question, partly to make a point about the disappearance of the old English pub, but mainly to get very, very drunk indeed. The pub crawl attracted a lot of advance publicity in the national press: 'Says Mr Ingrams intensely: "We are very worried about pubs – the way Betjeman is about churches".'

It had all started with an Ingrams article in *Isis*, praising 'pubs with fine historic names, in which men in cloth caps down countless pints of beer while they discuss fishing, politics and other relaxing topics' (a highly romanticised undergraduate view, of course; the said cloth-capped worthies were probably discussing burgling the newsagent's – but to continue:) 'The Landlord, previously red-faced and jovial, who wore braces and rolled his sleeves up, is now a dapper little man in a suit with smarmy hair and a clip-on bow tie.' Ingrams went on, quoting Belloc: 'When you have lost your inns, drown your empty selves, for you will have lost the last of England.'

Soon after this article appeared, Foot was thrown out of just such a plush, ritzy pub for eating a packet of chips. The nationals became interested on account of his relationship to Michael Foot, and published his retort: 'Eating chips is a basic individual liberty like walking down the street – I often eat chips for my dinner.' The pub crawl resulted. Wrote Ingrams: 'If this survey is of any value, it is of value to the man who hates drinking in a mass of duffle coats and college scarves.' No mention of the man who hates drinking in a mass of well-brought-up students earnestly slumming it in the public bar. The brave souls chosen to undertake the crawl were Ingrams, Rushton, Jack Duncan (obviously), and two other friends named Peter Holmes (now a drama teacher at Westminster School) and David Webster. All of them got fantastically drunk, and there was a lot of singing in bars with cloth-capped men. Duncan was later found fast asleep in a laundry basket in Pusey House Chapel.

Another of Foot's bright ideas as *Isis* editor was to publish reviews of university lectures, written mainly by himself and a man named John Davis, who later became Warden of All Souls. Some were complimentary, some were not: 'Mr Plamenatz's lectures are academic in the worst sense of the word. He fails to place Hobbes and Hegel in their historical context, so that it is difficult to see the concrete significance of their work, its typicality or otherwise. And he fails to relate their work in any meaningful way to our own political thought, and the problems both in theory and practice that we face today.' Or: 'If these [other commentators' points of view about Dante] are interesting, then I should like to hear more about them than Mrs Roaf's cosy-prosy evasions. If they are not interesting, then I don't mind if they're left out; as it is, the net result is dull and void.' Mrs Roaf, who'd probably never been cheeked in half a century, promptly had a nervous breakdown. The proctors moved in and Foot had to back down. He later resigned as *Isis* editor, but not before Ingrams had contributed a huge article attacking pseudery in all its forms. Alan Coren, incidentally, was one of Foot's successors.

All this tilting at the establishment – be it the academic establishment, the Labour Club establishment, the Oxford Union establishment or the brewing establishment – followed the *Salopian* pattern of using mockery to try and drive people down a certain cultural path, away from fakery, pomposity or humourlessness. Says Andrew Osmond: 'We didn't mock people for being Conservative, though we were mostly all Labour. We mocked people for taking themselves too seriously, for pretension, for any kind of humbug.' The sudden success of *Beyond the Fringe* and the pomposity-pricking style of Peter Cook was seen as a vindication of all they stood for. Says Ingrams: 'Those people were doing what we were doing. It wasn't so far removed. Wells knew Dudley Moore and that lot.' Cook and the *Beyond The Fringe* group were actually no older than Ingrams, Rushton and Wells, but were ahead educationally by virtue of not having done National Service. 'The fact that they did do that show and that it was such a great success inspired us all,' says Ingrams. 'It certainly inspired Usborne to start his magazine.'

As with their more famous contemporaries in the fledgling satire movement, Ingrams and his friends' humour was largely directed outwards at the world, and revealed little about their own day-to-day lives, other than what could be gleaned indirectly from their fervently expressed opinions. One exception to this, however, was a large piece, written ensemble, that took over a whole issue of *Mesopotamia*. It was a version of the *Rake's Progress*, starring John Wells (as drawn by Rushton) as 'Little Gnittie', a *Candide*-style fresher on a guided tour of Oxford. A drawing of Wells as Gnittie, pictured in a parody of the *Daily Express* crusader logo, can still be seen on *Private Eye*'s masthead to this day. Wells was a natural choice for the role; he was, after all, still the outsider in the group.

Gnittie starts in 'Bloodyland', where an upper-crust character called Oz (clearly Osmond) shows him how to avoid going to tutorials. In an attempt to become more grown-up, Gnittie grows a beard. 'Beards give charm to the chinless. Beef to Bambini. Psensitivity to Pseuds. Panache to Poofs. Weight to Weeds. Verve to Virgins.' Then comes the vexed question of sex. Gnittie is introduced to 'The Expert'. The Expert is clearly a caricature of Ingrams. 'Yes,' says The Expert, 'come and meet the birds.' There follows a large number of cartoons of various female types by Rushton. ' "Women?" enquired Gnittie, who was rather embarrassed; "No, no", said The Expert, "just girls".' Behind him is a poster on the wall advertising 'The Pok Pitter. Be pock-marked for only 7d! Girls love that pitted face! 3 days free trial (deposit, 17 monthly payments of £27–10s)'.

Clearly, a degree of jealousy was creeping into his comrades' perspective of Richard's romantic success. In his last year, Richard contributed a poem about his daily life to Foot's *Isis*, part of which read:

> . . . But all the same I ride a bicycle
> Down to that little sweet shop in St Giles'
> And then ride back again. How nice it is
> To read the same *Observer* with a cup
> Of steaming home-made Maxwell House and smoke –
> Appropriately – a *Bachelor* cigarette.

This last line was something of a fib.

9 The Leader of the Gang

The Ingrams gang used to meet every day in a Cypriot-owned greasy spoon called the Town and Gown. 'That's what we were – his gang,' says John Wells. 'He's a natural gang leader, a very attractive personality to men and to women.' Osmond, Wells, Duncan, Jay, Foot, and Rushton, when he was in town, were the regulars; sometimes Grey Gowrie, nicknamed 'Groinbrush', and later to become Minister for the Arts, would turn up. Usborne was not included, for he was a businessman and therefore didn't count, an attitude that still divides the staff of *Private Eye*. There was also one regular female member of the gang, John Betjeman's daughter Candida, who had been introduced by John Wells. Candida was not a student, but was doing a sculpture course at the local Tec. She describes their chosen meeting place: 'The Town and Gown was a very small, oily chip shop off the High, a real lorry drivers' cafe with neon lights and absolutely filthy food. We just merged in there through our scruffiness, although we were often the only people in there. We had a table which was just ours. We had lunch there every single day. We never changed the venue, ever, in three years – there was no question of it.'

This conservatism, and this inclination towards ostentatiously working-class culture, carrying with it a converse distaste for anything bourgeois, were typically Ingrams values. Besides, the much smarter Grill over the road was already occupied by the rival Christ Church 'bloodies'. 'Richard had the same egg and chips fry-up every single day,' says Candida. 'I was aware even then that it was very unhealthy, this absolutely disgusting food.' 'Breakfast there was appalling,' agrees Osmond, who was obviously getting up a little later than Candida; she'd referred to the same meal as 'lunch'. 'But the thing was,' she explains, 'you could just go to the cafe and know they'd all be there. That's where the week's *Mesopotamia* and things would be cooked up.'

Candida Betjeman was madly in love with Richard. 'When she first saw him,' says Paul Foot, 'she fell off her bicycle. And she was the most beautiful woman in Oxford.' Blonde, well-bred and sought after, Candida only had eyes for Richard. 'They were a good-looking bunch,' she recalls. 'Foot and Gowrie had a lot of women buzzing around them, Jack Duncan wasn't bad either, but nobody – *nobody* – compared to Richard, because he had such wonderful eyes. He still has. I didn't mind the rough face, it was those eyes. And he had a certain saintliness about him. Of course we were all brought up pretty strictly compared to nowadays. I believed in mortal sin and things like that. Nobody was smoking dope then, for instance, at Oxford. So I suppose part of this faint holiness he exuded was a puritanical streak. Not that I even really identified that saintliness then, I was just trying to make him fall in love with me, which he quite clearly wasn't going to do.

'John Wells was my best friend, he lived in a little flat above a sweetshop in St Giles, and I used to spend an awful lot of time there complaining to him that I was very much in love with Richard and he wouldn't even look at me. Poor Wells, he had the most awful time hearing all these sob stories. In those days one loved unrequited love, because you sat and wrote poems about it. I wrote a lot of poems about Richard. He had this red jersey that I used to write about, and red socks.' Both items, no doubt, riddled with enormous holes. Poor Candida was almost as much in love with unrequited love itself as she was with Richard. After eighteen months pining for his red sweater she transferred her affections to Glyn Worsnip, who also spurned them. She was to leave Oxford unfulfilled. In fact the only sexual excitement to come her way during the whole three years was when Noel Picarda came round to her flat and heard her singing 'Love for

Sale' in the bath. When she climbed out he said, 'You've got it, kid', and leered.

For his part, Richard preferred a more knowing type of girlfriend, such as the self-assured Fiona Douglas-Home. When she drifted off after his first year, there were plenty of potential replacements. Says Paul Foot: 'Richard was tremendously sought after by women. He had a number of affairs at Oxford and lots of girlfriends. He not only looked absolutely wonderful but he was so funny as well.' Says John Wells: 'He was thought of as the expert on girls. There was a beautiful redhead called Caroline Threlfall whom I'm pretty certain he had an affair with, and there were girls who just used to crawl over his lap. There was one French girl whom he had a long affair with.' Then there was Susan Andrew. 'Gosh, a real star undergraduette,' says Jack Duncan, his eyes misting over.

'It's true, I had lots of girlfriends at Oxford,' concedes Richard, while vociferously denying any of the above-named involvements. He had discovered the pleasures of being surrounded by adoring women, and soon became enough of an expert to paint an authentic portrait of Lady Margaret Hall, then a girls-only college, for *Parson's Pleasure*: 'Sylph-like wispy girls with no shoes on who flit out of their rooms carrying kettles and flutes; you expect them to dart away at your approach like startled squirrels,' he wrote daintily. Rushton describes the Ingrams lifestyle a little more bluntly: 'I think he was knocking-up most of the glamour at Oxford, and there were some very glamorous women there – I used to enjoy going up to Oxford myself, because there's always something faintly erotic about intelligent women. I think he was very badly behaved by the standards of the late Fifties. He was getting his end away all over the place – that was the impression I got. I was extremely jealous, as nothing at all was happening to me. As the Sixties dawned I felt that I'd been blackballed by the permissive society, whereas Ingrams – very quietly and decently – was having the time of his life. And I raise my hat to him.'

Richard's principal love was Faith Anderson, not an Oxford student but an actress and dancer from Nottingham, one of a group hired by Ken Loach to take part in a play at the Edinburgh

Festival at the end of Richard's second year. Crucially, she was a Catholic. Everybody remembers Faith vividly – 'she was blonde and incredibly sexy,' says Richard – but confusingly they remember her not as Faith but as Tina, her real name and also the name of her role.

'Tina was very pretty,' says Wells. 'A proper hoofer, obviously trouble in 1960. Ingrams kept her photograph on his mantelpiece, and I remember him saying "that's my bird". He was definitely committed to her. He was taking a plunge into the working class.' Candida Betjeman had particular cause to remember Faith Anderson. 'She'd obviously done it – I mean, nobody else had in those days. You could tell. She gave me a terrific inferiority complex. She was grown up. She used to come and visit Richard – a bit of a showgirl, very glamorous, and I knew I didn't have an earthly chance.' That relationship, too, was destined to fizzle out, when Faith was involved in a car crash. She was confined to hospital for some months, and fell for one of the doctors.

If Richard was spectacularly at ease with the opposite sex, the same could not be said for the gang as a whole. There was an awkwardness with women – no doubt the product of single-sex education – that manifested itself in *Parson's Pleasure*, where girls were invariably referred to as 'fruit', 'skirt' or 'totty'. This communicated itself to Candida Betjeman: 'They used working-class descriptions of women – "birds" and so on – to mask their embarrassment; they were all highly embarrassed. They put sex in a separate drawer. They were very laddish. But they never made passes at me, none of them . . . Actually that's not quite true. But I'm not telling.' Oh go on. 'No no, I'm not going to,' she blushes.

In print, women were treated with a mixture of desire and reverence. The glamorous Caroline Seebohm, who shared digs with Margaret Callaghan (and frequently took tea with Richard), was consistently fêted. Her performance in *The Provok'd Wife* was summed up with the words: 'Acts well, and was neither rattled nor, unfortunately, disrobed.' In its early days, *Parson's Pleasure* even invented a beautiful undergraduate, Suzanna Harcourt, the subject of gushing tributes which masked a shortage of real-life women in the authors' social circle. Perhaps it was this mixture of awe and chivalry towards the opposite sex that saved the young Esther Rantzen from any punishment in the review columns.

The social life of the gang tended to revolve around principally masculine and working-class pursuits, largely inherited from the army, such as playing darts and drinking like fishes. The pub visited was, of course, always the same one – the Duke of Cambridge, on the corner of Little Clarendon Street and St Giles, which had two tiny bars and was run by a ferrety woman with protruding teeth. Naturally, they always used the public bar, for economic and social reasons. 'We drank a great deal of beer,' says Willie Rushton, 'and frequently got very drunk. National Service had given us very solid heads for it. We'd all drunk a considerable amount for two years before we came out into civilian life. We played darts all the time – we'd discuss the magazine over darts – and we were also very heavily into pinball; we judged a pub by the standard of its pinball machine, whether it was a Williams or a Gottlieb. Jack Duncan was a master of the tilt.' Says Duncan of this semi-working-class existence: 'I think it was most important to them that you had to be at one with the lower classes – particularly Foot and Ingrams. There was always something that made Richard sympathise with the downtrodden.' Foot, although he did tag along to the pub, didn't go in for the heavy drinking. A wise move perhaps, as all that alcohol eventually took its toll. Rushton explains: 'I'm teetotal now, because of diabetes. But I'd had enough anyway. The hangovers were getting worse. They were appearing two mornings later.' Ingrams, too, drank himself to a point where he was forced to give up. Of all those who took part in the great *Isis* pub crawl, only Jack Duncan is still piling back the pints.

When the pubs closed, they sat up all night drinking coffee, as students always have done and always will do. Sometimes they went to see Ingmar Bergman films. Sometimes they went to parties, where Chris Barber or Bill Haley played on the gramophone; the same old student parties that everybody's been to – 'You know, a bunch of people in a room full of smoke, drinking beer and red wine, and chatting up the birds,' says Andrew Osmond.

Richard was always the only one who refused to dance, but he did have a party trick – he could put his cello over his lap like a guitar and play 'Living Doll'. 'I remember walking back with him through North Oxford,' recalls John Wells with fond nostalgia, 'and him looking up at the stars and saying, "Wonderful to think that on some remote star there are two men walking back from a cabaret, completely pissed out of their minds, one of them holding a cello".'

Oxford was perhaps Richard's happiest time. The friendships he established there formed the framework upon which he built the rest of his life, both socially and professionally. The jokes of *Private Eye* are recognisable as the jokes of Ingrams' gang at Oxford, the magazine's views those of a radical English patrician family dipped in the sergeants' mess and allowed the opportunity to ferment among like-minded Oxford undergraduate souls. For the first time, at Oxford, Richard was able to construct a formidable social barrier against the demons of misery and loneliness that had troubled him at West Downs, at Shrewsbury, and in the army. For Andrew Osmond, this is critical to an understanding of Richard Ingrams' character: 'At the heart of the matter is a web of male friendships, very English in style, and very much a creation of his own, on which he is dependent. Take it away and the night would close in.' Except that Richard's friendships do not really form a web; rather they resemble the spokes of a wheel, in that although all these friends know each other well, he turns a different aspect of his personality towards each one. In some cases they come away knowing a different man from the one perceived by the others.

The friend who has reached closest to the heart of Richard Ingrams is Paul Foot. He is the serious, intimate friend, privileged to be allowed to see Richard's dark side. According to him, 'Richard's been unhappy all his life. He's a very melancholy man. He's always got a lot out of life, but there has always been a great streak of melancholy in him, which none of us have ever been able to probe. In those almost halcyon days he came into my family for the summer holidays; the first summer, I remember, he came down to Cornwall when my grandfather was still alive. My

101

grandfather had a great big house, and we stayed there, and we stayed with my uncle John, and we would go walking together. I would always take a book; the summer of '59 was absolutely wonderful, and we would sit for hours on Cornish cliffs, or the hills of Bodmin Moor; and I was always amazed by the fact that he could just sit for hours without doing anything. He could cope with his own resources. I could never do that – I always had to be doing something, or talking to somebody – but he had this great internal resource, which flowed with his melancholy and with his religious commitment, which was always deep. From really very early in his youth, he had a religious commitment which as an atheist I've never understood, of course. I don't think anybody's ever reached that part of him. I certainly never did.'

Cavernous depths indeed; but shout into a dark cathedral and the echoes will give you a rough indication of what lies where. Perhaps, as they sat on the cliffs, Foot skittish, Richard drawing on his great well of solemnity, more of the inner Ingrams was being revealed to Paul Foot than he likes to give himself credit for. Richard himself remembers the summers he spent as a guest of the Foot family with equal affection. 'Footie's parents were always abroad with the diplomatic service, so we went off to stay with the Rt. Hon. Isaac Foot, his grandfather. He was very keen on Bach in his old age, so I used to sit and play the piano to him; then I had to read his old speeches back to him after dinner. He was a real bibliomane – he had this huge house stacked with books. Every single room was full of books – he obviously couldn't part with any book. He'd even keep the instruction leaflet from an aspirin bottle, because it contained the written word. Michael and Paul were both like that – they inherited this bibliomania.

'I remember going to see Michael on Lord Beaverbrook's estate, where he'd rented a house. My first introduction to politics was through Footie's family – they spent the whole time discussing the bomb. All his uncles were very anti-nuclear; Michael got Paul into CND. At this stage, Paul was liberal, not left wing. He'd been president of the Liberal Club. But he'd been very heavily influenced by "Kek", and he was much more interested in plays and poems than politics. Then in my last year at Oxford, I was in digs at 99 Woodstock Road, and living above me was a man called Williamson, a Welshman whom I hardly knew; but I used to hear this man engaged in conversation late into the night, and it kept me awake and annoyed me. I discovered later on that he was a Marxist economist, and the noise I'd heard was Footie coming round to see him – he was converting Footie to the cause. Williamson's now a professor at Cardiff, by the way.'

Inevitably, as Foot's political ambitions widened, he drifted further away from Richard; their professional life together was intermittent at Oxford and has continued to be so ever since. Initially, they had done everything together – compiling magazines, writing sketches, and attending auditions together, at which they would perform a scene from John Mortimer's *The Dock Brief*. 'We were both failed actors,' attests Foot. 'We both played in the OUDS *Coriolanus*, ninety hours rehearsing for one line in my case, and five lines in Richard's case. We weren't any bloody good, either of us.' In time, Foot decided that acting was not for him, that he'd rather change the world instead; but despite this divergence, the emotional bond between himself and Ingrams remained powerfully intact. Andrew Osmond points out: 'Notice how the two of them are complete opposites; that's the secret. Paul's unquenchable enthusiasm, his rubber-ball irrational optimism, was always deeply delightful to his world-weary friend.' Says Candida Betjeman (now Candida Lycett Green): 'Foot did become increasingly politically committed and earnest, but he was still able to laugh at himself. He and Richard used to tease each other all the time.'

Richard forced himself to go to the Oxford Union to see Foot in action, and in May 1961 he and Osmond were the tellers on the night Foot won the Union presidency. In an astute valediction to Foot's Oxford career published in *Isis* in 1961, Grey Gowrie wrote: 'Foot will probably not make a practical politician. Like his uncle Michael he is a first-principle boy. In spite of his great attention and attraction to facts, which saves him as a political journalist, his socialism is armchair. Like many others whose most passionate concern is the well-being of the working class, he is little at ease with its members and he is totally hopeless abroad.'

103

If Paul Foot was privy to the dark side of Richard Ingrams, Willie Rushton's job – as it had been before the interregnum of John Ellis – was to keep the bright side as bright as possible. As Candida Lycett Green recalls: 'He was jolly, funny, enthusiastic, and he constantly cracked jokes that made you rock. He was very chubby – I've got pictures of him at the Edinburgh Festival and he's got no chin.' Rushton, who had indeed ballooned in size during his army days, was now a familiar sight in Oxford with his broken umbrella and pork pie hat. 'Being a sort of honorary member was the best way of getting a university education,' he explains. 'It suited me down to the ground. I also went to St John's College Cambridge sometimes, using my father's old John's scarf.' According to Alan Coren, 'Willie hasn't changed at all as far as I can see. He has the most originally surreal imagination of all of them, but he's such a lazy bastard.' Ingrams feels the problem to be more organisational. 'He's a brilliant fellow, Willie, he has a fantastic flood of ideas, but he always had difficulty harnessing it all.'

The arrival of Foot meant that the Rushton–Ingrams relationship would never be as close as it had been at Shrewsbury; but they still saw each other often, got on well, and had a laugh together. Asked whether he thinks there is any sadness inside Richard, Willie replies: 'No, I don't think so. He's thoughtful, maybe, rather than melancholy.' Perhaps he has seen a different Richard Ingrams from that perceived by Paul Foot? 'No, Richard's the same to everyone. It's one of his strengths.'

Andrew Osmond, in common with both Willie Rushton and Richard Ingrams, had suffered the loss of his father at an early age. 'My father died when I was eight,' he says, 'so Richard and I were always seeking clues to our fathers. They were both very respected and well-liked men, so we always felt their absence. One of the few times I've seen him really angry is when someone insulted his father. He was always very curious about his father, always trying to find out things about him, always intrigued by his wartime career.' Partly because of this connection, Osmond was the only friend, apart from Foot, privy to Ingrams' darker corners: 'Richard was a very funny fellow, but he could also be quite melancholy and depressed about certain things. I was always well aware of that, and occasionally he let me see that side of his personality. I've been conscious on several occasions of really trying to cheer him up, because his natural melancholy was threatening to overwhelm him. His pessimism would make him much more prudent than I ever was at that age, because he was always aware that the worst could happen. He had an aura not only of melancholy but of vulnerability to disaster – a lot of people don't glimpse that much. I worried less, I was more irresponsible and carefree.'

Osmond was indeed a wilder sort. On one occasion, driving down the Broad full of gin and *joie-de-vivre*, with his hand pressed permanently on his car horn, he was pulled up by a police constable. 'How old are you?' inquired the officer. 'Twenty-one,' replied Osmond. 'Those figures should be reversed,' commented the plod wittily. This was of course only the ostentatiously knockabout behaviour of the upper-crust young officer type. 'I had taken the officer route at school,' explains Osmond, 'captain of this and that.' Ingrams tamed Osmond to some extent, by example and by education. 'He indoctrinated me into music. Any knowledge or enthusiasm that I have for classical music came entirely from Richard. Of my desert island discs, I'd have to say of at least seven out of eight that I first heard them through Richard Ingrams.' The two would spend long hours together practising Brahms concertos so they could play them to their friends. It was the Ingrams family teaching habit surfacing again.

Osmond was considered a great wit at university, and so managed to combine, in lesser measure, the appeal of both Rushton and Foot. Lesser, as evinced by the fact that Ingrams never bothered to seek Osmond out during the holidays. Nevertheless, the similarities between the Ingrams–Osmond friendship and the Ingrams–Foot friendship are intriguing. Both men are alone among the gang in calling their friend Richard and not Ingrams. Both men identify the same prevailing trait in Richard's character: as described by Osmond, 'his melancholia and pessimism, which drive him to look for laughter and make him such a demanding and possessive friend' – qualities which also help make him the

105

natural editor he is. Yet Foot and Osmond could not be more different; Foot scruffy, enthusiastic, crusading, always with a bee in his bonnet; Osmond scrupulously tidy, well-groomed, laid back, carrying himself with careful dignity, still visibly an ex-Gurkha officer.

The fastidious Osmond had a great deal of difficulty coming to terms with the condition of Richard's digs. 'His rooms at 99 Woodstock Road were indescribably scruffy and dirty. Every so often one of us would make an effort at clearing them up because you couldn't even get across the room for old coffee cups, records, half-finished essays; the floor was inches deep in gunge and rubbish. He lived in the most indescribable squalor.' Richard's sartorial habits were unusual to say the least. In winter he would wear several shirts at once, take them off for his daily bath, then put them all back on again. If he needed specific items of clothing, he wrote to his mother and asked her for them. 'Could you send please (heigh ho!) a shirt and collar (white) and studs and a pair of black shoes.' All his life Richard has had to be looked after sartorially. At one stage the dons of University College held a vote as to who was the scruffiest student in the place. Richard was not impressed to find himself out in front as one of the two leading candidates, along with Jack Duncan. Duncan remembers Richard's further 'surprise and indignation' at winning first place.

One crucial need that Andrew Osmond's friendship could fulfil, where the companionship of Paul Foot was perhaps less adequate, was in the area of religion. Richard's Protestant upbringing, tempered by his mother's Catholic strictures, had left him uncertain and teetering on the brink of conversion. He made friends with Father Michael Hollings, the university's Catholic chaplain, who took him through the first stages of formal instruction into Catholicism before Richard backed off. As a fellow Christian, Osmond alone was privy to the details of this semi-conversion, whereas those such as John Wells had no idea it was taking place. 'He and I would often discuss deep matters of religion,' says Osmond, 'and I remember him telling me that one day he would become a Catholic. He reacted very sharply against logical positivism – we'd all been spoon-fed that we could only trust the evidence of our senses, and we'd all swallowed it. Richard found this very arid, and developed a huge contempt for those philosophers. That's when he started turning to people like Chesterton and Belloc.' Also, as Richard explains, 'I was increasingly warming to Catholicism as a result of reading the testament. I found it very persuasive.' So why did he not go through with the conversion? 'I don't know. I think partly through living on my own, and partly through really working hard, I was getting quite intense, but then I left Oxford and that intensity collapsed.'

Richard's distaste for logical positivism did not intrude on the cordial relationship he enjoyed with his philosophy tutor, Peter Strawson, who had been greatly amused by the *Isis* pub crawl. Nor did it compromise the clear benefits he perceived in studying the subject. 'Wasn't it MacNeice who said that if you read philosophy at Oxford then you never believe anything that anyone says to you again? If it's done well, it trains you to think about the meaning of what people say and analyse what they're really saying. Since most people talk balls all the time, it is a useful training.'[1] Unfortunately, though, Richard wasn't actually very good at philosophy. It was his first venture outside the classics for years. 'I was just hopeless,' he admits.

After two years of messing about, Richard studied intensely in his last few terms. 'I revised, hard, for the whole of the last year, lots of translations and things. I worked very hard indeed.' Andrew Osmond, however, paints a very different picture. 'We were pretty cavalier about work, and took the most appalling liberties. One went to lectures, but lectures that one liked – Isaiah Berlin and so on – which were nothing to do with one's subject. Richard never had his heart in his studies, they never seemed of any importance to him. He just did enough work to get a third.' Once again, one is left with the unsettling notion that different people were seeing different sides of Richard. Osmond, for instance, claims never to have seen Richard drunk. He is quick to play down the picture of the well-oiled, highly-sexed best mate painted by Rushton; his Richard Ingrams, despite a jokey surface layer, was a deeply spiritual individual. Part of this is just the protectiveness of the true friend, but there

107

is more to it than that. Ingrams didn't like anyone to grasp the whole. Obviously, an intelligent man like Osmond is aware that there are a number of apparent contradictions inherent in Ingrams' character; he points to 'Richard's extraordinary mixture of reserve and authority', for instance. In many ways, Ingrams' authority is exercised through that very reserve, which hides his own personality while awing others into gabbling out the details of their lives.

Jonathan Cecil, the occasional member of the gang who occasionally sat up late into the night at Woodstock Road, describes Richard as 'an enigma. A highly social being who yet seemed detached. He was not usually a leading light in the conversation – a difficult feat with Peter Jay in the room – but his laconic comments then as now were always drily amusing.' There was always a feeling that Ingrams was somehow in control. 'John Spicer, who was a nice quiet undergraduate, would only get going far into the small hours, when he was unstoppable, while the rest of us flagged. Ingrams could be extremely droll – although not unkindly – at the expense of "the late night Spicer", as he dubbed it. The measured, precise and low tones with which Richard delivers witticisms on *The News Quiz* today are not the result of maturity, but sound exactly as they did when he said that, over thirty years ago.'

Perhaps Richard's most interesting friendship over the years has been with John Wells. It had not fully developed at Oxford, but the future pattern had been seen set there. At the time they were introduced, Wells was a successful late-night cabaret artist, in the words of Jonathan Cecil, 'a toothy youth with a honey voice'. Ingrams and he had instantly hit it off as collaborators – Wells's multiplicity of voices and freewheeling improvisational style perfectly matched by Ingrams' dry, sniping wit and gift for editorial discipline – and their work quickly outstripped Ingrams' previous efforts with other writers. Like many who create more easily together than they do individually, each man became jealous and slightly dismissive of the other and his solo work, these emotions tinged with – but sometimes obscuring – a more honestly felt admiration. Wells has always believed himself to be something of an outsider in Ingrams' gang; he points out that he never went to Shrewsbury, but then neither did some of the others. He is something of an outsider because that is where Ingrams likes to keep him. Ingrams and Wells are what has been described as 'frenemies', best friends who are eternally and subconsciously working out their frustrations with each other on anyone who will listen. When Wells described his first impression of Ingrams as 'an incongruous baboon-like figure', and 'a mild-mannered orang-utan', the statement contained both affection and the need to ridicule. Inevitably, each man has the capacity to hurt the other; but it is in Richard's nature never to admit it, and in John Wells's nature to admit it freely.

As the outsider in the group, Wells was most keenly aware of the extent to which they had become a gang, led by Richard, all of them falling into line with Richard's world view. 'After Oxford, I started writing an Oxford novel,' he admits sheepishly. 'The image I had of Richard was of looking out of my window down St Giles, and Richard was standing on the pavement with a bike in one hand and his arm round a girl, looking up and talking to me. It was a summer's day, and all the people walking along the pavement were just flowing round him, like a stream around a rock. That was what I respected; he was his own man. He seemed to know what was going on. He seemed to have a very clear idea of what was right and what was wrong, that we slavishly followed. There was always this clear sense of the importance of distinguishing right and wrong, not as complex as a moral code.' More of a moral perspective, perhaps.

Wells has railed at Richard's refusal to reveal himself further than in simple moral terms. 'Ingrams was fond of talking in comic voices at university; it served as a defence against intellectual, emotional or political commitment – any statement made in a comic voice can carry the force of a straight statement, but at the same time contains its own ejector seat if things get too hot,' he complains.[2] This is *Private Eye*'s style, contends Wells, reflective of Ingrams' personality; but how much of his apparent irritation at this defensiveness stems from the fact that Ingrams never allowed Wells himself into the deeper recesses?

One of the major pieces of grit in the cogwheels of the

Ingrams–Wells friendship was the tricky business of class. Most of the gang were of course patrician – the type to be described as 'upper class' by the middle classes and 'middle class' by the upper classes. Duncan was working class, and therefore entirely acceptable by virtue of being one of the salt of the earth. Wells, however, was straight-down-the-line middle class, the son of a Bognor Regis vicar and educated at Eastbourne College. Ingrams thinks this gave him a regrettable inferiority complex. Wells thinks this gave Ingrams a regrettable superiority complex. Wells has striven to raise his status in society, and now moves in circles considerably more socially elevated than Ingrams does, a feat achieved on the back of his remarkable capacity to entertain. He writes ostentatious articles for the *Evening Standard* on what to pack for country house weekends. 'Wells has got very good qualities, but he's a ghastly snob,' says Ingrams, who finds this leapfrogging of his own position irritating and risible. Wells, conversely, thinks that Ingrams is the snob, and refers to him and his patrician friends as 'Lord Snooty and his pals'; because he is a patrician, thinks Wells, Ingrams wishes to keep him in his proper place.

Wells always tried to stand slightly apart from the mocking patrician standpoint of Ingrams' satirical work. 'He caresses nothing more passionately than the status quo. The sergeants' mess and the similar British pub have only served to confirm the patrician prejudice, to find everyone obsessively comic: royalty, aristocracy, arrivistes, students, politicians, journalists, pooves and the lower-middle classes. The greatest crime, because the most embarrassing, is romantic idealism. How the starry-eyed Trotskyite Foot stood it I shall never know.'[3] Foot, though, had a private line.

What must have irked Wells especially about his climb to a position of friendship with royalty is that once he got there, he was still being laughed at from below as he had once been from above. For Ingrams is not a snob in the traditional sense of looking down on those beneath him and looking up to those above; his mother and the army curbed any instincts in that direction. Rather, so possessed of patrician confidence is he (as opposed

110

to prejudice – but a fine dividing line) that he takes nobody and nothing seriously, from kings to cabdrivers, if they fall outside that domain of old England that produced him and which he has been prepared to spend his life defending.

Yet there is genuine affection between the two men. Asked by the *Telegraph* Magazine for a feature they were preparing to name his 'soul mate', Wells nominated Ingrams. 'I don't know why,' harrumphed Ingrams, before his face cracked into a grin, and he conceded that Wells was 'a good friend' indeed. Wells told the *Telegraph*: 'If I get a bad notice, he is on the telephone within minutes wondering whether I've seen it, saying how very cruel people can be . . . and that he feels he really has to read it out to me in full.' Only friends do that. 'I suppose I see him as a challenge. It's harder to make him laugh than anyone I know.' Wherein, of course, lies the secret of their joint success. Ingrams must have cared deeply for Wells in his way, for he invited him home to Cheyne Row, and on holiday to Suffolk, to meet his beloved Sefton Delmer. There, Wells was treated to a rare flash of the other Ingrams. 'He has placid depths,' admitted Wells, 'a familiar feature in great men.'

By the summer of 1961, all Richard's friendships had coalesced, as friendships invariably do when you are about to leave university, and the gang lay in a field near Aynhoe, enjoying a liquid picnic. Andrew Osmond takes up the story: 'We were lying there in the sunshine and Willie said, "What are you all going to do when you leave this place?" We all had our different plans, and he said, "You're all mad. We should do a magazine. The public would buy this stuff." And we all said "Yes, Willie, have another drink".' Despite the discouraging reaction, Rushton had undoubtedly struck a chord. There was no question that what they were doing on *Mesopotamia* was part of a progression, from the *Salopian* through *Parson's Pleasure*, which would be very difficult to abandon, all of them scattering into merchant banks and accountants' offices as the grey men were preparing to do. It was up to Richard, as the editor and the leader of the gang, to seize the reins and take decisive action.

In fact Richard had already decided that a conventional career

111

was not for him. His inheritance lay untouched in his bank account, ready to be put to good use. The founding of *Private Eye* magazine was, it seems, inevitable at this point. Except that Richard then sprang a surprise. He left the gang in the lurch, and turned his back on jokes, satire and the world of magazines altogether. Instead, he said, he was going on stage, to forge a life on the road together with Jack Duncan.

10 Tomorrow's Audience

When not lying comatose in a laundry basket in Pusey House Chapel, Jack Duncan had established himself as Oxford's leading theatre director by a distance. Not that he was the obvious theatrical type; his blond matinée-idol looks sat oddly with a blunt northern outspokenness that verged on the antagonistic when faced with authority. As Grey Gowrie wrote in *Isis*: 'It is tempting to typecast him without much further comment as a sort of theatrical Andy Capp . . . in fact he is the best, perhaps the only first-class theatre producer there has been at Oxford for nearly a decade. His *The Miracles* was the college production of all time.' Duncan cast Richard in all his plays. In their first year, the two had performed and recorded an anthology of extracts about war from the point of view of the Other Ranks (naturally), which had come second in a BBC Radio competition and had been broadcast on the Third Programme. From that point on, they had stuck together theatrically like glue. *The Provok'd Wife* . . . *A Woman Killed With Kindness* (in association with the sylph-like ladies of Lady Margaret Hall) . . . Maurice Baring's *The Rehearsal* . . . *The Miracles* . . . right up to the triumphant apex of Duncan's Oxford career, *Tamburlaine The Great*.

Jack Duncan's productions tended to be extravaganzas, and unfashionably so. Method acting may have been all the rage, but nobody toyed with an orange or mumbled their lines in a Duncan production. For *Tamburlaine*, he employed a cast of over a hundred, in an outdoor acting area forty yards long, and cut the

113

play by half. Jonathan Cecil, who wasn't in it, remembers sitting in the audience: 'It was an amazing production. It was in St John's Garden, which is particularly lovely. They were all tearing about. It was so vital, every scene overlapped with another scene. It was unashamedly hammy, extrovert and theatrical. He's a bit of a loss to our theatre, Jack Duncan.' The reviewer from *The Times* supported Cecil's view, adding: 'Perhaps only Mr Wyndham Parfitt, Mr Richard Ingrams, Miss Wendy Varnals and Miss Romola Christopherson succeed in overcoming the difficulty of speaking Marlowe's lines clearly across big distances in the open air. But if Mr Duncan's production is not quite a triumph, it is certainly a brilliant experiment.'

Tamburlaine was played by Peter Holmes, he of the pub crawl, Gordon Honeycombe played the King of Soria, Osmond and Usborne were in there somewhere blacked to the waist, while Richard played Mycetes, the King of Persia. 'His idiot King of Persia was just cracking,' says Duncan, 'prancing round the place in a falsetto.' It has to be said that Richard was normally a lot happier in comic parts, such as those he played in revue with Wells, or in the ETC cabaret night, which he also produced. 'I don't think he'd be offended if I said that he was a pretty awful actor,' says Jonathan Cecil, 'but playing this effete king, screeching and holding on to his crown, he was very funny. Everyone was obsessed with Brando-style acting at the time, but Duncan let him overact as much as he wanted.' Willie Rushton thinks that Richard is 'one of life's great performers. He was a very good mimic. And *I* think he was a very good actor.'

Richard's first involvement with a touring show was at the Edinburgh Festival of 1960, where the OUDS (Oxford University Dramatic Society) put on a double bill: one extremely serious and worthy undergraduate play, a performance of Schiller's *Wallenstein* directed by Ken Loach, and one jolly, frivolous and rather old-fashioned student musical, *From Jacqueline With Love*, written by Richard Ingrams, Herbert Chappell and Patrick Cavendish, with additional material by Loach, Peter Holmes and Ian McCulloch. Richard played a Guards officer, not without irony, and earned good reviews, not least from Faith Anderson, who was

114

in the cast. The band included Bryant Marriott on drums, later controller of BBC Radio 2, and the cash was put up by another undergraduate, Richard Booth, now the millionaire second-hand book king of Hay-on-Wye.

More opportunity for minor celebrity-spotting was afforded the following year, when the double bill idea was repeated. This time the main feature was Aristophanes' *The Birds*, 'an especially long and dreary adaptation' according to Candida Lycett Green, who'd been recruited by Richard for the late-night revue. 'I remember singing in Richard's flat, and I didn't think anyone was listening, and I did a sort of yodel-warble, and Richard heard me and said, "My God, you can sing". Next thing, I was up on stage singing songs with Willie Rushton. That was when I knew everyone was seriously funny. It was incredible, just the most wonderful thing ever. We even got the giggles on stage.'

The 1961 Edinburgh show was drastically different. *Beyond The Fringe* had premiered at the 1960 festival, opposite the rather more traditional OUDS effort, and had opened in London in May 1961. Now audiences were hungry for satire (or anything approaching it), which suited the Ingrams gang, who followed Cook & Co.'s lead when they devised their 1961 show. It was written in a stable block near Thame, where Rushton and Osmond nearly died after leaving a gas tap on and going to sleep on the floor. When starvation threatened, Candida's mum drove up, threw open the boot of her car (which was bulging with food), and said 'I thought you might be hungry', the way well-brought-up mothers do. Eventually, all was ready, and the cast decamped to Edinburgh, where it was discovered that the script hadn't been cleared by the Lord Chamberlain's office. Andrew Osmond explains: 'In those days the Lord Chamberlain had to approve anything that went on the stage. There was a mad dash, first of all to write it all down, and secondly to get to the nearest branch of the Chamberlain's office, which was in Newcastle, where they crossed out a few rude words.'

'We all slept in a huge school dormitory,' recounts Candida, 'women at one end, and men at the other. Peter (Peter Snow, now presenter of *Newsnight*) had a girlfriend, and the only place

115

they could . . . er . . . get together, was in the shower, where everybody could see them through the curtain.' Those little model tanks in the *Newsnight* sandpit will never seem as authoritative again. The show itself took place in a church, and was a massive success. Their greatest triumph was to persuade Albert Finney, who was starring in a deadly serious John Osborne portrayal of Luther elsewhere at the festival, to come along after his performance and take part in a sketch. Osborne's play postulated the idea that Luther's theological ideas stemmed from his constipation; in the sketch, Finney, dressed in his monk's costume, sat straining on a lavatory. Ingrams walked past and remarked, 'Luther?' Finney replied, 'No – tighter'. Harold Hobson wrote a wonderful review, and the show was much lauded everywhere.

While most of the gang were content to rest on their theatrical laurels, Jack Duncan had not been idle, and had started working part-time at the National Youth Theatre even before his finals. He had also tried for the BBC, along with Osmond, Wells and Ingrams, but his great theatrical skills failed to impress Huw Wheldon and Donald Baverstock. After all, if ever there was an officer type it was Sir Huw Wheldon. 'So tell me, Mr Duncan, what aspect of contemporary life moves you most?' 'Well, on my way here, I heard that Newcastle had beaten Spurs. That moved me.' Exit Duncan, *sans* job. Like Ingrams, he was utterly unable to treat authority with the respect it craved. In the end the BBC job went to Wilfred de'Ath, who is currently on the run from the police, which says a lot for the BBC's powers of perception.

Ingrams, meanwhile, got involved in an undergraduate production of *An Italian Straw Hat*, which the management of the Lyric Theatre in Hammersmith unwisely agreed to take on. This one starred Glyn Worsnip, Caroline Seebohm, Jeremy Paul, Jonathan Cecil, Richard Ingrams, Piers Plowright, John Wells and Esther Rantzen, who played – some might say appropriately – the part of Clara, 'a mantis'. This time round the national press were not so fulsome, and booted the production from one end of Fleet Street to the other. The audience in the theatre actually started booing. Richard just laughed at the criticism, a reaction which didn't impress Jonathan Cecil: 'Some undergraduates, like myself, took acting deadly seriously as a possible career. Ingrams always seemed to think it was a jape or a lark. I'm sure he thought me a bit of a prig, but he was always charming and courteous.'

In fact, the acting bug had bitten both Ingrams and Duncan to the extent that neither of them could now conceive of taking on a responsible job, in much the same way that no responsible job could conceive of taking on either of them. True, they couldn't take the theatre particularly seriously, but then they couldn't take anything very seriously. Hence the concept of the Tomorrow's Audience theatre company. 'It's a cringe-making name now, of course,' admits Duncan, 'but the idea was to take theatrical anthologies on tour to schools around the country that didn't normally get any.' A mixture of acting and teaching, which was right up Ingrams' street; having fun while introducing the audience of tomorrow to modern theatre, or 'headmaster-bashing' as Richard put it. 'We saw it as Leavis-ite,' he explains. It was also, of course, Kek-ite, a theatrical version of the Frank McEachran teaching method.

As Richard remarked at the time, 'Teenagers abhor the sort of shows that have kept the theatre going until now. They want plays that mean something to them. It is no good pretending to them that life doesn't exist. Why hide sex and violence from them?' He and Duncan set to work devising *The Prisoners*, an anthology not unlike that which had succeeded in the radio competition, featuring the work of writers from Plato to John Mortimer, via the likes of Arnold Wesker and Brendan Behan. The theme of the whole performance was anti-capital punishment. The teenage audience was to be tempted with jazz records prior to the performance – 'That is the way to fetch them in,' said Ingrams – and the proceedings would begin with 'Jailhouse Rock'. Among the advisers signed up for the fledgling company were Nevill Coghill and Lord David Cecil, Jonathan's father. There were actors to be hired, scenery to be devised and created, transport to be arranged and bookings to be sought, but the first priority was to find Duncan somewhere in London to live. That was settled easily enough – he became a paying guest at Cheyne Row.

'The first thing she did was throw away my pyjamas,' laments Duncan of his introduction to Victoria. 'She said, "I'm not having these in the house." I mean, they *were* absolutely horrible. Torn and dirty.' There was no place for bluff, homespun Geordie pyjamas in the elegant surroundings of Cheyne Row. 'Mrs Ingrams lived in the basement kitchen cooking continuously for a succession of scruffy youths whom Richard would bring home – she used to be very amused by all these young lads that would turn up.' Foot, Wells, Picarda, Rushton, she fed them all when they came back after a hard evening at the pinball tables. 'She was just terrifically tolerant,' sighs Duncan. 'I've modelled my whole domestic life on Mrs Ingrams' kitchen. That was my dream room. She was like a second mother to me. I was terrifically happy there.'

It was while Jack Duncan was staying with Richard at Cheyne Row that their degree results came through; they were not good. It was like the Unit Selection Board all over again. 'Ingrams was appalled,' says Duncan, who was not at all fazed by his own congratulatory third. 'He'd shared tutorials at Univ. with one of the northern lot, a beer-drinking rugby type called Bob Stober, and Ingrams had more or less tutored him. When the results of the examinations came through, he'd got a third and Stober had got a second. He was utterly shocked and taken aback. If Stober had got a third, it would have been all right.' Not that Richard should have been particularly surprised. In one exam paper, Literae Humaniores – Plato's *Republic*, Aristotle's *Nicomachean Ethics* and others – he'd simply scrawled the word 'Balls' across the question sheet.

Despite his disappointing degree result, the only real relevance of which was that he'd wasted all that third-year work, Richard was desperately upset to have left Oxford, where he'd been so happy. 'I remember thinking when I left, that I never want to come back to this place, because I'll just feel so overwhelmingly nostalgic about it. I didn't think I could face ever coming back to Oxford. But now it means nothing to me at all, because when I went back, everything I knew had gone, all my friends had gone, all the dons, all the pubs and restaurants, it was completely different.' To a

118

great extent, Tomorrow's Audience was an attempt to offset that nostalgia, by converting his undergraduate triumphs into a career.

When Richard did return to Cheyne Row after Oxford, unattached once more, Fiona Douglas-Home and Faith Anderson long gone, he found Mary Morgan waiting in the garden. After all, Victoria never gave up. Mary immediately joined up with Richard and Jack Duncan as the costumier and secretary to Tomorrow's Audience. This did, admittedly, present one problem. 'She couldn't spell at all,' confesses Victoria, 'and they'd have rather sarcastic letters from headmasters saying that for an educational project, it was strange that their letters were spelt so badly.'

Victoria didn't seem to mind Richard spending several thousand pounds of his inheritance on founding a theatre company, much to the chagrin of John Wells, who was vacillating between a safe career in schoolmastering and a risky one in the entertainment business. 'Ingrams and I called him the Farter,' explains Willie Rushton. Partly because he could make a farting noise with the palms of his hands, and partly 'because he kept farting about between the two jobs.' 'Yes, well neither Ingrams nor Rushton nor Paul Foot actually *had* to work,' retorts Wells. 'All of them came from a class who could afford to float around a bit. When Richard started "Tomorrow's Audience", that was not an act of rebellion. The high aims of producing a touring theatre company which could somehow increase the number of people going to the theatre in the next generation was very typical, a very natural thing for a son of that family to do.'

The Kent and Cumberland education authorities bought the idea, as did a number of individual London schools. So Ingrams, Duncan and Mary Morgan piled into a minivan with six professional actors and set off for the north-west. They performed the show at over fifty schools, everything went swimmingly, and they were invited back for a second tour. Money was a constant problem; only the Ingrams nest-egg stood between Tomorrow's Audience and bankruptcy. Richard spent a lot of his time trying to get a grant from various Arts Councils, but always without success. The notion of two young men with manifest talent, seeking financial support for a sensible idea liable to propagate interest in the

119

arts, with a clear potential for future commercial viability, was just too confusing for them. Nevertheless, the company stayed marginally solvent, and the two decided to set their sights a little higher.

The Marlowe Theatre in Canterbury agreed to take them on for a two-week run. The first week was taken up with the *Prisoners* show, to little or no effect. For the second week, the lure of comedy proved too strong, and Spike Milligan and John Antrobus were approached for permission to stage the premiere of their new play *The Bed-Sitting Room*. Rushton was signed up to play the lead, and Ingrams slid onstage in another extrovert role, as the plastic mac man. 'He was excellent,' says Rushton stoutly. Duncan's production was a massive success. Ken Tynan, the idol of the Potter–Trodd set at Oxford, made it his lead review of the week, setting it above all the London openings. Bernard Miles inquired about transferring the show to the West End. Tomorrow's Audience, it seemed, could not fail.

While Ingrams strode Duncan's boards across the country, the rest of the gang, leaderless, had scattered to the winds. Wells, opting for safety, had secured a suitably upmarket job as a schoolmaster at Eton; Foot had achieved a correspondingly downmarket posting on the *Glasgow Daily Record*. Rushton continued his part-time work on the *Liberal News*, where he was soon joined by Christopher Booker, fresh from Cambridge. Andrew Osmond, characteristically, decided to join the Foreign Office, and went to France to learn French for the entrance exam. The vital spark needed to bring them all back together was eventually provided by Peter Usborne, the businessman from Balliol, who'd been there in the hayfield when Rushton had made his chance remark. 'Nobody had really taken Willie seriously except me,' he says. 'I went to New York after university, and ended up working on *Time-Life*. I had a job lined up as a trainee in advertising, at Mather and Crowther near Waterloo Bridge. But Willie's idea kept preying on me.' When he reached Mather and Crowther, Usborne soon realised that it was not a place where a man could make his first million. 'So I rang everyone up, and sent them all ten-page letters. I spent most of my lunchtimes standing in a telephone

Richard in the arms of his mother;
PJ, who had been paid a penny
to keep quiet, poses obediently
at her skirts.

Leonard and Victoria Ingrams
(and friend) enjoy their declining years,
all the while steadfastly refusing to
own one of those newfangled cars.

PJ shoulders the burden of
(in ascending order) Richard,
Rupert and Leonard junior.

The Ingrams boys at home:
(from left) PJ, Leonard,
Rupert and Richard.

The young Ingrams
confined to a wheelchair,
after unwisely stepping
out of a first-floor
dormitory window in his sleep.

Shrewsbury in the 1950s: Rushton and Ingrams plot their meteoric rise to power, observed by the suspicious face of authority.

'Four Merry Matrons, Here we stand, Eager to offer a helping hand, With fists, wrists, twists and lysts.' The young Ingrams (second from left) is forced humiliatingly into nurses' uniform at Shrewsbury School. History, sadly, does not record exactly what a 'lyst' is.

An early but perceptive Rushton effort, from *The Salopian*.

The illustration which won Ingrams the Shrewsbury School
Headmaster's Drawing Prize, *Les Joueurs de Bagammon*.
The models, in fact, were PJ and his mother.

THE PSEUD

There is a tribe that in the world exists
Who might be called the pseudo-culturists.
Who think they can to heavenly realms aspire
By warbling Handel in the concert choir ;
He who acclaims as masterpieces all
The tawdry paintings of the mad Chagall
Who quotes from Blake or from Professor Freud,
This man I label with the title " Pseud. "

OTIS.

The Pseud makes his début,
in the pages of *The Salopian*.

The blunt end: Ingrams and
John Ellis pose for a snap
in the hills above Inchon.

booth by Waterloo Bridge, looking up printers and trying to find out about lithography.'

Booker, Rushton, Wells, Usborne and Danae Brook, one of the girls from the Edinburgh show, convened in The Bunch of Grapes pub. Wells was unwilling to give up his job at Eton; but Booker and Rushton, it transpired, had already made tentative plans to set up a British version of the French satirical journal *Le Canard Enchaîné* (provisionally entitled *Bent*), along with Bruce Page, a colleague on the *Liberal News*. They were both keen on Usborne's idea. Nobody, however, had any cash. A drunken telegram was sent to Osmond in Paris: 'MESPOT RIDES AGAIN STOP COME HOME STOP UZ'. Osmond left Paris at once, bearing £450 – he knew what his friends were after – and tracked them down to the King's Head and Eight Bells, Richard's local. By the time he got there they'd completely forgotten that they'd actually sent him the telegram.

Osmond's return was the catalyst; so embarrassing was it that he'd actually turned up with the money that they really had to go ahead. Names were discussed endlessly. Usborne wanted *The Yellow Press*, and to that end had already purchased reams of yellow paper, which explains why the first issue was such a horrible colour. The others rejected this, and they also rejected *The British Letter* (a reference to Booker and Rushton's French inspiration), *The Flesh is Weekly* (a pun), *The Finger* (suggested by Osmond in reference to the famous Kitchener poster), and *Tumbril*. Rushton rejected Ingrams' suggestion of *The Bladder* because his grandmother was dying of a bladder disease; 'I think he still broods about it sometimes,' says Osmond.[1] Finally, because everyone was so bored by this time, Osmond's second suggestion, *Private Eye*, emerged victorious.

When it came down to doing the actual hard work, however, there were only two takers, Booker and Rushton. Osmond wasn't really a writer but he did have a car, so he was made sales manager. Usborne didn't do jokes, he was a tycoon. Wells went back to Eton. Foot hadn't even bothered to come down to London at all. As for Richard? 'My feeling was that my theatre thing was much more worthwhile and important than the *Eye*.' According to John

Wells, 'If he'd been devoting himself to the magazine full time, he would have been the leader, but we thought of him as being rather knightly, off with Duncan doing good causes.' When Richard was in town, he did join in part-time, writing the odd line here and there. His local was often used for joke-writing sessions, for it fitted the model of the ideal public house established at Oxford. 'The King's Head and Eight Bells was a nice old place,' says Rushton, 'with sawdust on the floor, and settles. It's changed considerably since then – now it's like an airport lounge.' In 1961 it had a dartboard, and the right sort of pinball machine. 'Rushton and Ingrams were addicted to that pinball machine,' recalls Jack Duncan. 'Either that, or Booker and myself used to take on the pair of them at darts.' Then they would all go back to Cheyne Row, where Booker would bang out jazz and boogie-woogie on the piano, and Victoria would feed them all without a murmur.

Booker, fashionable and self-possessed, was unrecognisable from the golden-curled Fotherington-Thomas of Shrewsbury School. It was he who grasped Richard's mantle of leadership and assumed the editorship of *Private Eye*. He wrote almost the whole magazine single-handed, while Willie laid it out and drew all the cartoons. The first three issues were put together partly at Cheyne Row, partly in Osmond's flat, but mostly in Willie's bedroom at Scarsdale Villas, where the carpet was laced with streaks of Cow gum. 'It was chaos,' says Willie. 'It looked like the floor of a betting shop . . . although it still looks not much better.'[2]

Four hundred copies of issue one were printed, and placed in honesty boxes in a small handful of restaurants and coffee bars in Earls Court and South Kensington. This was Osmond's stamping ground, described memorably by Patrick Marnham as 'the land of striped shirts and hair lacquer where, after games of rugby and squash, public schoolboys faced up to grim reality and each other's sisters.'[3] Says Richard: 'The early *Private Eye*s have a flavour of that Kensington world.'[4] The public schoolboys removed 350 of the 400 copies from the honesty boxes. None of them left any money. 'We didn't care. We wanted to be told we were brilliant,' says Osmond.[5] The *World's Press News* was informed that 5000 copies had been distributed and paid for, and they believed it. Copies were sent to celebrities including Ken Tynan and Peter Cook, who wrote back expressing enthusiasm and suggesting an idea from an American magazine, the now famous photo-bubble covers.

Not everyone was delighted by the rude new organ. *Private Eye* was printed by Rank Xerox in Cricklewood, and when Lord Rank found out he put a stop to it at once. Candida Lycett Green, who had taken work as a sub-editor at *Queen* magazine, did the stapling in the evenings. When her boss Jocelyn Stevens heard about it he sacked her on the spot (an unwise move, as he spent the next thirty years being subjected to the Potter–Trodd treatment). Mary Morgan volunteered to help, and offered the use of her van and her house at Pavilion Road for stapling purposes when Tomorrow's Audience was in London. 'She was an unpaid lady helper and she was quickly absorbed into the group,' says Andrew Osmond. 'She had bags of energy, she was very cheerful, very jolly, totally committed to the magazine and to Richard. It was a very happy relationship at that time.' *Private Eye*, too, began to flourish.

Sadly, the same could not be said for Tomorrow's Audience. For when Richard and Jack Duncan attempted to realise the lifesaving profits from *The Bed-Sitting Room*, they made a horrible discovery. They had been represented throughout by a business manager called Peter Rawley, a fat man in a suit who smoked cigars, drove a Jaguar and alarmed headmasters. Osmond had known him at Brasenose College: 'None of them knew him when they took him on. When I heard they'd hired him through an advertisement in the press, I was appalled.' Jack Duncan explains what happened: 'We were fairly naive. We thought that there was a standard agreement that if you first put on a play, you were entitled to something like one per cent of all gross receipts for the next two years – so we thought we were in for a lot if it did the West End, which it did. We found out, however, that it had been negotiated as one per cent *of* one per cent, so we got a total of £140, and that spelt the end of Tomorrow's Audience.' The company went bust, taking Ingrams'

123

money with it. Peter Rawley went on to become a successful Hollywood agent. British libel laws militate against outlining his transactions in further detail; suffice it to say that Peter Rawley is an outstanding agent and an utterly fine chap.

Richard was, not unexpectedly, bitter. 'That was a bad experience for him,' says Osmond. 'I remember riding on a bus with him, and him saying, "I will *never* do anything else again that involves my own money". He never put any money into *Private Eye*. He refused to own any shares, and when some were made available to him he passed them over to Mary. He has a sharp business brain, but after Tomorrow's Audience he fundamentally doubted his own business ability, and wouldn't take any risks with his inherited capital.' Jack Duncan moved into a flat with Osmond and Gordon Honeycombe, and got a job as a childminder in Dulwich. 'I had a fairly awful time,' he remembers. Eventually Melvyn Bragg, who embarrassingly enough had been turned down by Duncan at an Oxford audition, got him into broadcasting, and he spent some time in television; but it was never quite his forte in the same way that the theatre had been. Recalls Jonathan Cecil: 'Jack Duncan was very much his own man – I don't think he could have existed in something like the RSC or the National. He was great fun. I acted in a management in-house video once, and Jack Duncan was directing it. He was very embarrassed. He's a real lost talent.' Duncan now lives in York, where he runs a second-hand bookshop. Victoria Ingrams still drops in to see him on her journeys between London and Scotland.

Richard had only one option left upon the collapse of Tomorrow's Audience – to throw himself full time into *Private Eye* magazine. Had he not, after all, been the inspirational editor of *The Salopian, Parson's Pleasure* and *Mesopotamia*? There was, of course, one drawback. *Private Eye* already had an editor.

11 We've Decided I'm Taking Over

Private Eye had been launched in October 1961, right in the middle of the satire boom. This was not entirely a matter of mere good fortune, as there was an element of chicken and egg in the *Eye*'s fashionability: egg, in the sense that *Beyond the Fringe* had influenced the *Eye*'s direction and had created an atmosphere in which it could flourish; chicken, in the sense that the two were part of the same social trend, in which the first highly sceptical and aware generation of post-war-educated public schoolboys was unleashed into society. The remarkable self-confidence and fearlessness of the early 1960s satirists came not from having surveyed a weakened political world and discovered themselves capable of mastering it, but had been instilled into them young by the very establishment they now mocked, the establishment they had been taught to assume command of in due course. That the satire boom was a by-product of this trend and not its inspiration is confirmed by the retrospective application of the label. According to Christopher Booker: 'In October 1961 everyone was talking about *Beyond The Fringe* as being a satire show, whereas when it had first come on in May, if you look through all the reviews, the word "satire" doesn't appear. It's very interesting how suddenly "satire" was the word of the moment. When *Private Eye* was actually first being discussed in the summer of 1961, there was no such thing as the satire boom.'[1]

Private Eye subsequently took off because both public and press were hungry for anything that might be described as satirical. The early history of the magazine is well documented, most thoroughly in Patrick Marnham's *The Private Eye Story*, but it is interesting to dredge up one or two old cuttings and see what the newspapers made of the *Eye*'s protagonists at the time. 'Christopher Booker, bespectacled with bantering talk and mauve striped shirt; Richard Ingrams, a big fellow with a caveman look; and the cartoonist William Rushton, rotund and quizzical,' ran one description. Ingrams himself was described, pejoratively and as a result sloppily, by columnist 'Mr Martell': 'He is tallish, young, immature, unkempt and slovenly in appearance, and not very sure of himself. I am afraid I have to admit I liked him, despite the despicable and scurrilous kind of journalism in which he is employed.'[2]

Richard had joined *Private Eye* permanently after the collapse of Tomorrow's Audience, but Booker was unquestionably still in control. He was a highly visible editor, fashionable and flamboyant; despite claiming to detest the Swinging Sixties, in many ways he epitomised the period. When he married the aristocratic Emma Tennant in 1962, there was a drag act cabaret at his wedding. 'If he could have had a sports car and a blonde he would have done,' says Barry Fantoni, an artist who later joined the *Eye*. An early BBC Radio interview reveals that if anyone deserved Mr Martell's tiresome 'immaturity' tag, it was Booker. Asked what he would do if he made a great deal of money from the *Eye*, Booker said: 'I'd like a sort of really modern house with glass walls and things, on Lake Como in Italy. And an aeroplane to fly to and from London. It's a funny thing about our society, that real talent never gets rewarded. And people when they're young – I'm not talking about myself at the moment, but one does see young writers who could use a lot of money and who are very talented, and doing a fabulous job of work, and never getting paid enough; but you also see, on the other hand, people who have made a reputation when young getting to the age of forty or fifty and doing very bad work, getting lousy articles in newspapers and so on, and getting enormous sums for them.'[3] Christopher Booker attained the age of fifty, and bought a house with stone walls near the M4.

From the beginning there was friction between Booker and Ingrams, both culturally and professionally. Richard, for instance, would not smoke pot, and followed pop music routinely and unenthusiastically: 'I sort of stuck with the Sixties up to about the Beatles and then I lost interest. When all those Jaggers and people came along, I thought, this is too much.'⁴ Richard was keen to impose editorial discipline on the *Eye*; it was largely owing to his influence that the magazine began to be published at identifiable intervals, once every two weeks. Booker's style was erratic, unreliable, sometimes ingenious, sometimes sloppy. He was the sort to rip up an entire article on a whim, start again and still be thumping away on the typewriter in the small hours, while more sober souls slumped heavy-lidded around him, waiting for him to cross the finishing line. Sometimes, he would smash up a telephone or two. He was the complete antithesis of the Ingrams style. On one occasion, he reviewed an Errol Garner concert for a Fleet Street paper, without realising that the concert had actually been cancelled.

Although Ingrams himself would deny it, and although it was his own fault, he must surely have resented conceding the unofficial leadership of the gang to such a character as Booker. In what he felt was a fair-minded attempt to settle the issue very early on, Ingrams wrote to Foot with the connivance of Usborne and offered him the editorship of *Private Eye*. Foot said no. 'I wrote back this pompous letter, saying "I've become a socialist – I'm part of a movement now",' confesses Foot sheepishly. 'I wanted to bring about the revolution, which unfortunately up to now I haven't been able to achieve.' A crisis was thus averted, but not permanently. The showdown with Booker had merely been put on ice for a while.

In his letter to Foot, Ingrams had stressed the need for editorship 'from the left of centre'. Although this was partly intended to entice Foot back to London, there was a political debate going on at the *Eye* too. Naturally enough for 1962, there was a general anti-Conservative consensus. Says Richard: 'We resented everything Harold Macmillan stood for. We regarded him as a slippery, fraudulent old snob, who stood for all that

127

was wrong with Britain. If only, I thought, we could get rid of all those earls and Old Etonians and bring in Harold Wilson and the Labour Party, then there would be a new dawn. Looking back it seems incredible that I could have been so starry-eyed. For whatever faults Macmillan may have had, they were more than matched by Wilson.' Quite how to bring the Conservatives down, however, was a matter of dispute. Booker was a fervent Liberal. 'I remember him jumping up and down when Eric Lubbock won Orpington,' says Willie Rushton, 'and I thought, "You can't be serious".'

The arrival of Ingrams full-time had unquestionably added more satirical bite to *Private Eye*. Andrew Osmond describes the nature of the contributions made by the three men: 'Chris Booker was brilliant, but I don't think he was ever really an editor. We led a very ragged existence, writing the *Eye* in the middle of the night. He was very good at the jokes. He wrote the early issues from end to end. Willie did the covers, the drawings and the layout; he wouldn't ever write much, except one-liners, but ask him to think of a cartoon about anything and it would come up in minutes. But it was Richard who turned the "yah-boo-sucks" element into something more pointed. Richard pushed us into being braver about insulting public figures, so straight away his influence stopped it being just a sort of whimsical, undergraduate frolic. The jokes were quite radical, political and outrageous.' Among the public figures targeted were Chris Chataway, Dominic Elwes, Tony Benn (Stansgate as was), Lord Snowdon, Jeremy Thorpe, Jocelyn Stevens of course, and – the *Eye* always ready to bite the hand that fed it – Ken Tynan. 'Our line,' says Booker, 'was simply that whatever was the received wisdom, we were against it.'[5] This almost anarchic desire to provoke the complacent was a more deeply-felt Ingrams urge than his relatively naive disaffection with the Conservatives, which would later be transferred to governments of any and every hue.

Another target, right from the off, was *Punch* magazine, the *Eye*'s declared rival. The first issue of *Private Eye* contained an 'interview' with Mr Punch: 'Q: And what about your staff? A: Oh, much the same, you know. Still got Figgis the librarian, for instance – been with us since 1899 – checks the jokes to see whether they've been in before . . .' Alan Coren joined *Punch* in the autumn of 1963, the magazine perhaps stung by the *Eye*'s constant attacks into hiring someone rather younger than Figgis. 'The *Eye*'s obsession with *Punch* was all about destroying your father,' he reckons. 'In fact Bernard Hollowood, the editor, reminded me of Richard – a shire radical obsessed with cricket.' For the most part, however, *Punch* came to be staffed by grammar school boys, of whom Coren was a typical example. It is ironic that what the public perceived as the 'establishment' humour magazine should have been staffed by outsiders, whereas the 'anti-establishment' humour magazine should have been staffed by those from a quintessentially establishment background; but from that very contradiction derived *Punch*'s obeisance and *Private Eye*'s confident criticism of the status quo.

Despite the presence of the Cambridge interloper Booker running the Oxford gang, the mood of those putting the *Eye* together was by and large a jolly one. The magazine's chief social aim of maintaining the Oxford atmosphere had succeeded very well, and Booker had a strong enough link with the group through his Shrewsbury school days to make his presence perfectly acceptable. The two defaulters from the gang, Foot and Wells, were teased mercilessly. Candida Lycett Green relates: 'Foot was getting involved with the *Socialist Worker* people in Glasgow. So I used to have to send him postcards inviting him to stay for the weekend, and make up a four to play tennis – really embarrassing upper-class postcards.' Wells was subject to correspondingly downmarket approaches at Eton. 'I'm surprised Wells hasn't thanked us more for breaking up his career,' says Rushton. 'He simply wasn't designed as a schoolmaster.'

It is interesting to note that the two who were still holding out against the lure of continuing their Oxford social life, Foot and Wells, were the two who had not served in the ranks, and had never cared for the heavy drinking sessions. Increasingly, the King's Head and Eight Bells was becoming the nerve centre of *Private Eye*, with layout in the garden studio at Cheyne Row and catering by Victoria. Eventually, though, even this patient soul began to get bored with it all. 'There were books, apples and glasses trodden on, people's garments. It was quite incredible. That was the *Private Eye* lot. Eventually I told them that I couldn't bear another winter and that I was going to sell the house.' On their free days, Richard and Willie would hang around the studio and paint all over the walls. 'We used to paint while having alcoholic binges,' recalls Willie. 'We painted the most brilliant murals based on Van Gogh.' By now, Mary Morgan – Morgo for short – had joined the drinking crowd. Jack Duncan recalls: 'Mary was around Cheyne Row all the time. We all liked her, but I think she very much had her eye on Richard from the start, and she got him. He was a drinker, and most of the people were – Booker and Willie used to have a few as well. She could hold her own in the company he kept – it made her one of the lads. More marriages are made in pubs than in heaven. She came across as reasonably capable, a good sort.' In the summer of 1962, Richard and Mary announced their engagement, to the quiet satisfaction of Richard's mother. Victoria had got what she wanted in the end.

Another new member of the *Eye* staff, or to be more precise another loose strand from the past folded neatly into the present, was Willie's young cousin Tony Rushton. 'Tone' had been itching to get in on the new project: 'I wanted to be in it from issue one, but I was doing my finals. My last exam was on a Tuesday in June 1962, and I started on the Wednesday, as general dogsbody.' In fact it was not Willie who had recruited his cousin, but Peter Usborne, who'd already 'borrowed' Tone to help organise a deb's dance and found him useful. The fact that Tone had no skills of any relevance to a magazine, as regards written content or business administration, was neither here nor there; he was family. Eventually, it was decided that Tone should take over the job of laying out the magazine, which was taking up too much of Willie's time. 'He was no good at all,' says Richard, 'he was hopeless. But rather like that bit in *Reggie Perrin* where Reggie started a shop which sold useless things, like paintings of the Algarve by his brother-in-law, and it was a tremendous success, well, in the same way Tone's hopeless attempts at layout were acclaimed by all the designers in the Sixties as a sort of brilliant new type of
130

layout. I believe books about layout now feature Tone as being one of the great innovators. Men came from America to interview him, and he's won prizes.' The fact that Tone was never replaced, even when the *Eye* could afford a professional designer, is one hundred per cent Ingrams: the joke was too good to spoil. 'It was always worrying if Tone went on holiday, and someone else had to come in who'd always be very good, and you suddenly saw how the *Eye* could look if it was well designed. It was always a matter of great concern to me – I was always quite relieved when he came back.' The joke was to prove commercially effective: a cheap production style suggested rebelliousness, independence and integrity.

If Tone benefited from such old-fashioned British values as nepotism and amateurism, he suffered from the corresponding Ingrams-led patrician distaste that labelled him, on account of his purely functional job, as a 'boxwallah' or clerk. If there'd been a tradesmen's entrance at the *Eye*, Tone would probably have had to use it. Furthermore, he suffered, as he has done all his life, from being a year or two behind the others at Shrewsbury. 'I'm still the kid cousin even now. At school the stratification was so clear cut.' As a mere boxwallah, Tone saw another side to the affable Mary Morgan: 'She wasn't very likeable with me. I never felt at ease with her.' Mary was not being malicious, but was falling into what would become a lifelong pattern of reflecting – or attempting to reflect – Richard's attitudes and behaviour. Richard's amused contempt for the clerical vocation, echoing his Oxford contempt for the grey men, was just another joke, a laugh at Tone's expense. Mary misinterpreted it and, lacking her husband's charm, sailed uncomfortably close to snobbery.

A year into its existence, the finances of the *Eye* remained extremely precarious. It was still only a small-scale operation, with five salaried staff. Besides Tone and Mary Morgan there was a secretary, Elizabeth Longmore, while Booker and Rushton paid themselves first £5, then £7 10s a week. Unlike Richard, who still had a few thousand in the bank, both men had a fair bit riding on the magazine, as they had cut the cord binding them to the *Liberal News*; in Rushton's case he had been sacked before he could leave, and his parting cartoon strip contained a variety of characters standing at odd angles, forming the words 'Fuck Off' to anyone looking at the paper from a distance. Usborne was still combining *Private Eye* with a proper job, while attempting to unleash various big ideas on the business world: at one stage he suggested a Euro-edition of the *Eye*, and rather fruitlessly shipped some copies to Munich. He also flew to Paris to talk to the editor of the successful satirical magazine *Le Canard Enchaîné*, which sold a third of a million copies regularly. Monsieur l'Editeur was optimistic for the *Eye*'s chances, but added, 'You will have to wait until you are all aged forty-five. That is because your friends in government will not come into power until then. We on *Le Canard* survive by getting the hot potatoes from our friends in power.'[6] He was wrong – the British old boy network was to move a lot faster than that; but even the relatively pessimistic forecast of a wait until 1982 encouraged Booker, Rushton and Ingrams to stick at it. Gradually, their circulation crept upwards, although Osmond, as the notional owner, could still see no sign of any profits on the horizon.

By 1962 the *Eye*'s young satirists had attained an aura of minor celebrity, and were invited to guest as editors of the *Sunday Times* Atticus column, a page in *Queen* and a special satire supplement for the *Spectator*. A book, *Private Eye on London*, was specially commissioned. Richard was also hired on a permanent basis as the theatre critic of *Time and Tide* magazine, the editorship of which passed to one W.J. Brittain. After a few weeks the editor's minion Iain Sproat (now a Conservative minister) sent a pompous memo down to him: 'Mr Brittain asks me to remind you that you are writing for a great magazine, and not for yourself.' Richard was sacked, and immediately launched a readers' competition in the *Eye*, the object of which was to get as many bogus letters into *Time and Tide* as possible; one point was awarded per letter, with extra points for 'particularly risible' efforts. 'Our aim is – sink *Time and Tide* by Christmas' trumpeted the *Eye*, with that mocking relentlessness that all who crossed Ingrams' path got to know sooner or later. Brittain had every letter checked. Still they got in. One from Mr James Chenevix of Cheyne Walk called for the return of Sir Anthony Eden, 'a man of stature who could raise our standard of statesmanship to the height that our country needs at this time'. Of course, to W.J. Brittain and Iain Sproat, such a letter did not seem risible at all, which is why – as opposed to Richard's sacking – *Time and Tide* entirely deserved its premature demise.

Another publisher who thought he might enrich himself by taking on a bunch of youthful satirists was Gareth Powell, a millionaire delivery boy turned soft pornographer, who was an entirely different proposition from W.J. Brittain. Despite opposition from his fellow directors, who like many of the country's newsagents felt that the *Eye* might be a corrupting influence placed next to their honest, wholesome pornography, Powell wished to take over the distribution of the *Eye*. In return he lent the use of a cavernous office in Seven Dials, at 41 Neal Street. The magazine's first permanent premises proved to be a Victorian warehouse, piled high with unsold copies of books about Leonardo da Vinci. There was a humorously impressive panelled boardroom adjacent, where Richard and Tone worked the postal franking machine together in a misleading and short-lived burst of fraternity. 'There was no distinction between editorial staff and boxwallahs in those first few months,' sighs Tone wistfully. The nearby Seven Dials pub proved to be of a suitably spit-and-sawdust variety, with pinball machine, dart board and the requisite complement of red-nosed old men, and it gradually took over from the King's Head and Eight Bells as Gang HQ. Everyone drank beer. Richard moved on to whisky. '41 Neal Street was the nicest office we ever had,' recalls Peter Usborne. 'Then one night someone forgot to lock it up and Gareth Powell kicked us out.'[7] That someone being none other than a certain Richard Ingrams. Once again, the *Eye* was on the move.

Throughout its early nomadic existence, *Private Eye* had been gradually attracting more and more occasional contributors. Timothy Birdsall, a talented young cartoonist, had become a regular. Now it suffered its first defection. Andrew Osmond, who'd still seen precious little in the way of profit, had been quietly taking the Foreign Office exams in his spare time. In the summer of 1962 he sold *Private Eye* and left to become a diplomat. Ingrams

133

remembers the pressure from Osmond's family: 'His father-in-law was a very respectable type of man and kept saying that he must get a proper job, that he was wasting his time.' Osmond's view is predictably slightly different: 'I didn't have any more money, that's why I sold it. As usual when you're the banker, you're actually going down for more than anybody realises, because I wasn't paying myself. Our circulation was 18,000, and we thought that if we could get it to 50,000 it would pay for our lifestyle, which was pretty modest. But it was easy to see that getting there would mean that somebody would have to open up their wallet. They were trying to persuade me to stay but they didn't really need me any more.' Professionally, perhaps not. Osmond had only ever written one joke for the magazine: 'Losing the hairs in your ears? Try earwigs.' Socially, however, there was considerable disappointment at losing one of the founder members of the gang. Osmond generously split his £1000 profit from the sale between himself, Rushton and Booker.

Spirits were raised, however, by the revelation that the new owner was to be none other than the young King of Satire himself, Peter Cook. 'It wasn't a philanthropic gesture at all,' admits Cook. 'I'd been very annoyed when the *Eye* had come out. My plan had been to bring a magazine out as part of the burgeoning satire empire I had in those days. The magazine was basically going to be like the *Eye*, so when the *Eye* came out it pissed me off no end. So as soon as it got into difficulties, I swooped.' Cook in fact, had been an early *Eye* target, satirised as Jonathan Crake, a bright young Cambridge wit who ends up hitting the bottle in middle age and copying old jokes out of *Punch*. He has since been known to drink the occasional lager for breakfast, but is fortunately still a very funny and original man.

The centrepiece of Cook's satire empire was the Establishment Club, a former Soho strip joint at 18 Greek Street that he had bought up with the help of Nick Luard, previously treasurer of the Cambridge Footlights. On the strength of *Beyond The Fringe*, which was still running twice nightly, ten thousand people had been persuaded to pay two guineas membership fee before the club had even opened. Cook and Luard brought in a resident cast of young Cambridge satirists – Eleanor Bron, John Bird, John Fortune – and teamed them up with a more experienced stage actor, Jeremy Geidt. Every night the four would perform satirical sketches to the young and fashionable of London, Cook would stroll over after the eleven o'clock performance of *Beyond The Fringe* to act out the role of lordly proprietor, while in the basement bar Dudley Moore would play jazz piano with his trio. 'We paid him a ludicrously small wage,' grins Cook, 'but he was surrounded by the best-looking birds in London.' Upstairs was a club reading room and a space for art exhibitions. Cook had an intuitive eye for appropriate performers, persuading the likes of Barry Humphries, Frankie Howerd and Lenny Bruce to appear. The Home Secretary, however, banned Bruce from entering the country, for his 'sick jokes and lavatory humour', a phrase immediately adopted by the *Eye* and advertised on its masthead.

Cook's idea was to merge the *Private Eye* crowd and the Establishment Club performers, to form a sort of School of Satire. 'I thought it would be a good idea to mix John Bird and John Fortune, who were very funny, with Ingrams, Booker and Rushton, so I moved *Private Eye* into the club.' The waiters' changing room became the magazine's new offices, not an entirely satisfactory arrangement on account of the number of waiters wanting to change. The only way out of the 'office' was across the stage, so it had to be vacated by 6 p.m. when the club opened, by which time Booker was often only just getting started. A feeling of resentment began to build up, as the *Eye* crowd became aware of their status as poor cousins. Far from smoothing over the situation, Cook's weekly 'satirical lunches', at which the two groups were supposed to spark each other off, merely exacerbated the divide. Recalls Richard: 'John Bird thought the Establishment people were serious political satirists, whereas *Private Eye* was frivolous by comparison. They took themselves very seriously.'

Taking oneself too seriously was a major crime in *Eye* circles. *Private Eye* disapproved of the Establishment Club in much the same way that it disapproved of the establishment itself. Richard Ingrams wrote, a few years afterwards: 'There was a deep mutual

135

suspicion between the two camps . . . Everyone was suffering from the consequences of being fashionable. While it was nice to be successful, there was also a feeling that it was not quite right for satirists to inspire such general acclaim. When Malcolm Muggeridge wrote in the *New Statesman*: "One is struck, at the Establishment, by the general air of affluence. One looks around instinctively for Princess Margaret, or at any rate the Duke of Bedford", he touched an exposed nerve. The tendency, as a result, was to go to yet greater lengths to shock people.'[8] The *Eye* itself, of course, was not immune to this temptation. When Rab Butler was described as 'a flabby-faced old coward', many thought it was a blast of eighteenth-century satirical freshness, but in retrospect it lacked wit.

There were exceptions to the uneasy atmosphere backstage at the club – Jeremy Geidt was generally popular, and Booker as a Cambridge man found it easier than his fellows to get on with the opposition – but before long the experiment was deemed a failure. Cook and Luard moved the *Eye* yet again (the subscription department excepted), just four doors up the street this time, to a tiny office over a betting shop and strip joint at 22 Greek Street. Luard, as a suit-wearing old Wykehamist Guards Officer, was not the sort to engender confidence in the 'other ranks' atmosphere of the *Eye* office, but he set about making changes nonetheless. He interviewed all the staff, established proper wages, changed the masthead to its current design, and, most crucially, attempted to build an editorial board of Cook, Rushton and Ingrams around Booker's rather ramshackle editorship. Although irrelevant in practice, this gave Ingrams yet more ammunition with which to fight Booker's 'hopeless procrastinations'. The number of tetchy arguments began to outweigh the good times. Luard recalls: 'They weren't a happy little band of satirists. Booker was once locked out of the office by Ingrams and he came to me to complain.'[9] There were policy divisions over religion (Booker was an atheist), abortion (Booker was pro, Ingrams was anti), and, somewhat pretentiously, over Mozart (Ingrams pro, Booker anti). Booker claims that he demanded of Ingrams what he wanted to do with his life. 'I want to edit a magazine,' Ingrams replied. 'Little did I realise which magazine he had in mind,'[10] says Booker.

Who knows how long *Private Eye* could have carried on with Booker as pied piper, leading Ingrams, Rushton and the others up and down the hills and dales of the small hours in an alcoholic haze, with a straggle of birds and boxwallahs in tow? A major upheaval was, however, on its way. The satire boom was about to reach its apogee with the unexpected arrival of Ned Sherrin, David Frost and *That Was The Week That Was*. The destructive potential of television with its seemingly limitless supply of cash and its capacity to swallow up writing and performing effort was almost completely unknown in 1962. It was now about to visit itself on the hitherto self-enclosed world of graduate satire.

Willie Rushton was one of the new programme's first signings. He'd been spotted in a cabaret at the Room At The Top in Ilford which had been organised by Willy Donaldson, later to find fame as Henry Root. Donaldson had brought together a cast of Rushton, Ingrams, John Wells, and – bizarrely – Barbara Windsor, and booked them to perform a satire show in a nightclub perched at the top of an Essex tower block. Wells's dedication to Eton had been steadily weakening for some time, and he had started to send contributions in to the *Eye* under the name Campbell Murdoch. The nom-de-plume was essential; he had been warned by the Eton authorities that they had disapproved of his predecessor, John le Carré, because 'he had friends in London'. Now he took the plunge, and appeared under his own name for the first time. After all, how would anyone at Eton College find out who was heading the bill at an Essex nightclub?

The Room At The Top turned out somewhat predictably and disastrously to be a chicken-in-the-basket venue, as Rushton and Ingrams discovered when they turned up in tweed jackets. 'I don't *believe* it,' said Babs. One night the Krays came to see the show. 'We thought they were frightfully nice,' said Rushton. 'We couldn't understand what Barbara was panicking about.'[11] Needless to say the revue was a flop, but the long arm of TV was present, and Rushton's ebullient performance was good enough to secure him an invitation to take part in *TW3*, and thence to a lifelong showbiz career. For Wells, too, the Ilford show had a profound effect on his decision to opt for a regular career in comedy, but in a rather different manner. When he got back to Eton he discovered that the authorities there knew all about his activities, and he was asked to leave.

'Willie never came back to the *Eye* on a regular basis,' says Ingrams sadly. 'He had his career mapped out. He always wanted to be in showbiz and regarded the *Eye* as a stepping stone. He went off as soon as *TW3* started, and became a TV personality overnight.' Willie was not the programme's only capture from *Private Eye*. Christopher Booker, the visible face of the magazine, was taken on as chief scriptwriter. He took Timothy Birdsall with him. Willie hired Jack Duncan to work on his sketches and deliver them back to him in camera-scripted form. John Wells, too, directed his writing efforts enthusiastically at the programme. The only person the BBC weren't interested in, apparently, was Ingrams; whereas they had been attracted by the obvious extroversion of the other young satirists, they had failed to spot his quieter talents. The effect on the *Eye* was disastrous. The new show offered bountiful wages of £80 a week, compared to the magazine's fluctuating £5–£15 a week. It sucked up the *Eye* satirists' time, attention, and many of the jokes which should have been destined for the printed page. Booker's timekeeping became even more erratic. *TW3* rapidly became so successful, though, that nobody seemed to care.

The prime mover in this mass recruitment drive had been the presenter of *TW3*, the young and highly motivated self-publicist David Frost. Today, the mere mention of his name is anathema to many of the comedians of his generation, from *Private Eye* to Python. Peter Cook calls him 'the bubonic plagiarist'. Everybody quotes the Kitty Muggeridge description of Frost as 'the man who rose without trace'. Frost freely admitted to being no jokewriter himself, but he had an uncanny ability to spot comic talent and marshal it in his service. In his defence, he undoubtedly gave scores of young writers and performers their opening in television; but many of them rapidly came to resent their discoverer, who appeared to have none of their ability, yet who smoothly sucked up their best material like a vacuum cleaner, growing bigger and bigger on the pickings of other people's wit. Says Ingrams: 'There was something ungentlemanly about a man who was so obviously on the make. His astonishing industry ran counter to the spirit of public-school amateurism which characterized *Beyond The Fringe* and *Private Eye.*'[12] Yet in the same breath, Ingrams speaks of Frost's mysteriously endearing charm. Of course, the lure of television accounted for much of the undignified scramble to join him on *TW3*, but his personal charisma and enthusiasm must not be discounted as a motivating force. He was a master of hype. Looking back now at *TW3*, as Richard says, is like looking back at the early *Eye*: 'Hard to explain what all the fuss was about.'[13]

Torn between staying to save the magazine and the pain of being left behind, Richard wrote some sketches with Jack Duncan and achieved partial acceptance as a junior in Frost's jokewriting squad. Booker had become Frost's right-hand man, and used to go round to his flat in Victoria for writing sessions; occasionally, Richard was allowed to join them. One day, he was writing there for Frost when the great man decided that he was going to the lavatory. 'All right, David, I'll carry on,' said Ingrams; but no. Frost summoned him to stand in front of the open door. There he was expected to compose jokes, in full view of Frost, to the accompanying splashes of defecation. The humiliation was just too much. All Richard's hatred of being pushed around over the years came welling up again. John Wells maintains that, along with his failure to secure a commission in the army, this single episode was one of the main turning points of Richard Ingrams' life.

What made the episode so hurtful was not just the humbling of a patrician before a voracious parvenu. Frost and *TW3* threatened to destroy the Oxford social life that Richard had striven to preserve, the security blanket of friends and laughter that he had drawn up about him. He had stolen their private jokes. Also, in appropriating the services of the gang wholesale, Frost had inverted the natural social order that had developed over the years; Richard, the innate leader, had been cast in the junior role, while Booker's unnatural precedence over him had been made official, and Willie had been promoted from court jester

139

to king. On top of that, not only had *TW3* destroyed their independence, it was corrupting their values. When John Kennedy
was shot, the entire *TW3* team colluded in a glutinous tribute to
the great man. Richard recalls: 'There were special songs about
him by Millicent Martin. Frostie intoned a solemn eulogy. They
were then invited over to America to do it on US TV, and they
were fêted all over New York. Now it would make them all cringe
with embarrassment.' Mere jealousy? Of course, there had been
some measure of jealousy from Richard throughout, but now it
had been transcended by deeper emotions. Frost and *TW3* had
mounted an assault on everything that he stood for. His capacity
for stubborn resistance had been stirred.

There had been other graphic indignities. On 24 November
1962, Richard had married Mary Morgan. After the wedding date
had been set, the first episode of *TW3* had been scheduled for
the same day, so the gang all had to go and work at the BBC.
Even the best man, Willie Rushton, was unable to turn up. Cast
off from the general revels, Richard and Mary honeymooned in
Ireland, and then moved into a flat in Bramham Gardens off the
Earls Court Road. For Richard, with Osmond gone, and Rushton
and Booker seemingly on the verge of going for good, it was a
deeply uncertain period. He had to steady the ship, and he had
to steady it at Booker's expense. All he could do to the television industry was glare at it from a distance, but *Private Eye*
magazine he could do something about.

'In 1963 Booker was having less and less to do with the
Eye. Then he got married and went on a sort of open-ended
honeymoon. *TW3* was going into a new series in the autumn and
I thought that this was hopeless. The whole thing was going to
fall apart. Booker just wasn't behaving like an editor,' complains
Richard. Often, Booker had kept Mary waiting in the delivery van
until 4 a.m., while he wrestled with his copy. So while Booker
honeymooned in Scotland, Richard took his chance and organised
his editor's dismissal. As Booker told the BBC: 'I was going to try
and spend the summer writing a book, and the idea was that I was
to come back at the end of that period and resume my post; but
my colleagues got together as the day loomed for me to return,

and I think they decided that I'd been rather a difficult colleague in some ways . . . I got a letter in Scotland saying "Booker, do not come back", which rather horrified me, I have to say.'[14] Booker put it more brutally to Philip Oakes: 'I left because they hated me.'

It should be stressed that this was not a one-man putsch. Willie Rushton, whose name appeared next to Richard's on the dismissal letter, says: 'Ingrams is not as ruthless as people suggest. It wasn't like *Richard III* – "First of all I take out Booker, then I take out Rushton, then I become rich and famous and found *The Oldie*". Almost everything that happened was chance. We were on a roll, and as you will when you're on a roll, some people fall off and some people don't.' Andrew Osmond concurs: 'Although the coup occurred after I'd gone, it was inevitable. The early issues had been chaotic. Richard put discipline into it, which is easily underestimated. He wouldn't let it spill into his private life.' Barry Fantoni, the new cartoonist, recalls: 'I did like working for Booker because it was very spontaneous, and there was something maniacal about his behaviour, which was great when it was going well, but on his off days it wasn't so good. He had a very volatile temperament. So while he was away Richard sent a round robin, asking everybody to sign it.'

Richard was undoubtedly the prime mover behind this missive. Rushton, his main co-signatory, had never even seen the word 'obdurate' before, let alone used it. Yet there was no doubt that the rest of the staff were with him, even if some feigned ignorance of events. 'I actually thought the round robin was a birthday card,' lies Barry Fantoni blatantly. 'I thought how sweet, he's asking me to sign his birthday card or something. No one told me what a round robin was. I finally discovered that I'd actually been an instrument, as indeed everybody else was, in his being purged.' Tony Rushton is less diplomatic: 'Booker was getting to be a pain. Peter Usborne was very aware of that, and I was aware of that, and when Richard and Willie were coping without Booker, the idea that he didn't come back didn't seem so extraordinary.' Richard had already contacted Peter Cook, the proprietor, and obtained his permission – not a difficult task, as Cook always agreed with the last person he spoke to. 'I always remain above or below the politics of the magazine,' he points out.

When the full weight of what had happened sunk in, Booker was furious. He saw his own editorial style as perfectionist, 'a struggle against the more anarchist tendencies inherited from *Mesopotamia* and lazy Oxford days . . . Without my capacity for taking pains, I am convinced that *Private Eye* would never have become established. I thought of the magazine as my baby . . . and I was horrified to have it snatched from me. I took the view that it would lose a good deal of its character and backbone, and that it would decline in quality and circulation, and I was not wholly wrong.'[15] The flame of Booker's anger still burns, a tiny pilot light deep within. 'He's perfectly pally now, old Booker,' says Ingrams. 'But deep down there it still rankles.'

At the time of Booker's sacking, sales had already passed the profitable 50,000 mark, reflecting the national rage for satire; but now that the craze was being led by television, it had become dangerously ephemeral. The dire predictions with which the departing Booker had shaken his fist at the *Eye* were all about to come horribly true.

12 Cook Saves the Day

It was time for a new structure, a new gang. Booker and Osmond had gone, Duncan had all but gone, and Rushton and Wells were only present when showbiz commitments allowed. A new editorial board was constituted, comprising Ingrams and Rushton, but like its predecessor it was more or less a sham. *Private Eye* could only be run by one editor, autocratically, and from the start it was clear that Richard Ingrams had restored himself as leader. He may have been leading only a rump of his old Oxford brigade, but he set about restoring the quintessential Oxford atmosphere of clubbish hilarity to the tiny offices at 22 Greek Street. 'It was jolly, happy, a very funny place,' recalls Tony Rushton fondly. Peter Usborne, who'd quit his advertising job to become full-time business manager, reflects: 'I thought Richard was helpful and kindly and rather brave. He'd made himself effectively editor of the magazine, and he was very nervous, sitting there alone with a little notebook, ringing people up trying to find stories. I had my doubts to start with. But he was very successful all right.'

Usborne shared the right hand of two cramped rooms with Tone. The furniture was second-hand and shabby, but there were a number of comfortable deep armchairs to get lost in, their springs long deceased. Editorial was on the left, containing Richard, Barry Fantoni, a number of battered typewriters, and Wells and Rushton on their occasional passing visits. In between lay a desk and typist which together masqueraded as a reception, and concealed a cubby hole containing the franking machine used for the dull work

143

of sending out subscription copies. On the windowsills, pigeons sat in lines facing the tall blank wall of the Prince Edward Theatre opposite. Down below, pimps, gamblers, tarts and strippers of various nationalities dawdled in Greek Street. Patrick Marnham noted the details in his history of the *Eye*: girls from the Naked City strip club in the basement pushing through the crowds with little vanity cases and expressions of disgusted indifference, the barkers crying out constantly, 'Live Show. Live Show. Twelve lovely girls. They're naked AND they dance. Come along in boys. Live Show.' One of the strippers held a degree in English Literature from Somerville, but liked the job and the wages it brought too much to find respectable employment elsewhere.

Richard never cared for Soho and these ostentatious pleasures – it was simply a place that Cook and Luard's business machinations had brought them to – but at least the area didn't suffer the curse of bourgeois respectability, and it suited the magazine's rebellious image. As a result of the lack of office space, the local pub became the *Eye*'s jokewriting centre. The Coach and Horses easily fitted the bill as defined by its predecessors, boasting as it did in Norman Balon the rudest barman in London. 'It can never be underestimated, the daily lunch routine at the Coach,' says Fantoni. 'It was very, very important. A lot got discussed, a lot of banter, a lot of jokes. We played draughts all the time.' Ingrams explains: 'Everybody was on top of each other, so we all went to the pub and had big discussions about what the great organ of satire was going to do next.' Bottles of wine, whisky and beer would be brought back for alcoholic writing sessions in the afternoon.

In search of a new collaborator and friend, Richard had fallen on the unlikely figure of Barry Fantoni, a cheerful Italian-Jewish cartoonist from South London with a Beatle haircut and a big nose. Fantoni had arrived during the last days of Booker, as an art school graduate whose first exhibition at the Woodstock Gallery had caused something of a stir. 'The exhibition was of satirical pop art paintings, of Kennedy, and Kruschev, and Marilyn Monroe; and the most important of them was the Duke of Edinburgh in his underwear, surrounded by five or six of his famous uniforms, done as a child's cut-out. I'd read all the issues of *Private Eye* at art school, and I thought it would be the obvious place to publish something like that. So I came to the offices and walked up the stairs, and there were Ingrams and Booker and Willie Rushton who was making a cup of tea, and Usborne, all the familiar names in the cast of 1963, plus all the Sloaney women. And then Tony Rushton said he'd be kind enough to come and look at the pictures.' What Fantoni hadn't realised, of course, was that an audience with Tone was actually one notch below 'go away'. The pictures caused a splash in the papers, however, when the entire exhibition was bought up by an American collector. Richard, who was in charge of contributions at the time, generously commissioned Fantoni to paint Usborne's door. Before long he was also painting a regular satirical cartoon in the magazine, and has stayed on the *Eye* staff ever since.

Fantoni's achievement in breaking into the ex-Shrewsbury and Oxford inner sanctum of *Private Eye* should not be underestimated. Apart from Ian Hislop twenty years later, he is the only man to do so. According to Christopher Booker: 'He just interpolated himself. The rest of us all knew each other. He was a complete outsider and he is now one of the collaborators and at the heart of the magazine. Remarkable. I feel fondly towards him for that reason among others.'[1] True, the *Eye* was at a low comic ebb when Fantoni happened along, but his genial enthusiasm masked a determined ability to get in with people.

Ingrams' own relationship with Fantoni is one of the most interesting of all his friendships. Fantoni was working class, which immediately touched on one of Richard's familiar weak spots: 'The lower and upper classes have always had a lot in common,' says Fantoni. 'They hate the middle classes with the same kind of relish.' Fantoni was also a very entertaining man, always an important quality as far as Richard was concerned. In other respects, though, he was the antithesis of everything Richard regarded highly. He pointedly refused to behave like a working man who knew where he stood in the *Eye*'s ordered universe; rather, he behaved like a middle-class professional, always pushing, publicising himself, trying to better his lot. There was no

145

constancy with Barry, who would be gripped by wild enthusiasms for people and pastimes, then drop them again. The result was that Richard treated Fantoni very badly for what he wanted to be, always putting him down as an upstart; yet remained fiercely loyal to Fantoni for what he was, refusing to allow anyone else to be rude to him, and banning any unkind remarks about him from the magazine. When one member of staff was going to put a Fantoni quote from a daily newspaper into the Pseud's Corner column, Richard was heard to growl, 'Take it out or you're sacked.'

Explains Richard: 'People often underestimate Barry, including me, because he's so often a pain in the neck, in that he's a persistent self-promoter. He would spend the whole time on the phone to producers. He was on *What The Papers Say* simply by ringing up a girl he had worked with, endlessly, saying "When am I going to go on?" And he was on the God slot. If he does a book, he'll ring up reviewers and diaries, absolutely non-stop, badgering them, and it works. Barry proves that anyone can get on telly if they want to. Only once, of course . . .' In fact Fantoni is a veritable polymath. In his time he has written a successful series of Chandleresque novels about detective Mike Dime, presented a dubious Sixties TV show called *There's A Whole Scene Going*, and has turned himself into the country's leading expert on Chinese horoscopes. He has been, at times, an actor, a pop singer, a jazz musician and the *Times* pocket cartoonist. His chief talent, though, is as a comic collaborator, a foil for others like Ingrams to bounce off. Paul Foot uses the analogy of the second fiddle to describe him; you wouldn't necessarily wish to hear it solo, but without it the orchestra would fall down. 'Barry is a very funny man,' says Richard. 'A brilliant collaborator. I've written so many things with him.' Alone among the *Eye* contributors, Fantoni is an expert on such downmarket areas as pop music, television and football. Richard's undoubted regard for Fantoni's useful abilities, and his fierce fraternal protectiveness of him, ran contrary to his unease that Fantoni's persistence worked where it shouldn't have, in securing a place in the exclusive *Private Eye* club.

In return, Fantoni felt a similar affection for his employer,

146

together with a corresponding amused scorn for the patrician peculiarities of his behaviour. 'Ingrams loathed any kind of physical contact. The more I felt he was irritated by physical touch, the more I'd go over the top and throw my arms around him in an Italian way. He used to hate it. It was like teasing an old man. Even now, I still occasionally go up and give him a big cuddle, and he'll say, "Don't do that! Don't *do* that!" So I say, "Come on big boy, give us a kiss!" ' Fantoni also echoed Richard's own protectiveness towards him. 'One of the reasons I was employed, as a lower-class employee, was that I could speak the language of people who had come round to beat him to death. He once wrote a piece about a crook, who then got a hit man to come and bash him up. Someone down on the switchboard rang up and said there was a problem, so I went down, and there was a man there so huge that he couldn't get through the doorframe – I'm not joking, he had to come in sideways. He'd been paid by the hour, 'cos he kept looking at his watch. I had to do the whole accent and everything.' Fantoni managed to negotiate with the heavy for two hours, until the period of heaviness for which he had been employed finally elapsed.

In one respect, the arrival of Fantoni put the cat among the pigeons, in that he precisely resembled a cat among pigeons with the female staff. It transpired, in due course, that he had actually been expelled from Camberwell School of Art for a number of unexplained experiences with women in the clay bins. His technique, frequently successful, was to laugh women into his clutches. Once Richard is said to have walked into his office to find Fantoni rolling around the floor on top of one of the secretaries. Richard simply stepped over them without a word, went over to his desk, and carried on working. Fantoni himself couldn't think of a riposte, so no one said anything. The incident, however, spoke volumes about them both. Sometimes, Fantoni's approach could be rather more direct; on one occasion he crept up to Richard's secretary as she bent over the photocopier and goosed her. Unfortunately, it was a case of mistaken identity: the object of his lust turned out not to be Richard's secretary at all, but Tone, dressed in similar jeans and jumper.

147

Such mishaps apart, Fantoni had a field day at the *Eye*, which appeared to have a policy of hiring rather glamorous women of varying abilities. Tessa Reidy, one of the more talented female employees, remembers: 'The women were "the birds". We were decorative, pretty, we made the tea, we were the prop-up gang to keep the lads in comfort.' A nice, well brought-up girl, Tessa arrived for her interview at the *Eye* in a state of trepidation, thinking the members of the editorial board would all be trendy drug addicts. Instead she was directed to the Coach and Horses, where Ingrams and co. were watching the Test match on TV. 'They were all glued to the cricket and nobody said a word to me. Eventually Norman Balon, the landlord, said "You're here about the job?" and I said "Yes". So he said "You'll do", and I was hired.' Sometimes the lads were more particular about a lady's credentials. Gill Brooke, an attractive dark-haired girl who had applied previously to run the new classified advertising section, had been rejected for the job after a brief, stern interview. So desperate was she to land the position that she turned up again the following day in a blonde wig; nobody recognised her and she was hired immediately. She arrived for work on her first day minus the wig, and nobody said a word. Needless to say, it didn't take Fantoni long to have his wicked way with Gill. When Tessa Reidy arrived in due course, she was warned to be wary of Barry; his attentions, it seems, came with the job description. Instead, Tess married him, and they lived happily ever after (well, nearly).

Richard and the Oxford lot may have loved to be surrounded by pretty women, but unlike Barry they would never have dreamed of laying a finger on them, such was their code. 'They all seemed very remote, very masculine, and very English,' says Tessa. 'They weren't very good at communicating with women.' (One exception to this rule was Nick Luard, the Cambridge-educated co-owner of the magazine, who had wooed and married the *Eye*'s original secretary Elizabeth Longmore.) 'But they were such original, bright people, who wouldn't button down to anybody else's rules and laws, who just lived their lives the way they wanted to. They could do whatever they wanted.' This admiration, coupled with the wit and gentility of Richard and most of his colleagues, was the key to the loyalty with which the *Eye* 'birds' stuck at their relatively mundane tasks. Tessa, who enjoyed the advantage of being Catholic, was the first person to undertake the necessary task of organising Richard's chaotic office life. Before her arrival, his filing system used to consist of great piles of paper, from which he'd invariably pull out something near the bottom; the pile would then collapse, where it would be left, splayed across the floor.

Women found the idea of looking after Richard especially attractive, and he in turn, with his religious morality, found them especially untouchable on account of his newfound married status. Says Fantoni: 'Every woman I've ever spoken to has always said that they like him in the same way they like gay men, because they won't get molested. It's just nice to be with a cuddly good-looking man who's not going to cause any problems.' Adds Tessa: 'The fan mail used to pour in, because he used to do a bit of telly – he was deeply attractive on the telly, because his pockmarks didn't show, he's got a nice voice, and they couldn't see that he was scratching his bum and his shirt tails were hanging out. There was this one lady called Beryl who was about fortyish, who used to write him titillating letters and send photographs of herself in a bathing costume, which used to embarrass him something rotten. He'd be horrified at the thought that his wife knew about these fan letters.' Some women, such as Jilly Cooper and Germaine Greer, allegedly tried to entice Richard into bed. Cooper is said to have pointedly shown Ingrams around a hotel room; Greer, who according to one female member of staff 'turned into a girly, stupid woman' when she was with Richard, apparently tried to seduce him in the lavatory of a London-to-Brighton express. He remained, as always, coldly unamused.

The winter of 1963 was freezing in the little offices; there was snow outside and only one fan heater within. Everybody wore thick jumpers, stamped their feet and drank a lot to stay warm. There was a thick fug of cigarette smoke and a constant chatter of laughter and teeth across the two rooms. Sometimes there would be an impromptu jam session, everybody imitating a different musical instrument. Lyrics would be improvised: 'Oh Princess Margaret with your titties so white, won't you be my lady tonight.' It was an enjoyable time, Oxford revisited, although unknown to them all it was actually the lull before the arrival of a nasty squall.

Although he was now more contented than he had been in the Booker days, Richard had never fully recovered from the betrayal that *TW3* represented, when his friends had deserted him *en masse* for the prospect of fame. Previously, as at Oxford, his social life and his professional life had been indivisible, staffed by the same characters, all sharing the same jokes. Now he had been made aware that others had different priorities, and could not always be relied upon. Furthermore, he had become a married man, and did not wish to fritter away his evenings in the tacky surroundings of Soho. He and Mary would sometimes drive out to Berkshire, to go for walks on the Ridgeway. One day, they bought a tiny, venerable cottage with deep thatched eaves in the village of Aldworth. Eventually, they withdrew from urban life altogether. John Wells recalls: 'They had been living a rather conventional existence in London, having us round for dinner parties and so on, and then they suddenly moved out there and disappeared. That was the beginning of the big shut off.' The 'shut off' was not just physical, although it's true that Richard would dash off to Paddington at five every evening, issuing a breezy 'Haven't you got a home to go to?' to his staff. It was also emotional; Richard now firmly divided the entertainment and conversation that the *Eye* wits had to offer from the love and loyalty that Mary, whatever her faults, could provide. His colleagues found his true feelings even harder to grasp.

In due course, he would abandon the cello for the organ of his local church; wearing a pair of ancient leather pads, he played for the Aldworth cricket team – which is when the *Eye* crowd would be invited up to Berkshire, to take part in an annual match; and he bought a dog, to accompany him on long contemplative walks across the Ridgeway. He also had a huge bed specially made. 'It has to be a big bed,' Mary told John Wells, 'because Ditch is like an old dog. He does like to burrow round and round the bed and make a place for himself.' As Richard settled into the role of rural gentleman, they sold the little cottage and moved into a much bigger house, equally ancient and picturesque, that nestles (no question about it, that's what it does) on the edge of the village. The cost was borne by family money, held in trust, which paid for it outright. 'I thought, wow, this is serious money – untold wealth to most of us,' says an envious Tony Rushton. The purchaser of the original cottage was Tony's increasingly rich cousin Willie, impressed by his friend's new lifestyle and keen to emulate it; but such a way of life was not already imprinted on Willie's soul, as it was with Richard. Willie soon sold the cottage on to that quintessentially rural figure, Marianne Faithfull.

The apparent contrast between Ingrams the uncompromising satirist, burster of reputations, and Ingrams the organ-playing rural gentleman, has been frequently remarked upon. In fact they are two sides of the same coin. As an unspoilt vignette of the English countryside, Aldworth represented everything Richard fought to defend against the new barbarism. He had merely transmuted himself into something he had long admired, the Englishman at one with his countryside. Work in Soho became a series of sallies into enemy territory, lancing the pompous, the insincere and the betrayers of Old England, from behind the *Eye*'s citadel walls of camaraderie. The lack of financial commitment so envied by Tony Rushton gave Richard the independence and freedom from everyday responsibilities to say what he liked. It helped, too, of course, that if one kept one's London social life to a minimum, there was less chance of meeting one's targets. (As Paul Foot said when he happened to bump into Enoch Powell, 'I liked him. Oh God, I *liked* him.')

Around this time the *Sunday Times* profiled the editor of what was still regarded as a minority concern, the unglamorous fag end of the satire movement when put beside the likes of *TW3* and the Establishment Club. 'Richard Ingrams, editor and anchor-man, is a massive slow-moving aristocrat. His face is covered with scars and razor cuts, his clothes with tears and loose threads. He is the least successful, and nicest, man in satire – even now he only just earns a living wage from full-time *Private Eye* work. He commutes with dogged regularity to a country cottage, keeps clear of London life because he finds himself disconcertingly unable to attack people after he has met them, plays cricket, and keeps snapshots of his pleasant-looking wife on his desk. His colleagues declare that Ingrams' qualities of character, the steadiness he inherits from his upper-class Chestertonian Catholic background, have kept the magazine alive. Christopher Booker is a very different character. Ingrams has found himself, Booker has not.'

As the *Eye* gradually began to transcend the merely social reasons for its founding and became an important publication in its own right, there is no question that Richard consciously wanted it to be part of the old English satirical tradition, that literary and journalistic tradition of radical campaigning and pamphleteering. It was very much his influence that led the *Eye* away from being merely a collection of jokes, as it had been under Booker, and towards news stories and gossip. Richard loved gossip, particularly embarrassing gossip about people who took themselves too seriously. 'It was always our intention that it should be a paper of information as well as jokes,' he says. 'The only trouble was that we had precious little information to print.'[2] Explains Andrew Osmond: 'Richard instituted a new gossip section in the magazine, and eventually he got the gossip to fill it. It just came his way, because of the waters we swam in.'

Private Eye may have been the junior partner in the satire movement, but because of this journalistic element it unquestionably had the biggest long-term impact. There had been minor scoops in the early days, such as the discovery that Lord Beaverbrook's famous wartime appeal for aluminium pans to build Spitfires had been a bit of a PR fraud; but the *Eye*'s biggest story, which famously shook the establishment like an old carpet until all kinds of dirt dropped out, was the scandal surrounding the Conservative MP John Profumo. This had begun in the last days of Booker, when various rumours that were flying round London were speculatively gathered into two pieces. The first, 'Idle Talk', disguised the Russian spy Vladimir Ivanov as Vladimir Bolokhov, and Christine Keeler, the mistress of both Profumo and Ivanov, as Gaye Funloving, a good-time girl adapted from an existing *Eye*

character. The second, a big Timothy Birdsall cartoon entitled
'The Last Days of Macmillan', showed nude girls and cabinet
ministers by a palatial pool, David Frost as 'Juvenile', the court
satirist, reporters as a flock of geese being led in the wrong direction by Lord Boothby, and a sign on a pillar reading 'Per Wardua
ad Astor', a reference to two of the main characters in the affair,
Lord Astor and society osteopath Stephen Ward. Firing blind,
without having the faintest idea what they were writing about,
they had fortuitously hit the mark. George Wigg raised the *Eye*
article in the House of Commons. Ward came round to the *Eye*
offices and confessed all – how he had introduced Keeler to
Profumo at a swimming-pool party at Lord Astor's house, and so
on. 'He thought we knew everything, you see,' says Willie
Rushton, who had received him. 'So he came and spilled the
beans entirely, which was wonderful. He said, "I can see from
this that you know everything; I'd like to give you my side of the
story", which of course nobody else got.'3 The *Eye*'s circulation doubled instantly.

After Booker's demise, Richard was determined that the
government should not be allowed to sweep the Profumo scandal under the carpet. 'My eyes had been opened,' he says. 'It
wasn't the bonking that shocked, but the dishonesty, and the
sacrifice and trial of Stephen Ward as a scapegoat. I felt very
angry. I thought the *Eye* should lash out and be abusive.' That it
succeeded was partly the work of the veteran left-wing journalist
Claud Cockburn, whom Ingrams now recruited to fill the gap left
by *TW3*'s depredations. Cockburn had started a fiercely iconoclastic publication himself in the 1930s, entitled *The Week*, which had
built up an influential circulation despite having been started with
no money, printer or distributor. Sefton Delmer had lent Richard
a copy of *In Time of Trouble*, Cockburn's autobiography, and the
old man had immediately joined the pantheon of Ingrams' heroes;
except that he turned out to be very much alive, pottering around
the town of Youghal in Ireland in a battered overcoat and hat.
Richard took Mary on a pilgrimage to seek him out on their
honeymoon. They took with them a letter of introduction from
Donald McLachlan, the editor of the *Sunday Telegraph*, for whom

Cockburn used to write. McLachlan had described Cockburn as 'a highly eccentric recluse, living on the edge of the civilised world, in conditions of extreme climatic change'. This last mysterious remark turned out to be a reference to the appalling floods and gales which, Cockburn frequently claimed, prevented any deliveries getting in or out of Youghal. In fact he had often just been too lazy to do any work.

'Cockburn lived up to all my expectations, being highly amusing and full of charm,' wrote Richard. 'He is, despite his eminence, entirely without pretensions, and despite his intense commitment, always amusing.' He had been neglected in recent years because 'he was a victim of the youth cult . . . that the over-forties were only fit for the scrap-heap . . . It seemed to me that what *Private Eye* wanted was some old blood.'[4] Richard persuaded the old man to return to England and the *Eye*, to join the editorial board for a while, and even to edit the magazine when he was away. 'Claud's line was very left-wing, very savage,' says Richard. 'He produced this issue which included a cartoon of Stephen Ward being carried away saying, "For God's sake, say something, even if it is only goodbye".' When Ward committed suicide, he died in hospital with Cockburn hanging on the other end of the phone.

After Cockburn had 'guest-edited' the magazine, Richard returned from holiday to find that 'all hell had broken loose'. *Private Eye* had linked Lord Boothby with Harold Macmillan's wife, listed the Duchess of Argyll's lovers and named Sir Dick White, the head of M16. Soon afterwards the security services visited the offices in the person of Colonel Sammy Lohan, Secretary of the 'D' notice committee. Lohan, a jovial military figure with a bristling Kitchener moustache, warned the staff about the Red menace and told them that in future they would be bound by 'D' notices telling them what they could and couldn't print; but the notices, fortunately, never arrived.

Cockburn wasn't finished. When there was a good story, such as the death of a man in police custody, he'd investigate it. When there wasn't, he was prepared to lash out in any direction. He even attacked Albert Schweitzer, for being 'too good to be true'. Says Richard: 'Funnily enough, after the article, a lot of

154

anti-Schweitzer material did come out. So there *was* a case against him.'⁵ Cockburn didn't need facts. He said: 'All stories are written backwards – they are supposed to begin with the facts and develop from there, but in reality they begin with a journalist's point of view and conception, and it is the point of view from which the facts are subsequently organised.' How very different from the stated aims of that other celebrated *Eye* journalist, Paul Foot, with his great, crushing wall of meticulously-researched information, and how very similar to the John Birt model now so derided by the left. Like Richard's father Leonard, the fearless Cockburn had been on Hitler's death list, and he undoubtedly became an idealised father figure to Richard in many ways.

The same could be said of another of Richard's 'old men' brought into the *Eye* to fill the gap left by Booker, Malcolm Muggeridge. Muggeridge had been an *Eye* target in Booker's time, when he had been lambasted as 'Lord Buggeridge of Snide', and had complained that the *Eye* used a bazooka rather than poisoned arrows; but under Ingrams, such former targets were treated with the respect that their status as literary and journalistic elder statesmen deserved. Muggeridge had been sacked in 1957 from the editorship of *Punch*, where articles about Winston Churchill and about the Church had threatened to give that magazine a direction. His fatal crime had been to be rude about Cheam, where Prince Charles had been sent to prep school; unfortunately it turned out to be the proprietor's home town.

Muggeridge had tried, vainly, to link *Punch* to its own radical past, and to the same eighteenth- and nineteenth-century radical literary traditions that inspired Ingrams. Now Richard gave him a second chance at the helm. Muggeridge too became a guest editor. He felt, he said, 'like a respectably retired whore who has been given one night of freedom to walk down Piccadilly and see if she can still draw a whistle.' His *Private Eye* would be 'as *Punch* would be, in a good, true and beautiful world.'⁶ He invented the 'Colour Section', the black-and-white news page which still opens the *Eye* today, with its masthead of a well-endowed gentleman on a donkey; this erotic detail was stolen from *Punch*'s traditional cover frieze, which had finally been dropped by Muggeridge's successor there, Bernard Hollowood. It was, said Richard, 'a symbol of the vigorous satirical *Punch* of the old days, which Malcolm had fleetingly revived.' He considered Muggeridge to be 'one of the few journalists who has a genuine contempt for power and the people who pursue it . . . he was at once adopted as a kind of uncle to be rung up for advice about a tricky cover or a nasty libel action.'[7] Muggeridge was equally fulsome in his praise for the young man who seemed to want to be his nephew: 'In a sane world, Richard Ingrams would be editor of *The Times.*'

Although scarcely an 'old man', the poet Christopher Logue was another respected senior figure taken on by the *Eye*. He too was an articulate radical, who had been jailed for taking part in an anti-Vietnam demonstration, organised by eighty-nine-year-old Earl Russell and declared illegal by Henry Brooke, the Home Secretary responsible for banning Lenny Bruce. Brooke issued summonses against a number of prominent supporters of Russell, including Logue, Robert Boult, Arnold Wesker, John Papworth and – of all people – the sexologist Dr Alex Comfort. They were charged *in advance* with breaching the public order act, and bound over to keep the peace by not going on the demo. 'I'm not going to be bound over in recognisance of my good behaviour when I'm behaving well anyway!' shouted the outraged Logue, who promptly became prisoner 6459 at Drake Hall Prison, Staffordshire, for a month. Russell only got a week, 'because they were frightened he was going to die on their hands,' says Logue. The prisoners' job – 'some wit allocated it' – was to help demolish one of the biggest armament factories of the Second World War.

Logue had been hired by Ingrams on his release from jail, when Richard had been editor in charge of outside contributions under Booker; the Establishment Club hired him too, to write song lyrics. Ironically the radical Logue ended up originating the *Eye*'s least offensive column. 'Ingrams asked me what I'd like to do. I said, well, look, I have this collection of absurd and funny clippings that my father gave me, that I've been keeping for ages. Why don't I just rewrite them, sticking to the facts but changing the names – these are after all mostly humble and modest people

156

– and let's see how it goes.' The cuttings collection ran out after three issues, but Ingrams advertised for readers' contributions, and Logue went on to edit 'True Stories' for thirty-two years.

Like Muggeridge (who was a late convert), Logue is a Roman Catholic. The attraction for Ingrams is easy to see – Cockburn and Muggeridge were living embodiments of the traditions he sought to be a part of, and Logue shared some of their attributes. Logue says: 'I suppose all of us – Muggeridge, Cockburn, myself, and similar contributors – were anarchic idealists, either of the left or of the right. "Troublemakers". Richard and I both *believe* very strongly. We're disinclined to analyse. I think it's very difficult to analyse, and that is what passes under the word "temperament". I regard Ingrams very highly, and I'm annoyed when I see him attacked in the newspapers. I want to defend him.'

As *Private Eye* gradually became more radical and campaigning, it inevitably began to make enemies. Some quarrels were trivial. Dr Jonathan Miller, an early contributor himself, who went up the wall when his name was carelessly appended to a supposedly anonymous piece he'd written about 'pooves'. The letter he fired off – 'You stupid bloody irresponsible cunts' it began, and continued in much the same vein – still hangs in a frame on the office wall. Other adversaries posed more serious problems, particularly when they took to the libel courts. The comedian Terry-Thomas and author Wolf Mankowitz both obtained damages, the latter when his novel *Cockatrice* was described as 'a lot of cock written in a trice'. Little-known author Colin Watson was paid £750 after being described as 'a little-known author'. One Alderman Tarbit, the Liberal candidate for Rotherham, also sued after a piece written by Noel Picarda described him as being 'keener on the good things in life than the bad things in Rotherham' (it's hard not to be, one would have thought). Tarbit died a fortnight later, before he could reap his inevitable a financial reward, indirectly giving rise to the legend of the Curse of Gnome. Libel invariably posed a problem, because any joke, however manifestly nonsensical, sounded like a serious and defamatory statement when read out for the seventeenth time by a po-faced lawyer in a court of law. In the *Eye*'s early

157

days Andrew Osmond had asked a lawyer friend to leaf through each issue and say which, if any, of the articles were libellous. He announced that they all were.

The nearest *Private Eye* came to judicial ruin during this period was when Randolph Churchill sued over a cartoon concerning his forthcoming biography of his father Winston. The *Eye* suggested that the book was actually being written by teams of underpaid researchers – 'never was so much written by so many for so little' – and would gloss over the more dubious episodes of Winston's career; 'an abominable suggestion', according to Randolph. Of course, it later transpired that the *Eye* was absolutely right, but this did not prevent the full majesty of the law descending upon the magazine. Randolph issued thirteen writs, against each and every employee, including the girls in the office, served by a man posing as a buyer of back numbers. At first this was thought a colossal joke, and a display window was mounted at 22 Greek Street showing the offending article, the writ and a special Rushton cartoon, 'The Great Boar of Suffolk', depicting Randolph as a pig. Said Richard later: 'Little did we know that every movement at No. 22 was being watched by private detectives.'[8] A few hours later, an injunction arrived banning the display, and a sign had to be put up reading 'Killjoy was here'. The *Eye* lawyers spluttered famously: 'You did not inform us that the pig was excreting.'

Both Cook and Luard were away during what seemed to be heading for a financial crisis, Luard on his honeymoon with Elizabeth Longmore in Paris, where the bride's grandmother had paid for them to occupy the bridal suite at the Ritz for an indefinite period. After just two days of wedded bliss, Luard was recalled to London by an urgent message. 'The boys had panicked,' he said.[9] It soon became apparent that their every move was being dogged. Peter Usborne left the *Eye*'s defence dossier in a restaurant. It was returned a few days later with a pencilled note appended: 'I think this is yours. Randolph Churchill'.

Despite this provocation, there was an admirable refusal to take the whole nonsensical lawsuit seriously. Hauled up in court over the business of the display case, Willie Rushton even made the judge laugh, by providing a commentary on the footsteps of

Churchill's QC, as they approached along the flagstones outside:
'*Ten* guineas, *twenty* guineas, *thirty* guineas, *forty* guineas . . .'
Luard persuaded Churchill to settle out of court, in return for a
full-page apology in the *Evening Standard*. He and Willie, who on
account of his relative fame was the most impressive companion
Luard could muster, went to see Churchill at his Suffolk home,
bearing the original Rab Butler 'flabby faced coward' print (Butler
was an old enemy of his) as a gift. Randolph introduced them to
the teams of researchers that the *Eye* cartoon had dared to suggest existed, then began to get steadily drunk on whisky while
various of the researchers were ordered to read aloud from the
incomplete manuscript. Nick Luard recalls: 'Finally he asked us if
we wanted to see the garden. It was pitch dark and pouring with
rain but he found a torch and led us outside. There we stood in
the mud, looking at a rosebed in the torchlight.'[10]

The notoriety of such episodes as the Churchill case and the
Profumo scandal ensured that by the tail end of 1963 Richard
Ingrams' *Private Eye* was a going concern. The circulation was
pushing six figures, and the magazine was finally turning in a
small profit. It was at this point, however, that the satire boom
suddenly collapsed, and everything went wrong.

Satire, still a buzzword in the summer of 1963, was condemned
by the vagaries of fashion to be considered near-obsolete by Christmas. It was a spectacular collapse, rendered all the more so by
the fact that the two mammoth foundation stones at the base of
the structure were the first to be pulled away, starting with the
Establishment Club. Peter Cook recalls: 'I was in New York in
1963 and it went down the plughole while I was away. Nick Luard
had wanted to do a big format showbiz mag called *Scene* magazine.
I'd seen dummies of it and it looked pretty good. The problem
was really my greed – he could either have done it as Cook &
Luard, or he could have done it on his own, but I thought, well,
it might just work.' It didn't. *Scene*, replete with a young Tom
Stoppard as theatre critic, devoured money like an obese, pam-
pered princeling. 'It appeared to us that *Private Eye* was being
starved of cash,' complained Tony Rushton, as more and more
Cook-Luard resources were diverted to feed the little monster.

'We were so naive,' says Cook, 'we even put everything in the same company. *Scene* lost so much cash, it took the Establishment Club with it.' In the final days, Elizabeth Luard had to pawn her jewels to pay the club's wage bill.

Soho's protection racketeers had often called round to the Establishment to extort money in the past, only to be utterly defeated by Cook's silly voices and refusal to take them seriously. Now that such a famously profitable venue was in clear financial trouble, the Soho sharks moved in. The club was bailed out by a Lebanese 'businessman' calling himself Raymond Nash, and his partner Anthony Coutt-Sykes, who'd added the 'Coutt' because he thought it made him sound impressive. 'Nash was a traditional Soho type,' says Cook. 'He never drank, never smoked, and always carried a briefcase full of cash. He was later sent to jail for gold smuggling in Tokyo. Nash came out to New York and promised me that nothing would change, but we all knew he'd wreck the place. When I got back it was just absolutely different – filled with very heavy men, the atmosphere was so bad. The Establishment was something you just couldn't revive. He was a crook, and a tough crook at that.'

As Cook-Luard imploded on itself, and its business dealings were unravelled, it transpired that Cook had never owned *Private Eye* at all, and that all the shares belonged to Luard. Says Cook: 'I was very cross indeed. I sent over a famous New York lawyer called Sidney Cohn. I thought if anything should emerge from the shambles, I should like to retain the *Eye*. And somehow or other he did it. The *Eye* never knew how close it got to going down the tubes. Nick [Luard], although a remarkably nice man, didn't actually do any jokes – and there's nothing less attractive than a tycoon who's suddenly lost all his money. We didn't have a pension fund to steal from in those days.'

Next to go was *TW3*, when the BBC's Director-General Sir Hugh Carleton Greene banned the programme in November 1963, in a cowardly and stupid reaction to the prospect of a general election the following year. *TW3*, says Richard, had 'blatantly defied the corporation's obligation to be fair and provide balance. From that point of view it was doomed from the start.'[11] To

160

make matters worse one of its prime movers, the immensely talented Timothy Birdsall, died of leukaemia that summer.

The satire boom had been stopped dead in its tracks. *Private Eye's* circulation crashed from a peak of 95,000 to 19,000. Usborne, overprinting, was caught on the hop. 'At that time the *Eye* became the last thing to be seen carrying,' he says.[12] The *Eye* was, according to the *Sunday Times*, 'the last and dying echo of the satire boom'. Cook himself thought it 'the most ephemeral part of the satire movement.'[13] Even its owner did not expect it to survive; and yet somehow, like one of the little mammals that hid in cracks and crevices, and managed to survive the destruction of the dinosaurs, it did.

Part of the problem was that despite the achievements of Ingrams in reasserting morale and persuading veteran radicals to lend their journalistic expertise, the magazine's comic content still had not completely recovered from the loss of Booker and Birdsall, plus the heavily reduced input of Willie Rushton and John Wells. Comedically speaking, points out Tony Rushton, 'It was amazing we got away with it, because if you look at those issues now there is nothing in them. They could be condensed into a couple of pages in *Private Eye* today.' Ingrams, Fantoni and occasionally Willie Rushton were trying to write the bulk of the magazine by themselves, which meant that – according to Willie – 'It went through some terrible periods. We really didn't think it would last.' Economically, a crisis loomed. David Cash, who had joined the magazine at the start of 1963 to do the accounts, remembers: 'We had virtually no money in the bank. We nearly went under when the *Eye's* popularity suddenly went off the boil.' Cash and the two Sloaney secretaries who formed the subscriptions department had spent the year marooned above the doomed *Scene* magazine, in the *Eye's* one remaining room at the Establishment Club. Now that the club had collapsed, a home had to be found for them too. The entire staff took fifty per cent pay cuts and looked for other jobs; Usborne had to go and work at *Which?* magazine during his off weeks. The slate at the printer's lengthened. The bank manager loomed.

Then, one day in 1964, Peter Cook walked in and saved

161

the day. Ingrams had ultimately lost the battle to keep morale up. 'We'd almost forgotten about jokes, we were so depressed,' recalls Peter Usborne. Cook's protracted tour with *Beyond The Fringe* in America had come to an end, so he had come home to grasp the despairing hand of the last surviving offspring of the satire movement, just as it disappeared beneath the waves. Says Barry Fantoni: 'I don't think I'm being unfair, but if it wasn't for Peter Cook arriving from America and introducing all the brilliant, brilliant ideas he had at that time, we would simply have gone under.' Willie Rushton goes one further: 'He brought it back from the dead. That magazine had extraordinary recuperative powers.' As a humorist rather than a journalist, Fantoni tends to be relatively unimpressed by the journalistic strides the *Eye* had made under Ingrams: 'The circulation collapse would have happened whether Ingrams or Booker were there, because people had grown tired of satire; but Richard was over-enamoured with and seduced by the great names of Fleet Street, which he always had a strong romantic hankering for.' Cook, on the other hand, went straight for the jokes.

Cook wrote only one series of pieces himself, a parody of quasi-masonic cults featuring Sir Basil Nardly Stoads and the Seductive Brethren, but he dictated many others at breakneck speed. His appearance in the office was always like an electric shock. He would stride up and down, tall and loping, embarking upon impromptu lectures about enormous snakes, 'many of them millions of miles long', or he would impersonate a zoo keeper attempting to recapture a very rare type of bee which had become intractably lodged in a lady's undergarments. Possibly the best young comedian ever, Cook was the first man to discover quite how funny an animal the bee is. He also invented the catchphrases 'not a million miles from the truth' and 'my lady wife, whose name for a moment escapes me', as uttered by the immortal writer of letters to the *Telegraph*, Sir Herbert Gusset. In the wake of the collapse of the John Bloom package tour company, he put 'The Raft of the Medusa' on the cover, with one of the cannibal survivors saying, 'This is the last time I go on a John Bloom holiday'. Even Ingrams agrees that 'Cook

162

saved the day. I was very uncertain about what to do until he arrived.'

Cook's ability to leave everyone in stitches was not confined to the pages of the magazine. The BBC *Tonight* programme once featured an African dance group comprising a troupe of near-naked women who jiggled around in time to music. The next day Cook rang Television Centre claiming to be Sidney Darlow of the Sidney Darlow Dance Ensemble. Recalls Richard: 'He said he'd seen these black women, and he wanted to know why he couldn't go on the telly with white women, and they'd do exactly the same, they would just dance around with no clothes on, and how they were really beautiful, just as beautiful as these African women, and why couldn't they be on the BBC? And this woman from *Tonight* was rabbiting away, trying to justify it, without daring to admit it was because they were black.' Cook also telephoned the Foreign Office claiming that the Russians were coming through the drainage system at his house, and demanding to be put through to increasingly senior and increasingly despairing officials.

On the financial side, Cook immediately injected £2000 of his own money, and persuaded various celebrities to lend £100 each. Dirk Bogarde, Jane Asher, Bryan Forbes, Peter Sellers, Anthony Blond, Bernard Braden and Oscar Lewenstein were among those who gave generously, along with Lord Faringdon, Britain's only gay communist peer, a man who once began a speech in Parliament not with the words 'My Lords', but with 'My Dears'. Some, like Sellers, were ultimately repaid; the remainder became 'shareholders' in the magazine, in return for a case of wine every Christmas. (Peter Cook still owns the majority of shares himself, but never receives any money for them. Despite their enormous value on paper he believes them to be practically useless, as he is committed to offer them to the other shareholders at cost – £1500 – should he decide to sell; although whether this restriction is legal is open to some doubt.) Cook also tried to raise finance from America, by writing to *Playboy* offering them a concession on *Eye* articles written by himself and 'Willie Rushton, our fat cartoonist'. Hugh Hefner remained somewhat unimpressed. 'He told me to piss off,' says Cook.

Like Cockburn and Muggeridge, Cook took a turn at guest-editing the magazine, with similarly alarming results. Richard returned from his 1964 holiday to discover that Cook had named the Kray brothers. 'Either the charges are true,' Cook had written, 'in which case the newspapers should have the guts to publish them . . . or they are untrue, in which case they should stop scaring the people with this horror movie of London under terror.' Cook himself made sure he was on a plane to Tenerife before publication day, leaving Ingrams' kneecaps in the firing line. It was some years before Cook edited another edition, when, during the *Oz* trial, he put a Steadman drawing of a fully-frontal nude Judge Michael Argyle on the cover.

New contributors followed in Cook's wake. Gerald Scarfe had already arrived, as had Wally Fawkes and George Melly, creators of Trog, who had defected from the *Spectator* after the editor had turned down a particularly hard-hitting cartoon showing a doctor refusing an abortion to a pregnant woman with a Thalidomide baby: 'I'm sorry, but the ethical position is quite clear. Thalidomide was a legal prescription, but what you suggest is an illegal operation', ran the caption. The cartoon subsequently appeared in the *Eye*. Now other artists followed, Ralph Steadman, Michael Heath, Bill Tidy, Larry, Hector Breeze and Nicholas Garland among them. Cook's most impressive catch, however, was to persuade Barry Humphries to contribute a regular cartoon strip, drawn by Garland. 'The Adventures of Barry McKenzie' was about an Australian living in Earls Court. 'I thought an Australian *Candide* would be a good idea,' says Cook. 'Sort of "An Arsehole Abroad".' Humphries introduced *Eye* readers to the world of Australian slang, including such colourful phrases as 'splashing the boots', 'shaking hands with the wife's best friend' and 'pointing Percy at the porcelain' (urinating), and such useful expressions as 'chunder', 'liquid laugh' and 'technicolour yawn' (vomit).

Richard remembers: 'Barry McKenzie was very successful, and helped lift the circulation up out of the doldrums. Humphries himself was a very wild, hard-drinking man in those days. It's difficult to remember now, but Edna Everage actually began life as a very ordinary little suburban housewife with a handbag.' The cross-dressing comedian from Melbourne found the *Eye* office a puzzingly refined place: 'It was a funny atmosphere – it was always rather raffish. Ingrams had the air of a prefect about him – slightly slovenly dress, shaving cream on the lobes of his ears, a pint of beer whenever possible.'[14] One wonders what manner of outback educational establishment Humphries had attended, where the prefects were quite so boozily ill-shaven.

If the relationship between Ingrams and Humphries was guarded, then Ingrams and Cook themselves hit it off from the beginning. Like Ingrams, Cook came from a well-to-do background: Radley College and Cambridge, his father a District Officer in Nigeria. He had gained a head start on the rest of his generation by managing to avoid National Service, rather dubiously claiming an allergy to feathers. Paul Foot, who came to London soon afterwards, remembers the chemistry between the two: 'Cook and Richard, improvising together, were brilliant. That's the thing I remember about *Private Eye* more than anything else. The joy of working there when Richard was editor was the tremendous amount of laughter, genuine laughter, that went on all the time. The whole thing was one huge joke. To be in the next office and hear the laughter of Cook, Fantoni and Ditch . . .'

Each man had a huge regard for the other. 'Cook's got a very searching awareness of humbug,' says Richard, pleased to identify one of his own cardinal virtues in his colleague's make-up. 'I almost always agree with his interpretation of people's motives. He latches on to the slightest inconsistencies. The funny thing about the *Eye* is, you would almost always get a consensus about whether someone was genuine or not.' For his part, Cook is equally fulsome in praise of Ingrams' editorial qualities, but according to one of Richard's long-standing secretaries, 'He was a little scared of Richard. In later years, when Richard had stopped drinking, he could be a little judgemental when Cook was pissed.' Sad, more likely, at the waste of talent, than puritanically unforgiving.

With *TW3* out of the way Willie Rushton continued to be largely diverted by his performing career but John Wells, who had only been a writer on the show, was freed to concentrate more on the

165

Eye. Fantoni and Ingrams, although first-rate humorous writers, were both essentially collaborators, good at shaping, colouring and editing the material of others as it was written. Together they had perhaps lacked the drive of an undisciplined individualist. Now both Cook and Wells, who joined the notional editorial board, were able to provide that comic thrust. A second floor was added to the office, to accommodate David Cash; the editorial side moved upstairs, where Barry painted a giant pop-art mural, and – joy of joys – a Gottlieb pinball machine was purchased from the editor of the *Listener* (who, it seemed, shared the *Eye* boys' love of public bar culture). Wells describes the atmosphere on the new editorial floor: 'There were a lot of concrete stairs, grey-painted wastepaper baskets and broken furniture. The office had a red door, with the name of the previous owner still on it, Isidore Green. So I wrote on it, "No, door is-i-red". There was a great deal of drunkenness and a lot of broken typewriters. Everybody used to come back after lunch pissed and people like Alan Brien [the journalist] used to come in and lean against the door talking for hours. It was a very scruffy, fairly alcoholic place, with very much a yahoo public school feeling of having to fight very hard to get jokes in. I remember feeling exhausted at the end of the day, just trying to get stuff in.'

Boisterous and competitive it may have been, but the old drive had been restored. Cook's surreal genius, harnessed to Ingrams' Beachcomberesque facility for building a family of characters, regenerated the magazine to a position where the modern *Eye* was clearly beginning to take shape. There was a regular editorial column, by fictitious press baron Lord Gnome, an early character partly based on the old *Parson's Pleasure* joke, who also sported various characteristics of Lord Beaverbrook and Lord Thomson. There was Glenda Slagg, based on Jean Rook, a Fleet Street columnist who wrote according to the principle of naming a celebrity, then coming down violently for or against them for no apparent reason. Then there was Inspector Knacker of the Yard, whose name came to Ingrams in a dream. 'I thought this was a brilliant name, and I remember trying to explain it to the head of comedy at the BBC, Michael Mills, a man with a beard.

He wanted to put on a *Private Eye* show. He said, "Couldn't this man be called something else?" I explained that the joke was based on the expression knacker's yard, and he said "Yes, I can see that, but it would be better, I think, if he had another name".' *The Private Eye Show*, unsurprisingly, never came to pass.

Characters dreamed up by Cook and Rushton are easy to spot by virtue of their names. Richard explains: 'Rushton names tended to be compounds and usually involved trousers in some way. Voletrouser would be a typical Rushton name, or I might mention Lobethrust in this connection. Cook thought of names like Sir Herbert Gusset, Sir Arthur Starborgling and Spiggy Topes, the leader of the Turds. The Turds were inspired by an article about the Beatles by Maureen Cleave; we had a woman called Maureen Cleavage, and her article started off, "I want you to meet four very young and very exciting Turds . . ." That was Peter Cook at work.' Neasden FC, the world's worst football team, was a Fantoni speciality, the obsession with Neasden arising from the fact that the *Eye*'s printers were located near there. Lunchtime O'Booze, another journalist, started life as a defrocked Catholic priest devised by Rushton; the compound name gives its author's identity away. It's an easy game to play; Lord Gnome's personal assistant Emmanuel Strobes, for instance, must surely be one of Cook's.

Private Eye was still viewed with huge suspicion by the wider world. W.H. Smith still banned it, refusing even to read a copy, on the grounds that 'it probably isn't very nice.' It was banned too in Australia, and in South Africa, where its anti-apartheid jokes were condemned as 'vicious and repulsive filth'. In 1964 the *South London Press* reported the story of a landlord who had beaten up and robbed one of his tenants, a student, after discovering that he had advertised in the *Eye*. The student sued and lost, as the magistrate considered the mere fact of his having advertised in the *Eye* sufficient evidence of bad character to make his testimony wholly unreliable. The magazine's circulation was still at a frighteningly low ebb below the 20,000 mark; but its influence on society remained disproportionately strong. The *Eye*, and the *Eye* alone, had survived the cataclysmic end of the satire boom, Cook had

167

grabbed it by the scruff of the neck, and it was beginning the slow, hard climb back to popularity. At the end of 1964, the government was finally due for re-election. It was the first big test for the new *Eye*. Could satire really bring down a prime minister?

13 That's Enough Swinging – Ed.

The appointment of Sir Alec Douglas-Home, Fiona's uncle, as leader of the Conservative party produced 'an outbreak of hysterical rage in the *Private Eye* office which has never been paralleled,' claims Ingrams. 'He was a half-wit who looked and behaved like something out of P.G. Wodehouse.'[1] Towards the end of 1963, Harold Macmillan had announced his decision to retire; his successor was an Old Etonian aristocrat who had abandoned his title and was now forced to fight a by-election before he could take his prime ministerial seat in the Commons. Macmillan was wise to get out when he did. Defeat for the Conservatives appeared inevitable; Macmillan himself was widely perceived as corrupt and snobbish. 'He had a fatal weakness for country houses and the people who live in them . . . his cabinet gave the impression of being a grown-up Etonian "Pop",' maintained Ingrams.[2] A wave of scandals had undermined his government's claim to the secure respectability which was its principal selling point: Profumo, the Vassall affair (with its implications of homosexuality), the resignation of Charles Fletcher-Cooke MP (for lending his car to a former borstal inmate), and the celebrated case of Margaret, Duchess of Argyll and the 'headless man'.

The Duchess of Argyll's divorce action, in which reference was made to photographs of the naked Duchess *in flagrante*, wearing (somewhat ambiguously) nothing other than 'a pearl necklace' and accompanied by a lover whose head had been omitted from the shot, of course had nothing to do with politics; but so closely had

169

Macmillan aligned his government with the aristocracy that its image was tarnished by implication. To quote a pertinent Trog cartoon in the *Eye*, 'we've never had it so often'. What the nation really wanted was a young, dynamic JFK figure. Harold Wilson, with his mac and pipe, was the nearest British politics could come up with.

To make sure of Sir Alec's ascendancy (or descendancy, perhaps) to the prime ministership, the third safest Conservative seat in the country, that of Kinross and West Perthshire, was selected for him to contest. 'It consisted of 2000 square miles of bracken inhabited in the main by sheep and pheasants,' recalls Ingrams.[3] Home was ushered around this spartan terrain, pausing in hamlets to utter pre-arranged and patently absurd slogans for the benefit of a willing press, such as 'I lived among miners for twenty years'. This remark occasioned a particularly vicious Scarfe illustration of blackened, wretched miners suffering at the coalface, while hundreds of feet above a gormless Home blasts away aimlessly with a shotgun at passing flocks of birds.

In response to the outrage of Home's selection, with a flash of comic inspiration it was decided that *Private Eye* would stand against Sir Alec in Kinross. Willie Rushton, the best-known member of staff, would be the candidate, and the electoral slogan – rather less inspirationally – would be 'Death to the Tories'. Bernard Levin, Rushton's colleague on *TW3*, wrote the election address, which was duplicated and sent out by the *Eye* girls. The entire office decamped north for the campaign, and Paul Foot drove over from Glasgow to join them. Their base was a mansion borrowed from the publisher John Calder. Despite the widely-held perception articulated by the *Eye* that Britain was being 'strangled by the class system', this was no act of revolution, Foot or no Foot. The young, articulate patricians in their mansion had come to attack the old, stupid patricians in theirs. On arriving at Calder's home, however, Richard and co. were in for an unpleasant surprise. In the innocent manner of Perthshire in the 1960s, Calder had left all his doors unlocked. Two Fleet Street journalists had let themselves in, polished off the contents of the drinks cabinet, and were now staggering about the property, sloshed out of their minds. One of them, George Gale, was discovered wearing a top hat and tinkling away at the piano, a misdemeanour for which he was to pay over several years with the *Eye* soubriquet 'George G. Ale'. Alcohol continued to play a major role in the campaign: at Rushton's first public speaking engagement, at a hotel in the village of Killin, the Irish hotelier was so drunk that his antics entirely dominated the newspaper coverage. 'I still dream of it and wake with a chill hand clutching my bowels,' says Rushton.[4]

The campaign was one of Willie Rushton's last major contributions to the *Eye*, although he has continued to draw the odd cartoon and appear on *Eye* records ever since. The jolly boy who had beaten Richard to the Shrewsbury wicketkeepership was, to all intents and purposes, bowing out of the gang. 'Everyone who leaves *Private Eye* gets a Rushton portrait. I didn't,' says Willie. 'But I'm very proud of the *Eye*. We came up with a bloody good idea, actually. I think I knew then I'd never come up with a better one. It's kept many people in pensions and homes, and raised their children, I mean it's been quite a good little enterprise really.' Willie had the talent to dominate British comedy in the decades that followed, but not the self-discipline. Richard thinks his career has been a little disappointing since. 'Who-ho-hoa' mocked the *Eye*, in imitation of his appearances as a celebrity on radio and television.

The *Private Eye* candidate at the Kinross by-election managed to poll forty-five votes – after all, the majority of people in West Perthshire had never heard of this cocky London magazine – but any damage that was inflicted on Home was done for the benefit of the press. Fleet Street dutifully ignored Home's manifest unsuitability for the job and swung its weight behind him, but the country wasn't listening any more. *Beyond The Fringe*, *TW3* and the Establishment Club, all R.I.P. themselves, had prepared the new prime minister's coffin for him; *Private Eye* continued to bang in the nails. When the *Aberdeen Evening Express* inadvertently captioned a picture of the great man with the incorrect title 'Baillie Vass', a nickname was born. Sir Alec's lieutentants were not spared either. Edward Heath was successfully nicknamed 'Grocer', as a result of his keenness to negotiate

171

away the food pricing difficulties obstructing Britain's entry to the Common Market. Quintin Hogg suffered at the hands of the *Eye*'s new merchandising arm, Ingrams International Designs, which offered for sale by mail order a 'Stuff your own Quintin Hogg cushion set'. Hogg sued, on what grounds it would be difficult to imagine, and duly walked away with £1511.

The Conservatives, nevertheless, went on to their doom in the general election. Some commentators dispute the influence of the satire movement on Home's defeat – again, there is an element of chicken and egg, if one chooses to regard satirical attacks as the result rather than the instigation of spreading disaffection – but Home certainly saw himself as a man in the wrong place at the wrong time. As he reportedly put it, he was 'laughed out of office'.

Private Eye celebrated his defeat with a grand competition, offering a cine-camera for the most ludicrous letter elicited from any of the new intake of MPs. The winner, J. Thompson of Newcastle upon Tyne, had written to his MP as follows:

> Dear Sir,
>   As the reputation of 'Private Eye' becomes more notorious, several MPs have taken to writing letters to this nefarious publication.
>   I would like your personal guarantee Sir, that you do not intend to indulge in this form of indecent exhibitionism.
>   Yours faithfully etc.

The MP in question replied gullibly:

> Dear Mr Thompson,
>   . . . I do not hesitate to give you complete assurance that under no circumstances whatsoever will a letter bearing my signature appear in the pages of 'Private Eye'.
>   Yours faithfully,
>   E. Popplewell

Popplewell's letter, signature and all, was duly printed in the *Eye*'s pages.

For a few brief weeks, now that Labour was in power, all seemed well with God's universe, and the Swinging Sixties

were at last freed to begin in earnest. Contributors of the calibre of Spike Milligan, Bernard Levin, Alan Brien and Tariq Ali
began contributing regularly to the magazine, and joining in the
carefree atmosphere of fun. On one occasion, when a reporter
from the *Daily Mail* was interviewing the young *Eye* editor,
Tariq suddenly appeared in the doorway wearing only his shirt,
tied around his loins, and intoned in an Indian accent, 'Time for
your meditation, Master'. Ingrams cottoned on quickly enough
to improvise some Beatlesque nonsense on the importance of
daily meditation, and the excited journalist swallowed the bait.
On another occasion Tariq telephoned Wells, pretending to be
from Pakistan TV, and explained that the great satirist Mr John
Wells was most respectfully requested to be the subject of the
first-ever televised satellite link-up with Pakistan. Unfortunately,
due to the time difference, the hapless Wells was persuaded to
report for his interview at 3 a.m.

Ingrams decided to marshal the growing number of celebrities,
journalists and politicians who wanted to be associated with the
Eye by inviting them all to a fortnightly lunch, where they could
meet each other and perhaps divulge a little information; 'People
with a strongly developed anarchic streak . . . who like nothing
better than to throw a few spanners in the works now and then.'[5]
Punch already had such a lunch, at a grand table with port
and cigars. 'Richard decided to have an alternative,' explains
Barry Fantoni, 'that would be very downmarket. In a pub, with
beer and rotten food.' The Coach and Horses, where the breath-
takingly rude Norman Balon had taken over as landlord from his
father, was the obvious place. Barry Took was one of the earliest
guests: 'It was a ghastly room, with a rickety table,' he recalls with
a shudder. 'And the food was always the same.' 'I can't think why
the food never varied,' suggests Ingrams innocently. 'It consisted
of melon, followed by steak and chips, followed by treacle stodge.
I always regarded it as a test of stamina for the guests, whether
they could get through this disgusting food. If they failed on the
stodge, which a lot of them did, it would always lower them in
my opinion.'

Norm is unequivocal as to why the menu was the same,

week in, week out. 'It was Richard's idea. He wanted it like public school food. *Every* week, by design.' This notion is so quintessentially Ingrams in conception that Norm is clearly telling the truth, while Ingrams has either forgotten, or is lying to avoid retribution from all those dissatisfied customers down the years. Norm himself would never worry about the feelings of the guests. He once remarked to the Labour MP Willy Hamilton, who had politely asked to find the *Eye* lunch, 'Fuck off. I'm on the phone'. Hamilton left and did not come back. In fact, so amusing did Richard find Norman Balon that he employed him to umpire at the *Eye* cricket matches, safe in the knowledge that he had no idea whatsoever of the rules; but woe betide any opposition cricketer who questioned one of his entirely random decisions. Norm has since made myriad appearances in the pages of the *Eye*, as the landlord of the Lamb and Flag, Sir Herbert Gusset's favourite watering-hole, and in the cartoon strip 'The Local'; he puts these constant references down to 'lack of imagination'.

The early *Eye* lunches were alcoholic affairs, at which Richard would invariably sit next to the best looking girl present and become increasingly tipsy, without – of course – ever once transgressing. As more and more influential celebrities were attracted to these lunches, they soon became an important source of stories. The new intake of Labour MPs proved much more talkative than their Conservative counterparts: 'The average Labour MP will tell you two or three malicious stories about his colleagues within five minutes of acquaintance,' confirms Richard.[6] One of the guests was a young Mrs Thatcher. 'Ingrams said she wasn't bright and wouldn't get anywhere,' laughs Norm scornfully.

The *Eye*'s increasing attraction to the famous was to come in spectacularly useful when the magazine came under financial threat. In 1965 Lord Russell of Liverpool finally sued over an earlier Cook piece that had satirised him as 'Lord Liver of Cesspool', after Cook had spotted his book *The Scourge of the Swastika* on sale in a dirty bookshop, sandwiched between copies of *Miss Whiplash* and *Rubber News*. (What has never been established is exactly what Cook was doing in the bookshop at the time.) Russell's book, which detailed Nazi atrocities, had been

174

serialised in the *News of the World*. 'It was thoroughly prurient, full of naked people, titillating in the most horrible way,' complains Cook. The *Eye*'s lawyer Michael Rubinstein advised Ingrams to take the court case to the bitter end, for the first time ever, but his advice turned out to be disastrous. Cook recalls: 'Lord Liver produced all these war heroes in court so lots of people with no legs came in, which rather swayed the jury to some extent.' The *Eye*'s legal team unwisely told Ingrams, Cook *et al.* to stay silent and leave it up to them. At one point the magazine's QC David Turner-Samuels stood up and quoted the *Times Literary Supplement*: 'Lord Russell's works could be said to be pornographic'. David Hirst QC, for Russell, jumped up and finished the quotation: '. . . but they are not'. Convinced by their silence that the *Eye* staff were cowards, the jury hammered the magazine with an award of £8000, including costs.

'It was a colossal sum, far beyond our means,' says Ingrams.[7] 'The experience was enough to make me determined in future to settle out of court. The case had shown just how poor an impression *Private Eye* makes in a court of law. A satirical article which would set the table on a roar across the road in El Vino's takes on a terrible solemnity when read out in the heavy courtroom atmosphere. Lawyers sometimes talk of a case being laughed out of court, but I have never heard of it being done.'[8] The *Eye* stared ruin in the face, but once again Peter Cook came to the rescue. He organised *Rustle of Spring*, an all-star fundraising show which took £3000 on a single night. 'There was a glittering cast,' he remembers wistfully. 'Dudley, Spike, probably Lulu and half a Bee Gee.' In fact the great and the good turned out in droves to appear in the show: Moore and Milligan apart, there were contributions from Peter Sellers, Roy Hudd, John Bird, Manfred Mann, George Melly, Bob Monkhouse, Bernard Braden and others. Bernard Delfont provided a theatre *gratis*, and even David Frost graciously came out of the cubicle to lend a hand. Readers, led by John Betjeman, sent in further unsolicited contributions totalling £1325. Ingrams and Cook toured the country to raise the *Eye*'s profile, and the target was finally reached in June 1966.

If the arrival of a Labour government had helped to confer a small measure of legitimacy and celebrity upon the *Eye*,
the political honeymoon itself was short-lived indeed. The new
government quickly proved itself grotesquely incompetent, and
Richard Ingrams was one of the first to become disillusioned.
Characteristically, he revelled in the *Eye*'s own discomfiture.
The magazine attacked those 'young men, who pretended to be
tough-minded realists, [and] were in fact soft-minded romantics;
who had found a comfortable high-minded faith in strutting about
in the jackboots of "dynamism", talking "tough" military jargon
about "making break-throughs", "blasting aside the cobwebs of
reaction and complacency" and "getting Britain moving".' In fact,
Labour rhetoric had proved to be so much empty Kennedy-style
jargon.

In 1963, when Sir Alec Douglas-Home had been announced
as leader of the Conservative party, the *Eye* had affixed an
Usborne-style plastic record to its front cover, entitled *His
Master's Vass*. Cook, Ingrams, Wells, Dudley Moore and Willie
Rushton (as the prime minister) had launched into a splenetic
attack on the Conservatives, so enraged in parts that it teetered
on the verge of breaking the obscenity laws of the time. Peter
Cook, for instance, interviewed as part of a parody voxpop: 'As a
trade unionist, people often ask me why I am voting Conservative.
The answer is because I am a stupid cunt.' Now, it was Labour's
turn, and the *Eye* gave away *BBC Radio Gnome*, starring the
same cast, except that John Bird had replaced Willie Rushton as
the new PM: 'I am constantly reminded of the words of my great
predecessor Ramsay McDonald: "Oh Christ, what are we going
to do now?"'

Wilson's connivance with American policy in Vietnam was
attacked in a Scarfe cover illustration showing the prime minister
on his knees behind President Johnson, tugging the president's
trousers down to a half-mast position, tongue at the ready.
'Vietnam: Wilson right behind Johnson' ran the heading. 'I've heard
of a special relationship, but this is ridiculous,' complained the
president. George Wigg, who asked for the attendance of Labour
MPs at *Eye* lunches to be monitored, was witheringly referred

176

to as 'a slack-jawed, bleary-eyed bag of condemned offal'. Tony Benn's record was held up as 'an unmitigated disaster'. Foreign Secretary George Brown, a man so drunk he had once allegedly mistaken the Papal Nuncio for a woman and asked him to dance, became the source of a famous *Eye* euphemism when his behaviour was officially excused on the grounds that he was 'tired and emotional'. Most damaging of all the new attacks, however, was Mrs Wilson's Diary, a regular airing of the homespun philosophy of the prime minister's wife. Devised by Cook and written in harness with Ingrams, then later by Ingrams and Wells, the diary proved not only extremely popular but extraordinarily accurate. Cook recalls: 'It was my first experience of the phenomenon whereby you make something up, and Downing Street begin to think you've got inside information, that people are leaking facts to you. Harold Wilson was quite sure that somebody was informing to us, because Mary had done exactly this or thought exactly that. I think we have the same thing now with the diary of John Major – it's thought that material is leaked to us.'

Mrs Wilson's Diary eventually became a successful stage musical, first at the Theatre Royal Stratford, then in the West End. The production was directed by Joan Littlewood, with lyrics by John Wells. 'Wells is excellent at lyrics,' suggests Ingrams, 'anything where discipline is imposed by the form.' *We're happy in harness/So have a Wincarnis* ran one of the more memorable lines. Reviewer Harold Hobson hailed the play as the first political lampoon to be staged since Walpole's day, although he feared that the portrayal of Wilson as intellectually limited would do wonders for his image. Cleverness, said Hobson, 'is the one thing the British public fears most in a Prime Minister.'[9] Mrs Wilson reacted to the production by saying that if she ever met John Wells 'she would like to bite him';[10] while her friend Tom Driberg MP, who had played a part in staging *Mrs Wilson's Diary*, was given the cold shoulder thereafter. So chaotic was the London first-night party, held in the Coach and Horses, that the well-known heavy drinker Jeffrey Bernard managed successfully to get himself locked in the pub overnight. The incident inspired a West End play of its own many years later, *Jeffrey Bernard Is Unwell*.

177

There is little doubt that Harold Wilson felt upset and betrayed by *Private Eye*, and failed to realise that the satirists too had a feeling of betrayal. Says Ingrams: 'To those like me who had been brought up on the idea that the troubles of Britain sprang from the fact that the Tories were in charge, and that they would largely disappear once the Labour party got in, the advent of Harold Wilson was a climactic event. Consciously or not, the satire movement had been working with Wilson.'[11] The initial attacks on the prime minister were fairly gentle, as Ingrams and his fellows struggled to adjust to the scale of their naivety, concentrating largely on the contrast between his banal suburban Pooterishness and his Kennedyish aspirations. Abrupt economic decline and the collapse of sterling in 1966 brought about anger, 'more intense for the wild hopes that had preceded it.'[12] Wilson was subsequently caricatured as Wilsundra, after Dr Emil Savundra, whose insurance company had collapsed spectacularly. From then on, 'the magazine's attacks on Wilson were as savage as any on the Tories'.[13] Wilson tried to offer the olive branch, inviting Richard and Mary Ingrams to a party at Number Ten, attended by Cliff Michelmore, Iris Murdoch and Morecambe & Wise. As the assembled gathering stood about awkwardly with their glasses of wine, Gerald Kaufman leaned over to Richard and whispered earnestly, 'Jack Kennedy's parties at the White House had nothing on this!' The resulting mental picture of Cliff Michelmore and Gerald Kaufman at opposite ends of Marilyn Monroe beggars belief.

Ingrams' disillusionment with Wilson anticipated the public's inevitable sense of creeping disappointment by a few years, which far-sightedness inevitably affected sales of the magazine; but he always regarded merely commercial concerns as secondary to editorial independence. 'The good thing about the *Eye*,' he says, 'is that the editor has supreme power, and the boxwallahs are treated with contempt, and Cook and the shareholders never show any muscle.' Ingrams always insisted that advertising revenue, which accounted for sixty per cent of the income of most magazines and often ended up influencing the editorial policy, be kept to a maximum of ten per cent. If more people wished to advertise than there was space, then rates were simply increased until the ten per cent ceiling was reached. 'Adverts were always kept right away from the copy,' says Tony Rushton, 'the *Eye* had to be completely editorially led. That's not just Richard's philosophy, it also came from Claud Cockburn, who regarded admin as an evil necessity.'

Depressed by this anti-profit spirit, Peter Usborne finally left to make his million, via the Fontainebleau Business School. His brainwaves were all gathered together and left in a file marked 'Usborne's mad ideas', but Richard kept him on the *Eye*'s payroll to see him through his course. In his stead, the bulk of the administration was left to Tony Rushton and David Cash. Cash is a calm, quiet, dome-headed man of extreme efficiency who ghosts about the *Eye*'s building, 'and invariably comes into your office at exactly the wrong moment with some footling query,' barks Ingrams. Says Tone: 'Like me, Dave Cash has always been in awe of Richard, felt inferior to Richard, because that's the way Richard makes people feel. But Richard's manner has been essential to the success of the magazine.' A private school boy who hadn't been to university, Cash feels that Ingrams' attitude to him is a wary one, born of not knowing where to place him.

It never once occurred to the long-suffering Rushton or Cash to try and place ads in the centre of the magazine, but Richard insisted on treating them as if that was their sole purpose in life. Sheila Molnar, who joined the *Eye* as company accountant ('I wasn't a qualified accountant, I was a temporary secretary – nobody at the *Eye* is qualified for the job they do') describes how Richard would toy with his boxwallahs: 'You always had to pretend it was very much a game with Richard, that it wasn't really a business meeting, because he still liked to think that the magazine fell from one issue to another without any real organisation – which wasn't the case at all, there were actually a lot of backroom people keeping things going. He'd refuse what Tone or Dave wanted just for fun. He'd be at a meeting and he could see that a particular decision was necessary, but because Dave Cash wanted it he'd say no, and it was just amazing to watch him. He would be laughing at them, and they'd get really

179

irate, and he would enjoy that. In the end he would give in of course, a few weeks later, but he would just do it to wind them up, to see the boxwallahs running up and down getting in a terrible tizzy.' Despite this sport, the staff didn't seem to mind much. Tessa Fantoni, who had to type the entire magazine on an intermittently faulty electric typewriter, describes the *Eye* as 'very small and haphazard. We liked it because it wasn't a vast organisation and there weren't any rules and regulations.' According to Patrick Marnham, Ingrams drank, smoked, made a lot of noise and made girls giggle. 'The sheer high spirits of the office in those days were entirely to his taste and very largely his creation. Some afternoons he would skive off to watch flamenco. Others, he would fall into a light sleep over an empty bottle of whisky.'[14]

It is ironic that the magazine which, along with *Oz*, epitomised the swinging London culture of the 1960s, should have been organised like a nineteenth-century colonial outpost run by put-upon clerks, under the command of a District Commissioner who was incapable of taking the whole thing seriously. The *Eye*'s attacks on Labour were probably perceived as coming from a fashionably hard-left perspective, but in fact as well as incorporating an understandable disillusionment with Wilson's performance they reflected the editor's own distaste for the tawdry cultural values dear to many of the *Eye*'s readers. Says John Wells: 'In 1964 there was a Mass for Vass rally. We called on everybody to come out in ironic support of Douglas-Home. This extraordinary collection of people turned up in Greek Street on a Sunday morning, all carrying placards, and I remember Ingrams pulling up the window, and his horror at seeing his readers, all ghastly people with beards and sandals.' Ingrams had experienced the ultimate nightmare, for him, of doing a piece of work and discovering that it had been enjoyed by a person with a beard.

Richard Ingrams was simply not culturally at one with the 1960s. Ian Hislop, the *Eye*'s current editor, reflects: 'You had Fantoni presenting *There's A Whole Scene Going* on TV, there was Booker getting excited about modern architecture, Foot was going round saying "The revolution's here!", and all the

while Richard was striding round looking at old churches.' Adds
Barry Fantoni: 'Richard almost never gets angry, but he got really
angry with me in 1965 when I said that one day Roy Lichtenstein
would be on everybody's walls and Rembrandts would be chucked
in the cellar. I can understand his anger, looking back. I was talking
rubbish. But I did believe it at the time. That's the only time he's
ever shouted at me. I was quite shocked. Still, he *was* drunk.'

Alcohol was one of the few remaining social links connecting Ingrams to the fashionable Soho world, and that link was
disturbingly cut in 1967 when he was forced to give up drink
altogether on medical advice. 'He used to be an amazingly large
drinker,' says Norman Balon of his client. 'He used to put it
down by the ton. Every week he used to have a big cardboard
suitcase filled with booze which he got from Kettner's wineshop
for the weekend.' Paul Foot concurs: 'When Richard got married
I remember being shocked when he and Morgo said they drank
a bottle of wine each every night, when they first went down to
Aldworth. Then one day, I remember Geoffrey Spencer, a doctor
we knew, saying that if he drank any more he'd be dead within a
year.' Even Andrew Osmond, returning to London from abroad,
had noticed a slight physical tremor.

Barry Fantoni takes up the story: 'The doctor had just told
him, and I was in the pub, and Richard was standing by the flap
that comes up and down in the Coach and Horses, and he was
gripping it, clearly in a state of shock. I asked him what was the
matter, and he said, "I've just been told by my doctor that I can
never drink again". He said it was his liver, and that if he drank
again, he'd be dead. It was an unguarded moment of candour,
'cos he wouldn't normally talk about himself in quite that way.'
Not to Fantoni anyway. 'So I said, well, it'll be a tough journey
– I'll give up drinking as well and make it easier. Actually, I quite
fancied the idea of an alcohol-free month, and I thought if there's
someone there drinking Perrier it'll make it easier. In the end it
worked out that I didn't drink for six years.' With the help of
Barry's brave gesture, Richard never touched another drop. His
friends, like Paul Foot, pay tribute to his iron will-power. According
to Norm, rather more prosaically, 'he got the fucking wind up – he

181

shit himself'. The *Eye*'s official historian Patrick Marnham prefers to believe that 'the drama of this abrupt conversion probably appealed to him'. Maybe it did, but if so, the drama was scripted not by Richard but by Dr Spencer; such dire warnings are hardly uncommon in the medical profession's repertoire.

Jack Duncan is another who applauds Richard's incredible stubbornness and refusal to give in to the lure of alcohol. 'I admire him immensely for it. I remember standing with him in the pub opposite the Theatre Royal where *Mrs Wilson's Diary* was on, being astonished by his will-power as he stuck to these bloody shandies. He regards drunks as laughable, feeble creatures now, but he never stopped going to the pub or refused to buy you a beer – I've always really admired that.' Richard confirms that his inability to join in a convivial drink contributed to his social isolation, and to his wariness with strangers. 'I only like the company of my friends. When they are convivial, I find that I can become intoxicated with them, which is strange. I start acting as if I've been drinking. People think I have, but it's not true.'[15] Despite the continued importance of these old, London-based friendships in his life, and the fact that his wife had stayed firmly by the roadside while he had boarded the wagon, Richard withdrew further from Soho. *Eye* press day had always been on Sundays, with a traditional lunch at Jimmy's Greek Restaurant, where the cover and any last-minute jokes would be decided; now it moved to Mondays, and the lunch was abandoned. Sundays would henceforth be reserved for Aldworth and his wife.

Mary Ingrams left the *Eye* when their first child, Fred, was born in 1964. Almost immediately afterwards, on 28 February, Richard's brother Rupert was killed in a car crash. He was twenty-four. Returning from a party – where he hadn't had anything to drink – he fell asleep at the wheel of his van, which left the road at a corner and smashed into a tree. His wife, Lady Davina, spent a year in Stoke Mandeville Hospital, and was left permanently paralysed below the waist. She is now confined to a wheelchair. 'I think if he had lived he would have been bankrupt,' rationalises Victoria, who loved her son very much. 'Rupert was a brilliant, marvellous young man,' says Paul

Foot. 'He was fantastically good looking, his wife was absolutely beautiful. They were beautiful people.' In her unsentimental and economical way, Victoria gave Rupert's old suits to Jack Duncan.

For Richard, standing at the funeral with his ten-day-old son in a cradle, it was to be just one in a line of tragedies that were to bedevil his family life and erect more fences about his melancholy soul. The effect of Rupert's death was more cumulative than direct, as the birth of his son exerted an emotional pull in the opposite direction. 'It was a nightmare thing, because I had to go and identify his body, which was very badly disfigured . . . but I was so taken up by Fred's arrival into the world. I still see Rupert's wife occasionally – she's very nice. Their children are grown up now.'

Christopher Logue, as a childless Catholic, became Fred's godfather. 'I think I let him down,' ponders Logue. 'I'm rather an indifferent godfather. I think Ingrams would have liked me to play more of a part in that role than I did. I should have gone and visited them in the country. But I don't really like the country much – I never know what I'm doing in the country.' 'Logue was a very good godfather,' says Richard, loyally.

Richard's second child Margaret was born in May 1965, and was nicknamed Jubby, after Lewis Carroll's jub-jub bird. Says Richard: 'I was keen my children shouldn't have the same relationship with me as I had with my own parents. When they went to boarding school, we therefore chose schools close to home so I wouldn't lose touch, and it made a tremendous difference. My relationship with them is far more intimate than my relationship ever was with my parents. I particularly liked reading to my children – partly for my own pleasure of course.'[16] How very English and patrician of Ingrams, troubled by his own unfortunate experiences at boarding school, to send his children not to day schools, but as boarders to schools that were close at hand instead; Fred's was a Catholic school, for both he and Jubby were brought up in the Roman Catholic faith. Despite this distance, Richard's children grew up to enjoy an especially warm relationship with their father. According to his secretary Tessa, 'He was the most lovely natural dad I've ever seen – a very warm father to his children. I remember being very envious of his kids, thinking they were very lucky.'

The effect of Richard's retreat into crusty, rural, organ-playing family life upon the *Eye*'s brand of radicalism was exacerbated at the end of 1965 by the return of a somewhat chastened Christopher Booker. The chameleon-like Booker, so sharp and well-adjusted in external appearance, had changed once again: he too had eschewed the Swinging Sixties, to an even greater degree than Ingrams. 'In his new manifestation,' says Richard, 'Booker appeared as the sworn enemy of all that was new, dynamic and trendy – the Swinging London craze.' His fashionable marriage had disintegrated in December 1964. Now he returned in search of income, seemingly content to take a subsidiary position under Ingrams, back where he belonged in the heart of the gang. 'In retrospect, I recognise that Ingrams was undoubtedly put on this earth to edit *Private Eye*,'[17] he says, like a defendant in a Chinese show trial. Ingrams refused to credit him until the hundredth issue.

Astonishingly, Booker now found God, for which abrupt conversion he earned the soubriquet The Deacon. In his time away from the *Eye* he too had fallen under the pervasive influence of Malcolm Muggeridge, upon whom he would descend during periods of impecuniosity. He had, according to Willie Rushton, been 'Muggeridged'. Ever the faddist, Barry Fantoni soon got religion as well, and was even heard to utter the ludicrous statement that the Devil had inspired him to attack the Royal family. 'Booker was previously this ridiculous Sixties figure, into pop music and such,' snorts Ingrams, 'then he and Fantoni were confirmed into the Church of England and converted to classical music. Barry and he became deeply religious and used to sit around listening to Mozart. The religion only lasted for a bit. Barry never stays long.' When Richard went away on holiday he allowed Booker to take over the editorship; partly because of Cook's dangerous irresponsibility with regard to the Krays during his last trip, and partly because of the personal competitiveness he shared with Wells, his official deputy on the editorial board. Still, when the cat is away, the mice must play. Booker's 1966 issue attacked sexual permissiveness and dismissed Ingrams himself as 'a leftie'.

184

Relaxing (if that's the word) with Thieri Njine.

Ingrams' acting abilities given free rein
in Jack Duncan's celebrated production
of *Tamburlaine the Great*.

A sober beginning to the great *Isis* pub-crawl:
(from left) Jack Duncan, Willie Rushton, Richard Ingrams
and Peter Holmes.

Two bulldogs (Osmond and Ingrams)
carry off an unfortunate student (Wells)
in another *Mesopotamia* photo-joke.

PARSON'S PLEASURE

Free inside —
New
Plastic gnome

Editors · · Paul Foot & Richard Ingrams

Price · · · · · · · SIXPENCE

Once upon a Mesopotimeia

Animated Picture by Varis Vee & Mount Vernon, New York, U.S.A.

The pamphlet-sized Oxford magazine *Parson's Pleasure*, kept alive for so long by the kindness of Michael Foot.

The altogether classier and glossier *Mesopotamia*, brainchild of Peter Usborne.

University College, Oxford: Ingrams' sketch of his own first-year room.

There was a little boy
called Gnittie . . .

"Who is this little man, Cedric?"

"We don't think this is funny."

'Yes,' said the Expert,
'come and meet the Birds.'

Little Gnittie (Wells)
meets the Bloodies,
the Grey Men
and the (very familiar-looking)
Expert on Birds,
in the pages of *Mesopotamia*.

At University College, Oxford:
Ingrams, Foot, and Foot's
soon-to-be inspiration.

Mary and Richard Ingrams
in the first throes of wedded bliss.

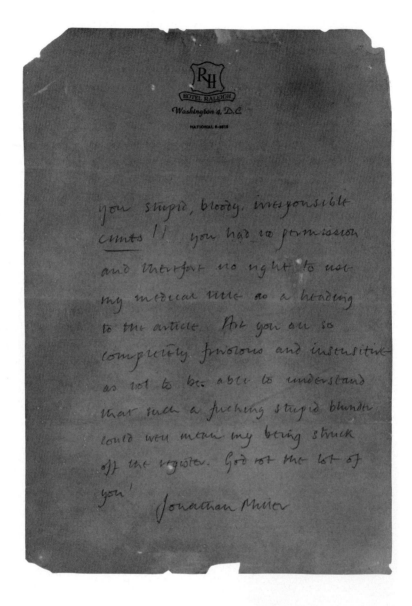

Dr Jonathan Miller's famously angry letter
to the *Eye*, after they had identified him as
the author of a humorous piece about 'pooves'.

The *Eye* was reported to the Press Council for its cover attack on Wilson – an illustration of a £1 note captioned 'Yours for 5/-', with the Queen's head saying 'Bloody Harold can pose for the next one himself'.

That these relentless assaults on Wilson were not fatally perceived as Conservative propaganda was partly because the *Eye* also increased its attacks on the government from a genuinely hard-left perspective, with the arrival around this time of Paul Foot. Attracted by the lure of national newspapers, he came to London to work on the pre-Murdoch *Sun* and the *Telegraph* in 1964, but spent much of the next three years working for the *Eye* on Sundays. In 1967 he moved to Greek Street full time, and the Shrewsbury reunion was almost complete. Despite Ingrams' lack of interest in giving the magazine a party political position, and what he regarded as the flippancy of the *Eye*, Foot realised the importance of the magazine as a platform, and admits that he was attracted to it 'like a bee to a honeypot'. He explains: 'It's independent publishing. It's independent of any kind of profit motive or shareholders' interference or advertising pressure. This is very important.'[18] There were no sub-editors to plague him, the editor was happy to leave his copy intact, and the feed-back he got from *Eye* readers was better than that he had received from the national press, taking him one step closer to realising his ultimate aim of inspiring the proletariat to rebel.

Foot took over the Illustrated London News section at the back of the magazine from Claud Cockburn and renamed it Foot-notes; not without friction, as Foot was a Trotskyite, whereas Cockburn was a Stalinist. Unlike Cockburn, who felt that the best way to establish the truth of a rumour was to make it public, Foot relied upon a barrage of factual research; and unlike Cockburn, who worked alone, Foot recruited journalists and politicians to his cause. Disaffected *New Statesman* staff, who disapproved of Harold Wilson and their own new editor Paul Johnson, began to feed in political stories: apart from *Eye* regular Alan Brien, this group included Alan Watkins, Richard West, John Morgan and Andrew Roth. After one boozy lunch, Brien and Morgan had a fight to decide which of them was the more working class.

Foot's sources were impeccable: a junior government minister and the head of a government publicity office began to leak him embarrassing information, as did members of Wilson's cabinet and a number of officials at the Treasury. A second full-time journalist was taken on in the shape of Patrick Marnham, a charming, secretive, scruffy and highly intelligent law student. Needless to say, Marnham was not a professional journalist; in fact he was a typical Ingrams appointment, being Catholic and well-spoken with a family history of serving the royal family in a medical capacity (his father had attended to the king's posterior). Richard immediately spotted this gaunt young man's ability with a pen, and appointed him to assist Foot. The result was a flow of first-rate stories, relentlessly exposing corruption and crime in high places, and beating Fleet Street to the punch time and time again. The *Eye* was about to enter a golden period.

Foot's feverish enthusiasm never failed to inspire Richard's strong natural sense of justice. The political provenance of Foot's material was irrelevant – 'He wouldn't propagandise, it was always stories,' stresses Ingrams. 'In fact his politics held him back, if anything. Foot had no-go areas – he would never criticise trade unions, for instance. But Foot's work wasn't really hamstrung by his prejudices. His actions were only slightly compromised, not by what *he* thought, but by what he thought the comrades would think of *him*. For a long time he would think twice about going out for lunch in a restaurant, in case he was seen and it was reported back.' Perhaps that's hardly surprising after all those Candida Lycett Green postcards asking him to make up a four at tennis, but nonetheless there is something ridiculously Wodehousian about Foot's attempts to distance himself from his origins. His Trotskyite group would entertain themselves by going off to Skegness for weekend jamborees, of the sort that one can easily imagine being broken up by Roderick Spode. Still, there is no denying Foot's enthusiasm was infectious. 'We'll really get them this time!' he would shout with earnest joy, when some particularly unpleasant morsel of official corruption arrived in the office. 'He's been really getting them since 1967,' says Fantoni laconically.

By the latter part of the 1960s, despite Richard's own ambivalent position, much of the *Eye*'s humour could be said to have been homing in on the government from a right-wing perspective, while almost all of its journalism homed in from the left. It is difficult to imagine such admirably impartial diversity occurring in any other magazine, or under any other editor than Ingrams. Sales, as he had predicted, began to take care of themselves. 'We would watch the ABC [circulation] figures with great concern,' says Foot, 'because the survival of the magazine depended on whether it was 25,000 or 30,000, it was absolutely crucial; but the fact is, that what went into the magazine had no connection with the circulation. It was what each individual wanted to put in.' This policy was about to pay off. Richard Ingrams was about to turn his small-scale, cheaply-produced rag into one of the most highly successful, massively influential cheaply-produced rags this country has ever seen.

14 The Ring of Truth:
An Editor at Work

'No one should doubt that *Private Eye* is Ingrams' operation. He has done it against overwhelming odds,' acclaimed Paul Foot in 1971. Foot was speaking at the end of a period when *Private Eye* had become a national institution, surpassing its merely fashionable notoriety of the early Sixties; and Ingrams was indeed entitled to claim the lion's share of the credit. It was not so much, as Christopher Booker had suggested, that he had found the job he was born to undertake. Rather, he had created that job in his own image; and where he now led, the *Eye* staff followed, and in their wake, the educated and aware middle classes of Great Britain. Ingrams had brought to bear that rare combination of professional qualities fundamental to any who would lead a satirical magazine: the journalistic instincts of the news editor and the humorous instincts of the comic editor.

Of course, any satirist must learn to get the mix right; satire involves a journalistic identification of those errors, hypocrisies and vanities of our supposed betters, which can successfully be held up to comic ridicule. The frequent failing of such programmes as *Spitting Image* and *Weekending* is to become sidetracked by their own political agenda, then attempt to apply humour retrospectively. All too often, the resulting attacks contain the banal catch-all assumption that our masters are motivated wholly by a combination of stupidity and evil, fatally blunting their satirical thrust. Coming from the English humorous tradition, Ingrams knew that a story had to be intrinsically entertaining, and a joke

188

about someone intrinsically funny, before it was worth considering for inclusion; that successful satire involves finding jokes which point in the right direction, rather than pointing oneself in that direction before attempting to add a humorous gloss to one's opinions. Christopher Booker complains: 'I was always asking Ingrams, "But what are you trying to say?" which used to irritate him. He preferred to write the jokes first, and work out what he was trying to say afterwards.'[1] Or, to be more accurate, which of the jokes he'd written happened to enshrine points worth making.

Essential to this kind of judgement was Ingrams' detachment. Although he disliked authority, particularly when exercised for its own sake, and although he could be assiduous in vengeance, he had no real political axe to grind. 'I never had a campaigning feel. We exposed shits for fun,' he says. As he told *Campaign* magazine in 1976, 'I do what I do for a laugh. I enjoy reading *Private Eye* and I write it in order to read it.'[2] His primary purpose in producing the *Eye* was to keep together a group of friends, and to have fun, as directed by him, in their company. Added Barry Fantoni in the same interview: 'He doesn't treat the magazine as a way to earn money or make a reputation. He doesn't use it as a stepping stone. In many ways he's like a great amateur. The *Eye* reflects all aspects of his life and all aspects of his life are reflected in the *Eye*.'[3] (A tautologous statement, and a tautological one as well, but the sentiments were accurate.) Readers were irrelevant, and only there to be goaded, as when many complained at a singularly long and unfunny correspondence perpetrated by Larry Adler. Their protestations merely prompted Ingrams to include more and more of Adler's ramblings.

This disdain was central to Richard's editorial style, which in both the journalistic and comedic areas of the magazine reflected the confident exclusivity of his social life and the in-jokes that it bred. Readers constantly exposed to the magazine would learn its private language which derived from Richard and his friends' own conversations, and thus obtain honorary membership of the club. Only *Eye* readers referred to the *Guardian*, with its notoriously inept proof-reading department, as the *Grauniad*; only *Eye* readers knew that 'Ugandan discussions' referred to

189

sexual intercourse. Richard explains: 'That expression arose as the result of a story told at an *Eye* lunch by the poet James Fenton. He'd been at a party, given by some journalists from the *New Statesman*, and he'd been chatting to a lady journalist present, who'd said to him very excitedly, "James, James, you must come upstairs, they're talking about Uganda." Soon afterwards he did go upstairs, and he discovered the lady journalist *in flagrante* with a wooden-legged black man. We were going to put the story in *Private Eye* in full, when an emissary came round from the *New Statesman* to say that the black man was the former head of the Ugandan Electricity Board, and that if we mentioned the wooden leg he would be immediately identified by an Obote hit squad. So we took it out.' Ian Hislop, Richard's successor as *Eye* editor, encapsulates Ingrams' ability to latch on to memorable stories in this way: 'He converts causes and energies into jokes and catchphrases and ways of looking at things, so that they catch on. That's his genius.'

In much the same way that the comic pages of the *Eye* had developed a cast of regular characters, so Ingrams devised a type of 'repertory journalism' for the news pages, featuring the same targets week in week out. Funny stories are invariably twice as funny if you know – or feel you have come to know – the butt of the tale; Ingrams consciously took this principle to extremes. He once parodied a John Junor piece, in which Junor – whom he was friendly with – had reminisced about an old colleague from the RAF; variations on the piece were run again and again in the *Eye*, inexplicably and persistently describing a 'white-haired boy in a Nissan hut near Deal'. Junor was utterly mystified by the joke, and never realised that his mystification was itself the joke. Ingrams would almost weep with laughter at the thought of the elderly Scottish editor's puzzlement on reading another instalment. Then there was the case of Ron 'Badger' Hall, an obscure *Sunday Times* journalist whose doings were invariably featured in scrupulous detail: 'Nobody ever knew who he was, and nobody could understand why every single issue of *Private Eye* would feature this man Badger Hall. But I liked that,' says Ingrams simply.

This was the Beachcomber and Peter Simple influence coming through again. Although it had been Willie Rushton who had introduced Richard to Beachcomber, he and Booker had gravitated more towards *Mad* magazine around the time the *Eye* was founded; their Aesop cartoon strip had been half-intended as a tribute to the *Mad* style, with every little joke thrown in. Richard had subsequently reinvented the *Eye*, implementing many of Beachcomber's comic devices wholesale: 'He [J.B. Morton] was the first person to do a column which consisted entirely of spoof newspaper items. He wrote most pieces as parodies of journalists' reports, with silly expressions like "allegedly", and this business of putting in people's ages. I think it was thought to be a way of preventing a writ, that every newspaper piece seemed to end by saying "Sir Arthur Starborgling is 67"; I don't think papers do that any more, but *Private Eye* keeps on doing it.'

If Morton was the primary influence on Ingrams' comic style, then the main role model as editor – perhaps unconsciously – was Harold Ross, the long-serving chief of the *New Yorker*. He had started his own magazine from nothing and built it into a national success; he too inspired an enormous degree of loyalty from his staff; he too imposed a strongly-held personal morality on his magazine; he too consciously mocked his readers; and he too was almost helpless domestically, in equal need of constant mothering. Ross was a convinced anti-intellectual, a posture Ingrams has sometimes been accused of striking, and in the margin alongside a reference to William Blake once wrote 'Who he?', a phrase which Ingrams adopted for his own use in the pages of the *Eye*. If there was a difference between the two, it lay in leadership style. Ross talked constantly, and drove his office forward, leading from the front; Ingrams was quieter, more powerful, a brooding presence at times, who never needed to cajole, such was the force of his personality.

Like Harold Ross, Richard Ingrams was blessed with an excellent visual sense and an artist's eye for cartoons. The inferior cartoon editor frequently settles for an illustrated verbal joke; Richard always plumped for the punchy visual gag where possible, such as the early *Eye* cartoon of two RSPCA men trying to force a comatose giraffe into a small van. Bill Tidy, who drew the successful Cloggies strip, about the lives and loves of a team of Lancastrian clog dancers, worked for him for many years: 'I was always a bit scared of Ingrams, but I liked the kind of . . . well, *woolliness* he had about him. He wore the same green jersey for twenty-two years. He wasn't slow, but detached, like a retina. He was an excellent judge of cartoons, and always tried to avoid desert island and dinner-in-the-oven gags, all the conventional areas. I remember one of mine he chose, a bunch of tough men coming down the street holding these placards which said "Campaign for Real Bastards". *Private Eye* took that one, but *Punch* wouldn't have done. He spotted The Cloggies from a one-off, and suggested the strip. I said, "I don't know anything about it". He said, "Neither will anyone else".' The Cloggies' days were numbered, however, from the moment that Tidy fatally introduced a clog dancer with a beard.

Barry Fantoni puts Ingrams' visual sense down to his skill as an amateur painter. He took a delight in seeing a joke emerge from a drawing as it was executed, so Barry would often sketch out his cartoons in front of Ingrams, on a napkin at the Coach, or wherever they happened to be, in exactly which state they would be put into the magazine. Ingrams felt that cartoons often lost their spontaneity somewhere in the business of fine-tuning; more pains-taking artists such as the great Michael Ffolkes were frequently enraged when their roughs were used without permission. The best cartoons in the *Eye* often represented the victim; this was Ingrams the humorist emerging over Ingrams the satirist, for as the saying goes, the satirist rides with the hounds, while the humorist runs with the hare.

Whereas Richard manifestly retained absolute control over individual contributions such as cartoons or news stories, the comic prose of the magazine was generally written collectively. 'I always think that jokes are better written by people working in collaboration,' he says. 'There are very few people like Beach-comber who can actually be funny sitting at a desk on their own. The rest of us rely on working up a hysterical atmosphere in the company of other people.' On the *Eye*'s editorial floor each piece would be acted out by the protagonists, the parts spoken aloud, while one person held the pen and wrote it all down. Ingrams would be the director, tracing some sort of narrative through the hilarity. The performance finished, the piece would be read aloud to general applause. As Patrick Marnham related in his book, 'The management of the collaboration is a difficult matter. Too many participants and the atmosphere becomes too competitive, resulting in one person's jokes being elbowed off the ledge, and consequent ruffled feathers.'4

Behind this apparent collectivism lay an absolute autocrat who was not prepared to share real power. When John Wells joined the editorial board he fully intended to take on his share of editorial responsibility, unlike his predecessors, who had simply recognised the reality of Ingrams' *de facto* editorship. Ingrams was having none of it. In March 1966 the 'Editorial Board' credit was replaced by a notice that Wells had become 'Creative Editor and Literary Influence' to Richard's 'Editor-in-Chief'. 'Editing the magazine with Richard was unbearable,' says Wells. 'I couldn't get anything past him at all. Eventually I credited myself as "Stylistic Influence", as a joke.' This sarcasm washed over Ingrams like the sea over a rock, and from May 1966 Richard was credited as sole editor. In February 1967 these credits vanished altogether, as if such an obvious statement of fact was superfluous. The fact that his editorial rival had been John Wells probably made Ingrams all the more determined to assert himself in this way.

'He is quite ruthless,' confirms Paul Foot. 'To be a good editor you need that streak of utter ruthlessness. He is an exceedingly good judge of other people's stuff – editing is his speciality – but his judgement is the only judgement that matters. That sort of dictatorial approach is actually an advantage for many editors. He was a total dictator at *Private Eye*, quite against any democratic discussion about what should go in.' Andrew Osmond agrees. 'It was pretty demanding to create a magazine and keep it going and hold all these volatile erratic hacks together. But Richard's authority was absolute – he settled quite happily into the habit of command. He was completely autocratic, like all the

193

best editors.' How much of his unhappiness at West Downs and in the army, one wonders, had been because this natural capacity for leadership had been ignored or stamped on, casting him in the unhappy role of follower?

Like all successful autocrats, he was invariably decisive. 'He always knew his own mind,' says Auberon Waugh, who joined the *Eye* in the Seventies. 'He never discussed reasons, just said yes or no. If people quarrelled with him, he was capable of switching on this disapproval, which was quite disconcerting.' More than that, he could actually be frightening in his self-belief. Recounts Christopher Logue: 'I was once walking along with Auberon Waugh, and Auberon said to me, "Are you afraid of Ingrams?" So I said, "Yes, certainly. I'm afraid of Ingrams because I think if he thought that I'd done something wrong and he had to condemn me to death, he'd do so without a second's thought. He'd regret having to do it, but he'd do it, and that would be the end of it." And Auberon said, "You know, I think you're completely right", and we continued walking in silence for some time.' 'As an editor you need to be a despot,' says Ingrams in self-defence. 'There isn't time for too much democracy.'⁵ Acts of Ingrams' editorial ruthlessness have included dropping regular contributions suddenly when he has felt them to have outlived their natural lives, or if his authority has been undermined in any way. He once dropped the Great Bores of Today series for a while, because a Michael Heath cartoon of naked men in a sauna was included against his instructions (whereas, if anything, it should have been dropped for its shocking absence of perspective). Any objections were brushed aside. 'Richard is amazingly thick-skinned,' says Paul Foot. 'Most of us are plagued by doubt in our judgements. But Richard, never. That is his strength and his weakness.'⁶ Richard agrees that obstinacy is a failing. 'I find it hard to change my mind and admit I've been wrong,' he says.⁷

Some of the fear that Ingrams inspired among his colleagues derived from his inscrutability and his capacity for remaining silent. Many would interpret his silences as judgements against them. 'Ingrams rather likes power,' says Christopher Logue, 'and he is susceptible to it. He likes to silence people with a look. I used to go to lunch at the Coach when I was around, and people didn't want to challenge him. He is quite a frightening man.' James Fenton attempted to unravel the Ingrams facial mask in the pages of the *New Statesman*: 'His face poses an absorbing problem of interpretation – what are those expressions that disturb its uneven surface? Was that a smile? Was that interest, annoyance, worry, fear?' No, explained Richard, it was the expression of a man desperately attempting to feign interest in the conversation of James Fenton.

Richard's fear of bores is legendary. 'He has a very low boredom threshold,' explains John Wells. 'The phrases "That's enough – ed", or "Continued on page 94" are genuine indicators of his boredom.' According to Barry Fantoni, 'Any conversation with Richard is eight words maximum. You get in, you get out. Unless you're gossiping, then you can go on all day.' Says Ian Hislop: 'One reason Richard is a good editor is that he doesn't mind telling people that he's bored by something that they've written. Somebody could put a huge amount of work into a story, but they still had to interest him straight.' For many, fear of Richard was the fear of boring him and not being able to tell that boredom lurked behind those impassive features. To compensate, they would try harder to impress him, and their jokes would get better as a result.

Richard's yen for collective humorous endeavour sat ill with the prevailing competitive jealousy at *Private Eye*, should one person ever rise above the common herd – in much the same way that human nature has always militated against collectivism. The chief complaint directed at the editor by his staff was that he gave no credit to others for their efforts, and kept them all down. 'He's never credited anyone,' objects John Wells. 'You worked for him out of a mixture of loyalty and privilege at being accepted into his magic circle. The crackle of *Private Eye* in the early days was due to the passionate collaboration of people desperate to keep it going; I think on the whole Ingrams underestimates the amount of help he got from other people.' Ingrams defends himself against this charge: 'The trouble is that the *Eye* was always anonymous and so the editor got most of

195

the publicity. Other people like Fantoni and Wells didn't, so in a way they were right to feel aggrieved.' The aggrieved parties retort that the editor hardly struggled to disabuse the media of their simplistic notions. 'Richard loves publicity about himself. He thinks he doesn't, but he does,' laughs Christopher Logue.

There are points worth making on Ingrams' behalf. Individual credits for articles had had to be dropped, partly to avoid legal identification of specific culprits, and partly because of the space that an ensemble credit on every comic piece took up. Ian Hislop, who as the new editor benefits from a lazy press attributing all *Eye* work to him in much the same way, points out that Richard never credited himself either. Other controversial magazines, such as *Viz*, tend to employ the same system of anonymity. Ingrams' new magazine *The Oldie*, on the other hand, is fulsome in its accreditation of individual contributors. Besides, explains Auberon Waugh, Ingrams does praise people: 'The mere fact that he's prepared to go on with you means that he approves. "Yes", he will say. That is the height of praise from Ingrams.'

This may be true, but there is no denying that the system of collective endeavour worked both as a means of ensuring that everyone grew to their full comic potential, and as a barrier ensuring that nobody could apply that potential elsewhere. For someone politically opposed to dictatorial state socialism on a national level, Ingrams ran something perilously close to it in his work. When Barry Fantoni went off on a tour of Britain as *Eye* poet E.J. Thribb, Ingrams announced that Thribb had died, and stopped running his poems. When Fantoni collected his Colemanballs column into a book, nobody cared, because none of the others were interested in sport. When Barry subsequently raked in £90,000, everything changed; the resentment towards Fantoni from the other writers was palpable. It wasn't the money, it was the status. All the early contemporaries on the *Eye*, not just Ingrams, were jealous of each other's success, in the guise of principle. Ingrams attempts to defend this attitude in meritocratic terms: 'These are people who were never really much good on their own. That applies to Fantoni, Booker, Wells, and I suppose to me. I never thought Wells was much good on his own. Booker's got a naturally satirical mind, but if you take him out of the *Eye* milieu you get no feeling of that. Equally with Barry – he seems to be just this man who does Chinese horoscopes.' That's not the point, though. They should have been *allowed* to be good or bad in their own right.

All comedians everywhere, since the first neolithic stirrings of comedy, have been jealous of their contemporaries' work, and the *Eye* writers were no different. It should be stressed, though, that Ingrams' particular insistence that no one break ranks was not principally due to a petty desire to deny his friends any of the credit. There was another, more important reason. The old gang that the *Eye* represented was something that Ingrams loved dearly, and was genuinely frightened of seeing broken up. The *TW3* episode had alarmed him. Whatever permutations of faces the *Eye* went through, he always kept some semblance of the gang together. This attitude crept out frequently in interviews. 'It is very important to keep up this little gang, this little clique of people with all their in-jokes,' he told Edward Whitley.[8] 'A good magazine is a sort of gang, and I'm the gang leader, and you have to have that,' he told BBC Radio Four. John Wells recalls: 'I was asked by Nigel Lawson, who was then editor of the *Spectator*, to do the press column; and I've still got the first column that I did, which has got Ingrams' handwriting on it – he'd written "cock", "balls", and so on, with such incredible savagery that it cut right through the page. It's the idea of anybody deserting the gang. You've got to be loyal to him – it's a gang boss attitude.'

Richard once described loyalty as 'a minor virtue';[9] but it is, according to Andrew Osmond, 'the virtue he admires above all others. Richard is a great orchestrator of friendships. He thrives on them, draws something from them. Richard's friends have always been very very important to him. Because *Private Eye* was the extension of a multiple friendship, the friendship came before the jokes in the magazine. He held this sacred and would get very saddened if anybody quit. He would get quite irrationally cast down.' If a really beloved friend left the gang, Ingrams' sadness would be deeper but his revenge would be no more than token. Rushton's punishment for leaving, as he sees it, is that he has never been invited to a *Private Eye* lunch, a slight that Richard probably is not even aware of having perpetrated. If someone's defection was a genuine betrayal, however, and their friendship was less deep, his revenge could be relentless. Peter Jay, for example, took the Maxwell shilling (or in his case, the Maxwell £100,000) and went to work as bag-carrier for the fat crook. 'Jay was a close friend of ours,' says Foot, 'but Ingrams could never forgive his association with Maxwell and his libel action against us. Richard fastens on to people like Jay, who have betrayed him, and attacks them consistently.'

Christopher Logue is unsure about the morality of demanding such loyalty. 'It's that kind of loyalty which is in some sense corrupt. It's not sufficiently clear what you are loyal *to*. I can understand the kind of loyalty that Richard demands from people because, as the editor of *Private Eye*, he was in a very exposed position and had to take a lot of risks, and he did quite justifiably have to upset a lot of people, so I think that he was entitled to ask for loyalty. And I did give it to him gladly myself. But remember that the motto of the SS was "Loyalty is their honour".' To be fair, this is not strictly applicable, as Richard never demanded loyalty to his principles, only personal loyalty from his friends; but there was a fine line beyond which the loyalty demanded ceased to be a virtue and became simply a mark of subordination. Occasionally Richard overstepped that line, albeit for reasons that were entirely well meant.

Yet Richard got his loyalty, and it was given freely. He didn't need to impose it; people just fell in love with him. It is still there within the gang, although Booker, one suspects, will never forgive him. One need only talk with Barry Fantoni and John Wells to realise that while he drives them mad with frustration, they love him dearly too. Outside the gang this affection is, if anything, even more marked. The girls in the office all fell head-over-heels for Richard, one by one. His three secretaries, Tessa Fantoni, Liz Elliot and Maggie Lunn, were all besotted with him; and he loved them back, in a Dr Who sort of way. Tessa and Barry used to fuss around Richard, and buy all his clothes: 'We used to go and buy his trousers on trips to

Simpsons, or to the sales to get cashmere V-neck sweaters. He only had one tie, a William Morris design he took from our mail order at the *Eye*. He always wore exactly the same things: grey flannels, check shirt and V-neck pullover.' He would wear these clothes until they visibly began to fall to bits about his person, whereupon Tessa and Barry would go out and replace them. 'All his old clothes used to be left in the office. They never got taken home or thrown away. Trousers with ink leaks, shirts, shoes, anything that was discarded just got left there. Some shoes are still up on the office shelf.' In 1969 Barry bought himself a pair of green corduroys from Beale and Inmans. 'He really liked them, so we had a pair made. That set him off on the corduroy tack. He's never looked back. Virtually the only other trousers he's had since has been the bottom half of his collapsing funerals suit, all held together with safety pins.'

Maurice Richardson said of Richard that he 'always dresses and looks as if he has spent the night on somebody else's sofa.' Many of his jumpers look as if they have been attacked not by moths but by sabre-toothed tigers. 'Dad is an intellectual,' offers his son Fred, 'he forgets mundane things like new jumpers. And Mum always did everything for him, cooking, washing, ironing, buying underwear.' Richard is not best pleased when these sartorial deficiencies are pointed out. 'He doesn't give a damn about it,' says John Wells, 'and if you draw it to his attention he gets very angry.' His staff never did draw it to his attention. They just mothered him through sartorial crises, like some bewildered professor. 'He used to come shuffling in,' remembers Maggie Lunn, 'and he'd always broken his specs, and we girls would spend hours with tweezers putting them back together, and it'd be "Oh, what could I do without you?" And that would make you feel wonderful, obviously. He's brilliant at getting people to do things. That's why he's such a good editor – he can really get people to do anything, and make them feel important about it.'

This ability was not confined to relations with his staff. 'He had a way of gathering people around him who were part of the establishment,' marvels Liz Elliot. 'The people who used to come in always amazed me – MPs and that sort of thing – and

199

they gave information loyally and happily, because they believed that he was on the side of right; which I think he was, most of the time.' Christopher Logue is again somewhat sceptical about this capacity to inspire loyalty. 'I'd say to him: "You are in fact a sort of full-time seducer. You don't actually go to bed with people, but you seduce people all the time. You're very charming, and you're very good-looking, and people are afraid of you. And that's why women are so drawn to you".' Seduced or not, the *Eye* girls' feelings for Richard were genuine, and they were reciprocated. 'I think Richard loved me, in a paternal sort of way,' says Tessa. 'I was very fond of him, I must say. He was so pleased when Barry and I got married.' Adds Liz Elliot: 'His editorial judgement was absolutely brilliant. We'd have followed him through the Red Sea.' Parted, or unparted? 'Either.'

Maternal instincts aside, the quality most cited as worthy of admiration among Richard's employees was his fearlessness, often in the face of overwhelming odds. Says Paul Foot: 'His recklessness – or courage – is one of the great features of journalism in our lifetime.' Insists Auberon Waugh: 'Richard is somebody who isn't to be cowed. The most fatal thing to do to him is to try to frighten him or to worm your way into his good grace. He just laughs in people's faces and renews his attack. He reacts to any threat very violently and in the opposite direction.'[10] 'He doesn't mind what people think, which is very rare,' adds Ian Hislop. 'Most people don't have his sort of backbone, and they pull back – they're very worried about losing famous friends, and he never minded that.' It was of course his own personal knot of unfamous ones that he didn't want to lose. Andrew Osmond recalls: 'He would say, "If we're going to have to offend this person and it's going to cost us money, then we're going to offend them. Don't tell me we can't afford it". Which was exactly as it should be. You can date the decline of *Punch* from the day it started to be run as a business, by a businessman, William Davis. It just stopped being funny or dangerous or interesting from that point.' In 1969 Andrew Osmond abandoned his sensible career in the Foreign Office to write thrillers with an FO colleague, one Douglas Hurd. He also returned part-time to take over the management of the *Eye*. 'In the years after I came back, the magazine had a golden period. That was when Paul Foot had the back pages and we pushed the circulation on up from about 30–40,000 into the hundreds of thousands.'

The combination of Foot and Ingrams was, from a journalistic point of view, a devastatingly successful Jack-and-Mrs-Spratt mix. Ingrams was intuitive in approach, with an editor's nose for a good story; 'An editor's job is not to know stories, so much as to sniff them out,' he wrote. 'It's a question, as someone has said, of remaining bored until the right moment.'[11] If there were obstacles to checking facts, he let his instincts do the checking. Did the tale, he would ask himself, have the 'ring of truth'? Foot, on the other hand, was assiduous and methodical, and disinclined to rely on instinct. Ingrams was mischievous, Foot earnest. Ingrams wanted to stop the world changing for the worse, Foot wanted to change it for the better. Ingrams was a motivator, Foot could not have been more motivated. Almost the only attributes they shared, it seemed, were journalistic bravery and an immense regard for each other's abilities. Together, they pulled off some of the biggest scoops of the period, earning the tribute from Liberal leader Jo Grimond that *Private Eye* was becoming more accurate than the Fleet Street papers.

Ingrams' propensity to go for a story purely on instinct has attracted a battery of criticism. Esther Rantzen, one of the victims of the 'ring of truth', reacted bitterly: 'I think he now believes himself to be infallible. I think if he puts the finger on someone, he believes them to be utterly corrupt through and through. I think he now knows that he can detect the ring of truth at probably a range of some hundreds of miles, because as far as I know he doesn't meet his targets.'[12] Why rely on instinct, say Esther and others like her, why not just ring up and check the facts? A lot of fact-checking does go on, counters Ingrams; 'but most people I've rung up slam down the phone or tell me a pack of lies. I was criticised for not talking to Esther Rantzen, but the very few times I've talked to that woman, I've just had to listen to a lot of absolute rubbish.'[13] 'A lot of information is simply denied to us,' confirms Paul Foot. 'Facts are not just there to be picked off trees. In any story worth its salt, you fall short of proving it to the hilt. You do have to publish things without being certain. You need an editor who says, "Well go ahead and publish".' Foot cites the case of Sir Richard Marsh, whom he telephoned to check facts about a medical company of which Marsh was a director. Marsh refused to confirm or deny the facts, but immediately obtained an injunction stopping the *Eye* article; he never offered any defence, even after the story was ultimately published. Repeated protestations of innocence, if sufficiently furious, have always reinforced Ingrams' innate belief in a story.

Most journalists who have worked at the *Eye* back the Ingrams method. 'Richard liked a saying that I used to quote, that we were merely shepherds, shepherding the facts towards the desired conclusion,' says Peter McKay, now of the *Evening Standard*. 'It all went back to Cockburn and Muggeridge. They both said in one form or another that it wasn't any good just dealing with facts, because you couldn't ever get at the really important ones, you had to take a chance. All the powerful interests had defences against you ever finding out facts that would embarrass them. People always used to say, "If only you'd picked the telephone up", but of course every time you tried it they said "Fuck off, of course we're not going to talk to you about this", so he was right. Richard was quite an unworldly man, but unworldly people are often acute in some areas. He had a very acute ear for humbug. The ring of truth became a great joke, but there's no doubt that on the profit and loss account he came out ahead.'

Paul Halloran, an *Eye* journalist of later vintage, also pays tribute to the Ingrams instinct. 'When he was on form he was bloody marvellous. He used to read the newspapers to find out what was in them, and he knew instinctively when something wasn't right. He'd tear something out of the paper and say, "This doesn't sound right". It was usually very unwise not to listen, because you'd seen it work so many times before, and invariably you'd find something in it – it's a gift he's got. But there are a lot of myths about the ring of truth. A lot of what Ingrams did was to trust the judgement of the people who gave him the stories.

He made an intelligent assessment of their abilities and motives. Some mistakes got made, but mistakes are endemic in journalism, and to make them is no bad thing – as long as you acknowledge that they are mistakes.' Ingrams himself tends not to lose much sleep over the mistakes that were made, but he does regret one specific error of judgement. When the KGB were hawking salacious photographs around Fleet Street of Commander Courtney, a Conservative MP, all the papers turned them down. So did the *Eye*, but Ingrams decided to run the story of the abortive sale anyway, a piece that had much the same destructive effect on the Commander's career as publication of the photographs would have done.

Ingrams' older friends are uneasy about the ring of truth. 'He's definitely got some kind of instinctive sense,' says John Wells, 'that's why he got Maxwell and all those people. It's like a litmus paper. If you say anything hypocritical or dishonest in front of him, he's going to laugh at you. If you expose anything to him that is bogus, he will instantly sniff it, and ding! ding! the alarm will go. But the alarm can go off unnecessarily.' Says Paul Foot: 'The ring of truth is not enough on its own – I don't think Richard really believes it is either – there must be a factual basis as well. I'm not entirely inclined to trust his instincts. As journalists, we want things to be true. On the other hand, there's a defeatist and pusillanimous view that nothing can possibly be published unless it's proved to the hilt. It's that latter view which is by far the most current in journalism generally, and in British journalism in particular. All journalistic decisions hover between these two extremes. The great contribution of *Private Eye* – Richard's great contribution – is that it's tended much more to the first of the two, it's been much more ready to publish. Although of course there are plenty of times when you can show that the ring of truth simply didn't work, and they got egg all over their faces.'

If the ring of truth did fail its master once or twice, it tended to be over the smaller stories, one-off incidents that depended on the word of a single individual. Bigger stories of corruption and crime involving a number of participants provided the *Eye* with a battery of successes from the late 1960s onwards. *Eye* readers were the

203

Richard Ingrams

first to read about BP's sanction-busting in Rhodesia, eight years before the national press got hold of the story; the first to read about the Heath government's secret talks with the IRA; about the 1971 Payola scandal, when disc-jockeys were bribed to play certain records; about Meyer Lansky and Israeli links with the Mafia; about the racist ideology behind South Africa's pioneering heart transplants; and about the rise of a young Belfast politician called Ian Paisley. When the Ronan Point block of council flats collapsed in East London, an *Eye* article triggered off a series of contributions from high-powered consulting engineers, architects and so on, proving controversially that safety standards were being applied inadequately to council housing.

Undoubtedly the most famous *Eye* achievement of this period was the uncovering of the Poulson scandal. A young reporter on the *Bradford Argus*, Ray Fitzwalter – later boss of Granada Television – drew the *Eye*'s attention to the strange activities of John Poulson, a Wakefield architect. Paul Foot went to Yorkshire in 1970 and followed up the story. 'As I filled in the gaps between the things that Ray told me, all sorts of curious little sidelines to the story arose, and new kinds of corruption seemed to grow upon the central wart of it. Eventually we published an article over three pages in the *Eye* – that's getting on for 4000 words, I mean it's an enormous article, probably the biggest article ever published in *Private Eye* up to that time – called The Slicker of Wakefield. And no one paid the slightest attention to these remarkable facts about the corruption that was going on throughout the whole of the north of England, taking in representatives from both political parties, councils throughout the whole area, and so on. The whole thing could have been covered up for ever. Then, by a mixture of bad luck, incompetence and greed, Poulson was declared bankrupt, and the fact that he'd given coffee pots to ministers and bribed the Home Secretary all came out in public. Maudling, the Home Secretary, had to resign, and that was generally speaking put down to the *Eye*. But it was the ability to run the story again and again, fortnight after fortnight, to forge the thing in the consciousness of that fairly wide section of middle-class opinion which reads *Private Eye*, that established the matter as a national scandal.'

204

The British legal system, which had previously regarded *Private Eye* as an unpleasant nuisance, began to see it as some sort of vermin to be stamped out. Ingrams unwisely went to court in 1969 when sued by Hugh Farmer and Dennis Cassidy, two *People* reporters who had written a piece about an anarchist ex-con using the services of a Glasgow prostitute; the *Eye*'s allegation was that the prostitute had actually been hired by the two reporters themselves. Farmer and Cassidy's detailed alibi was that they had been eating a quiet meal in the Epicure restaurant on the night referred to. Although the *Eye* was able to prove in court that the Epicure had in fact been closed all day, the court found against the magazine. The *Eye* had to find another £10,000, and once again was forced to throw itself on the generosity of its readers with its 'Gnomefam' appeal.

Despite such setbacks, Fleet Street rushed to follow the *Eye*'s lead and a whole raft of investigative teams was set up by the nationals. Bereft of stories, newspapers like the *Guardian* took to lifting *Eye* stories as 'exclusives'. A piece commissioned by Ingrams from a freelance, which led indirectly to the head of the Flying Squad and the head of the Obscene Publications Squad being tried on corruption charges, was stolen just before press day by *People* reporters waving wads of cash. The *Eye* seemed to be getting all the best stories first. According to Patrick Marnham, the magazine had become 'a pacemaker for the national press.'[14] Fleet Street columnist David Wynne-Morgan reckoned that as many as eighty per cent of investigative journalists on the national papers were now feeding material to the magazine. According to newspaper editor Derek Jameson, the *Eye* was 'the rubbish dump for those stories that Fleet Street can't use for one reason or another. Either they are dangerous legally, or else the proprietor happens to be a mate of the victim, or whatever. We all know as editors in Fleet Street that the minute we say "Sorry cock, I can't use that, my goodness you must be joking," we know with total certainty that within a matter of days it will be in *Private Eye*.'[15]

Private Eye's journalistic reputation leapt even further forward with the arrival of Michael Gillard and the start of the

'In The City' column in 1970. The column was Foot's idea, and it was written with the crushing weight of factual detail that had become Foot's trademark. Incomprehensible to outsiders, it soon became essential reading to the police, the Bank of England, and the Security Exchange Commission in Washington. 'Nobody here wants to admit they read the bloody thing, but of course they all do,' admitted a NatWest spokesman in *Institutional Investor* magazine. Gillard possessed, in Paul Foot's words, 'a memory like a filing cabinet',[16] and his contacts were exceptional. Like Patrick Marnham, he was extremely secretive; he wouldn't allow anyone to take his picture, he always used a *nom de plume*, and even his closest contacts didn't know his phone number. 'He looked like a Mafia man, with a dark suit, a moustache, a low voice and these ever-present dark glasses,' says Ingrams. Gillard had been thrown out of the *Express*, after revealing secret links between the head of Rothmans and the South African prime minister John Vorster. It was the kind of investigative journalism that the *Express* could not tolerate on its own cosy pages; but it was perfect for *Private Eye*. There was no political pro- or anti-City bias about Gillard. He just 'exposed shits for fun,' as Ingrams had it.

The *Eye* journalists were rewarded in the public arena for their successes: Foot was made Journalist of the Year, and Christopher Booker and Candida Lycett Green, who were also working for other publications, jointly won Campaigning Journalists of the Year. Yet there is no doubt, as Paul Foot insisted, that the editor can take the bulk of the credit for the blooming of the *Eye* at this time. He had augmented his gang with an eclectic collection of specialists, and created the unique conditions in which they might flourish. Despite his laid-back and often reserved image, the sheer force of his personality made him a natural commander of this strange assortment of people; he was a man of huge editorial talent, instinctive rather than self-taught. He did, according to Barry Fantoni, secretly yearn for the filthy glamour of the national press: 'He harboured romantic ideas about Fleet Street, and its great names, although he never actually worked there.' What he was really dreaming of, though, was the brave old English campaigning journalistic tradition; not the grubby reality of Fleet

Street, where he would have been cast down by mediocrity and compromise, as he had been so often in life.

Although he had not really recognised it yet, Ingrams was inherently a nostalgic conservative, with a burning desire to hang on to any persons or moments capable of papering over the cracks of a naturally melancholy life. His editorial style was largely determined by his colossal attempts to hang on to a precious nostalgic happiness, as personified by that group of friends which had saved him and lifted him, first at Shrewsbury and then at Oxford. Most people recognise the inevitability of splitting up, moving on, waving goodbye to old pals. Not Ingrams. His gang was pulled this way and that by the army, by the pressure to find sensible jobs, by the lure of television and its prospect of fame and money. There had been endless permutations, one or two casualties along the way, and one or two additions; but somehow, he had managed to hold the nub of the group together. Except that, now, the guns of *Parson's Pleasure* had become the bigger guns of *Private Eye*, and when they fired, everybody listened.

This was not the apogee of *Private Eye*'s success – he was to take it on to yet bigger things, but it was the apogee of his contentment with his position as editor. Now, over a long, long period, the edifice he had built to protect his personal and professional lives began slowly to crumble away.

15 Eyes Right

In 1970, Richard's third child, Arthur, was born. 'Mary had been having pain all the time, which was not natural,' says Victoria. 'She hadn't been well with hepatitis and she wanted to make sure that the baby would be all right. Instead of going to her ordinary doctor, she went to a very posh doctor in Reading, and he never discovered that the afterbirth was underneath the baby. He never did a scan, and never discovered anything until it was too late. She had a Caesarean, but it was too late, Arthur had lost oxygen. He should have died there and then, of course. But you know how they keep them alive. Arthur could never sit, see, or do anything. Mary was wonderful with him.' Mary, who was virtually confined to the house by the new arrival, found it hard to conceal her deep sense of upset. Richard, however, reacted to the birth of a severely brain-damaged son with the same stoicism that had characterized the death of his brother. Prior to the birth, he had been smoking forty a day. Following Arthur's arrival, he was riding his motorbike over the Thames at Goring on the way to work, when he lobbed both the packets he had with him into the river. It was a cleansing gesture. He hasn't smoked since.

Ingrams was not one to offload his personal suffering onto others. His staff knew little about Arthur. Bravely, he ensured that life at the *Eye* continued at a jolly pace, and rang to the sound of laughter when he was in. On dull days, he would stand up and announce, 'Oh, this is boring, let's all go out to tea', and take the entire office off for the afternoon, abandoning telephones,

208

letter-opening and joke-writing in mid-flow. There was a new office now. The magazine was expanding at a rapid rate, and had outgrown the cosy premises at 22 Greek Street. A plush reception area with expensive framed prints and a glossy receptionist, a well-appointed boardroom, superbly-equipped offices, absolutely none of these things were considered for a moment by Ingrams. In fact the *Eye* moved a few doors up the road to No.34. There was an extra floor, but the premises were just as seedy. Tessa Fantoni remembers: 'It had exactly the same atmosphere. It was still another revolting office, but this time it was above a Chinese. The street door was unlocked, so you'd go into the lavatory and there'd be some junkie standing on the loo fixing themselves up.'

Indoors, the usual chaos prevailed. Edward Whitley described the offices as 'piled high with newspapers, *Who's Who*s and all sorts of press-cuttings, like a lopsided Dickensian film set'.[1] The previous tenant had been The Kinks' and The Who's old producer, Shel Talmy; he had left his furniture behind, which pleased Barry no end. Generally speaking, the boys were happier than the girls, who'd been hoping for something a little more salubrious. 'It was as if we had a palace to walk around in,' marvelled Tone.

The mail order business had suddenly and unexpectedly collapsed, but the *Eye* was flourishing commercially nonetheless. Sales were high, and *Eye* books were doing well. The newspaper misprints sent in by readers (an idea originally suggested by Fritz Spiegl, the Liverpool composer) had already been collected into two volumes by MacDonald, under the beguiling title, *What The Papers Never Meant To Say*. The same publisher brought out a 'Best of the *Eye*', entitled *Private Eyesores*, in 1970; this sold well enough to encourage Quartet to move in and publish a second 'Best of' book, outrageously described as *The Best of Private Eye Volume One*. In order to outflank this bickering, Osmond and Cash set up the *Eye*'s own publishing arm. They followed this by setting up an in-house distribution company, after discovering that their distributors Moore-Harness had been forcing smaller newsagents to take *Private Eye* as part of a package involving pornographic magazines. Then the pair started planning a company pension scheme. To Ingrams' continued and profound

209

disinterest, Osmond and the boxwallahs were transforming the *Eye* into a lucrative operation.

The classified advertising pages had taken off after a shaky start when the columns had been colonised by perverts using a secret code to pick each other up, and were now bringing in steady revenue: Ingrams banned all sex ads. A self-confessedly rival publication, *Oz*, proved short-lived, despite the best efforts of Her Majesty's judiciary to publicise it by arresting its editors. Flush with the success of a brace of free plastic discs, there was even an *Eye* album, entitled *Private Eye's Blue Record*; although this venture, put into the hands of Cook, Wells and Barry Humphries, came rather unstuck when the protagonists did nothing about it until the last minute, then got drunk and attempted to improvise the whole thing. The results were less than inspiring.

After years of ridiculing Harold Wilson, the *Eye*'s plastic records had found a new comic target in the shape of Edward 'Grocer' Heath, the newly-elected prime minister. It had been a tough campaign for Heath: schoolchildren had repeatedly shouted 'Grocer' at him during his public meetings. *Just For The Record* (1970) and *Hullo Sailor* (1971), featuring respectively John Wells and Willie Rushton as Mr Heath, were full of innuendo: Peter Cook, for instance, as Idi Amin, telling an interviewer: 'As I wrote to your Queen, Mr Heath'. A pop song of the day was nicely corrupted to: 'Grocer Heath, Grocer Heath, can't you hide those awful teeth? Grocer Heath, tell the truth, is it true that you're . . . aloof?' 'No, no,' replied Grocer, 'I think I'm as warm as the next man.'

Much of this was the work of Peter Cook: 'Every time someone goes out of power we think, "Oh my god, what are we going to do?" Heath was definitely the most boring one to think up,' he complains. Eventually, Mrs Wilson's Diary was replaced by a weekly letter from the managing director of 'Heathco.' to his staff, written by Ingrams and Fantoni. 'Looking back on it, you think, how did you ever milk anything out of that time?' ponders Barry. 'What we did was to put a little piece at the end of each letter about the plastic beaker automatic dispensing unit – the

PBDU – a machine he's bought from the Japanese, and why for heaven's sake do people keep using it as a dart board or sitting on it? That was what was funny about the Grocer, and also what made him so dull, that he had a failed grasp of what was happening politically, but was fixated on tiny things like items of new technology.'

Like Wilson before him, Heath refused to acknowledge his own declining fortunes, and reacted bitterly against the laughter of *Private Eye* and its editor – to whom he had ironically presented the 'Irritant of the Year' award at the 1969 *What the Papers Say* awards. The nickname 'Grocer', it seems, particularly infuriated the prime minister. Says Richard: 'The Grocer always had a tremendous chip on his shoulder about the *Eye*, and he thought we were public school snobs. He was on some radio show with Hislop recently, and he said "*Private Eye* could never forgive me for the fact that I didn't go to a public school" – which is an incredible remark for a man who'd been prime minister to make. He thought that because he was called Grocer this was *Private Eye* being snobbish, but in fact he was called Grocer because much of his career was concerned with groceries – all those early Common Market negotiations when the whole thing seemed to revolve around what we would have to pay for cat food and that kind of thing. His greatest achievement was the abolition of retail price maintenance.'

Eye-watchers seemed inexplicably confused by this swing from attacking Wilson to attacking Heath with equal energy. The Monday Club revealed that the magazine was really a front for the International Socialist Party, while almost in the same breath – or type of breath – the *Worker's Press* condemned it as fascist. In fact, of course, the *Eye*'s politics were primarily cynical, deriving from a universal distrust of politicians. Ingrams identified with the views of A.J.P. Taylor on this issue: 'The Germans greatly admired Hitler and look where it got them. The Italians thought Mussolini was wonderful and the result was disastrous. The great advantage in a democracy like ours is that we assume that our politicians are awful, and the fact is that they invariably are.' Auberon Waugh put it more strongly when he said

211

that it is a healthy (and very British) attitude to regard politicians as social and emotional cripples. This is not entirely hyperbolic – anyone who has attended an Oxbridge College will have had the misfortune to meet a significant proportion of the governing elite of his or her generation, and will remember them as largely inadequate characters who sacrificed a normal adolescent social life in order to attain power and status, and to foist their views on everybody else. It is of course the inevitable downside of democracy that those who work their way up the hierarchy to the top are not those best equipped to lead us, but those best equipped to work their way up a hierarchy. Says Ingrams: 'On the whole, the people one admires in politics lack the ruthless ambition that makes more successful politicians unpleasant.'[2] Jo Grimond was one he admired. Sir Oswald Mosley, with whom Mary and he had dinner once, was an extreme example of the latter type. 'Mosley talked about what needed doing in the country, when what he really meant was that he wanted to do these various things himself and there was no question of anyone else being consulted.' OK for a magazine, apparently, but hardly appropriate on the national stage. 'Then he started to wave his arms, and it all became slightly hypnotic and quite frightening.'[3]

Ingram's refusal to rally to any political standpoint has come in for criticism. According to Alan Coren, 'The causes that the *Eye* espouses aren't real causes. They're done for the comedy implicit in them – that's why it's very hard to get to the bottom of what their politics actually are. *Private Eye* picks up on a very English attitude of putting down, and that's fine if your culture is healthy. But if your culture is very vulnerable, as ours is at the moment, it makes it a sort of celebration of failure. I get depressed reading it. I think, they're probably right about all this, but it's not actually helpful.' That assumes, of course, that satire should be constructive, which is extremely debatable. In fact the *Eye*'s neutral political stance validates its campaigning journalism, so that it is taken seriously in a way that the *Socialist Worker* could never be.

Ken Tynan was another who felt that the Ingrams *Eye* was a purely negative force. In the early 1960s he had written a dismissive note to Ingrams saying 'When are you going to get a point of view?' Ingrams had promptly pinned the letter to the *Eye* noticeboard. In fact, Tynan could hardly have misunderstood the *Eye*'s editor more comprehensively. Ingrams' point of view was clear and distinct, and drove the *Eye* forward for a quarter of a century. Tynan had confused the deliberate absence of clear political affiliation with the absence of a point of view, and had allowed the magazine's comic voice to obscure its serious message. 'To the core, *Private Eye* and Richard Ingrams are British and patrician,' wrote John Wells. 'Kenneth Tynan should have recognised this, comic voices or no comic voices.'[4] 'Obviously the magazine had a point of view – it was the patrician point of view.'

At the polling booths, Richard had as little time for Edward Heath as he did on the printed page. He voted for Harold Wilson in 1964, 1966, 1970 and 1974. In 1979 he was torn between Callaghan and Thatcher, finally plumping for the Conservatives, with whom he stayed in 1983 and 1987, before drifting back leftwards again. In 1992 he didn't vote. None of his previous choices had been enthusiastic ones; he was sensible enough to feel uncomfortable about embracing any party's entire package of policies, and to be aware that there was little chance of them being carried out efficiently. 'Richard does not care about politics,' says Christopher Logue. 'He's a gent.'[5] They were, however, interestingly populist choices. '*Private Eye* is a weather vane of middle-class opinion. As far as I am concerned, this is a criticism,' says Paul Foot.[6] 'In the 1960s, Richard was a social democrat, in the 1970s he hovered between the two, in the 1980s he became a Tory. In the 1990s he's wandering back like most people, all the while having utter contempt for the government. He's like eighty per cent of the population.' For Foot, rooted to his spot on the far left, it was irritating to see Ingrams drift back and forth ahead of the tide, apparently vague and inconsistent.

While it is true that Ingrams has been inconsistent in mere party political terms, there is a profound consistency underlying these contrary voting patterns, and underpinning *Private Eye*'s political outlook; and that is his relentless distrust of the fashionable consensus. Explains Ian Hislop: 'He can't bear unthinking consensus, from blind support of the police in the old days, to blind canonisation of Freddie Mercury now. Fashions have changed – we've now got a liberal consensus, as opposed to when the *Eye* started up, a very set suburban consensus.' Being anti-consensus in 1964 fooled many into thinking that Richard was a socialist, including Richard himself. In fact he is and always has been an arch-conservative, with a small 'c'. Hence his identification with a substantial swathe of middle-class opinion that has always distrusted being told that something is good for it.

It was this broad identification with conservative middle-class opinion that made *Private Eye* so attractive. Where Ingrams diverged from, and excited, middle-class opinion was in his radical compulsion to support the underdog. 'All my instincts are radical,' he told Naim Attallah, 'a radical instinct being one that automatically sides with the underdog, the dispossessed or the poor – the Palestinians, the Catholics in Northern Ireland, those who are in a minority. It is a basic instinct I hold, coupled with a mistrust of the rich and powerful, and I have come to the conclusion that it is quite rare. Most people are fundamentally obsequious, including journalists, which is very sad. I think and hope my own instincts are too powerful to be seduced, for it is always right to be suspicious of the powerful and wealthy. My great hero, Dr Johnson, said that the insolence of wealth will creep out, and I like that very much.'[7] Ingrams' other great hero, William Cobbett, was of the same mould, a radical but not a revolutionary: 'He spent his life attacking politicians. He was forever being put into prison for libel. He wasn't revolutionary like Paine, who, though I admire him, was head-in-the-clouds. Cobbett was different: a sensible man who felt a strong antipathy to the Establishment and consensus thinking.'

So where does that leave Ingrams' own political point of view? 'Since I'm suspicious of, and distrustful of, the powerful, and these tend to be right-wing, Conservative, Fascist people, that makes me, as their enemy, left-wing. On the other hand, I don't particularly identify with the Labour party. The whole idea of Marxism is abhorrent to me, the great mystery of our time being how many clever people have managed to give their

214

allegiance to Russia. I used to think a lot about who would be in the Resistance if Britain were occupied by a foreign power, and I often assess people in that way.'[8] Quoting the author Malcom Lowry, Ingrams reckons that he is 'a Conservative Christian anarchist'. A Tory anarchist, he says, 'is someone who disbelieves in revolution, in other words who accepts the system as it stands on the grounds that any other system is bound to be, if not worse, at least as bad as the present system; and who distrusts anyone who disapproves of anyone who seeks to subvert the system. It is anarchical in the sense that it disapproves equally strongly of all politicians.'[9]

To this convoluted definition might be added the familiar word patrician. There are hundreds of minority causes worthy of espousal, but the radical Palestinian and Northern Irish Catholic causes have a long history of patrician support. Ingrams' general willingness to assault the establishment derives from the confidence of his class and from the knowledge that his attacks might improve the status quo but will not – and must not – destroy it. 'This radicalism is unique to the British patrician classes,' says Alan Coren. 'His is a counter-culture which has so much confidence that it knows it will continue, irrespective of what happens and irrespective of what it does. European culture has generally drawn its intellectuals from elsewhere, but in Britain intellectuals have often been drawn from patrician culture and have been destructive of it – like Byron, Shelley and Mary Godwin. Evelyn Waugh tried desperately to get in and be part of that. It's one of the reasons for the survival of British society.'

So, despite a superficially leftward swing by *Private Eye* after Edward Heath's election in 1970, the magazine's underlying trend was to react against the fashionable consensus and move right, into territory occupied by Christopher Booker and by Auberon Waugh. Round-faced, bespectacled and slightly baggy, Evelyn Waugh's son had joined the *Eye* in February of the same year, after being sacked from the *Spectator* by Nigel Lawson; in a moment of boredom at the printer's, he had altered George Gale's name on the contents page to read 'Lunchtime O'Gale'. Lawson eventually had to pay him £600 in compensation. Shortly afterwards, Waugh also lost his other job, at *The Times*, when an anti-Islamic article caused an enraged mob to burn down the British Council Library in Rawalpindi. His new *Eye* column began as a parody of Alan Brien's *Times* diary; Waugh even sported an Alan Brien-style false beard. The column soon took on a life of its own, however, and outlived Brien's diary by a decade.

The hallmark of Waugh's diary was the use of astonishing and frequently right-wing vitriol against public figures for comic effect. For example Shirley Williams, the instigator of comprehensive schools, was described as having 'done more harm to this country than Hitler. As long as there is breath in my body I shall seek to punish, torment, humiliate and ridicule this loathsome, pig-headed woman for the damage she has done to her country.' Northerners, the working classes, old age pensioners, the unemployed, any target declared taboo by the liberal consensus was fair game for Waugh. He was prepared to live and die by the pen; his friend Naim Attallah, the Quartet publisher, recalls: 'I read a profile of Auberon Waugh in the *Guardian* written by Polly Toynbee, and I have never ever seen a more vicious piece written about anybody in my life. I read it and I was sick. I talked to Bron about it, but he didn't seem to care. If the same piece had been written about me, I'd have gone crackers. In fact I've often wanted to sue people, and Richard and Bron have been furious with me for even thinking of it.'

What particularly appealed to Ingrams' love of stirring placid waters was Waugh's willingness to attack the *Eye*'s own camp-followers in the same direct style. *Eye* supporters such as Alan Brien and Bryan Forbes were, as Patrick Marnham puts it, 'nibbled by the new dog.'[10] Waugh was – and still is – openly dismissive of most of his new colleagues. Booker, he thinks, is 'mad as a hatter. And he can be a bore. He doesn't realise when he's being boring. He was pompous and he was on the make. But he's found his legs now on the *Sunday Telegraph*.' Then there's Fantoni: 'Always crawling around and sucking up, although there's no harm to him'; and John Wells: 'Nobody really likes Wells'. Ingrams, the terrible shadow of boredom forever lurking at his shoulder, gave Waugh a certain leeway. 'He never minded me being rude about Wells or about Booker,' says Waugh, 'but *not* Barry Fantoni. You were never allowed to make jokes about Fantoni. *Any* joke – even if I said what a splendid artist and philosopher Fantoni was. Jokes about Charlie Douglas-Home were always taken out too, but then Ingrams knew – which I didn't know – that he was dying.' Today, Richard has the odd twinge of regret about Waugh's vitriol: 'I did feel uneasy about one or two of his personal campaigns against individuals, and I think probably I should have been stricter with my blue pencil, looking back on it. Because I think he does pursue personal vendettas against people out of malice, and that is regrettable.'[11] Be rude, not malicious, is the Ingrams creed.

Twinges apart, Ingrams forged one of his greatest friendships with the spiky columnist. Waugh fitted the increasingly fixed pattern of Richard's attitudes and interests perfectly. He was of the same class; he had even at one stage briefly wooed Mary's younger sister Selina. He was old-fashioned, and sometimes wore his father's clothes. He represented a link with Oxford. He was a Roman Catholic. He was entertaining, and kept bores at bay. He had that searching awareness of humbug that Richard so admired. Like his editor, he had opted to remain isolated from metropolitan life, which prevented him from clouding his conscience by meeting his targets. Their families got on well, and Bron soon became a regular visitor at Aldworth. As if in parody of the dichotomy between Ingrams' own acerbic pen and charming personality, Waugh's writing was twice as acerbic and his personality even more charming. On one occasion, he flicked an unstubbed cigarette end out of the Greek Street window and set a passing woman's hat ablaze. The victim stormed into the *Eye*'s reception and was directed up to Waugh's office in a rage; only to emerge, smiling sweetly, shortly afterwards. This juxta-position is not unusual, of course. After all, is it not always the inoffensive, avuncular television presenters who have backstage tantrums and are caught in suspenders and stockings with a pile of cocaine up their noses? The reverse is true of the apparently shocking Mr Waugh.

There were small but marked differences between Richard and

217

his new friend. Christopher Logue explains: 'Although Auberon can be much ruder in print than Ingrams, he is not frightening in the same way. If Auberon attacked me I'd expect quite a lot of very witty denigration – but I wouldn't expect him to kill me if he was in charge, because he hates power.' Waugh had been given power in the army, where Ingrams had not, and thus never saw the other side of the tracks. Says Richard: 'I always thought the slight gap between me and Bron is that I had that experience and he didn't, and that in a sense he has always been on one side of the fence and is actually rather embarrassed about all these other people struggling along.' Waugh, conversely, feels that Ingrams romanticises the working classes: 'He thinks back to his days in the Royal Army Education Corps, and sees them as rows of earnest faces trying to spell "cat".'[12]

Although he represented a noticeable swing to the right, Waugh also got on tremendously well with Paul Foot, in the way that all patricians who don't believe in consensus politics clearly do. Both men laid into Grocer Heath from opposite directions. 'They would agree on most issues,' says Richard – a hardly uncommon bond between the far left and the far right – 'and of course they came from the same class.' Foot defends himself against any charge of collaboration: 'For all his right-wing, upper-class opinions, which I find most distasteful, Bron Waugh is nevertheless an extremely sceptical man whose instinct is to laugh at everything that's put up in front of him. He is utterly infuriating to establishment figures, I mean to my certain knowledge he has driven them into paroxysms of rage and fury by his ability to see the absurdity in them. I'm quite open about it – I was for many years and still am a friend of his. I like his sense of humour, and I think in the same way that although he finds all my political opinions utterly distasteful, he has a certain respect for the challenging nature of my journalism.' Only an extreme left-winger would announce a touching friendship with someone as if he was confessing all before the Praesidium of the Supreme Soviet.

Between them, Foot and Waugh landed the *Eye* in court again. Foot and Gillard had exposed the Home Secretary Reginald Maudling's corrupt involvement with the Real Estate Fund of

America, whereupon *Observer* journalist Nora Beloff wrote a memo to her editor suggesting an article whitewashing the Home Secretary. The *Eye* obtained the memo and printed it, causing Beloff to sue; not for libel, as the content of the memo was incontrovertible, but for breach of copyright. That case fell to pieces, but unfortunately Waugh had subsequently nicknamed her Nora Ballsoff, and had written that she was 'frequently to be found in bed with Mr Harold Wilson and senior members of the previous administration, although it is thought that nothing improper occurred'. This was obviously meant as a joke – the judge even laughed at Nora Ballsoff – but the *Eye* was nonetheless found guilty of libel and ordered to pay £5000. Despite healthy sales hovering around the 100,000 mark, the award was a major setback; the resulting 'Ballsoff fund' raised £1300 from readers including Michael Foot, Tom and Miriam Stoppard, and the headmaster of Eton.

There were victories as well as defeats, however, in the libel arena. The *Eye* set its own little legal precedent in the much-referred-to case of Arkell v. Pressdram (the name under which the magazine publishes itself). Lord Goodman wrote to Ingrams on behalf of Mr Arkell, the retail credit manager of Granada TV, who had been accused of corruption: 'His attitude to damages will be governed by the nature of your reply.' Ingrams sent back a wordy reply culminating in the sentence, 'The nature of our reply is as follows: fuck off.' Mr Arkell was never heard from again.

Despite Foot's great affection for Waugh, he was becoming increasingly unhappy about the direction in which the *Eye* was drifting, much of it influenced by Waugh and the new-style religious Booker. As early as September 1969, the young Irish Republican MP Bernadette Devlin had appeared on the cover, shouldered by two supporters in such a way as to reveal her knickers. 'This should get a rise out of Paisley', read the bubble caption. Foot had let that one pass, but two years later Bernadette was back on the layout desk; this time holding her illegitimate baby and talking to Harold Wilson, saying, 'I'm going to call him Harold because he's a little bastard'. Foot reacted by withdrawing his

219

labour. Unless the cover was dropped immediately, he informed Richard, there would be no Footnotes column that week. 'Richard couldn't believe it,' recalls Foot. 'We had this terrific row. Ultimately, he said, "Well, if you feel that strongly, we'll change the front page".' For Ingrams to cave in to any threat was almost unheard of; such was his regard and affection for Foot. Nonetheless, both men knew deep down that Foot's days were numbered.

Foot also tried to foist his politics on the magazine's administrative side; he objected to Leo Thorpe & Son, the *Eye*'s printers since 1962, on the grounds that they were non-union. A year or two later the *Eye* moved its business to FebEdge, printers of the *Socialist Worker*, whereupon a Mr B.W. Coppock of the National Graphical Association called at the office, demanding that Tone and his assistant join up, otherwise FebEdge wouldn't print the magazine. Normally, one would have expected Ingrams to issue an Arkell v. Pressdram-type response; but again, out of respect for Foot, he grudgingly capitulated. Richard's principal response to the hard left was to produce two new characters, both humourless jargon-spouting socialist bores: the short-lived Len Trott, and the famous Dave Spart, he of the catchphrase 'Er basically . . .' Neither was actually based on Foot – Len Trott sounded suspiciously like Ken Trodd and Dave Spart was based on *Oz* editor Richard Neville – but the politics satirised were indisputably Foot's.

In the summer of 1972 *Private Eye*'s cover featured a joke about Angela Davis, the black socialist revolutionary who had been arrested in the United States. 'That was particularly revolting,' complains Foot, 'when she was on trial for her life. Booker was responsible for it. Richard and I had a terrible row. It was one of the things that made up my mind I should leave.' In Patrick Marnham's history of the magazine Foot further attacks Booker's influence on the *Eye*: 'Under his influence there was a tendency just to add a satirical gloss to the *Sunday Telegraph*.'[13] In August, while Foot was on holiday, the *Eye*'s customary attacks on the Conservative government were tempered with jokes about the striking dockers and 'the Pentonville Martyrs', five of the strikers who had been jailed for refusing to appear before the Industrial Relations Court. On his return, Foot announced that he was leaving to join the *Socialist Worker*. 'I just couldn't bear being associated with these attacks, stemming from Richard's prejudices,' he explains. For prejudices, perhaps one should read 'views not in accordance with my own'. Foot had made a sterling contribution to the *Eye*, not only in terms of the stories he had brought to the magazine, but in widening its outlook. Sadly, he was not prepared to see that outlook widen in other directions. His tendency towards political extremism (for what is an extremist but someone who cannot laugh at his own point of view?) had proved incompatible with his colleagues' sense of humour.

'It was terrible to leave,' says Foot. 'Their laughter was so infectious. In many ways, it was the most uncomfortable decision I've ever made in my life. I felt I was abandoning Richard. I did feel a sense in which I was deserting my friend. He obviously felt that. He was very shaken. Especially as I went off into total, penniless obscurity. I suppose that, as I wasn't leaving to go and benefit myself in any way, that softened the blow. But it was a blow to him. It was a blow to me too.' A profound gloom settled over the editor. There was a farewell dinner in October 1972, and Richard was presented with a John Kent cartoon showing himself, Booker and Fantoni in a pulpit, casting out Foot; but Foot's departure had been nobody's choice but his own. He always missed the *Eye* after he left, sometimes contributed articles, and made a brief, futile attempt to rejoin the magazine in the late 1970s. The political gap had widened even further, though, and he could not settle. He is still Richard Ingrams' best friend.

Foot was not the only socialist incapable of handling the *Eye*'s broadening political outlook. When the print union NATSOPA was satirised as NOTSOBA in 1973, and its corrupt practices were exposed, following years of spineless inactivity from national papers held to ransom by the unions, Claud Cockburn said he thought that *Private Eye* 'reeked of the *Daily Express*'. The right-wingers, it seemed, could laugh at the right, but the left-wingers could not laugh at the left. Another blow followed in 1974 when Andrew Osmond decided to leave, this time for good. There was nothing political about Osmond's defection – he had merely done all he could with the business side – but Richard's depression was tangible. He had recently completed a novel with Osmond, under the pen name of Philip Reid (their two middle names), about a journalist who is force-fed LSD and framed. In order to write up the LSD trip, it was decided to try some of the stuff, a task for which Ingrams had unilaterally volunteered Osmond; Richard's theory was that the LSD trip had permanently warped Osmond's mind. Certainly it is hard to imagine the debonair Gurkha officer hallucinating – try to imagine Douglas Hurd on a skateboard and you will have some measure of the incongruity entailed.

Once again, the gang was contracting, but this time there was a distinct feeling that this was more than just another fluctuation, that the *Eye* was fundamentally changing. Foot, for one, feared that it was becoming more trivial, an opinion shared by one or two of the old guard and made known to Ingrams. Sniffing the merest hint of a threat, he did what he generally did on such occasions: he deliberately threw the cat among the pigeons. New blood was needed at the *Eye*, but there were no more members of the old gang left to recruit. Instead, Ingrams had one or two exciting new candidates in mind. If the old guard had thought that Waugh's sniping at them was bad, they had a major surprise in store.

16 A New Type of Dog

Nigel Dempster arrived at *Private Eye* in 1972. A dapper former City figure and beau of the débutantes' ball circuit in the 1950s, his financial career had crumbled and he had become a society journalist instead. During the 1960s, while working on the *Daily Express* William Hickey column, he had furnished the *Eye* with anonymous stories about the rival Charles Greville column in the *Daily Mail*. When poached by the *Mail* in 1971, he had done an about turn, and had started to send in stories attacking the *Express*. At around the same time, the *Eye* had started its own gossip column, put together by Patrick Marnham under the heading Grovel. Invited to an *Eye* lunch, Dempster confessed to being the author of the anonymous stories, and was asked by Ingrams to become a part-time member of staff, and in due course to take over as Grovel himself.

Peter McKay, Ingrams' other new recruit, officially joined the payroll in 1975. A rotund Scotsman who had begun his professional life phoning in fish prices from the quay in Aberdeen, he was now working for the *Sunday Express*, and his keenness to attack the *Mail* was seen by Ingrams as a nice counterbalance to Dempster's efforts in the opposite direction. In the amateur world of *Private Eye*, the two new recruits were out-and-out professionals. It was like throwing two piranhas into a pool of koi carp.

From the start, both men began to provide accurate and highly damaging revelations about fellow journalists, society figures and celebrities that their own papers were unwilling or unable to print. Says Dempster: 'We were at a time when Fleet Street newspapers simply refused to print stories. Editors were terribly scared and cowardly. They were extremely wary of running stories which might offend proprietors or whatever. But Grovel had enormous, naughty, intimate stories about the worlds which *Private Eye* readers didn't really know: a lot about the Royal family and about rich, privileged people. I can remember being assaulted at Jonathan Aitken's house by the Ambassador from Iran. He shouted, "What more can you write, having revealed that the Prince of Wales has got herpes!" Grovel was financial, sexual, about bad treatment of relatives, that sort of thing. It had the first story about Princess Margaret and Roddy Llewellyn, and it had stories on Charles and all his girlfriends. When we got a writ from Lord Wigg, we paid out £8000, but I raised £9000 from various people, like Lord King and Peter Cadbury,' claims Dempster. 'We had our revenge when Wigg was picked up for kerb crawling. Grovel was personality journalism at its finest.'

Dempster and Ingrams had a high regard for each other. 'I thought Dempster was very good, in the heyday of Grovel. He had a very good eye for people who were shits,' explains Richard, full of admiration as usual for anyone who shared his searching awareness of humbug. Dempster was an entertainer, and Richard was in need of entertainment. He was also a flatterer, and took to calling Ingrams Lord Gnome, after the *Eye*'s fictional proprietor. This appropriation of the title annoyed the old guard, amused Richard, and by all accounts appealed to Mary Ingrams, as the soubriquet Lady Gnome still managed to sound faintly aristocratic despite being a joke. For his part, Dempster appreciated Ingrams' fearlessness: 'He always believed my stories. Even though he's never been a Fleet Street journalist, he understood journalism, and you got a feeling that you were safe with him. If you did do something terrible, there would be no recrimination.' Ingrams exerted his characteristic magnetic pull of loyalty on Dempster, who would take his editor out for a £20 lunch at the Gay Hussar Hungarian restaurant every Friday, despite being paid just £10 a fortnight. Clearly, it was a labour of love, and for many years it was very hard labour indeed.

224

'I did Grovel by myself, week in week out for a long time, and was rather relieved when McKay arrived because it meant I didn't have to work so hard. McKay used to come to the *Private Eye* lunch, listen to the Grovel stories, and then run them in the *Sunday Express*. I eventually got very angry with McKay, and very angry with Richard for inviting him. McKay is one of the great thieves of our time, and he's a great journalist because of it. The only way of stopping him doing that was to get him to work for *Private Eye* itself.' Before long, McKay was writing no fewer than six sections of the magazine, and collaborating on a lengthy cartoon life of David Frost. Where Dempster appeared cool and aloof, McKay was always jovial, laughing and chortling. 'Get back in your boxes!' he would cry at the boxwallahs, echoing Ingrams' attitude. Like Dempster, he provided a fund of entertaining stories for his editor's lunchtime amusement. Ian Hislop recalls: 'There's a side of Richard that's very interested in gossip. He's very "old Fleet Street" – he likes being at a table where men are telling each other stories. That's what he loved about McKay and Dempster. They would sit and tell him stories about the Duke of Devonshire throwing cheese at someone. There were anecdotes I must have listened to three million times – that sort of El Vino's hack legend stuff. Richard loves that.'

There were, however, crucial differences between Richard and his two new jesters. All three enjoyed mischief-making, but in each case this was tempered by different motivations. In Richard's case his personal morality came into play; he disliked the hypocrisy of his targets, and wanted to see the gap between their actions and their stated intentions exposed. 'We don't want to know about people's private lives unless there is an element of humbug involved,' he said.[1] 'There are certain baddies in pursuit of whom one has to go out on a limb. I do it because nobody else is doing it. People come to me and say, how can you write those things about those individuals – doesn't it cause a lot of distress? I think this is the purest humbug. Undoubtedly if I went back through the magazine there would be things I would wish to remove, but not in most cases. When people say lampooning of

225

public figures should not be allowed, they are usually thinking of their own lives.'[2]

Unlike Ingrams, Dempster loved to move among his targets. He was motivated by a desire to climb in society, and sought to amuse his highly-placed friends and patrons by rooting out good stories about their friends, rivals and enemies. He was unabashedly snobbish about it. 'I've always thought that the poor, spotted creatures in technical colleges actually want to know what's going on in Buckingham Palace or Woburn Abbey,' he drawls.

Peter McKay's interest was at least partly salacious. McKay was journalism incarnate, motivated by a professional desire to convert the amusing misfortunes of others into money, an approach considered by some of his new colleagues to border upon malice. It was a tabloid approach, and they didn't like it. 'Dempster has a cold eye, like a fish on a slab, but he has a warm heart,' wrote Patrick Marnham in his history of the *Eye*'s first two decades. 'McKay has a merry twinkling eye, but for most people, he has no heart at all.'[3]

The magazine's sudden upsurge in journalistic activity, and the increase in stories that were personally rather than politically embarrassing to their targets, disturbed the satirists. A rift quickly opened between the old guard and the new. 'From a position of unassailable morality, Ingrams uses utterly immoral people to attack other people's morals,' complained John Wells. 'Do you tell readers about Rio Tinto Zinc, or about some peer shagging a starlet?'[4] The choice, said Wells, was Ingrams' responsibility, and he was abusing that responsibility. Looking back today, Wells is more reflective, but the message is the same. 'When he was at Aldworth, Ingrams had this wonderful Jack Russell called Missy. It used to run along in front of you when you were walking, and it used to pick up pebbles. Then, when it came back at the end of the walk, it would shake all the pebbles out for him. And I thought, we're all his dogs really, and he doesn't treat his dogs very well, and occasionally he employs very dangerous dogs like Dempster who then bite him in the arse. There was a time when he really, genuinely enjoyed the company of Nigel Dempster. He has been close friends with some of the shits of the century.'

Booker's reaction was if anything stronger, exacerbated by his long-standing resentment over Ingrams' usurpation of his job. He publicly attacked the coarsening editorial standards of the *Eye* and spoke of a growing streak of cruelty in the gossip. When Ingrams had to appear in a major court case, he wrote in a timely *Spectator* article that *'Private Eye* is on its day a strong candidate for the most unpleasant thing in British journalism'. The *Eye*'s gossip, he said, was 'repulsive and salacious'.[5] Ingrams dismissed this as yet another example of 'Booker's admirable tendency to bite the hand that feeds him'.[6] Bearing in mind the cruelty of the early *Eye*, and the viciousness of some of Auberon Waugh's previous assaults on his victims, it is tempting to discern crocodile tears in this newfound concern for the magazine's targets. Waugh himself remained cautiously ambivalent: 'McKay would cut your throat and destroy all chance of friendship for two lines in the *Daily Express*. But he is interesting and unusual,' he said.[7] Logue was sniffy. 'I was always slightly disappointed that we began to have a gossip column. I'd rather have cigarette advertising.'

Patrick Marnham, the man who had started Grovel in the first place, found himself in a difficult position. Not unnaturally, he prefers to believe that standards of gossip fell gradually as his own involvement lessened, before slumping dramatically when he withdrew from the magazine altogether. *'Private Eye* has changed a great deal since its beginnings. An interesting contrast is the difference in its treatment of the Profumo case and the Cecil Parkinson case. Its attitude in the Profumo case was completely original and rather pleasant, in which it said that the real victim of it all was Stephen Ward. In the Parkinson case it completely irresponsibly published the name of Miss Keays to no point at all really, it never bothered to establish any public interest. That's one illustration of how the *Eye*'s attitudes have become much more conventional and much more like the general attitude of Fleet Street, which is, if it's a good story – print it.'[8] That there was no 'public interest' in the extramarital liaisons of Cecil Parkinson, given the Conservative party's stated position on the importance of the family, is debatable to say the least; one can

227

only conclude that nostalgia has influenced Marnham's view.

Marnham returned to the attack when Martin Tomkinson, a journalist who was sacked from the *Eye* in an argument over his financial dealings, published an article in Richard Branson's short-lived *Event* magazine, accusing Dempster and McKay of sitting on a story that showed a *Daily Mirror* executive in a bad light. A very minor scandal indeed, if it could be called that, but Marnham wrote: 'The final stage was reached when . . . *Private Eye*'s influence was capable of suppressing news as well as circulating it.'[9] He cited Richard Ingrams' close links with Fleet Street, particularly his friendship with Sir John Junor of the *Sunday Express*, as an unhealthy influence on the magazine. With hindsight, this is nonsense. One thing the *Eye* can be proud of is its track record in *not* suppressing stories, however close to home the subject matter. Junor was relentlessly attacked by the magazine, precisely because of his friendship with Ingrams. Links with Fleet Street were the *Eye*'s life blood. What Marnham really meant by 'the final stage' was the final stage of his own *Eye* career. If this was a prediction that doom would accompany his leaving, then doom failed to materialise. Marnham's departure was conspicuous by its inconspicuous effect on the magazine.

Internecine rivalry apart, the crux of the matter lay in the definition of who was and who was not a public figure. Both sides broadly agreed that public figures were fair game; but they differed as to the qualifications for inclusion in this category. The old guard preferred to confine their attacks to politicians, industrialists and public servants. The new boys widened the net to include aristocrats, celebrities, almost anyone in a position of influence. As long as there was an element of hypocrisy involved, that was all that mattered. 'I would say that if details of your private life do appear in the newspapers,' maintains McKay, 'then it is a random penalty you must pay for leading an enjoyable secret life. We all lead such lives to some extent, even Ingrams. For many people the fear of discovery is part of the illicit pleasure,' he adds unconvincingly.[10] Whether true or not, this is very much a mainstream Fleet Street attitude, and in this observation at least Marnham was correct.

McKay and Dempster openly scoffed at the objections of

their new colleagues, complaints which the working-class McKay put down to snobbery. 'Booker always professed to hate gossip because he maintained all his smart friends were being insulted,' he says. McKay considers that the satirists badly overreacted. 'Wells came in one day and said, "That's it – Dempster's killed a man". Dempster had put some item in Grovel about this man's family, and the man had died. But he was about ninety! His death was nothing whatever to do with Dempster.' McKay breaks into a gurgling laugh as he recounts the tale.

Wells may indeed have been overreacting; but the affair did emphasise the need, when dealing with more vulnerable targets, to be especially accurate. 'These characters they create with their funny nicknames are real people, do exist, and sometimes have been personally hurt,' complained Esther Rantzen.[11] One target, an official of the Campaign For Real Ale called Mike Hardman, was referred to variously as 'barrel-shaped', 'firkin-shaped' and 'malodorous'. Hardman complained to the BBC that he did not deserve to be attacked because he was a 'small pebble on the nation's beach',[12] a point which seemed to sum up the position of the old guard.

Yet whatever the rights and wrongs of Hardman's case, his point is specious. The public importance of a target is, eventually, irrelevant. John Poulson was a small pebble on the nation's beach. What matters is whether the story itself is in the public interest; that is the sole criterion upon which the matter should have been judged. The sad fact is that many of the Grovel stories were not actually of interest to the public, not because they were personally damaging, but because they were boring. The aristocratic legover tales so beloved of Nigel Dempster were of interest only to the dedicated reader who was prepared to peruse them week after week, and so ease himself into the Grovel world.

While the debate raged, Ingrams did what he had intended all along: he sat back and enjoyed it. It wasn't really a case of divide and rule – he didn't need to do that. It was just another layer of entertainment to stave off boredom and depression. Barry Fantoni explains: 'He really liked the idea of setting all the hacks against each other. There'd be nothing more thrilling for Richard than to

229

know that one hack was getting at another hack's throat.'[13] Often, he'd encourage the new dogs to turn on each other. At one stage, four journalists – McKay, Dempster, Carla Dobson of the *Mail* and Lady Olga Maitland of the *Sunday Express* – attacked each other in their respective papers. Entertained as Ingrams may have been by the filthy glamour of the press, he still essentially held Fleet Street – and its values – in contempt.

By the mid-1970s, the *Eye* staff had fragmented into three groups – the journalists, the jokewriters, and the boxwallahs – in a faintly uneasy coalition. The days when everyone would go off together to the pub at lunchtime were a thing of the past. In general, however, the outlook seemed healthy; the magazine was proving popular with over 100,000 readers and sales were still rising. Yet as the attacks on individuals and their little hypocrisies and inconsistencies began to mount up, so did the list of *Private Eye*'s influential enemies. For the politicians satirised in the past, an *Eye* article had often been no more than water off a duck's back. For the new targets – TV celebrities, the rich and, most tellingly, fellow journalists – such attacks were harder to stomach. Now the victims began to fight back.

17 They're Real People and They Hurt

It was John Wells who once said, *'Private Eye coughs and men's trousers fall down.'*[1] Clive James, as an *Eye* victim, saw the matter from a different perspective, and famously remarked that the magazine 'sent people's children crying home from school'; to which Auberon Waugh caustically replied, 'It would probably be better to suppress all news of any description rather than make a young child, anywhere, cry on the way home from school.'[2] 'Of course a lot of people get upset by it,' pitched in Paul Foot stoutly. 'What use would it be if people weren't upset by it? That's the whole point of it, that it upsets people.'[3] Foot did not share his former Shrewsbury colleagues' misgivings about gossip columns, as long as the targets were powerful and rich.

Richard Ingrams, the 'nicest man in satire' of 1963, found himself increasingly coming under media fire during the 1970s for what was seen as a new line in indiscriminate personal attacks; but Ingrams' technique had always been to identify individuals and cast them as soap opera characters in his columns. It was the scope of these columns that was changing, to include media targets like Clive James who had access to their own columns with which to hit back. Bernard Levin, for instance, a former *Eye* supporter who had once praised the magazine as 'single-minded and unafraid . . . an enemy of cant and humbug', now found himself pooh-poohed for following the Bhagwan Shree Rajneesh (an Eastern guru known as the Bhagwash in *Eye* parlance). The *Spectator* gave Levin the chance to reply: 'Ingrams, himself corrupt, is unably to recognise

231

honesty in [others] . . . dealing in dirty little bits of gossip now constitutes practically the whole of Ingrams' life.' The *Eye* staff, he said, were 'marchands d'ordure', which doesn't sound nearly so impressive in English. Of course Levin looked pretty silly when it turned out that the Bhagwan had bought ninety-one Rolls-Royces with the money he'd fleeced from his supporters, and that he was wanted on charges of tax evasion; but the damage to Ingrams had been done, as it had been to Levin.

'I always viewed the function of *Private Eye* as analogous to a sort of weedkiller,' says Ingrams. 'In order to apply the weed-killer, you have to know who the weeds are.'[4] The weeds can be roughly divided into about four groups. The group that were doing most of the complaining were being attacked on the grounds of mediocrity and self-importance. Many of them were considered arrivistes; often they were communicators by trade, like Michael Parkinson or Esther Rantzen, who had risen swiftly by dint of their communicating skills, without necessarily having anything to communicate. The result, in the *Eye*'s view, was complacency. 'A lot of it was the level of their self-regard, of taking themselves seriously,' says Barry Fantoni. 'They didn't seem to have any self-critical faculties. Roy Hattersley would be another example, or Clive James.' Ingrams' favourite television moment of all time is the occasion when Michael Parkinson thoroughly lost his composure while being fiercely assaulted by Rod Hull and his Emu.

Fleet Street was the spiritual home of such banality and self-promotion. 'There is more humbug in Fleet Street than in the House of Commons,' said Richard. 'The big names of journalism tend to be more pompous and self-important about themselves than politicians, more lacking in the ability to take a joke.'[5] Ingrams shares the Auberon Waugh view that once a journalist thinks he's got something more important to do than fill up tomorrow's newspaper, he should pack it in and do something else. 'The person who has exemplified that for me is Harold Evans of the *Sunday Times*. He started off as probably quite a good journalist, but developed into someone who thought he was highly influential.'[6] A typical celebrity communicator, he was nicknamed 'Dame' in the *Eye*, after Dame Edith Evans. He sued in 1977 and received substantial damages; part of the settlement involved Evans being allowed to ghost a ludicrous editorial memo, to be signed by Ingrams, forbidding the *Eye* staff to attack him. His paper was lampooned instead as the *Sunday Dames*, and he ended up becoming a laughing stock. 'Look at him now,' Ingrams told the *Observer* in 1990, 'editor of some travel magazine in New York which nobody reads.'[7]

Several authority figures fitted into this category, politicians who had got to the top by dint of little more than an ability to promote themselves way beyond their abilities. 'I have an ethic,' says Ingrams, 'only in a very general sense, of saying that people who seek authority and power should be subject to ridicule.'[8] Much of the personal experience behind this philosophy went back not just to the indignities of *TW3* and the Frost era, but further, to the indignities of school and the army, and all the jumped-up dictators therein. ' "Knock, knock, knock. All you can do, Ingrams, is criticise". I can hear David Owen's voice whenever people say that. I'm sure he was a head boy. I can still hear David Owen-type people at school, saying to me, "Come along Ingrams, get up off your arse and do something, instead of just sitting there, knocking".'[9]

The second group of people that the *Eye* attacked also dated back to school and university. These were the Pseuds – Dennis Potter *et al.*, the pretentious heirs to the *Isis* tradition. This group overlapped with the first, as self-importance and humourlessness are often used as a defence by those who feel that they are breaking new intellectual ground, but at the same time do not feel entirely sure of themselves. Michael Palin remembers performing a comedy sketch on the BBC's *Late Night Line-Up*, after which Dennis Potter himself was interviewed. With breathtaking self-importance, Potter remarked that he had not come all this way to appear after rubbish like that. Pseuds, of course, were a traditional target, and Ingrams gave them a column of their own in the *Eye*, which was edited for many years by Christopher Logue.

A frequent visitor to Pseud's Corner was the *Eye*'s old enemy Jonathan Miller. Barry Fantoni explains: 'Miller is annoying because he talks rubbish. He used to come into the office and

233

do it. Miller's main offence was that he put Shakespeare into modern dress, which for Ingrams was the greatest sin that is known to man. Putting *Measure For Measure* into Steppenwolf outfits turns Richard into an assassin. That's the kind of thing that Miller does – he misses the point of something, and yet he's given control of it. You think, he can't possibly get away with this – that's how the bile works up.'

Another oft-quoted Pseud was Clive James. For instance: 'The characteristic mode of determinism is not investigation by criticism, but justification by description: an intellectual mode which might just as well be called anti-intellectual, since no matter how much information it aspires to deal with it can never arrive at a judgement.'[10] This was not so much pseudo-intellectual as badly written (Pseud's Corner was always a broad church), uncharacteristic for a writer of James's stature; manifestly, he had experienced the inclination to demonstrate an extensively polysyllabic vocabulary in the construction of his discourse. James used the *Times Literary Supplement* to fight back: '*Private Eye*'s crusade against barbarism is decisively hobbled by its own philistinism, and even though its editor undeniably knows how to put one of his own sentences together, it doesn't necessarily follow that he's equipped to criticise one of mine.'[11] This sounds suspiciously like a variation of the traditional nonsense that only a concert pianist is capable of reviewing a piano concert. James went on, rather childishly: '*Private Eye*'s enviable flexibility of stance was always dependent on its having no brains.'

Despite the accusations of anti-intellectualism, the *Eye*'s willingness to attack artistic pretension is one of its strengths. Contributors of the calibre of John Osborne and Graham Greene have joined in over the years. Compiler Christopher Logue, who can hardly be faulted for lack of intellectual stamina, reflects: 'Pseud's Corner is an accurately observed and previously unrevealed type of bad writing. We all knew about it before, but Ingrams was the one who thought it out. The column was in some ways a sinecure for me, but to compile it one did require a certain level of hatred of the pretentious idiots of this world. They never let me down, with their mastery of self-deception. Over ten years I was caught out by irony a couple of times. I got John Peel wrong, I think – I felt rather ashamed of that. But I was slightly deceived, because if the cutting came in clipped out of context, there was always a slight risk.'

Logue's Pseud's Corner did not merely concentrate on intellectual pretension; one extremely funny column lacerated the social pretensions of Dominic Lawson's wife Rosa Monckton, merely by quoting at length from an article she had written in *The Times*. A selection: 'While I love going to Berwick Street market and doing the shopping, I find I'm always exhausted afterwards and the thought of actually having to cook what I've bought is totally beyond me. Now I've found this really sweet girl called Jane who does it all for me . . . I always go to enormous trouble with flowers. I say to my display manager at Tiffany's: "Andrew, I'm having a dinner party tonight", and he does them. He's a most talented boy . . . Another wedding present was a frightfully formal hostess record book which had headings like "Food Given" and "Gown Worn". We've resisted using it so far, but now I think I will. After all, when you have as many dinner parties as we do, it's got to be useful to know what you fed people.' There followed a recipe for 'Dominic Lawson's hollandaise sauce', which was of course just the normal recipe for hollandaise sauce. 'Very good, wasn't it?' grins Logue. 'She lives in this little tiny world where they still carry on like that. That pretentious bag – can you believe it?' He leans back and cackles hugely.

A third identifiable group of *Eye* targets comprised both the corrupt and the immoral: two different things, but in Ingrams' eyes they tended to blur together. This was the area which found the *Eye*'s stance ranging from its most wholly admirable – bravely standing up to crooks like Poulson or Maxwell, for instance – to its most ethically dubious. There is a suggestion, albeit unproven, that the number of attacks on Esther Rantzen owed something to her presence by Desmond Wilcox's side soon after the break-up of his first marriage. The frequent targeting of Ken Tynan probably had more to do with *Oh, Calcutta* than with writing Ingrams a rude letter. Christopher Logue laments: 'I knew Tynan quite well, and although he said things which made him look pretty silly, nevertheless I was sorry that Ingrams took such a dislike to him. It had a lot to do with the fact that Ken was a theoretical fool for sexual liberation. He was in some sense an intellectual head of the libertarian sexual movement. But Ken was right to fight that battle. We no longer fight that battle, and we'll be in trouble if we don't do so. Natural censors who dislike liberty are gradually gaining power in our society. In fact, under other circumstances, Tynan and Ingrams would have been pals.'

Logue, himself a Catholic, believes that Ingrams' discomfort with breaches of conventional sexual morality stems indirectly from his all-but-Catholic upbringing. 'Sexuality is a very powerful, significant and important force in human life, and anybody who tries to deny this, which I think Ingrams would like to do, is one of those people who would like to deny that sexuality is power.' It is a failing of Ingrams that if he is unsympathetic to someone's moral code, he tends to dump them lock, stock and barrel into the enemy camp. 'Yes,' says Logue, 'but to a certain extent a satirist has got to do that.'

Ingrams set out his moral stance on marriage and sex to Naim Attallah: 'I was married in 1962, the year, according to Philip Larkin, "before sexual intercourse began". In those days chaps were expected to get married when they were about twenty-five. And they were expected to stay married. It seems to me a very sensible way of looking at marriage, the abandonment of which has caused untold problems. The permissive society may have a lot to be said for it but I count myself lucky that, like Larkin, I missed out. I wouldn't want to have affairs with lots of women. Men who behave promiscuously [in marriage] get into all kinds of difficulties that are better avoided. The idea that it's pleasurable to live that kind of life is quite mistaken. Plus, if you like women, you don't want to make them unhappy.'[12]

There is no question that this moral stance has influenced the *Eye*'s choice of targets. Influenced – but not determined. Ingrams believes strongly in moral right, but he stops short of righteousness. When a Dutch sailor offered the *Eye* photographs of a prominent British bachelor MP in explicit gay poses,

236

Ingrams refused to have anything to do with ruining the man's career. When he received stories about Jilly Cooper's husband Leo having affairs, he did not run them, in order to try and protect her from harm. When Paul Foot ran off and left his wife, Ingrams disapproved, but did not allow it to affect their friendship. Asked directly if he was a moralist, Ingrams replied: 'No. Well, I suppose I do condemn quite a lot, but I try not to be censorious.'[13] Nonetheless, when selecting stories and targets for the *Eye*, Ingrams cast his moral net very wide indeed. He could do this, because he practised what he preached. 'If you say, "What is *Private Eye* against?", it is basically against hypocrisy. I think you have constantly to consider, "Is that a charge that could be made against me personally?" And if you say, "Yes it is", then you shouldn't be making it.'[14]

The fourth group under fire in *Private Eye* consisted, quite simply, of Ingrams' own friends and colleagues. The likes of Wells, Booker, Waugh and Candida Lycett Green were all gleefully inserted into Pseud's Corner at their first slip. Germaine Greer had already been included in the column for a dreadful piece of nonsense: 'There was this girl in an exam I was invigilating who sat pitifully doing nothing. When she left she deposited a letter on my desk which ended: "Our minds are all so clogged on the dead ideas passed from generation to generation that even the best of us are unable to control our lives". I burst into tears.'

Wells's social climbing, Foot's left-wing views, Booker's right-wing views, all were ruthlessly pilloried in the *Eye*. 'We like to attack our friends as much as possible,' said Ingrams.[15] These attacks were mischievous ones, though, and were not intended to do any damage. Ingrams refused to run a story which revealed that Peter Jay had spelled out the name of a woman, using the first letter of each paragraph, in a *Times* leading article; he did not want Jay to lose his job.

This fourth category of targets is a small but important one: for it proves that the key to being part of *Private Eye* is not taking anything, including yourself, seriously. The *Eye*'s most fervent enemies have often been insecure people, who have not felt that they were getting the respect that they deserved.

237

Mrs Thatcher's favourite adman Tim Bell, for instance, who later went on to advise the mass murderer General Pinochet's favoured successor in the Chilean elections, reckons that '*Private Eye* is one of the great offences of modern life. It has no morality, it has no honour, and it does terrible damage to people. And the only way to neutralise this damage is to read it so that you can discount all those comments, because it's basically a pack of lies.'[16]

Very often men like Bell, who believe that they have done nothing wrong, are not only angered by the lack of respect shown, but confused as to the reason for the attacks and bewildered by their relentlessness. What they see as the legitimate protestation of their case, particularly through recourse to law, only seems to provoke the hornets' nest to further flurries of activity. 'Ingrams does harbour grudges,' says Barry Fantoni. 'He gets hurt and wounded like anybody else and he does find ways to get back at people. He will wait as long as it needs. But he prefers to get back at people intellectually. Lots of the arguments that we've had at the *Eye* have all been about the weakness of an argument, the weakness of an intellectual grasp.' Ingrams' relentlessness has a particular focus: 'The only people I *really* go after are people who sue, and their lawyers,' he says.[17]

Very often, the *Eye*'s targets are only able to reconcile themselves to the persistence of the attacks by ascribing them to some point of prejudice on the part of their author. In the same way that he was given credit in some quarters for every joke the *Eye* ever published, so Ingrams' prejudices were assumed to lie behind every news story. Jewish targets complained that Ingrams was a racist; working-class targets that he was a snob; pseudo-intellectual targets that he was a philistine; female targets that he was anti-women; homosexual targets that he was anti-gay; and sexual targets that he was a puritan. These are important accusations, because they have gained common currency through their sheer weight of numbers, and they need to be addressed carefully.

The culmination of this line of attack came in 1992, when *Spitting Image* regularly featured a Richard Ingrams puppet, elderly, dribbling, ranting aimlessly about Jews. Asked where they had got this notion from, one of the writers – a south London Labour council candidate – explained that it was 'common knowledge'. Ian Hislop, himself a former *Spitting Image* writer and by now the *Eye*'s editor, fired off an angry letter to the programme's producer:

> The idea that Ingrams hates Jews is balls. It comes this time from an anonymous profile in the *Guardian*, written by Jocelyn Targett. When asked by another journalist (*Independent on Saturday*) why he had written this, Targett replied that 'everybody knows it', 'he's anti-zionist' and 'it's sort of crept onto the record'. It later emerged that Targett had interviewed Barry Fantoni, a friend of Ingrams and a member of the *Eye*'s editorial team since the Sixties. Targett asked Fantoni if Ingrams hated Jews. Fantoni had to explain that (a) he was himself Jewish (b) no, Ingrams didn't and (c) there was a difference between sympathizing with the Intifada and voting for Le Pen. Targett ignored this and published anyway. The *Guardian* subsequently refused to print any letters in right of reply and have been taken to the ombudsman, proving that their vaunted moral superiority to other papers is somewhat tenuous.
>
> The anti-semitism tag is a dangerous one and I don't want it sticking to the *Eye* by proxy. We have Jewish reporters, Jewish humorists, Jewish cartoonists and Jewish lawyers and accountants. From Lord Kagan to Maxwell, if they are crooked and Jewish they go in. But this is equally true if they're not Jewish – Profumo to Asil Nadir, or Poulson to Barlow Clowes, or T. Dan Smith to the directors of Blue Arrow . . . you get the point.

All those who know Ingrams well are as quick as Hislop to dash such accusations. 'Absolute nonsense,' says Peter McKay. 'I never knew of any example of anti-semitism.' 'Impossible,' snorts Nigel Dempster. 'No!' Willie Rushton exclaims; 'All races, creeds and colours have their fair load of bastards, and if Ingrams doesn't like someone it's because that person's a shit.' 'He probably hadn't met many Jews when he was young,' admits Barry Fantoni. 'If he had, they'd have been the highly refined kind who played the

239

violin at his mother's house; but then, he's never been to a football match either.' Ingrams the anti-semite, confirms Fantoni from the horse's mouth, is a ridiculous notion.

In fact the smear seems to date back to 1967, to a series of articles written by Paul Foot condemning Israeli conduct in the Middle East war. At the time a mysteriously galvanised Noel Picarda had used the *Eye* offices to mount a famine relief operation for starving Egyptians. Two Labour MPs and Mordecai Richler, the Jewish novelist, had claimed that the *Eye*'s anti-Zionist stance was racist. Ingrams himself was not particularly motivated by it all: 'Personally I can't feel any great involvement in what is going on in the Middle East. People in this country seem too much concerned with the question of Israel and the Palestinians, which after all has nothing really much to do with us.'[18] He was, however, quite happy to give Foot free rein. Ingrams' own position, such as it is, is broadly in line with the same Arabist traditions of patrician England that saw the 'Ingrams peace' brought about in the Hadramaut by his uncle: 'Naturally I feel sympathy with the Palestinians when I see what is going on on the West Bank. I don't consider that the state of Israel has been a success. People such as Balfour who were responsible for Israel's coming into being were quite anti-Semitic and believed that creating a Jewish state would be a good way to get the Jews out of their own countries.'[19]

Despite such relatively innocent beginnings, the tag stuck. In 1975, for instance, Desmond Wilcox was attacked as a plagiarist when it was revealed that he had written a BBC book based on the scripts of other writers who were working for him. The Corporation had quietly paid out £60,000 in costs and damages to the offended parties. However Wilcox sued the *Eye* and won, after the judge took the view that his plagiarism had been 'guileless'. The battle lines have been drawn ever since, between the *Eye* on one side, and Wilcox and his wife Esther Rantzen on the other. Again and again Wilcox has returned to the accusation of racism. 'They're spiteful and anti-semitic,' he says. 'They're bully-boys who are better off punching the heads of children behind bicycle sheds or lavatories. They have a cartoon strip [*Corporation Street*, a regular strip concerning the BBC by Ken

240

Pyne] which frequently features my wife and myself and others, Terry Wogan, Sue Lawley and so on. At one stage that cartoon strip devoted itself to the anti-semite, spiteful, horrid biography of Esther and her family. It told lies about my elderly and much respected father-in-law, who's now nearly ninety. *Private Eye* has become a ventilation of the personal prejudices of Richard Ingrams.'[20]

Harold Wilson, prime minister once again after his re-election in 1974, was another who accused Ingrams of anti-semitism for attacking his friend Joe Kagan, a gesture which backfired when Kagan was sent to jail for the crooked business dealings which the *Eye* had exposed. When the magazine attacked Idi Amin, the Ugandan president in whose fridge human flesh was found, Ingrams was again accused of racism. Yet the *Eye*'s record of attacks on the apartheid regime in South Africa is consistent. Ingrams has employed black staff. Clearly the race accusation is without foundation.

A weary Ingrams reflects: 'I was quite upset when it was said that I hate Jews. I don't.'[21] Take Jonathan Miller for example, suggests Ingrams. 'Miller is paranoid about *Private Eye* and says it's like *Der Sturmer*. Of course it isn't like *Der Sturmer* at all, but if you can't see any reason why you should be attacked, if you think you're the great Dr Jonathan Miller, and how could anyone else think you're a ridiculous and absurd figure, then you persuade yourself that the only reason these people have got it in for you is because you're a Jew.'

The anti-gay accusation, often levelled in the same breath, is slightly harder to dismiss, partly because one of Ingrams' main accusers is Paul Foot himself: 'Richard is quite grossly prejudiced against gay people. There is no excuse for his attitude, I find it exceedingly offensive and irrational. It's not legitimate humour to laugh at gay people.' It's true that 'pooves', to use the phrase coined by Jonathan Miller, had been consistently laughed at during the 1960s by Ingrams, Cook, Wells, Fantoni and others. One article advertised 'Coming events' for gays: 'A gay moratorium (on November 7 all of us will just put on some nice clothes and go and walk about), a mass mince-in in Hyde Park, and a pretty candlelight demo in a King's Road bistro (service is very gay and the waiters all wear lovely fluffy jerseys).' An accompanying Michael Heath cartoon showed two utterly miserable homosexuals, one saying to the other, 'Are you gay too?' In later years Heath produced an entire 'Gays' strip, including the memorable cartoon of a man and woman walking into their immaculate living room and exclaiming, 'Oh no, we've been burgled by gays – the furniture's been re-arranged and there's a quiche in the oven!'

Heath eventually abandoned the strip out of a sense of guilt, which was a pity as it was a great favourite amongst gays themselves. The attitudes enshrined in all the *Eye*'s gay jokes were relatively harmless, culturally of their time, and had completely disappeared by the 1980s. It is interesting to note that in 1967, when such jokes were commonplace in the *Eye*, Ingrams was a hardline supporter of Leo Abse's bill to liberalise the homosexuality laws. Admits Foot: 'In those days one of his tests of an MP's decency was to ask, "How did he vote on the pooves?" If the MP had voted for the liberalisation of homosexual laws he was "fundamentally decent". If not he was "unacceptably right-wing".'[22] It is ironic that the man initially responsible for *Private Eye* being perceived as anti-Jewish – Paul Foot – should attack it for being anti-gay, while the man who started the anti-gay ball rolling – Jonathan Miller – should attack it for being anti-Jewish.

Putting this confusion aside, Ingrams' actual position on homosexuality seems to be a relatively tolerant one, but he finds it hard to come to terms with the physical realities of homosexual sex. 'My line is quite straightforward,' he says. 'I wouldn't want to be one. They don't have a very good time. I've been very pally with pooves like Anthony Blond and Tom Driberg. We've had one or two in *Private Eye*.' Driberg, the Labour MP for Barking, once even turned up to an *Eye* birthday party in partial drag. He was said to be able to seduce any man in the time it took the Greek Street lift to ascend to the third floor. There was a notice in reception which read: 'No male member of staff will take the lift on Wednesdays', that being the day that Driberg visited the office. Ingrams allowed him to compose a regular obscene crossword for the *Eye*, which was once won by the Archbishop of Canterbury's wife. Ingrams was extremely fond of Driberg, but was always careful to avoid the lift.

Like Ingrams, Barry Fantoni prefers to distance the emotional side of homosexuality from the physical side; these are views shared by almost all the *Eye* satirists of Ingrams' generation. 'I think he's quite right for finding the whole act of anal intercourse abhorrent,' says Fantoni. Ingrams regards promiscuous male homosexuals as addicts. 'You could never become addicted to women in that sense,' he says,[23] which isn't true. The promiscuity of male homosexuality derives surely from the naturally promiscuous tendencies of men, unfettered by the restraining presence of women; but as a non-promiscuous male Ingrams doesn't see it that way.

Another problem Ingrams has is with the politicisation of homosexuality. 'Homosexuality in my view has nothing to do with politics at all, it's a private matter. People have tried to promote the idea that homosexuals are a minority in the same sense as blacks or Jews, which is obvious nonsense.' Like many people of his generation, he is happy to be in the company of gays – a number work for his new magazine *The Oldie* – but prefers them to be discreet about their sex lives in the same way that he would be about his own. 'Richard is like Swift,' says Ian Hislop, 'liking individuals but hating the broad mass of mankind. He has loads of gay friends. One of his closest friends for ten years was Tom Driberg, whom he treated with absolute respect behind his back. And who does he like now? Stephen Fry. He's very split on the subject. Intellectually, they make him laugh a lot. But he greatly enjoys annoying the gay establishment.' Indeed, one must never forget the importance of mischief as a motivating force in any of Ingrams' pronouncements. When asked by Lynn Barber of the *Independent on Sunday* what he would have done if his son Fred had turned out gay, he merrily replied, 'Shot him'.

'He thinks that individuals being gay are very jolly but that overt proselytising gays are a bad thing for society,' explains Hislop. 'He doesn't like the idea that there is such a thing as "the gay community". Of course, there are plenty of gay right-wing old farts who don't want to be lumped in with all those clones down

243

the leather club.' Well, not in public, anyway. It's an amusing idea, Ingrams the defender of tweedy old English homosexuality against the identikit hordes of dreadful modern gays, with their 120-beats-per-minute music and their dress-sense-as-political-statement fashions. Ingrams' assessment of homosexuality is essentially cultural rather than sexual: as with everything else, his opinions are patrician and conservative, designed to protect the best of the status quo.

Like many heterosexuals, Ingrams is fascinated by the question of whether or not others are gay. John Wells remembers: 'We were having lunch at the *Spectator* and Graham Greene was present. Ingrams said that he wondered whether Lord Goodman might be gay, so I said, "What do you base that on?" and he said, "Well, Foot had to go round and have breakfast with him the other morning, and Goodman was still in his dressing gown". Even Graham Greene said that he did not believe this was absolute proof. I said that it was the old psychological problem that Ingrams could not face up to his own homosexuality, at which Ingrams launched such a kick under the table. I have never known him so violent. That's the problem. Most of us accept that everybody's not one thousand per cent heterosexual; he just will not have that.' Rather than the kick of a repressed gay, it was the kick of an old-fashioned conservative who had been genuinely offended by the remark.

The accusation of snobbery levelled at Ingrams enters similar territory, in that he is unquestionably aware and interested in the social class of others, perhaps unconsciously; he is broadly against changes in the status quo; and a cursory examination of the facts reveals that he is not prejudiced. As with the homosexuality issue, Ingrams faces a challenge to this last statement from within his own ranks. This time, the attacker is John Wells. 'Ingrams thinks that the aristocracy is very amusing. He thinks that the Royal family is laughable. He thinks all foreigners are funny – you get that in Beachcomber. He thinks working-class people are absolutely hilarious and he despises the middle classes. It's patrician prejudice. All he respects is this little tiny rather respectable gang of people who wear quite expensive suits and have their shoes made, who are like his father. It's a thin layer of society.' A thin but intractable layer, as Wells found out in trying to leapfrog it. One has to question, though, whether it is indeed snobbish to attack all other classes when one's own is so tiny. In the strictest sense, perhaps, but finding the whole of society and its internal jockeying funny is not the same as putting someone down because one believes oneself to be socially superior. Ingrams' view of the working classes, for instance, has been a romanticised one since his army days. Wells's view, one suspects, is heavily influenced by the nuances of his own mobile social position *vis-à-vis* Ingrams.

One *Eye* target who loudly considers himself to be the victim of anti-working-class snobbery is Derek Jameson, whose editing of a succession of extremely downmarket newspapers caused him to be nicknamed 'Sid Yobbo'. 'That's because I came from the East End,' complains Jameson in his thick cockney accent. 'The implication being, well, he's from the East End, he's a yob. Sid Yobbo, I mean that's not very favourable is it, it sounds like a gangster out selling second-hand cars somewhere, it sounds like a thug. I mean I'm a very highly literate, intelligent, sensitive person, but you wouldn't think that if you heard I was known as Sid Yobbo, would you? My names's Derek, but how could a yob be called Derek, ridiculous, whoever heard of Derek Yobbo? So of course it had to be Sid, didn't it. Now that is elitist, that is sheer pure snobbery.'[24]

Like Edward Heath, Jameson is so proud of his achievements that he cannot see how anything other than class prejudice could prevent somebody admiring them. 'When I edited the *Daily Express*, Ingrams called it the *Daily Getsmuchworse*, so I said to Richard, for Christ's sake, you know, I'm putting on circulation, I've turned the paper round, I've modernised it, we're doing much better, couldn't you make it the *Daily Getsalittlebetter*? So then he made it the *Daily Getsmuchworsethananyoneeverthoughtpossible*. And then he made it the *Daily TitsbyChristmas*, that was just before Christmas, and of course I will never ever at any time put nipples in the *Daily Express*, it's not that kind of paper.'[25] In fact, explains Ingrams, the 'Sid Yobbo' nickname was anything but an attack on the working class itself. 'Jameson was one of those people who traded very successfully on being a working-class lad from the East End. As he got more and more successful, so his accent became more and more coarse, so his origins became more and more humble.' So, it was the old suspicion of humbuggery all the time, then. 'I always thought that Jameson should get out of journalism and become a showbusiness personality, which is in fact what happened.' None of this convinces Jameson. 'You know they all went to Winchester School, don't you. They're a bunch of Wykehamists,'[26] he points out, displaying the accuracy that made the *Express* what it is today.

Ingrams is not a snob, but his opinions are almost entirely informed by the attitudes of his class. It's a confident class: after Lord Snowdon was made Constable of Caernarvon Castle, he was lampooned unstintingly in the *Eye*, then found himself seated close to Ingrams and Willie Rushton at a party a few days later. He protested vociferously and at length. 'Ingrams lay there rumbling like Krakatoa,' recalls Willie, 'then pronounced, "You must remember, Snowdon, that you are a very unimportant person. Utterly insignificant." Princess Margaret sank beneath the table like a U-boat.'

Alan Coren believes that Ingrams' class confidence is the key to his other attitudes. 'People are wrong to accuse him of racism or anti-homosexuality. It's nothing to do with that. It's about "people like us" and "people who aren't like us". He doesn't really understand "people who aren't like us", and he doesn't feel it necessary to understand.' Or, put more sympathetically, Ingrams doesn't like people who don't want to assume their proper place in relation to his culture, but who want to supplant it with their own. Says Coren: 'You don't always feel, from reading Richard Ingrams' *Private Eye*, a strong commitment towards the things it defends, because there's also the confidence that these things won't be destroyed anyway.' Coren believes that Ingrams' rudeness towards authority is therefore fraudulent, disguising deference, but this is not the case; Ingrams simply shows no respect for the system because he has an insider's understanding of it. As for the romanticising of the working class displayed by Ingrams and to a greater extent, Foot, 'It's like the eighteen-year-old

Etonian officers in World War One who wrote home saying, "The men never change their underwear but they're the salt of the earth." *Private Eye* is the officers' mess.'

Coren is one of Ingrams' chief accusers in another supposed area of prejudice, that of philistinism. '*Private Eye* has always viewed any serious stand as bogus,' he attests. He believes that the Pseud's Corner column is rooted in the refusal of Ingrams' class to contemplate emotion openly – a pretend toughness. 'Chaps don't blub,' he suggests. While it's true that Ingrams is not one to parade his emotions in public – his refusal to join the long list of John Cleese's admirers has a lot to do with Cleese's insistence on doing just that at every opportunity – this is a very narrow criticism of a column, and an attitude, with a much wider scope. Puncturing pretension has always been one of the *Eye*'s main policies. It is simplistic to put the desire to do so down to emotional immaturity or a lack of intellectual rigour. With the exception of Rushton, all the *Eye*'s founding fathers had exceptional academic records that reflected first-class minds. One of the prime movers in transferring the attack on pseuds from Shrewsbury to *Private Eye* was Christopher Booker, precisely for reasons of intellectual snobbery. Pseud's Corner is not the laughter of incomprehension heard from below, but the laughter of condescension heard from above.

Of all the accusations that have been hurled at Ingrams, most of them defensive and ill-thought out, only the accusation of puritanism is really hard to answer. 'Richard used to be very puritanical,' says Peter Cook. In March 1974 he banned the popular Barry McKenzie strip because too much sex and bad language had crept into it. 'Richard censored it when it got to lesbianism and pubic hair in a dentist's chair,' recalls Cook. 'He used to chuckle away when I frequently wrote obscene material, but he'd never put it in.' The strip's author Barry Humphries remains displeased to this day. 'Lurking in the atmosphere of that office was an innate conservatism, one felt. Everyone was fundamentally rather puritanical. This was the paradox, of course, of Richard Ingrams.'[27]

'Is there a wide puritanical streak in me?' ponders Ingrams,

247

enlarging the debate beyond the realm of disgruntled writers who have had their dirty jokes cut out. 'Some people use puritanical in the sense of being against promiscuity, divorce, abortion and so on. If that is the meaning of being puritanical, then I am, but if it means being against people enjoying themselves, then I'm not. I'm all for people having a good time, and all for them drinking and smoking, though I don't do either myself. There are a great many puritans around who conduct campaigns against things like smoking, even against dogs, and there are strong puritanical influences in society which I'm much against.'[28] Ingrams is right. He is not strictly a puritan; but what he has done, constantly, is to use his own moral values – which correspond to orthodox Catholic moral values – as a yardstick by which to judge other people, and that way puritanism lies.

Says John Wells: 'I do remember when Humphrey Burton was being constantly pissed over in the magazine because of his screwing around, and then there was a letter from an anonymous ex-mistress of his, and Ingrams laughed and said, "Great stuff, great stuff, put it in". And I said, "Come on Ingrams, if we start putting in letters from anonymous ex-mistresses, where will any of us be?" And he rounded on me with terrifying blue eyes, saying, "You speak for yourself". He was like Robespierre. In the same way that what *Private Eye* was doing was positively to shore up the old society, positively what Richard was doing with that gossip column was being extremely moralistic and tub-thumping, and saying "Thou shalt not screw around".'

Unlike many a prurient tabloid editor, Ingrams himself never wavered from the straight and narrow. Christopher Logue insists: 'I am sure that Ingrams has never had an affair with anyone at all. He's not that type. If Ingrams had an affair with someone, it would be a very serious matter indeed and everyone would know about it. It would be very easy to catch him out if he was an adulterer, but he's not. Germaine [Greer] set her cap at him. She really did. She didn't have a chance. Lots and lots of girls were all nutty about him. None of them had a chance.'

'I think he is just a fundamentalist,' says Esther Rantzen. 'He believes in heaven and hell, the goodies inhabit one, the baddies

248

inhabit the other, and the goodies write about the baddies.'[29] There is something in this analysis. Ingrams would see his clear-cut moral code as a strength, whereas Rantzen would regard it as a weakness. He is not and never was a prejudiced man, but he was certainly unforgiving. If you transgressed his moral rules it was hard to find a way back. In fact this crusading inflexibility was both a strength *and* a weakness. A weakness, from the perspective of those innocents who accidentally slipped under the wheels of the moral juggernaut; although the list of the *Eye*'s undeserved casualties is small and many of those clamouring to get on it are concealing the truth about their behaviour. A strength, because it enabled Ingrams to have the courage and the self-belief to go after the real baddies, the big fish that Fleet Street would never dare tackle. This was the 'faint holiness' that Candida Lycett Green had observed. In 1975, Richard Ingrams went after the biggest fish he'd ever been after, bigger than Randolph Churchill, or Lord Russell; even bigger, it seemed, than the prime minister himself. He was to be almost crushed in the process.

18 Prison Beckons

It all started with a newspaper story, on 26 November 1975. A requiem mass had taken place the previous day at the Jesuit church in Mayfair for Dominic Elwes, the forty-four-year-old play-boy, painter and former *Eye* target, who had committed suicide that September. Eulogies to the dead man had been read by Kenneth Tynan and the zoo owner John Aspinall. On the way out of the service Tremayne Rodd, the former Scottish scrum half and a cousin of Elwes, had gone up to Aspinall and punched him in the face. On reading the piece, alarm bells in Ingrams' head immediately began to ring.

Also in the congregation was Nigel Dempster, so Ingrams asked his gossip columnist to provide more details. It transpired that Elwes had been a member of the Clermont gambling club and a close friend of Lord Lucan, the missing peer. He had been approached by an Old Etonian journalist friend, James Fox of the *Sunday Times*, who wished to write a piece about the Lucan set. Elwes had persuaded his friends that Fox was a good sort, so they had co-operated; Elwes even painted a picture of a Clermont club lunch for the article. Unfortunately for Elwes, Fox found Lucan's cronies to be an unpleasant bunch. His article did not depict a noble brotherhood defending the honour of an absent member as they had been expecting, but a seedy gang of self-obsessed gamblers, who cared not one whit that their friend had been a near-bankrupt Nazi sympathiser and had attempted to murder his wife. 'If she'd been my wife, I'd have bashed her to death

250

five years before and so would you,' John Aspinall had told the police.

When the piece appeared, the Clermont set was furious. The leader of the group, the multi-millionaire-businessman Jimmy Goldsmith, was particularly incensed by an accompanying photograph showing Lucan with his arm around Annabel Birley, the mistress that Goldsmith kept openly in London while his wife and children lived in Paris. The implication for Goldsmith's status was obvious. Elwes was banished from all his favourite haunts and sent to Coventry by his friends. He was barred from the Clermont and from Annabel's nightclub, and from Mark's restaurant. Nobody talked to him. Distraught, Elwes fled to southern Spain, where by coincidence he ran into Nick Luard, the *Eye*'s former owner and a nodding acquaintance. Luard recalls: 'He was trembling, stuttering, rambling, almost incoherent. He was unable to eat, he had to be helped down steps, he kept dropping glasses . . . he clung to the hope that this would somehow change Goldsmith's attitude.'[1] A few weeks later, he committed suicide. His note is understood to have included the words: 'I curse Mark [Birley, owner of Annabel's] and Jimmy from beyond the grave,' but since the coroner never released it, this cannot be proved.

James Goldsmith was of interest to Richard Ingrams for another reason. The Slater Walker group, run by Goldsmith's friend Jim Slater, had recently collapsed with massive debts. The Bank of England had bailed out the company at a cost of £110 million of public money, on the dubious grounds of 'preventing a loss of confidence in the City'. Slater had gone, and Goldsmith had been appointed as the new, independent chairman. There were rumours, however, that Goldsmith's companies actually had a considerable amount of money locked into Slater Walker.

Quite separately, Michael Gillard discovered the interesting fact that Goldsmith's solicitor Eric Levine had once had close business ties with T. Dan Smith, the corrupt associate of John Poulson, though not in any criminal capacity. (Goldsmith himself, the lawyers wish me to point out, had never met T. Dan Smith in his life, nor had he ever had anything to do with him.) Levine had worked for a law firm called Paisner's, and had left suddenly in unusual circumstances.

Dempster and Gillard's information was pooled into two articles by Patrick Marnham, which not unnaturally drew heavily on the James Fox piece in the *Sunday Times*. Marnham did not know, however, that Fox had made a terrible mistake. He had reported a lunch that had taken place the day after Lucan's disappearance, when the Clermont set had gathered to discuss a plan of action to help their friend. Goldsmith, he had claimed, had been at the lunch; but this was not the case. Unknown to the *Eye*, Fox had gone abroad without realising his error, and the *Sunday Times* had been forced to make a profuse private apology to Goldsmith. Marnham now repeated the mistake, and compounded it by implying that the Clermont set had obstructed the efforts of the law to trace Lucan. He meant 'obstructed' in the literal sense, but of course 'obstructing the police' is a criminal offence. The *Eye* lawyer missed the implication, and the magazine went into print effectively accusing James Goldsmith of breaking the law.

Like a Dreadnought swinging round to set its sights on a pea, the entire financial might of the Goldsmith empire bore down on *Private Eye*. In the first salvo, no fewer than sixty-three writs were issued against the magazine and all the wholesale newsagents who distributed it. It had been done in a hurry; three of the firms named didn't actually take the *Eye* and one of them was owned by Goldsmith himself. It didn't matter. The frightened newsagents began to desert the magazine, promising never to distribute it again. Only seventeen of them stood firm. Among the writs directed against Ingrams and Marnham, Goldsmith's lawyers had dredged up a sixteenth-century offence called 'criminal libel', which appropriately enough had been used to imprison puritan pamphleteers. Goldsmith was determined that Ingrams should go to jail. 'I will throw them in prison,' he raged. 'I will hound their wives, even in their widows' weeds.'

Goldsmith's political views were extremely right-wing, and he had been a financial supporter of the Conservative party. As he dug deeper into the structure of a magazine he knew little about, he was horrified to discover the existence of Paul

Foot. As he told David Dimbleby in a BBC interview: 'One of the key people in *Private Eye* is Paul Foot. I quote him as follows: "A socialist society can only come about by revolution, if the masses, through general strikes and mass agitation, seize the means of production".' Dimbleby retorted: 'But may you not be making a very simple, but illogical step – which is assuming that Paul Foot's private views are the motive for *Private Eye*'s attack on you?' (Especially as Foot had actually left the magazine a few years before.) Goldsmith smouldered back: '*Private Eye* is in fact a club of journalists, who are not only working in *Private Eye*, but also working throughout the press. And when you start looking, and investigating these people, you find these sort of revolutionary views, people who want to destroy Parliament . . . I have started to realise that all the wit, the satire, is no more than the sugar coating to allow you to take the medicine more easily. The product is sheer poison . . . That's where this nation for so many years has been fed pus. Small subversive groups have been allowed to infiltrate all sorts of the activities of the nation, vital parts of the nation. I'm suggesting to you that the tolerance of extremists who are trying to destroy our society is not a virtue. I believe that it is cowardice and treason.' Goldsmith had added a McCarthyite sense of purpose to his vendetta.

James Goldsmith was one of the most powerful men in Britain, and not just because of his huge financial resources. After Mrs Thatcher had taken over the Tory leadership, she had been less impressed with Goldsmith than had her predecessor Ted Heath, and Goldsmith's links with the Conservatives had been allowed to drift. Instead, David Frost had introduced him to Harold Wilson and his powerful secretary Lady Falkender, who were back at Number Ten. By this time Wilson had become consumed with hatred for *Private Eye*, which had restored Mrs Wilson's Diary to prominence. According to Frost, when Goldsmith had been introduced to the prime minister, he had offered to rid him of 'this turbulent magazine'. Wilson fawned over the tycoon. Lady Falkender danced with him at Annabel's.

The *Eye* had been attacking Wilson with a vengeance since the slagheap scandal of 1974, when it had been revealed that

253

the family of Wilson's secretary (then plain Marcia Williams) had been negotiating land deals from his office. Wilson had responded by making Marcia a Lady. Still the *Eye* had come back at him, with a wealth of highly detailed information about the seedy camp followers who made Wilson's second premiership so undignified. There was of course Joe Kagan, who was not only corrupt but had links with the KGB. Wilson had retorted by making him a knight. There was Richard Briginshaw, the print union leader who was being sued for conspiracy to defraud by his own union, NATSOPA. Wilson made him a lord. Then there was the property salesman Eric Miller. After the *Eye* suggested his dealings were corrupt, Wilson in due course made him Sir Eric. Miller later committed suicide while under police investigation. It was clear that all this information was so accurate, and so damaging, that much of it was coming from a central source. MI5, it transpired, was using *Private Eye* to try and bring the prime minister down. Wilson complained that he was the victim of a plot, but the nation just laughed.

Ironically, the defender of Wilson and the left in this matter was Paul Foot, who considered that many of the *Eye*'s articles about Arthur Scargill in particular were being fabricated by the security services. It is to the credit of Richard Ingrams that he allowed Paul Foot to publish articles in the *Eye* casting doubt on the magazine's information. 'Actually the *Eye* had it both ways,' admitted Ingrams. 'At the same time that Auberon Waugh was accusing Harold Wilson of being a fully paid-up agent of the KGB, Paul Foot was writing about the MI5 plot against him. We did report quite extensively on the group led by Peter Wright. But it shouldn't be forgotten that the people with whom Wilson surrounded himself were a very rum lot, so the security services had a point.' MI5 plot or no MI5 plot, the information being fed to the *Eye* about Wilson was damaging. 'There was this fantastically good story going,' says Auberon Waugh, 'which was that elements in the security service thought the prime minister himself was an extremely grave security risk. I was glad to run it.'

Private Eye has always been somewhat out of its depth in

the labyrinthine and unprincipled world of espionage. There was always something faintly suspicious about Tom Driberg's great affection for the magazine, given that he was a double agent working for both MI5 and the KGB. Driberg would always insist on being introduced at *Eye* lunches as 'Mr Richmond', because, he explained, the lunches were being monitored by Harold Wilson's own government security people. When Driberg went away to Malta, the Tory MP for Arundel and part-time MI5 agent Henry Kerby suddenly became a keen supporter of the magazine. It was clear that, for once, *Private Eye* was floundering.

At the start of 1976 the battle lines had been drawn between Goldsmith and the *Eye*, as part of a larger war. On one side, Goldsmith and the government; on the other, *Private Eye* and the press, who were disturbed by the legal precedent of holding newsagents responsible for the contents of the publications they sold. Watching over the whole thing with the same amused contempt with which Ingrams regarded his feuding staff, were the security services. At the time, few people had a thorough enough knowledge of British society to comprehend the full picture. The case was to be decided by the one body of people in London society whose understanding of the matter was entirely negligible: the judiciary. As Ingrams said, the parties involved might just as well have hired two boxers to settle it.

Goldsmith thought it would be a simple matter to sweep aside this tiny publication, but he completely failed to realise how many roots the *Eye* had put down in English public life. This was because Goldsmith was not actually English: his grandfather was a German (the family name had originally been Goldschmidt) who had settled in England. His father had then emigrated to France and married a Frenchwoman, and Goldsmith himself had lived much of his life abroad. His accent was curiously Teutonic. When the *Eye* attacked, he proclaimed himself part-Jewish (and the *Eye* anti-semitic) into the bargain. Goldsmith's biographer Ivan Fallon wrote: 'Ingrams and Gillard were making the mistake, as many others would, of seeing Goldsmith through English eyes, as though he was an Englishman.'[2] Equally, Goldsmith was making the mistake of thinking that he understood England. In the isolated

255

world of Wilson's kitchen cabinet, he had been led to believe that attacking *Private Eye* would make him a popular hero. Goldsmith had ambitions to become a press baron, and to become involved in politics; he failed to realise how his un-English aggression was putting those ambitions in jeopardy. The English do not like to see a brave little Englishman being thrashed by a big powerful foreigner.

Goldsmith saw himself as offering leadership. He was a manic depressive, a superstitious man with an unusual fear of rubber bands. He had once been seated on a plane from Spain to Buenos Aires awaiting take-off, when he had spotted a rubber band in the aisle. He had promptly marched off the plane, accompanied by a group of Basque shepherds who had seen him emerging from first class and, presuming him to be an important man, had followed his example. Goldsmith was about to discover a fundamental difference in attitudes between Basque shepherds and the English middle classes.

In his own way, Ingrams was as intractable a personality as Goldsmith, not that he had any choice but to fight. The *Eye*'s offer of an apology along the lines of that made by the *Sunday Times* had been turned down. Paul Foot went to stay with Ingrams at Aldworth: 'We used to go for these great walks across the Berkshire Downs, and I remember once I said, "What are you going to do about this Goldsmith thing? It's going to finish you. It's going to get you evicted from your house, and everything". He just said, "My main problem is how I'm going to attack him next".'

It was the worst possible time for this nightmare sequence of events to be heaped upon Ingrams' head. Only a few weeks before, his elder brother P J had been killed. He had joined an expedition from Oundle School that was attempting to climb Mount Antisana in the Ecuadorian Andes. With one other master and five boys, he had walked up to the snowline in darkness, before crossing a snowfield at dawn to a height of 19,000 feet. As the party crossed a snow bridge and proceeded up a steep slope of soft snow, the weather had turned nasty. The party had been divided into two groups, each roped together, but both masters were in one group; P J had untied himself in order to cross over to the other group. Released from the rope, he had suddenly decided to climb the next eighty feet alone, to investigate what lay around the shoulder of the mountain. The other master urged him to turn back. P J took no notice, disappeared out of sight behind the rocks, and was never seen again. The Ecuadorian Air Force never found his body. 'Peter John's death absolutely struck Victoria to the heart,' says his old teacher Michael Charlesworth. 'She idolised her boys.'

A wooden bridge was built in P J's name, with a plaque, at Wylie Gill in Carrock Fell in the Lake District. Alec Binney came down to join Richard, his mother and the rest of the family at the Memorial Service. Fiona Douglas-Home thought that P J had committed suicide, for he had never recovered from the guilt he had felt at the death of the two boys in earlier mountaineering accidents; but P J was a Catholic, one of Victoria's boys, and that would not have been his way. Richard's daughter Jubby remembers him with fondness: 'Peter John was absolutely great. Really bonkers. He had a huge Mercedes and drove really really fast. I wasn't surprised when they said that he'd gone up a mountain and hadn't come back. He would drive his car around the corner at about 100 m.p.h. just to see if he'd make it. He was the sort who'd go down the Cresta Run.' Goldsmith tried to suggest that P J was still alive, the implication being that somehow it was all a stunt intended to drum up sympathy for Richard's cause. Relations worsened.

Another blow for Richard, once the trial had got under way, was the departure of his beloved secretary Tessa. She adored her boss, but was beginning to find the public schoolboys-and-boxwallahs hierarchy of the *Eye* a strain. 'The final straw was the day Michael Gillard asked me to get a newspaper, and I thought, I can't stand it any longer. I used to come home at night thinking, this is such a waste of my time in the end. But I suppose it formed me. It made me the person I am today.' Tessa left in 1976, to become a bookbinder. Her replacement was Liz Elliot. The week after she joined, her salary was halved, along with everyone else's, to pay for the army of lawyers needed to fight Goldsmith's army of lawyers. 'Nobody ever worked at the *Eye* for money,' says Liz. In fact one of Goldsmith's fundamental misconceptions was to see *Private Eye* as just a smaller commercial rival that could be ruined financially. 'If he had closed the magazine down,' explained Barry Fantoni, 'Christopher Booker, John Wells, Richard and myself would still have assembled in Greek Street on Monday afternoons and made each other laugh.'[3]

'Everyone just soldiered on penniless out of loyalty to this great man, Ingrams,' says Jane Ellison, who joined the *Eye* soon afterwards. 'It says something about his ability to command loyalty. It was entirely through admiration, and not at all through fear. He was such an attractive person that he inspired a protective feeling from his staff.' The readers rallied to the cause too, and money flooded into the new 'Goldenballs' fund, from the likes of Sir Alec Guinness, the Earl of Lichfield, Anthony Sampson, Professor Hugh Trevor-Roper, Reginald Bosanquet, the staff of Slater Walker, and a number of local Liberal and Labour parties. Goldsmith's business rival Tiny Rowland offered £5000, with no strings attached. There were fund-raising events, at which *Eye* supporters gave their services free. Nigel Dempster climbed into the ring at Chelsea Football ground with a wrestler called Johnny Quango (an odd title – one thinks immediately of a panel of four wrestlers, taking half an hour to decide on each move). There was just one notable defector. Booker, still brooding after all these years, virtually crossed into the Goldsmith camp with an article in the *Spectator* entitled 'Come off it, Lord Gnome'. Mary Ingrams never forgave him.

Ingrams' own account of the case that followed, entitled *Goldenballs*, cannot be bettered as a clear and well-written journalistic account of legal procedure. It is his best work. What follows is essentially a brief summary of a long and frightening sequence of events. A libel case, Ingrams learned, can only be judged criminal if a judge first deems it 'in the public interest' for it to be so. In the first of many court hearings, Mr Justice Wien decided that it was. He felt that the *Eye*'s offer to apologise had been indicative of guilt. Goldsmith had won the first round. Michael Gillard set out to see if he could find any more information concerning Goldsmith or his solicitor, Eric Levine.

Gillard approached John Addey, a jolly, entertaining PR man who was a regular at the *Eye* lunch, and whom Ingrams and Osmond had used as the basis for one of the characters in their novel. Addey knew Leslie Paisner, who owned the law firm that Eric Levine had left in 1969, seemingly under a cloud. Addey went off to question Paisner, and came back to the *Eye* lunch flushed with excitement, bearing good news. Paisner had told him exactly why Levine had lost his job and he proceeded to regale the assembled company (including the then Labour MP Brian Walden) with the details. In turn, Gillard had warned Addey that a mysterious letter had been received at the *Eye* offices denouncing him, and containing inside knowledge of his business dealings. Addey read the letter, laughed, and said it was so accurate that he might have written it himself. Patrick Marnham went to see Paisner, who declared himself to be on the *Eye*'s side and who freely confirmed Addey's story. Things were looking up.

On the eve of the court hearing, on 17 May 1976, Gillard's secretary at Granada TV, where he sometimes worked, took a message for her boss from an agitated, anonymous caller. 'I'm a friend. He will know who it is. Tell him that one of his main stories has collapsed disastrously. It will be murder for him tomorrow.' Meanwhile, Eric Levine had a sheaf of papers delivered to the *Eye*'s solicitors. They were signed statements by Leslie Paisner and John Addey. Paisner's read as follows:

> After Eric Levine left Paisner & Co., the firm of which
> I am senior partner, in October 1969, I have deliberately
> on a number of occasions seriously defamed him [here he
> recounted the story he had told Addey]. I hereby unequivocally
> acknowledge that all these statements and allegations were lies
> and without any foundation whatsoever. They were part of a
> vicious vendetta perpetrated by me on Eric Levine. I withdraw
> each and every one of them unreservedly . . . My relationship
> with Eric Levine had been a close one. His departure turned
> my feelings to hatred. Despite my attacks against Eric Levine,

259

he prospered. The success of his firm embittered me the more, particularly when I learnt that the successful Jimmy Goldsmith had become his client . . . When John Addey came to see me . . . I saw this as an opportunity . . . to ensure that Eric Levine would be ruined. I therefore told Addey a pack of lies about him and that I regretted the day I ever met him. John Addey yesterday confessed to me that all he told me was a pack of lies, fabricated to get information from me about Eric Levine for *Private Eye*, who were blackmailing him (Addey), and who were embarked on a campaign of vilification against Eric Levine.

Then, when Patrick Marnham called me to ask what I knew about Eric Levine, I saw yet another opportunity to bring about Eric Levine's downfall without being seen to be involved myself. I therefore repeated to *Private Eye* what I had told Addey and other seriously damaging statements.

All that I told John Addey and Patrick Marnham was a complete pack of lies from beginning to end and without any truth or foundation. I have withdrawn all these statements and allegations.

I am deeply ashamed of my conduct. Only now do I fully understand how vindictive it has been and what harm and damage I have caused Eric Levine. I now wish to put an end to the campaign I mounted against Eric Levine and ensure that he suffers no further damage as a result of the lies I have told about him.

Addey's statement had been sworn at Goldsmith's offices in Leadenhall Street. It referred to Gillard's initial request for Addey's help:

[Gillard] began, after friendly preliminaries, to talk about harmful information he had received about my firm and me personally – the former from, he suggested, a previous employee, and the latter about a homosexual liaison.

He then said he was pursuing an enquiry into a lawyer, Eric Levine . . . The plain implication was the threat that, if I did not help, *Private Eye* would print damaging things about my firm and about me personally.

The *Eye* staff were stunned by these documents. Gillard had

never mentioned homosexuality or attempted to blackmail Addey
– indeed, he had not even known that Addey was a homosexual.
Leslie Paisner was a respectable solicitor, nearing retirement.
The phrase 'pack of lies', which he used three times, was hardly
characteristic, but was to crop up elsewhere in the prosecution's
case. Clearly, something extraordinary had happened. Ingrams
immediately telephoned Addey to find out what. Addey refused
to return any calls at first, then left a message for Ingrams to
meet him at the Albany, at 12.45 on 19 May. Ingrams arrived
there to find Addey flustered and frightened. He begged Ingrams
to believe that he'd had no choice but to sign the statement;
Paisner had retracted in a state of collapse, so he'd had to
follow suit. 'This conversation never took place, OK?' he added
as Ingrams left.

The *Eye* found itself divided. There was genuine excitement
at the prospect of going to court, to see how Addey and Paisner
would react under cross-examination. At the same time, it would
surely bring about inevitable defeat. Peter Cook went to see
Goldsmith to try and bring about a settlement; he couldn't believe
anyone cared so deeply about who had been at lunch with whom.
Goldsmith refused to budge. 'He was a very unpleasant man,'
remembers Cook. 'He wanted an eye for an eye, a tooth for a
tooth.' Goldsmith had his surrender terms delivered to the *Eye*:
an apology, £15–20,000 in damages, an agreement not to write
about Goldsmith or Levine for five years (all articles thereafter
to be submitted for approval), and – a somewhat sinister request,
this – the names of all those who had furnished information for
the *Eye*'s initial pieces to be handed to him. 'Unless he gets the
names,' said Goldsmith's QC Lewis Hawser, 'he will move heav-
en and earth to identify them and he will hound them.' Ingrams
turned the offer down.

Before the case could come to court, there was another
bombshell. Harold Wilson resigned as prime minister, leaving
behind an honours list so controversial that the Honours Scrutiny
Committee refused to pass it. David Frost had been removed from
the list by Wilson himself. That left a knighthood for Eric Miller
and for the boxing promoter Jarvis Astaire, and peerages for Lew

Grade, Bernard Delfont, John Vaizey, George Weidenfield, Sir Joseph Kagan and James Goldsmith. These were all friends of Lady Falkender: Weidenfeld was her publisher and escort, John Vaizey her admirer, Goldsmith and Miller her dancing partners. 'We couldn't see what these fellers had done for Britain,' said Lord Crathorne of the Scrutiny Committee. 'We didn't like the cut of their jib.' Lady Falkender wrote to *The Times* complaining of anti-semitism.

Goldsmith had been given his peerage 'for services to exports and ecology'; but his company, Cavenham, was a tiny exporter, sending just 0.4 per cent of its output overseas. As for ecology, well, it was a big industrial concern. The only 'ecology' that could possibly be attributed to James Goldsmith was the removal from the planet of a magazine that he considered waste product. Goldsmith's friend Sam White, the *Evening Standard*'s man in Paris, also later claimed that Goldsmith had been honoured by Wilson to give him more status in the courts, and that the 'ecology' reference was a private joke between himself, Wilson and Falkender.

Goldsmith never got his peerage – he was demoted to knight by the Scrutiny Committee – and Jarvis Astaire got nothing at all. The press reaction was furious, and Goldsmith's political ambitions were destroyed at a stroke. 'By suing *Private Eye*,' wrote Ingrams, 'he had made the fatal mistake of becoming conspicuous.'[4] He had also underestimated Ingrams' power as a breaker, if not a maker, of men who do not keep their heads down. Unable to see this, he began to believe instead that there was a conspiracy against him, 'linking an unfriendly reference even in the *Financial Times* or *The Times* to a kind of imaginary central intelligence which somewhere revolved around Ingrams and Gillard,' as Ivan Fallon put it.[5] In this context he made the mistake of subpoenaing an entirely irrelevant Auberon Waugh, who when the case finally came to court lashed him with a stream of non-libellous but highly articulate abuse about his 'repulsively ugly face'.

On 5 July 1976 the parties finally assembled at the Law Courts, initially to hear an injunction that had prevented the *Eye* writing about Goldsmith throughout the honours list affair;

Ingrams remarked that spotting the immaculate, determined Goldsmith across the courtroom 'was like the first sight of the shark in *Jaws*.'[6] The *Eye* team immediately suffered an unpleasant, but not altogether surprising setback. Paisner and Addey were missing from court. Addey, it was explained, had fled the country leaving no address. In Paisner's place, Goldsmith produced a doctor who revealed that Paisner was 'extremely confused and disoriented', and medically unfit to give evidence. Immediately after the trial, Paisner resigned his job and emigrated to Israel. Goldsmith had won round two.

Goldsmith lost the next round, though, because the injunction was thrown out; Foot now wrote up the Paisner–Addey affair for the *Eye*, and Goldsmith applied to bring contempt of court proceedings against him. During the course of the week's trial, a curious change seemed to come over Goldsmith: he began to look as if he was enjoying himself as the focus of the glamorous media circus. Furthermore, he seemed to develop a sneaking admiration for Ingrams' refusal to buckle, as so many of his former adversaries had done. Barry Fantoni recalls: 'Goldsmith kept smiling at Ingrams in the court. As if he envied him.' Says Ingrams: 'I had the strong feeling that he was highly intrigued by us all, and was in a way envious of my own position – that he would have liked, in other words, to be the editor of *Private Eye*.'[7]

The next round, on 29 July, was the committal proceedings for criminal libel at Bow Street Magistrates Court, a purely formal interim stage designed to rake in a few more fees for the lawyers. Before this could take place, Gillard fired a shot back across Goldsmith's bows, suing both Addey and Goldsmith for slander, for the accusation that he was a blackmailer. The committal proceedings saw Goldsmith's only appearance in the witness box, ranting and raving about 'filth'. 'Do you mind behaving a little less theatrically, Sir James?' asked the magistrate, Mr Kenneth Barraclough.

During the next case (a further attempt to gag the magazine, heard by Mr Justice Goff on 9 August), another mysterious anonymous caller tipped off Ingrams, claiming that there was a spy in the *Eye*'s midst. Eric Levine had produced a bundle of confidential

Eye documents in court. 'There is nothing more demoralising,' said Ingrams, 'than the thought that someone whose loyalty you take completely for granted might be a traitor. You look with new eyes on people who have been working with you for years, and begin to harbour suspicions about them.'[8] Before Booker could be hoist from the yardarm, however, it dawned on Ingrams that the call had been a trick to lower morale, and that the confidential papers must have been stolen from the *Eye*'s bins. Not *'stolen'*, explained Goldsmith's embarrassed QC Lewis Hawser to the court; merely 'borrowed' by a highly reputable firm of private investigators m'lud, photocopied, and put back in the rubbish.

By the end of October 1976, there had been no fewer than eight court cases, and the main criminal libel hearing was nowhere in sight. Master Warren had thrown out the writs against the wholesale newsagents, Mr Justice Stocker had reversed the decision in Goldsmith's favour on appeal, and now *Private Eye* went to the Court of Appeal. Goldsmith was trying another tack to get Ingrams thrown into jail with the contempt case over Foot's article, heard before the Lord Chief Justice Lord Widgery and two other judges. After Lewis Hawser had addressed the court for an hour, Widgery confessed himself to be totally lost. In the true style of Beachcomber's Justice Cocklecarrot, he admitted: 'I'm bound to say that I've still got very little idea of what all this is about.' Eventually, Goldsmith's application was thrown out. It was gradually filtering through to the various M'luds that something suspicious had happened to Paisner and Addey.

Steadily, the whole case was becoming bogged down in the Dickensian procedural mire that passes for the British legal system. Both sides were getting tired. Ingrams came out in boils. 'The strain of an apparently unending stream of cases was beginning to tell. I myself could talk or think of little but Goldsmith. At night I dreamed about him. The obsession was plainly turning me into a bore.'[9] Being a bore was a far worse nightmare for Ingrams than any dreams of Goldsmith. As for Sir James, his finances were bottomless, but he had not reckoned on the time it would all take. His ambitions to be a press lord were suffering as his political ambitions had: an attempt to buy the *Observer* was vetoed by the paper's trust body. Instead he set his sights on the Beaverbrook stablemates, the *Express* and *Standard*, but the journalists there did not relish the prospect of a boss who sued newsagents for libel. The stock prices of Cavenham began to fall, as the company simply became unfashionable.

In December, the *Eye*'s appeal against Goldsmith's victory over the newsagents came to court, before Lords Denning, Scarman and Bridge. Denning spoke plainly and simply, as is his wont, in favour of the *Eye*: 'Common sense and fairness require that no subordinate distributor – from top to bottom – should be held liable for a libel unless he knew or ought to have known that the newspaper or periodical contained a libel . . . It would mean that all the firms who distribute *Private Eye*; all the bookstalls who sell it; all the public libraries who stock it; all the clubs and common rooms who take it; and everyone who hands it to his neighbour to read – each and every one of them would be liable.'

Scarman then came out, completely unintelligibly, in favour of Goldsmith: 'The Plaintiff's purpose has to be shown to be not that which the law by granting a remedy offers to fulfil, but one which the law does not recognise as a legitimate use of the remedy sought, see Re. Majory (1955) I Chancery at page 623 . . .' and so on. Bridge followed suit, with equally unfathomable gobbledygook: 'There is a breach of the rule *audi alteram partem* which applies alike to issues of law, as to issues of fact, and in a court of inferior jurisdiction this would be a ground for *certiorari* . . .' and so on. Goldsmith had won, the *Eye* was faced with a massive bill, and the main bout was still to come.

The criminal libel date was set for the 10 May 1977, at the Old Bailey.

The verdict against the distributors had been about class as much as about law. Denning was a countryman, and recognised Ingrams as one of his own kind. He plainly had little time for Goldsmith and his flashy suits. Other judges, on the other hand, knowing little about the case except that *Private Eye* was a satire magazine and that James Goldsmith was a businessman with a knighthood, tended to plump naturally for Goldsmith as a pillar of society. In truth, class is really only a matter of how far one has to go back up one's family tree to find a coal merchant; Ingrams would probably have had to go further than Goldsmith, but most judges naturally assumed the opposite. He began to fear that defeat – and prison – were inevitable.

Yet in the end, it was Goldsmith whose nerve failed him. He had been forced to buy up all the public stock in his own company to prevent its shares collapsing. His bid for the *Express* and *Standard* was tottering. In April 1977, the *Standard*'s editor Simon Jenkins approached Ingrams with a deal: Goldsmith would go away for £30,000, an apology and a handshake. He would leave the newsagents alone. He would drop the criminal libel and forget the Levine matter. Ingrams accepted. There had been thirteen hearings in the space of eighteen months, and now it was all over. On 16 May 1977, Ingrams and Marnham were called to the Old Bailey to plead not guilty and receive their formal acquittal. For Gillard, suddenly left to fight his slander case against Addey and Goldsmith alone, it was a betrayal. 'Ingrams grabbed the peace offer like a drowning man thrown a line. He lost his nerve. He had started to see the prison gates.'[10] Marnham was sceptical. 'The prison gates were clearly visible from my house in Abergavenny as well.'[11]

Ingrams denied that he had been scared of going to prison. After all, it wouldn't have been too dissimilar from West Downs. Nigel Dempster disagrees. 'He *was* frightened. I remember going to Bow Street for the committal proceedings – Richard had had a haircut and bought a new corduroy jacket – and we went to Bow Street that day in the sure knowledge that Richard and Patrick were going to prison. No doubt about it. Gillard was wrong. I don't see what else Richard could have done.' Outside the court, a journalist had approached Ingrams and asked him what frightened him most about the prospect of going to prison. The idea of being visited by Lord Longford, he had replied.

Goldsmith's biographer Ivan Fallon is in no doubt that Ingrams was the victor. 'In effect Goldsmith was acknowledging that Ingrams and *Private Eye* had won, that although he might be awarded the victory, finally it was he who had to leave the field.'[12] Goldsmith never did get his handshake. He never got the *Express* and *Standard* either. He had to settle instead for starting up his own news magazine, called *Now!*, which he openly admitted would not employ members of any left-wing political party. *Private Eye* absolutely crucified *Now!*: Ingrams renamed it *Talbot!*, after the recent decision by Chrysler cars to rename themselves 'Talbot' to prevent falling sales. 'It's a lovely idea, isn't it?' he says. 'Sellafield was another one, changing it from Windscale so that people would forget it was a terrible nuclear dump.' A new *Eye* record was brought out, entitled *The Sound of Talbot!*, starring Spike Milligan, Pamela Stephenson and the usual cast. 'Should John Aspinall be shot? A tiger talks!' it proclaimed. Every fortnight the *Eye* derided the newcomer for the plainly visible piles of unsold copies that were littering London. Ingrams laughs: 'I don't think I've enjoyed anything so much, particularly all the stories about how piles of *Talbot!* were being dumped into the sea.' The editor of *Now!*, Tony Shrimsley, protested: '*Private Eye* serves no more to inform or expose than hard pornography. Mr Ingrams is not just some puritanical eccentric who plays the church organ for relaxation. He is an evil-doer.' Sir James, though, closed down *Now!* and left the country.

Gillard won his slander case against Addey, and lost the same case against Goldsmith. Sir James was, after all, still a millionaire businessman, whereas Addey had been revealed as a homosexual. Gillard took it to the House of Lords, but his mafioso image did not endear him to Their Lordships. 'He may not have been a blackmailer, but he certainly looked like one,' said one colleague. Addey was described by the Court of Appeal Judges as 'a liar, not to be believed in any particular'. He was subsequently appointed a magistrate. He died recently. Paisner died in 1979. Eric Levine went into property in the USA. Harold Wilson hawked a full list of *Private Eye* informers around Fleet Street, compiled presumably with the help of Goldsmith's 'reputable firm of private investigators'; but no one seemed very interested.

It later transpired that the £5000 gift from Tiny Rowland

had been his response to Goldsmith's non-payment of a £10,000 wager; Goldsmith had bet him that Ted Heath would replace Wilson as prime minister by 1975. Goldsmith was also found wanting when he said that the *Eye* had lost more than £100,000 on their case, and that if their bill actually came in under that figure he'd stand the difference personally. The final amount was audited at £85,000, but Goldsmith still questions his liability to pay the balance. It was later confirmed that he had indeed had millions of his companies' money locked in Slater Walker, money that Gillard's investigations might have endangered.

'I think the Goldsmith case was the best thing that ever happened to *Private Eye*,' reckons Peter McKay. 'It did wonders for the circulation, because it was such a fierce row that it got into all the papers.' 'There's nothing that puts on sales so much as a great libel fight,' agrees Nigel Dempster. The *Eye* was indeed better known after the trial, but the famous Goldsmith sales effect is in fact a myth. The *Eye*'s sales had crashed in 1964, and stayed quite low until 1970. Between 1970 and 1974, they shot up to 117,000. Between 1974 and 1979, they fell back to 89,000 and stayed there after the trial. In 1979 they immediately recovered to 116,000, pushing on to 144,000 the next year and 190,000 in 1981. Of course there were other factors involved, but these dates correspond exactly to the various changes of government between Labour and Conservative. More of the *Eye*'s readers were left wing than right, and they simply found it harder to laugh at their own point of view. However damaging the revelations about Wilson, fewer people wanted to hear them than wanted to hear Mrs Thatcher lampooned.

Ingrams, tired but victorious, desperately needed a rest; but he was not to be allowed one. Further personal tragedy lay ahead. An off note was struck in one of his many visits to court. Alan Coren was a spectator in the public gallery: 'I went along with Stanley Reynolds to see Richard defend himself. And Mary Ingrams turned up with some sandwiches in a paper bag for Richard. As he was going into the witness box, she tried to get down there herself, with this brown paper bag containing his lunch. An usher said, "You can't do that", and she got rather

268

hysterical. It was quite early in the morning, about ten, and I realised that she wasn't drunk. There was something funny about her.' Now the alarm bells were ringing in Coren's head.

19 The Trouble with Mary

Arthur Ingrams died of pneumonia on 7 September 1977, aged seven. The blow to both Richard and Mary was a crushing one. 'It was a time of great stress,' recalls Richard, 'especially for my wife. As far as I was concerned it was far worse than the deaths of my two brothers. The whole business of having a brain-damaged son imposed a great strain, more so than on my wife because – and this is often difficult to grasp – a mother can love her child regardless of its physical condition while a father probably doesn't quite share that attitude. I felt affectionate towards Arthur, but because he couldn't speak or do anything apart from smiling like a baby, I couldn't feel towards him as Mary did. When Arthur died I think I inevitably felt a sense of relief, partly because of his own death and pain – or a sense of release, I should perhaps say.'[1]

As a couple, Richard and Mary were ill-suited to deal with grief. They coped with it not just in contrasting ways, but in directly conflicting ways. Richard buried it under layers of silent dignity, stubbornly refusing to display his emotions in public or allow his daily routine to waver. Barry Fantoni had just returned from holiday when it happened: 'I was working alone with him, and he just said "Arthur died", and that was it. Somebody else would have taken the day off, or wept, but he didn't.' It would perhaps have been better for Richard, at that moment, to have been alone with his thoughts on the Berkshire Downs.

Mary, meanwhile, was the one left in Berkshire. She had

270

friends to share her grief with, but very often her only memento of Richard was his dirty socks. 'It was doubly hard for my mother when Arthur died,' remembers Richard's son Fred. 'He was incredibly beautiful. She'd got to know him and love him. It would have been better if the doctors had let him die in the first place.' She began to resent Richard for his ability to disappear off to London each day, and for his unwillingness to talk when he got back in the evening. 'I don't think I can have been easy to live with,' admits Richard. 'I do sit in silence most of the time and I am anti-social.'[2]

Richard had always been a quiet husband, content to stare for hours into the recesses of his own mind. Mary once gave an interview to the *Evening Standard* in which she complained: 'He may have had lunch with the most exciting and interesting people and not say a thing about it. He might have had lunch with Margaret Thatcher, for instance. "What did she say?" I ask. "Not a lot," he says.'[3] Richard tried to blame it on the hassle of commuting. His secretary Liz, who took Mary's phone calls at the *Eye*, became aware of the problem early on: 'If Morgo had had a job, perhaps in London, it might have taken her mind off it; but instead she had somebody whom she imagined to be living the high life up in London, very high profile, utterly charming, and every woman saying "Richard Ingrams is my ideal of a sexy man". Then for the sexy man to come home and never say a word . . . even I might have been driven potty.'

If Richard's tendency to bottle everything up was making life difficult for Mary, it was as nothing compared to the problems he now faced with her. As a young girl, she had only been able to watch as her mother's manic depression darkened into serious mental illness. Now, to the despair of her family, that same unpredictable form of depression began to affect her. At first there had been just the odd moodswing, but after the traumatic birth of Arthur these had intensified dramatically. A worried Victoria, along with Leonard's wife Rosalind, had faced her with the possibility that in her obsession with Arthur she might be neglecting her other children. In an act of vicious retaliation she had cut both women off entirely from her family. Victoria was forbidden to see her grandchildren for nine years.

'Her manic depression crept on,' remembers Victoria. 'It started with the children, so Fred told me. Richard wouldn't believe it at first, but then it came to me. She shouted at me and I had to leave the house. I wasn't allowed to see the children again until they had grown up, and I never saw Mary at all.' 'It was an incredible situation,' recalls Jubby. 'When I was young I never saw my grandmother, never knew that they existed, all these people in my family. One by one, she banned them or refused to acknowledge them. I thought my family was just my mum and dad.'

Now, after Arthur's death, it got worse. Mary refused point blank to speak to her husband for eight months. Richard had to go and stay with Paul Foot. 'You would sometimes see a little sad bag with pyjamas when he was staying with Footy or his mum,' remembers Barry Fantoni. If the office tried to get through to Richard at Aldworth, Mary would slam the phone down. 'When I stayed there,' says Fantoni, 'it felt like they were two complete strangers. She'd make supper and talk about herself non-stop. He'd just sit there quietly. She went on to destroy every relationship that he held dear. She deliberately cut off myself, Duncan, Wells, Rushton, Booker. All the Oxford lot.' This is something of an overstatement. Foot, Waugh, Osmond and their wives all remained in favour. Nonetheless, Mary's edicts could be abrupt and dramatic. John Wells borrowed the Aldworth cottage for a week when Richard and Mary were away, to work with a composer on a new musical: 'We had to go back to London in a hurry. I did everything I could to clear up except for the fact that I didn't clear out the grate, and there was one pair of sheets which I hadn't changed. Mary didn't talk to me for eleven years. Rushton did something similar.'

Jack Duncan frequently made the trip to Aldworth to play for the village cricket team. 'We reckoned she used to have a little black book for no reason at all. One time I went up to play cricket, I'd been given a lift up by Peter Jay, and I needed a lift back. Footy and the others were all invited back for supper, and

272

a message from Mary was passed down that I was very definitely not to come. I've no idea why. I'd said nothing. I'd done nothing. I was left in the pub with no means of transport back to London.' Quiet public school manners were no match for the imposing, uncontrollable matron figure that Richard's wife was fast becoming. Duncan was lucky: a passing vanload of West Indian cricketers from Reading happened to pull in for a pint on the way home, and gave him a lift to Reading station.

Barry Fantoni shakes his head in wonderment: 'I remember when we were playing another cricket match, at Osmond's house in Minster Lovell. There were eleven of us in the changing room, and we'd *all* fallen out with her. We'd all been given the boot. I said that we should call the team "The Enemies of Mrs Ingrams". Richard would bring home his affections, people he liked, and she would stick the knife in and sever them and watch the relations rot. You'd need a degree in psychology to understand why she did it all.' Or perhaps it was simple jealousy of her husband, his job and his apparent capacity for calm, tipped over the edge of propriety by manic depression.

On the increasingly rare occasions when Mary swam in the *Eye* pool, it seemed to the staff that she affected a haughty superiority. According to Nigel Dempster, she refused to speak to him, a mere reporter, until he married a Duke's daughter. 'I remember a *Private Eye* outing, by train and ferry across the Channel,' claims Dempster. 'Richard and Mary drove back from their holidays in the Dordogne (where the increasingly profitable magazine had purchased a villa) in order to meet up with the hacks. Mary arrived and there were twenty-five to thirty *Private Eye* people and she would speak to no one except Auberon Waugh. We all thought she'd go round saying "Who are you?" or "How nice to see you", but she spoke to no one. We were all as nothing.' Richard himself, with fierce loyalty, vociferously disputes this version of events.

If she did come up for lunch in London, Mary often utterly missed the mood of those around her. Says Wells: 'I remember Mary sitting there, describing somebody as a "snoring bore". Richard said "Oh I don't know, I rather like him".' She had made an inadvertent faux pas, but instead of realising it, continued loudly: 'But darling, I thought you said he was a snoring bore.' The atmosphere curdled. According to Tessa Fantoni, 'She used to talk endlessly about her experiences in hospital, or if she wasn't talking about those she would talk about Marianne Faithfull, who was living in her village; and how she was saving "Droopy Drawers", as she called her, from suicide.' 'The trouble with Mary,' adds Maggie Lunn, another of Richard's secretaries, 'is that she became so charmless and snobbish that she couldn't get anybody onto her side, although it was probably quite a good side in a way.'

Eventually, there were very few people from *Private Eye* still permitted to visit the Ingrams household; Mary had many visitors of her own, but Richard's friends had to dig deep into their reserves of loyalty. Recounts Jack Duncan: 'What most of us who were on the black list had decided, was that our friendship with Richard was so strong that we weren't going to let her oddities interfere with it. So people used to just put up with her and be nice and polite to her. Nobody thought it was worthwhile to have a go.' According to Fred's godfather Christopher Logue, 'Mary had no judgement of character. She used to think, for instance, that the sun shone out of McKay's arse. Take one look at McKay, he's a fucking Gestapo agent! You wouldn't trust him a minute!' In fact there was a significant reason that Mary looked so fondly on the rear aspect of Peter McKay; for Peter's wife Helen had also borne a handicapped child. The Ingrams and the McKays socialised frequently, until one day Peter McKay left his wife. Thereafter Helen McKay continued to visit on her own.

Alan Coren met Mary Ingrams when Fred grew up and joined *Punch*. 'She struck me as being in the line of that county type of woman who is a bit odd – you know, when you read in the papers that someone's shot their next-door neighbour. It couldn't have been much fun going home to Mary. Richard's marriage didn't seem bonded by friendship. By suffering and love, yes. It has to be said that I saw them together only half a dozen times and therefore have no business making snap judgements about a marriage which lasted thirty years, but I don't think they liked one another very much.' There, perhaps, was the crux of the matter. Richard and Mary loved one another deeply, but they rarely shared a laugh. Even alcohol, which had once united them, now divided them. Much of their life together was still calm and content, but Mary's chief virtues of loyalty, supportiveness and tolerance were being increasingly distorted by outbursts of manic depression.

So why on earth did Richard let her get the upper hand? How did such a strong, stubborn, resilient character allow *anyone* to banish his mother from his children's presence, or leave his friends on the doorstep on a Berkshire night with no transport home? The answers are various. First and foremost, he was aware that Mary was ill, and that there was no point in trying to argue the toss rationally. 'I always saw that it was due to mental illness, which perhaps others didn't, and therefore, however unpleasant Mary was, I didn't treat it as if it was her; because if you took it seriously, you would think that she was deeply unpleasant, which I never did feel about her. The only alternative was to think that she was not responsible for what she was doing. I just hoped it would work its way out.'

Then there was the vitally important question of loyalty. Mary had stuck with him through thick and thin. She had always been there to darn his trousers, to fetch him his chocolate after dinner, to back him up, right or wrong. When his friends had all dashed off and disappeared, for the chance of greater glory on *TW3*, he'd always had Mary. However disturbed she had become, he owed her that. In his dogged, reticent manner, he was trying to show her some respect. In many ways too, he still needed her; she was the framework within which he lived his life. According to John Wells, 'Joan Littlewood, who can see through walls, said that Ingrams is somebody who needs a framework to live inside. He'd have gone to pieces without her. He's never once said an unkind word about her. If you look at "Dear Bill" [the Denis Thatcher letters composed by Ingrams and Wells], there was a lot of his marriage, and I suppose mine, in that: keeping your head down when the old lady goes bananas. I remember him saying that he treated Mary's rages like a kind of storm.

You just had to put your collar up and pull your hat down.'

Richard was of course famous for his inability to handle direct confrontation. For such a brave man, who stood unwavering in the full blast of Sir James Goldsmith's rage and took everything that could be thrown at him, Ingrams suffers inescapably from the patrician distaste for fuss and bother. When the *Eye* ran a piece alleging that Esther Rantzen had commandeered a BBC office for breastfeeding purposes, Rantzen called up and spent an hour hanging on, refusing point blank to get off the line until Ingrams took the call. Eventually she had to give up. When Ingrams had dropped the Barry McKenzie strip, its illustrator Nicholas Garland had similarly failed to get him to come to the phone.

On more than one occasion Tony Rushton made such dreadful, irredeemable mistakes with the *Eye*'s layout that Richard resolved to sack him. He could never bring himself to do it face to face, but had to do it in writing. 'I've got a letter from the 1970s sacking Tone,' says the *Eye*'s accountant Sheila Molnar. 'Apparently Ingrams sacked Tone, then Tone would come to work the next day and carry on. Richard would say "I sacked you", and Tone would say "I took no notice", and Richard would say "Oh, all right then".' As a substitute for confrontation, Richard would content himself with drawing up a parody of Ulsterman John Cole's unintelligible TV news reports, and inserting the phrase 'Fockin Tone' somewhere into the middle. The very depths of his emotional subconscious had to be stirred before rage would rise to the surface. Sitting in the Coach and Horses one day Gerry Lawless, an occasional Irish contributor to the *Eye*, had accused Richard's father of being a traitor. 'Get out! Get out!' Richard had shouted. Turning to the landlord, he added, 'Norman, this man is never to come into the pub again!' – and nor did he.

In general, though, Richard assiduously turned his face away from any squall, and allowed it to blow over him. 'My worst fault is cowardice,' he told Lynn Barber of the *Independent on Sunday*. 'I've been cowardly in sort of wanting to have a quiet life really, and not really facing up to things.'[4] This isn't strictly true; a lesser man would have admitted defeat and beaten a retreat from Mary, something Richard never did. If Ingrams had had to fight in the trenches, he would not have refused to go over the top into a hail of bullets; but he would have closed his eyes as he did so, so as not to see the mess. 'Besides,' he said, 'if I'm not getting on with my wife, then I've always got my children to talk to.'[5]

Richard's children, of course, were the other reason that he could never have abandoned Mary. 'I think the family unit was more important to him than anything else in the world,' reckons Barry Fantoni, 'and he could put up with anything she did in order to keep it together. I remember driving with him, and we both agreed that whatever happened, neither of us would ever get divorced. There are really strong measures by which he governs his life – a lot of them Catholic, of course. There might not be a great many of them, but they are immutable, as firm and solid as a mountain. He's a Buffalo,' adds Fantoni, switching effortlessly into Chinese horoscope mode. 'Charlie Chaplin, Peter Sellers, Walt Disney and Saddam Hussein. He's a sort of mixture of all them.'

Both Richard's children speak with great affection of the tolerance and good humour of their paternal upbringing. If his marriage had not ultimately succeeded, then his relationship with his children most certainly did. He was an intuitive father, the best sort. Recalls Jubby: 'I remember when Fred and I used to go to the pub in the village and get very drunk, aged about fourteen. We had these dogs in the house, and we had to get through the door without them hearing us and barking; so it could be a very time-consuming thing, turning the doorknobs quietly, shushing each other, crawling on our hands and knees, trying not to be caught. We'd get through three doors, this whole palaver would take ages and ages, we'd get to the next door, and there would be my dad in his pyjamas with a big grin on his face, saying "Hello". He never got cross about anything.'

For Richard's son Fred was reserved the special privilege of being taken to the Barbican to see four Jacques Tati films on the trot. 'Whenever the Marx Brothers films were on, we always used to watch them, and Danny Kaye. Always the funny films. Dad hates violence. He laughed his head off at *Airplane*.' Clearly, like many a father-and-son relationship, there was a strong element of nostalgia in Richard's friendship with Fred. When Fred was eleven, Richard bought a copy of *The Green Roads of England*, a guide published in 1920. The two of them set out to follow the Berkshire Ridgeway, from outside their front door, all the way to Dorset. One blazing July, with a knapsack full of pork pies and crisps, they set off for Lambourn, then on the next day to Avebury, where they stopped in a transport cafe for a fry-up.

From Silbury Hill to the Wansdyke ('You got the feeling that this was the capital of old England'), staying the night at the Golden Swan in Wilcot; across Salisbury Plain, through Shaftesbury, and down to Charmouth at the end of the week for a dip in the sea. 'I felt I was showing Fred what England was really like,' says Richard wistfully. 'We were pretty chuffed that we made it; we were sort of heroes, particularly Fred.'[6] If Richard could have frozen time to preserve just one day in his life, then up there, on the Downs in July, away from the cares and worries of feuding colleagues, unpredictable wives, predatory lawyers and half-witted judges, that would perhaps have been the day.

It was almost inevitable, after the scholastic hothouse of Richard's own education and his reaction to it, that he would fail utterly to put any academic pressure on his children. Rushton and he had once collaborated on a cartoon, showing a proud father introducing his son to a boarding school headmaster: 'I want him to have all the disadvantages I never had, Headmaster . . .' Richard sent Fred to Douai Abbey, a Catholic boarding school just nine miles from home, that was not entirely prepared for this attitude. 'Dad's got a very healthy lack of respect for people in power, and I've always had that instilled in me. I would say that such-and-such a master was a bastard, and he would just agree with me. If I got a bad report, he would just say "never mind". I was always very good at art – I used to win the art prize on parents' day – and I was good at cricket. Both made him pleased, and that was enough. I remember when my sister got a D and an E, and my mother said, "Oh well done, darling". Mum was totally unacademic, she had no idea what it meant.'

278

D does, at least, sound a long way from Z.

Jubby's schooling was wrecked by another in the series of personal tragedies that have been regularly visited on the Ingrams family like biblical plagues; only the Kennedys can know what it must feel like to be an Ingrams. First, Jubby fell off a horse and broke her back. Then, a tumour was diagnosed on one of her legs. She spent much of her childhood in hospital encased from head to foot in plaster, an experience from which her spine has never quite recovered. Her surgeon was Art Themen, a small middle-aged Anglo-West Indian who plays saxophone with the Stan Tracy band. Jubby fell crushingly, hopelessly in love with him.

'When he came on his rounds I'd be flat on my back with my Walkman. So I'd buy hip music that I thought he'd be interested in and leave the tape lying there, and luckily he fell for that one. He saw my J.J. Cale tape and said, "Oh J.J. Cale, great, I really like him"; and I was so happy, because I hated it, and I thought "Yes! It was worth £5.99".' Eventually, Themen was replaced on the ward by J.P.R. Williams, the rugby player. Jubby was devastated, but resolved to track Themen down. 'When I left the hospital I used to go and see all this ghastly jazz in these pubs in Barnes, when I was about fifteen. I hate that sort of music but I stood there at the back, hoping that he wouldn't see me. Once he caught me at the 100 Club, and gallantly dedicated a number called "Sheila" to me. It was awful, excruciating, really embarrassing.'

Like a true gentleman, Themen politely affected not to notice the schoolgirl who dogged his footsteps, and whose friends wrote him embarrassing notes revealing the true nature of her affections. In due course, Jubby grew out of it. In 1989, she had to go and see him about her back once more: 'I took my friend Nina Train, who's American, and she saw this little middle-aged man in a beige suit and a brown tie, and said "That's *him*? Is that the *guy*? Are you *crazee*?" It was so obvious, and he was standing there saying "Hello". I almost died.'

In 1992 Jubby's back gave way again and she was forced to have an epidural at Charing Cross hospital. 'It was still heart-fluttering to speak to Art Themen, even after all those years,' she admits. Jubby finished her schooling at Padworth, a remedial establishment in a beautiful Georgian mansion on a hill near Newbury. It had a wine cellar, where sixth formers ran up a tab and from which they could even take wine into their lessons. There were a lot of parties, and Richard and Mary exerted no academic pressure of any kind.

There is a danger, of course, that if a parent encourages a child to display a healthy disrespect for authority, then at a certain age that parent is lumped in with the authority being rebelled against. Without ever losing their enormous affection for their father, that is exactly what happened with Fred and Jubby. At sixteen, Fred begged his father to allow him to switch schools or leave altogether, but Richard for once said no; if Fred was to make anything of his education, and mature into a professional artist, then he must stay put. Fred now admits that his father was right, but at the time he concentrated hard on getting himself expelled.

Often he would play truant for days on end, vanishing to London to stay with Christopher Logue. 'I used to pitch up at his place at two in the morning. He used to send me the most amazing books; I've a signed David Hockney volume. And he gave me all sorts of good sound advice. He was a groovy guy in London, so I could relate to him much more than my parents. He was much more laid back. He used to write me very good letters, and I used to confide in him; about when I first fell in love, and that sort of thing. Mum always said that if they were wiped out in a car crash, I would have a most unconventional upbringing.'

Most of Fred's rebelliousness was merely mischievous, and directly inherited from his father. He shaved his head for two years, just to annoy Richard. Then, when he and Jubby left college, they posed naked for Katya Grenfell's book of photographs *Nude London*, again, purely to annoy their father. 'He was furious, depressed, annoyed and shocked,' says Fred. 'At least . . . I hope he was. I'd just been tattooed as well, with Japanese happy and sad Noh masks, and I wanted to show them off. I'm sure that really annoyed him too.'

The publisher of the book, Naim Attallah of Quartet, was an old *Eye* target for whom Jubby had gone to work. 'She came to

Cook and Ingrams – looking rather well fed
in the early days of his marriage – try to bale
the *Eye* out of its straitened circumstances
by taking their publicity roadshow to
Durham University.

The *Eye* office in the late 1960s:
(from left) Fantoni, Foot, Ingrams
and Booker clearly enjoying 'a golden period'.

Ushering in the 1970s with a variety of suitable wigs:
Tony Rushton is in the foreground on the left,
Ingrams is in the centre, Tessa Fantoni is to his left,
and Patrick Marnham sits next to her.

The intricate and delicately balanced relationship
between Richard Ingrams and John Wells,
captured in 1974.

A typical *Private Eye* lunch at the Coach & Horses
in the 1970s. Clockwise round the table, from bottom left:
Jilly Cooper, Frank Muir, Martin Tomkinson
(*Eye* journalist), Ned Sherrin, Patrick Marnham,
Sally Beauman, Anthony Blond, Anthony Haden-Guest,
Ann Chisholm and Richard Ingrams.

PJ walks towards his death in the Ecuadorian Andes.
Moments after this picture was taken he disappeared,
never to be seen again.

A new era is ushered in at *Private Eye*: Peter Cook (looking somewhat the worse for wear) gives his full backing to the man on his left, who on this occasion turns out to be Ian Hislop.

Ingrams' celebrated leather-clad pose to publicise the launch of the *The Oldie*. *Private Eye* is first in line to register its derision at the antics of its former master.

Lookalike

Dancer   Editor

Sir,
 I wonder if any of your readers have noticed the strange resemblance between well-known Oldie editor Richard Ingrams and the anonymous gay dancer pictured in City Limits. Could they perhaps be related?

Yours,
ENA B. RUSHTON,
London.

The girls cluster round as the Oldie bashes out another hymn: Maggie Lunn looks suitably adoring, while Polly Sampson hunts for a musical alternative.

Watching the cricket at Aldworth: Richard's creaking back, now retired, gets some much-needed support from his daughter Jubby.

Ingrams in clover, as beautiful young Deborah Bosley moves into his home.

Richard with his beloved
grandson Otis – named,
it is said, after the lift company.

me and said, "I'd like to be in it". I said to her, "Lay off. Never. Never. Your father will kill me". Eventually she was so insistent, she said "I'm doing it with Fred". I said, "You can do what you like, I don't want to have anything to do with it". Anyway, she went and had it done, and brought some polaroids to show me. I said, "Oh my God, if your dad sees those . . ." and I confiscated them. The next day I was going to New York, where I had to see a bank manager. And while I was there, the bloody things fell out on the table. He must have thought, "What a seedy customer this is, carrying this naked woman around." I'll never forget it.'6

'So one day I got an agitated Jubby on the phone, she said "I've just received a call from Father at *Private Eye*, somebody's told him about the book, and he's summoned me. What shall I tell him?" "I don't know what you tell him!" I shouted. Anyway, after lunch she rang me, laughing hysterically. She said, "Oh, Dad was great". He was having a whale of a time fielding calls from journalists, fabricating wild stories about who else was in the book. He did later admit that he disapproved, though. The book died a silent death, and he was pleased about that.'

This need to shock their imperturbable father probably secretly impressed him; he knew deep down that it clumsily masked the huge affection they felt. One-time *Eye* journalist Paul Halloran remembers the sixteen-year-old Fred visiting his father at the *Eye* offices: 'He came into the Coach at lunchtime and sat down beside his old man, and spontaneously put his arm around him, and kept it there, for the whole lunch.' Fantoni would have been amazed.

Sadly, Fred and Jubby's relationship with their mother was not of the same calibre, tainted forever by the family schisms she had imposed when they were young. Eventually, Fred got into art school in London, but fell foul of the authorities there; his grandmother Victoria found him in a crumbling flat in Camberwell without bedsheets or even a towel, and took him in. 'It was lovely having Fred,' says Victoria, 'and I think he was quite pleased too; there was always a meal for him. I hadn't got a lot of money left to give him, but I had a viola which I sold. In small ways, I was able to help him a bit. Mary was furious. She didn't find out for some time, and then when she did, if Fred was visiting home and she said awful things, he would take his plate away and sit somewhere else in the room. What's so nice, though, is that when Fred married, I thought I wouldn't see him, but he always comes to visit.' Fred Ingrams, crop-haired, muscly and strapping, lived with his tiny birdlike grandmother for two years. 'She's my best mate – a wonderful lady,' he says.

Fred and Jubby don't see their mother very often these days. 'It looks from the outside like my dad's a baddie,' explains Jubby. 'But his friends know that's not the case.' Victoria was briefly reconciled with her daughter-in-law in 1989, when she skidded into the oncoming carriageway of the M4 in driving rain, and was badly injured. 'When Mary found out she said "Why didn't you tell me?" She wrote to me at once, and got on the telephone asking if she could come round, as if nothing had happened. That went on for a while, then the depression came on again, as it always does.' Victoria Ingrams is an immensely resilient and strong-willed character, the sort to write off her car at the age of eighty-one without a murmur; but just like her son she was utterly incapable of facing Mary down, for fear of creating an undignified, ill-mannered scene.

Fred Ingrams reckons that, ultimately, Arthur's death and the consequent marital troubles made his father a stronger, wiser person. Stronger and wiser perhaps, but also less happy. Mary emerged a weaker, lonelier person, and their marriage was fatally wounded. The idealised image of rural family life which Richard had created about himself now began to dissolve; it became increasingly clear to his colleagues that things were not as they should be. Just as Richard preferred not to discuss his working life at home, so he preferred not to discuss his home life at work: this was not intransigence, merely an understandable desire for privacy in the face of tragedy, combined with the weariness of an easily bored man who has been asked too many stupid questions by colleagues. Secrecy, though, breeds curiosity, and unravelling Ingrams' home life became the main conversational topic of the *Eye* staff. 'You could have lunch with anybody at *Private Eye*,' says Barry Fantoni, 'and at the end of it the conversation would always go back to Ingrams. Even though you'd said you weren't going to do it, you would end up talking about him.'

Attempts to probe the truth were invariably rebuffed. 'It was the one thing you never discussed with Richard,' says Sheila Molnar, 'you just went round pretending you didn't know what was going on.' Willie Rushton unwisely tried the direct approach: 'Ingrams has an ability, when questioned, to switch off like a TV, little white dot disappearing and all. I sat him down in the Coach and said, "Come on, tell me, I'm a mate". I looked up. His eyebrows had narrowed. He was pulling a face which wouldn't have been out of place with the *Jaws* music. An amazing faux pas. I'd crossed the line.' The likes of Foot, Waugh or Osmond would have been privileged to hear the confession. The likes of Rushton and John Wells would not. 'He never confides or confesses. That makes a real gap between him and the others,' complains Wells.[7]

On one occasion, Ingrams agreed to be interrogated by Anthony Clare for his radio programme *In The Psychiatrist's Chair*. Sheila Molnar recalls: 'It was the only time I saw Richard terribly anxious. He was frightened of giving away too much, to the extent that Jane Ellison and I sat in the Coach and Horses and went through a sort of rehearsal with him. And if you listen to that interview, you'll find that Richard gives very little away. He was prepared to publicise the magazine, but he didn't want to reveal himself to the radio audience.' Another interrogator, Lynn Barber, found interviewing Ingrams 'like pushing a stone uphill.'[8] 'I don't think anybody knows him,' concludes cartoonist Bill Tidy. 'Perhaps there's no such person.'

As Fred and Jubby grew up, came into the *Eye* office and chatted openly to their father's colleagues, information about life at Aldworth began to leak through the back door. Stories spread further afield, and the press started to take an interest in the creaking Berkshire idyll. Richard Ingrams became more gossiped about than gossiping. Rather like the Royal family when their younger generation came of age, the Ingrams family mystique withered in the face of speculative and usually inaccurate press stories. Dempster and McKay refused to write about their boss in their respective papers, but one or two others dwelt at length on Richard's marriage. Richard was genuinely shocked; for he had done nothing wrong. Their interest seemed merely prurient, a fact he could not come to terms with.

Richard's devoted secretarial staff began to shield him from other gossip columnists' excesses. 'For years we protected him,' reveals Liz Elliot. 'Soon after I arrived, a piece appeared in a magazine saying that Richard's marriage was in trouble. I was new to the idea of what journalists were like, so I threw it in the wastepaper basket. I mentioned it to Patrick Marnham, and Patrick went berserk: he was into every single wastepaper basket. "Where's that piece? For God's sake, we've got to put it up on the wall!" ' Sheila Molnar remembers that 'when his marriage was going through a really difficult period around 1979, we actually cut out articles from *Boulevard* magazine so he wouldn't see them. And he never questioned why he received magazines with pieces cut out.'

An unkind soul might suggest that Richard Ingrams had been hoist by the petard of his own firmly-held principles, locked into a doomed marriage against all human instinct, not daring to leave lest he appear hypocritical under close journalistic scrutiny; but in fact it was his instincts, as much as his principles, that were keeping him *in situ*. Critics suggested that the *Eye*'s gossip column served merely to offload Ingrams' own unhappiness at his marital problems onto other people; but as far as he was concerned, there was no comparing his treatment at the hands of the press with *Private Eye*'s treatment of others, for the *Eye* confined itself to exposing humbug, which was hardly something he could be accused of. He was thoroughly determined to fight it out and hold his marriage together, and see off his critics in the process.

Ingrams was getting weary. His home life had ceased to provide a respite from the pressures of work, and his work life proved equally unable to furnish a respite from the pressures of home: for no sooner had Goldsmith been vanquished, than another massive, powerful, ruthless enemy came lumbering over the horizon.

20 The Beast from the Swamps

Richard Ingrams believes that the best *Private Eye*s were produced in time of adversity, especially in the late 1970s. Despite his personal troubles, he managed to keep the atmosphere of general office hilarity on the boil; except on those days when depression took over and he couldn't raise himself to orchestrate the jollity. There were new columns, two of them inexplicable to outsiders – a racing column by Jeffrey Bernard and a gardening column by Germaine Greer – and one which was a highly original variant on the Pseud's Corner theme of puncturing pretension. 'Ongoing Situations' was pure Ingrams, attacking the bastardisation of the English language into insecure, jargon-spouting officialese: social workers who claimed that 'Before there is a rape situation, there is nearly always a pre-rape situation', or academics who offered 'drama therapy courses which explore the individual in a verbal and non-verbal context'. One battle which, as a glance at the *Guardian* appointments page will confirm, the *Eye* lost hands down.

The magazine also went through an exceptional period for breaking news stories, naming Sir Anthony Blunt as the fourth man and exposing – thanks to Paul Foot – the case of Colin Wallace, an intelligence officer who had been framed for murder by the security services after threatening to make public the plot against Harold Wilson. Naming Blunt – a rare success for an *Eye* spy story – was a huge gamble, based on the fact that Blunt's lawyer had demanded a pre-publication copy of a new book that detailed the fourth man's activities without actually naming him.

285

Richard Ingrams

'It could have wiped the *Eye* out,' says Sheila Molnar, 'but Richard was very courageous. Everybody in the office, Gillard and so on, said, "This is it, you're going to finish the *Eye*". But he said "No, it has the ring of truth". He really had the courage of his convictions, and we ran with it.' It was revealed that the authorities had known for years that Blunt had spied for Russia, and that he had probably cost the lives of British agents; but Blunt was a knight, and the Surveyor of the Queen's Pictures, so they did nothing to punish him, other than to remove his knighthood.

An even more remarkable achievement was the *Eye*'s role in bringing to trial Jeremy Thorpe, the leader of the Liberal party, on charges of conspiracy to murder and incitement to murder. The story went back as far as 1975: in another case of Ingrams' mental alarm bells sounding the ring of truth, the *Eye* had picked up on a small report in the *West Somerset Free Press* about the murder of a dog on Exmoor. A professional hitman, Andrew Newton, had been arrested after trying to execute a male model called Norman Scott, who was out walking with his Great Dane Rinka. Newton shot the dog as it tried to defend its master, whereupon his gun jammed, enabling Scott to flee and raise the alarm. Scott claimed to the police that he had recently ended a homosexual affair with Jeremy Thorpe, and that certain elements in the Liberal party wanted him dead to avoid the matter being made public.

Auberon Waugh took up the story repeatedly in his *Eye* column, and Ingrams had the idea that Waugh should stand in the next election under the banner of the Dog Lovers' party. His slogan: 'Vote Waugh. A better deal for your dog.' As with the campaign against Sir Alec Douglas-Home, the intention was not to mount a serious electoral challenge – Waugh polled no more than a handful of votes – but to bring the matter to public attention. The implications of the case were very serious indeed, but the national press was refusing to touch it, for fear of offending the homosexual lobby. Says Ingrams: 'Again, it was a case of *Private Eye* opposing the standard humbug of Fleet Street, where you got people like Harold Evans and Anthony Howard thinking it was wrong of *Private Eye* to go after someone on the grounds that

286

it was wrong to go after a homosexual. That wasn't the issue at all.'[1] The *Eye* was not anti-gay, but anti-murder.

Paul Foot was having similar problems at the *Socialist Worker*, where they were unwilling to cover the story, so he investigated the matter for the *Eye*. It transpired that a large donation to the Liberal party by the patriotic businessman 'Union' Jack Hayward had gone mysteriously astray; at the same time, a comparable sum had been paid by persons unknown into the bank account of the hitman Andrew Newton. Newton claimed that senior Liberals had hired him to kill Scott. Harold Wilson's supporters alleged, bizarrely, that the *Eye* story was the work of South African intelligence; but in fact, the source of the *Eye*'s extremely reliable information this time was the police. They believed they had enough evidence to bring Thorpe to trial, but the Director of Public Prosecutions Sir Anthony Hetherington wanted to keep the case out of court. The police used the *Eye* to force Hetherington's hand. Thorpe followed Goldsmith's example and tried to sue Richard Ingrams for criminal libel, but this attempt at legal camouflage failed to deflect growing public interest in the matter. 'By resorting to law people simply draw attention to themselves,' says Ingrams.[2]

Thorpe's trial (and subsequent acquittal) in July 1979 was a celebrated farce. Thorpe, after all, was a prominent Oxford-educated politician whereas Scott was a homosexual and Newton a criminal. The matter of who had really hired a paid assassin to kill a blameless male model, and what had become of Hayward's money, was skated over in a judicial summing-up that instructed the jury not to believe a word that either man had said. The *Eye* published a memorable parody of Mr Justice Cantley's verdict, which Peter Cook performed on stage on behalf of Amnesty International and which was later released as an LP, entitled *Here Comes The Judge*. 'We have been forced to listen to the whinings of Mr Norman St John Scott, a scrounger, a parasite, a pervert, a worm, a self-confessed player of the pink oboe. A man who, by his or her own admission, chews pillows . . . On the evidence of the so-called hitman, Mr Olivia Newton John, I would prefer to draw a discreet veil. He is a piece of slimy refuse, unable to carry out the simplest murder plot . . . You are now to retire, carefully to consider your verdict of not guilty.'

Thorpe celebrated his acquittal with a church service at Bratton Fleming, Devon. As a parting joke, Marnham telephoned the local vicar claiming to represent a London gay rights movement, and informed him that they were sending a coachload of some thirty or forty activists to the service. The vicar stalled desperately, trying to think of liberal-sounding reasons for them not to come. It later transpired that he had wired up a sound relay to the village hall, so that the gay activists could be kept in tune with developments well away from Thorpe and his party.

The Thorpe trial damaged the Liberal party at the 1979 general election, and with the winter of discontent fresh in the electorate's mind Labour were doomed from the outset. The arrival of Margaret Thatcher at No. 10 Downing Street was a godsend for the satirists of *Private Eye*. It led to the creation of what became – in book form – the *Eye*'s most successful item ever: the Dear Bill letters. These were begun by Ingrams, Peter Cook and John Wells, but Cook soon dropped out. 'Richard and John work so perfectly together, I was superfluous,' he says. The letters, supposedly written by Denis Thatcher to his golfing chum Bill Deedes, were a Wodehousian concoction that utilised the strengths of the Ingrams–Wells partnership to best effect. 'When I work with Wells, he's much better at language than me,' explains Ingrams. 'He thought up amazingly lifelike Denis expressions. I provided political direction to the thing, otherwise he'd have just drivelled on about the golf club. I think it did wonders for Denis. Mrs Thatcher used to go round saying "Oh, everybody loves Denis", as if the *Eye* creation was the real thing. In fact the real Denis Thatcher wasn't at all like that, he was a hard-faced businessman.'

John Wells concurs. Working without Ingrams, he turned Dear Bill into *Anyone for Denis?*, a successful TV show and West End stage musical: 'When we were doing the play I got very conflicting remarks back, for example Mrs Thatcher came out of the thing saying "A marvellous farce" to the cameras. Then she said in private afterwards, "What a squalid little play". And similarly, Denis was very critical of the play because he thought it presented him as a bit of an idiot; but according to his friends, he rapidly grew into the role, and regularly offers people a "tincture" or a "snort". It's E.S.P. in a way. Or it may be just P.I.S.S.E.D.'[3] The real Bill Deedes complained to the BBC that although he did indeed play golf with Denis Thatcher and enjoyed 'the odd tincture' with him, 'we don't tell Richard Ingrams or *Private Eye* what we've done, so he must make it up.'[4] It was Deedes whose tenure at the *Telegraph*, coupled with his curious mode of speech, had given rise to the *Eye*'s editorial catchphrase 'shurely shome mishtake?' He described *Anyone For Denis?* as 'dishashtroush'.

If Dear Bill recalled the finest moments of past Ingrams–Wells collaborations, it also dredged up the worst aspects of their rivalry. The stage musical, all Wells's own work, was condemned by Ingrams as 'utterly and totally atrocious', in contrast to the 'excellent' stage version of Mrs Wilson's Diary, which they had written together. 'Wells very kindly insisted that I should take a cut in his play,' added Ingrams, 'and I said that I didn't want any.' Wells snorted back that 'Ingrams does not give credit, he does not like his friends writing plays and he does not want them to succeed.'[5] Rather, he does not like Wells writing plays or succeeding with them.

'Wells and Ingrams are inextricably bound,' explains Candida Lycett Green, 'like Rodgers and Hart, Laurel and Hardy, Gilbert and Sullivan, Morecambe and Wise. Which is bound to create fireworks.' Wells did indeed make a lot of money from *Anyone For Denis?*, since when Ingrams has tended to insist that Wells pay for any lunches they share. Wells is very much in the Dempster category of those-who-must-buy-Ingrams-lunch. There is another category, containing the likes of Fred and Christopher Logue, for whom Richard will always insist on buying lunch himself. 'I'm very fond of old John, though,' admits Ingrams gruffly, through several free mouthfuls.

During the 1970s, Wells had made the mistake of becoming friendly with Princess Margaret, who had taken to leaving messages for 'Jawn' (as she pronounced the word 'John') at *Private Eye*. Ingrams and Rushton had observed them chatting earnestly at a party, and stood barely two feet away, sniggering at Wells. 'I think there was an element of very slight snobbish jealousy there,' opines Wells. 'It suits Ingrams very well to laugh at drawing rooms, but when he's accepted in a drawing room he's as bad as the rest of us. His present gang is Auberon Waugh and my brother-in-law Alexander Chancellor, and the "Lord Snooty and his pals" aspect of their behaviour is really quite irritating after a bit. Still, as a collaborator, it is the most stimulating thing on earth to make him laugh. I really love working with him.'

Wells and Ingrams have since continued to play practical jokes on each other, designed mainly for public amusement, but always incorporating hurtfully accurate digs against the victim's weak points. Ingrams recalls: 'We rang Wells up and offered him a job writing a column on *The Times*, and invited him to lunch at L'Escargot. Wells got very excited, then we all booked a table at L'Escargot too. Wells duly came in and sat down, and he'd brought with him a whole lot of foreign newspapers to impress this guy. It was April Fools Day, and Wells was sitting waiting for this man to come, and eventually I went over and told him it was an April Fool. He took it in quite good part.' When Richard left the *Eye* unattended for a weekend, to visit Venice with A.J.P. Taylor, Wells took his revenge by slipping in a last-minute parody of *Death In Venice*, featuring Taylor as Aschenbach pursuing Ingrams' Tadzio round in a gondola: 'Just one Ingrami, save one for me, Delicious satirist, from Shrovesbury.'

'Richard likes to attack all his contemporaries,' explains Chief Boxwallah David Cash. 'It's not particularly vindictive or vicious. It's just a way of life. He enjoyed stirring things up, friends and enemies alike. But he had a good laugh – I don't think anyone ever fell down in tears.' 'He's been going so long he gets bored,' points out Andrew Osmond. 'He lashes out to keep himself interested.'[6] Of course, it wasn't just a case of Ingrams amusing himself at the expense of the others. By the turn of the 1980s, the jokewriting side of the *Eye* was like several well-worn marriages rolled into one, a group of old friends who managed to combine respect and affection for each other with relentless bickering. 'In fact,' says Ingrams, 'the interesting thing is how people have stayed on at the *Eye* despite the disagreements. Somehow it's all held together in the joke-making department.'

It is probably inevitable that any group of people whose speciality is ridiculing others will in-fight spectacularly, given time; take, for instance, the fractious Pythons, and John Cleese's need to attack the innocuous Terry Jones. Booker, with his constant vein of dissatisfaction, was a natural target for the others. Still full of original ideas, but something of a mystery to the rest of the staff as he glided in and out of the building without chatting to them, his close colleagues considered him irritatingly volatile. For example, he campaigned in the *Spectator* to uncover the truth about the deportation of Cossack prisoners-of-war to Stalin's death camps in 1945, then abruptly swung round and attacked those who had supported his initial stance. Marnham wrote scathingly about 'Mr Commissioner Booker, the man who appointed himself to whitewash Harold Macmillan's role in the deportation of Cossacks . . . do not forget that this same man once had genius and founded *Private Eye.*'[7] Says Ingrams: 'He changed tack in the most odd way, but then he's very easily influenced by the most disastrous people. Right now he's under the influence of Laurens van der Post, and goes to sit at his feet all the time.' The others got their revenge by lampooning van der Post every fortnight in 'Heir of Sorrows', a romantic mini-series about another of van der Post's disciples, the Prince of Wales. Bogus van der Post aphorisms littered the text: 'On top of the stone it is sunny, but there is always shade underneath' and other such wise words. 'I like old Booker,' says Ingrams, 'but I wouldn't regard him as a friend.'

Booker and Fantoni's joint religious conversion had now been supplanted by a new fad, as their unlikely alliance embraced philosophy instead. Jung was a particular favourite. 'It was just a religious substitute,' scoffs Ingrams, 'where they sat around analysing their behaviour and everyone else's behaviour.' This was not to say that Booker and Fantoni actually got on with each other. 'All the *Eye* people were frightfully spiteful to Barry, especially the Deacon,' says Barry's wife Tessa. 'He was our best man. You don't expect your best man to behave so badly. I would

sail in to protect Barry. Booker hated him acquiring knowledge.'
The latest in Booker's long line of wives was an Irish Protestant,
which brought his views into conflict with Ingrams' Anglo-Catholic
stance. 'Their entire views on Northern Ireland could almost be
seen through their wives' eyes,' sniffs Fantoni.

Booker used the *Spectator* to attack Ingrams once again,
when the *Eye* published Richard West's book of war dispatches,
Victory In Vietnam. The book included a description of the death
of Peter Duval Smith, a British journalist. His orphan daughter
was being looked after by David Leitch of the *Sunday Times*, who
unsuccessfully took out an injunction against the book to protect
her from reading it. The *Eye* pursued Leitch for costs. Booker
threw his weight behind the Leitch camp, for the best of reasons,
one would like to think. Wells had no time for Booker, describing
him as 'demented'. 'Booker is a bad influence on Ingrams,' he
insisted. 'All that unbalanced sentimental Mary Whitehousery.
And he shares with Waugh a peculiar kind of viciousness, more
sadistic than satirical.'[8] Waugh, of course, had no time for Wells
either.

Then of course there was Fantoni's spat with Wells. 'John
Wells wrote something called *Lionel: The Musical*, which was
about cockney Jews. He dragged me in, with a week to open, to
write the authentic dialect. I wrote every single word that was
spoken on stage. And we went to the first night, and I looked in
the programme, and I got a credit underneath Laundry.' *Lionel:
The Musical* was a huge flop, as Fantoni gleefully relates. Sometimes, however, Wells and Fantoni would find themselves thrown
together in alliance, against the Shrewsbury old boys: 'During the
joke sessions they would keep coming up with these fragments of
Shakespeare or Wordsworth or whatever,' says Fantoni, irritated.
'Shrewsbury is a tremendously snobbish school,' objects Wells. 'If
there are two of the Shrewsbury mafia in Greek Street, no one
else gets listened to.'[9]

One bright spot against all this bickering was that Richard
had managed to forge as close a relationship with Liz Elliot as
he had with his previous secretary, Tessa. 'I was very devoted
to Richard,' confesses Liz. 'I was extremely fond of him, and I'd
292

have done anything for him.' 'We all thought he loved Liz,' chips in Sheila Molnar. 'Not sexually, of course.' Liz took over the dual role of dealing with Richard's wife and looking after his wardrobe. 'I used to take his jacket to the dry cleaner's without him knowing. I'd say, "What's the fastest time you can do this in – can it be done really quickly?" Richard may not have noticed by the time it came back, but as least it didn't stand up on its own.' Maggie Lunn, who succeeded Liz some years later, observes: 'Liz was madly in love with him. I think he probably was with her. He does have these great loves with people, but nothing ever happens.' Says Liz: 'I was always thinking, what's going on behind those eyes? What does he think? Am I talking absolute nonsense? He did need a woman who could chatter on without taking any notice of him quietly sitting there.'

Against the background of all the office in-fighting, Patrick Marnham was commissioned to write the official history of *Private Eye*, for the magazine's twenty-first anniversary. He did quite a good job, especially on the early years, but of course nobody liked it, mainly because he had decided to leave and so gave the impression that the *Eye* was on its last legs. 'Marnham's book had an odd tone,' says Peter McKay. 'Not just neutral, but almost hostile; which was surprising for an official history.' Ingrams was deluged with staff complaints about the first draft and forced Marnham to listen to them. 'Marnham has no grasp on reality,' says Fantoni. Booker wrote in the *Spectator* that: 'The nicest thing one can say about his book is that it is at least a good deal better than the earlier draft.' Ingrams says exasperatedly, 'I tried to get Marnham to knock the book into shape but he got bored with it and he wouldn't.' Marnham refused to go on a publicity tour. Ingrams refused to pay Marnham's wages. Marnham walked out. Marnham complained about Ingrams to BBC Radio 4: 'If he's made a serious mistake, and it's perfectly obvious to everyone, he just will not change, he just becomes completely obstinate.' It was all getting rather messy. The *Eye* was beginning to bear less and less resemblance to the gang of Oxford students who had once gathered in a field near Aynhoe to drink wine and celebrate their friendship.

Amongst the reviews of Marnham's book, one, in the *Listener*, stood out: 'Does it really make a valuable contribution to our society to destroy both in our own eyes and in those of the world at large our major national asset of incorruptibility in public life – to replace it with a belief that the instincts of the piggery motivate our successful entrepreneurs?'[10] The author of this article, which accused the magazine of 'queer-bashing' and 'Jew-baiting', was none other than Robert Maxwell. Maxwell was an old enemy of the *Eye*: as a Labour MP he had urged his government not to come to the aid of the Czechs during the Russian invasion of their country, and the *Eye* had retaliated by calling him 'human filth'. It later transpired that Maxwell, who himself hailed from Czechoslovakia (his real name was Jan Hoch), had signed an agreement in 1947 to assist the KGB.

Maxwell had also founded the 'I'm Backing Britain' campaign of the 1960s, which had been laughed at in the *Eye*. Ingrams and Wells had been invited to take part in a television debate with him: Maxwell had delivered a long and moving speech about what it meant to be British, while Wells made accompanying violin noises. Ingrams had objected: 'But you're not even English – your name's not Maxwell, it's Hoch.' 'You were born English, I chose to be English,' retorted Maxwell to a round of applause. The BBC received a number of letters complaining that these jumped-up public schoolboys had been allowed airtime to insult such a great man.

In 1969, the directors of Rothschild's went over the accounts of Pergamon, Maxwell's company, with a view to a possible purchase by one of their clients. What they discovered horrified them. One of them, Rodney Leach, wrote: 'There came to my offices a stream of letters, voices and visitors telling nightmarish tales of betrayal, fraud and violence. Among the visitors was a nameless man with illustrious connections who asked me if Pergamon's structure lent itself to the laundering of KGB funds. I felt he knew the answer to his own question . . . We pulled out when we found the true state of Maxwell's company accounts. I shall never forget the moment that it dawned on us exactly how he was cooking the books – by creating bogus sales to his own private companies.'[11]

The matter was referred to the Department of Trade, who after a long investigation reported back that Robert Maxwell was unfit for the stewardship of a public company. It was now up to the DPP's office to prosecute; and as so often in the history of that dishonourable institution, no action whatsoever was taken. The greatest thief in history was free to continue his villainous career.

Over the following decade, the *Eye* frequently brought up the Department of Trade's report, as it repeatedly castigated Maxwell for his excesses. In particular, there was the publication of his 'World Leader' series of biographies, clearly paid for by the Eastern bloc, which praised the Romanian psychopath Nicolae Ceaucescu for his 'constant, tireless activity for the good of his country', and credited the Bulgarian mass-murderer Todor Zhivkov with building 'a prosperous and happy nation'. Then there was the 1981 industrial dispute at Pergamon, when Maxwell – avowedly a socialist – refused to negotiate a wage settlement for two years, then sacked his workers as soon as they went on strike. Maxwell responded to each and every criticism with a shower of writs.

The crunch came in the early 1980s, when Maxwell revealed his ambitions to become a press baron. His attempts to buy *The Times* and the *Observer* were rebuffed on account of his dubious history, as highlighted in *Private Eye*. When he finally succeeded in buying the *Mirror*, he was rewarded not with the respect he craved, but with a regular John Kent cartoon, 'Cap'n Bob', showing the *Mirror* as a galleon on the point of disappearing beneath the waves. Maxwell was determined on revenge.

Ingrams reflects: 'Having seen Goldsmith off, another hideous beast emerged from the swamps – probably even more hideous than Goldsmith – in the shape of Robert Maxwell.' The comparison was in part a valid one. Like Goldsmith, Maxwell was an *ersatz* English gentleman, with political ambitions and a desire to own a newspaper; like Goldsmith, he made the mistake of seeing Ingrams in commercial terms, as a smaller business rival to be defeated financially; and like Goldsmith, Maxwell resolved to destroy the magazine. '*Private Eye*,' he threatened, 'is a satirical magazine whose proprietor Mr Ingram (*sic*) is in the habit of going after innocent people. I am one of those. But he

295

knows if he steps out of line (here he thumped the table top) he'll be swatted like a fly.'[12]

The *Eye* had been running a series of photo lookalikes on its letters page, a device common to many magazines; some of them, provided by the *Eye*'s own staff, were credited to a fictitious 'Mrs Ena Maxwell'. One, for instance, observed a facial resemblance between Adolf Eichmann and the Duke of Edinburgh. Another drew a comparison between Maxwell himself and Ronnie Kray. Maxwell consulted his lawyers. Then the *Eye* published a news item, given to them by a senior Labour Party source, suggesting that Maxwell was bankrolling Neil Kinnock's international tours in the hope of a peerage. An accompanying cartoon showed Kinnock as the His Master's Voice dog, sat by a large horn gramophone bearing Maxwell's face. Once again, the full majesty of the law (which had so completely failed to do anything about Maxwell's criminal activities fifteen years before) bore down on *Private Eye*.

The *Eye* was on a hiding to nothing, because the Labour party source did not wish to go anywhere near court. The involvement of Peter Jay, who had recently been taken on as Maxwell's lackey-cum-secretary, further exacerbated the situation: 'Jay would ring me up, a personal friend, and say things like "Mr Maxwell has to have an answer by three o'clock this afternoon",' complains Ingrams. 'We went to court unwisely, on the principle that we weren't going to let such people beat us.'

It was not until 1986 that the case finally came before a judge. Maxwell, who was Jewish, played the anti-semitism card with histrionic skill. He held up the Eichmann–Prince Philip lookalike and started to weep. According to the following day's *Daily Mirror*, which under the editorship of Mike Molloy had swiftly become little more than a Maxwell fan club newsletter: 'Maxwell shook with emotion and banged his hands on the witness box as he said, "My family was destroyed by Eichmann" . . . It was several minutes before he composed himself, wiped his eyes and took a sip of the glass of water handed to him. He then turned to the Judge and said, "I'm sorry".' The headline read: 'Maxwell weeps over family massacre – publisher's fury at *Eye*'s fake letter.' Ingrams recalls: 'It was one of those extraordinary incidents, and nobody knew how to react to it. Some people thought it was funny, some people thought he was putting it on, and in a British court of law they all sat in solemn silence while he fished out his handkerchief and mopped his eyes.'

Worse was to come, as Maxwell turned to his own lookalike, the one that compared him with Ronnie Kray. Even the judge noticed that in the place of the usual 'Are they related?' caption, it was enquired, 'Have they anything else in common?' Said Maxwell: 'Mrs Maxwell and all of our children were utterly shocked to have me, their father, compared to a convicted major gangster.' (Not half as shocked as the day the Fraud Squad turned up to arrest one of the children at 6 a.m., I'll bet.) Ingrams tried to bring up Maxwell's criminal past and the Department of Trade enquiry, 'whereupon all the lawyers jumped up and said "This is most improper, we can't possibly have this referred to". It was a very good example of how, when anything comes to court, what you and I might think are the most important things cannot be mentioned.' The *Eye* lost, heavily, to the tune of almost a third of a million pounds. It was their biggest-ever defeat, and only the hugely increased sales of the Thatcher years saved their financial bacon.

Maxwell followed up his victory with two publications: *Not Private Eye*, a parody of the magazine, and *Malice In Wonderland*, a 200,000-word account of the trial (designed to look like Marnham's book, *The Private Eye Story*) which had taken just eighteen days to write and publish. Again, the anti-semitism card was played with relish: *Not Private Eye* featured large pictures of Nazi leaders conversing, doctored to include Ingrams chatting with Hitler. *Malice In Wonderland* was effectively a eulogy of Maxwell: it even included a gratuitous list of his recent business achievements. The illustrations, depicting all the celebrities who had successfully sued the *Eye* ('a shortened version of *Who's Who*,' exulted Maxwell), seemed somewhat extraneous at first, until one saw them as a *tableau vivant*, the backcloth of the great man's triumph, all redeemed by their saviour from their 'genuine fear' of Ingrams and the *Eye*. Its only value was as a distressing

297

insight into the courtroom world where reality, common sense and humour are left behind, to be replaced by paper-thin sensibilities, hyperbolic outrage and lachrymose manipulation of twelve good men and stupid.

The book's explanation of the *Eye*'s previous successes in bringing down villains was that 'if you fire buckshot at a football crowd, you are bound to hit a hooligan or two.' Especially a twenty-stone hooligan who's just bought the club in order to asset-strip it, one might reply. Any of the ordinary supporters of Derby County or Oxford United, the football clubs that Maxwell tried to fleece during the 1980s, could have told the authors at length just what sort of person Maxwell was. For the supposedly intelligent men who surrounded Maxwell without questioning his methods, who allowed him to take the banks for over £1 billion and to rob his own employees' pension funds of several hundred millions, there can be no excuse. As Rodney Leach of Rothschild's wrote in the *Spectator*: 'Some who closed their eyes or acquiesced in terror, will never be able to explain . . . how they came to sign this or that document. Others, who had nothing to fear but who lent their names to Maxwell, will have to choose between looking like fools or knaves. They will choose foolishness.'[13] *Mirror* editor Mike Molloy claimed that, in trusting Maxwell, he had made 'the biggest mistake of my career.'[14] The authors of *Malice In Wonderland* were John Jackson, Joe Haines and Peter Donnelly, with cartoons by Charles Griffin and David Langdon. They have yet to declare for knavery or foolishness.

Richard never forgave Peter Jay for acting as Maxwell's flunkey. 'I find it hard to stomach,' he said, 'and I feel we haven't much in common any more.'[15] Another great regret was that Paul Foot had also written for the *Daily Mirror* during Maxwell's reign. 'I did work there, but everyone knew I was against Maxwell,' explains Foot unconvincingly. 'I was in an equivocal position, but I did attack him in the Union.' Foot is kidding himself if he thinks that Ingrams forgave him because he retained his independence of mind. Ingrams was deeply saddened by Foot's presence in the camp of such a grotesque and unpleasant enemy, but loved his friend too much to let him go.

Sometimes Richard Ingrams misses Maxwell: 'Captain Bob was just a comic figure. One mourns his departure.'[16] When the great villain finally tumbled from his yacht and died, he was embarking on another legal operation against *Private Eye*, to counter the shocking allegation that he had been meddling in the *Mirror* pension funds. He would almost certainly have won. Ingrams reflects: 'It's funny, I think that the Law Courts are made to look like a cathedral, outside and inside, but I always think of them as being a great casino. I remember Bron [Auberon Waugh] saying that even a simple act such as eating a sausage could be made very sinister in a court of law.'[17]

Throughout the early 1980s, Maxwell's lawsuits and many other libel cases were taking up an increasing amount of Ingrams' time: 'I got more and more drawn into meetings. Obviously these libel actions involving large sums of money were very important, but I found it more and more difficult to concentrate on them. I always got very annoyed because you would spend an afternoon sitting in a lawyer's office, when you could actually be writing jokes.' All newspapers receive large numbers of libel writs, but by 1982 the *Eye* had received over 2000 of them, and the number was rising faster and faster all the time. The magazine's editorial policy had not changed, but the well-publicised boom in sales had drawn people's attention to the fact that *Private Eye* was now rich. Everyone wanted a slice of the pie. Most of the litigants were beaten back or held off with a (usually bogus and insincere) apology, but any that got through to court knew that it was virtually impossible to lose, such was the judicial contempt for *Private Eye*.

Most of those suing the magazine were journalists, a tradition that went back to the now extremely right-wing commentator Paul Johnson's winning a substantial sum when the *Eye* had suggested that his adulation for Harold Wilson might be temporary and insincere. 'It's partly because journalists are naturally mean and grasping,' explains Auberon Waugh, 'but also because they're the only people in the country who realise how the libel law works, how the plaintiff very nearly always wins.' Ian Hislop agrees: 'Journalists who produce bollocks themselves, inaccurate

299

features and mind-blowingly biased drivel, then get very pompous about others' work. Or TV people – Esther loses eight billion quid when she's working for the Beeb, then *we* have to pay *her*. The fact that the *Eye* has mostly been sued by journalists shows what a shitty profession journalism is. When I took over the editorship I was described by Nigel Dempster as "not a journalist". I took that as a compliment.'

Besieged on all sides by litigation, Richard Ingrams was getting too depressed to go on. Auberon Waugh thought he'd lost his bottle: 'I had this really big libel action coming up with Clare Tomalin, and I did an awful lot of work on it, and he promised he'd go through with it. And then he ratted.' Ingrams dreamed of mad schemes, whereby 'a whole mass of people gang together and start suing each other, just to flood the courts.' Except that the lawyers would still have won, for they hold a monopoly and can charge what they wish; they wouldn't have cared who was in court saying what, as long as their fees were sufficient.

One day, relates Ian Hislop, 'Ingrams said he had been looking out of the window during a very long lawyers' meeting, and they were describing some libel case that was coming up, and they were talking about Silvester.' This was Chris Silvester, a new recruit to the *Eye*. 'And he thought to himself, "I don't give a fuck about Silvester, I don't give a fuck about the story, I don't give a fuck about this room, I've got to stop doing this. When you don't care any more, you can't do it any more".'

It was time to jack it all in.

21 Hislop

When Richard Ingrams first encountered Ian Hislop in 1980, it is unlikely he realised that he was talking to his eventual successor. Yet he had spoken to various journalists of the need to bring new blood into the *Eye*, the reference had been spotted by Hislop's mother, and she had pointed it out to her son. Peter Cook had recommended Hislop to Ingrams as a promising young man worth meeting. On both sides, perhaps, there was a faint glimmer of optimism. Hislop was an Oxford student, who was convivial, funny, pugnacious and confident, sporting a characteristic quiff that would soon desert him. Unlike his fellow undergraduates, many of whom had been reading *Private Eye* since childhood, Hislop had lived much of his life overseas, and had been brought up on airmail copies of Alan Coren's *Punch*. Unlike some of his friends, who tried to combine writing comedy sketches with journalistic investigations into the doings of Nazi choirmasters, thereby attempting to emulate *Private Eye*, Hislop was an out-and-out comedy animal. He was the editor of *Passing Wind*, the best humour magazine in Oxford, which he wrote with his cartoonist friend Nick Newman – through whom he discovered the existence of *Private Eye*.

Hislop set out to interview his comedy heroes, among them the editors of various national humour magazines, which was by no means a stupid idea for a talented young jokewriter in search of employment. 'I interviewed Coren and he was so *serious*,' remembers Hislop, 'talking about S.J. Perelman and humorous traditions, and I'd just wanted him to be funny. Then I interviewed

Cook. We got completely pissed at lunchtime, and got thrown out of this restaurant at about 3.30. He said, "I think you should go home and sober up, and come back and do the interview at six." ' That evening they repeated the process. Staggering down the white line in the middle of the road, it had occurred to Cook that Hislop showed promise.

After Cook came Ingrams. 'He really made me laugh. I tried to make him laugh too, because when you're that young you're very arrogant. "You think you guys are funny? Hey – we're students, and we're *really* funny". And of course we weren't. But Richard laughed politely, and asked me to send him the mag. Apparently the evidence in print was strong enough to get some sort of interest up.' By entertaining Ingrams, he had managed to clear an important hurdle.

Hislop contributed occasional pieces to the *Eye* during his final year. The first to be accepted was a list of bestsellers in the wake of John Lennon's death: ' "The AA Book of John Lennon", "John Lennon's Yorkshire", that sort of thing. Then I started coming up on the train once a fortnight and doing an hour with Richard. I was getting £30 a time and felt very flush – I just didn't think you could be paid that sort of money for doing jokes. I didn't tell anyone.' The piece that really caught everyone's eye was a *Room Of My Own* parody about Bobby Sands, the IRA hunger striker whose idea of thoughtful political protest was to smear his cell walls with excrement: 'He has chosen a simple pastel brown to decorate all four walls. "I think the effect is very soothing," he says, "and it sets off the subdued grey of my blanket. It cost me next to nothing".'

Hislop had caught the *Eye* style quickly, but Ingrams held him at arm's length for a long while. Even when he left university a year later, he had to teach English and work part-time in a bar, to supplement the dribs and drabs he received from *Private Eye*. Ingrams was testing his loyalty, but Hislop was acute enough to realise that he was being tested. He was also being introduced very, very slowly indeed, for fear that he would be rejected like a transplanted organ by the *Eye*'s jealous jokewriters. In the 1970s Ingrams had diffidently tried to introduce a writer, when

Miles Kington had come in and penned a few desultory pieces. Kington had been instantly spotted for a cuckoo by the others in the nest.

Hislop was certainly not intended to be the vanguard of a new generation. The *Eye*'s jokewriters had formed a closed masonic society for twenty years because they preferred it that way. Friends, whatever their differences, write better together. In any case, Ingrams would soon have realised that Hislop was a professional loner, who kept his cards close to his chest. The only man to come into the magazine with Hislop – indeed the only man who even knew the destination of his mysterious trips from Oxford – was Nick Newman. Hislop's was a discreet introduction because, although the others hadn't spotted it, he was being groomed to take over.

At first sight, Hislop bears closer resemblance to Coren than to Ingrams. Putting aside any physical similarities, both are convivial, volubly witty, confidently expansive and straightforwardly middle class; by contrast, Ingrams' well-bred restraint appears to belong to a different world and a different time. Underneath these superficial differences, though, Hislop and Ingrams are bound closely, by shared circumstances and attitudes that cannot be entirely ascribed to having held the same job. From the first, Ingrams recognised echoes of *Parson's Pleasure* in *Passing Wind*, its size, shape and feel, its attitude, its independence. The more he discovered about Hislop, the more he realised that he had found a successor who would not merely keep the standard of jokes up, but would also employ them according to similar principles.

Both men approach their work from a moral perspective. 'It's one of the things I admire about him,' admits Hislop, 'one of the things that makes him different. The same would be true of Booker. It's a sort of moral involvement – which sounds absurd when you are doing jokes – in the essence of what you're doing, that you're doing it because in some small way it matters. There's this idea that the *Eye* attacks everything. It doesn't. It tries to find the things that are worthy of attack.' In Hislop, as it does in Ingrams, this attitude finds a natural corollary in his own personal behaviour. Although it's not a fact that he appreciates

303

being reminded of, you can guarantee that Hislop will never be found 'with my hand in the till or my leg over my secretary,' as he once put it.[1]

Both men have a strong sense of injustice, a dislike of pomposity and a hatred of hypocrisy and double standards. 'With Ingrams it's a sort of stoic anger, never displayed, whereas with Hislop it's naked aggression,' observes Barry Fantoni. 'Hislop was born in the year of the Rat, by the way. All Rats have got an aggressive undercurrent.' According to Fred Ingrams, 'Both of them see things in black and white. I wouldn't be surprised to hear if Ian was religious, too.' In fact Hislop is religious, at least by today's standards. He likes to play it down, but he is broadly Godfearing in the Ingrams sense of being happy with attacks on the Church, but unable to accept attacks on the Deity.

Both men lost their fathers at an early age, and both jealously guard their family privacy. 'Ian is almost paranoid about his home address and phone number,' claims sometime *Eye* journalist Christopher Silvester. 'Richard would be wearily unsurprised if a diary journalist got hold of his home number. If it happened to Ian, there'd be an inquisition. It's bad enough if I ring him socially at home. Ringing him at home on a business matter is almost a sin.'

Then, of course, both men are great comic writers, and natural comic editors. If there is a difference of approach, it is that Hislop is more conventionally left-of-centre. 'Richard won't hold back on what is perceived to be correct,' says Hislop. 'If there's a big consensus that you shouldn't do jokes about X, it's probably wrong – that's the Ingrams instinct. I agree in as far as, if something makes you roar with laughter, it's usually because there's some point to the joke. That's the whole point of this sort of comedy, making a point *through* the joke.' Within these constraints, Hislop shares the Ingrams sense of mischief; 'and in a way that's morally defensible in itself, because it stirs up complacency.'

For the first time in his professional life, Ingrams had taken the part of elderly paternal role model, of the kind he himself had so often looked up to. Hislop stayed very close to his editor's

side as Ingrams piloted him through the dangerous waters of
Private Eye, through the decorative, harmless goldfish of the
front desk, exchanging pleasantries, past the lurking piranhas of
the newsdesk, saying nothing, to a safe berth among the bigger
fish of the satire department. Unfortunately for Hislop, Ingrams
was about to give the pool one of its periodic stirs. The piranha
quotient was about to be increased.

At around the time that Ian Hislop was making his discreet
trips to Oxford station to board the London train, a mini-drama
was being played out elsewhere in the city. It would end with
Ingrams introducing to *Private Eye* a new journalist, beside whom
McKay and Dempster would seem to the old guard as sweet little
spring lambs. The story began when Wilfred de'Ath, who had
beaten Jack Duncan to the BBC job all those years ago, fetched
up in Oxford after a largely undistinguished broadcasting career.
He announced himself, by way of a classified advertisement, as
Private Eye's man in Oxford, and on the lookout for stories. Pretty
soon he got one, when someone suggested to the *Eye* that Canon
David Burgess, the Domestic Bursar at University College, was
a member of the Vile Bodies, a society pledged to re-creating the
debauched excesses of the 1920s. De'Ath furnished the magazine
with a piece accusing Burgess of all kinds of misdemeanours, for
which he had no evidence of any kind. Publication of the story was
an utter disaster: numerous Oxford dignitaries rallied to Burgess'
defence, and Burgess' solicitor – the *Eye*'s old enemy Lord Goodman – even sued the magazine himself. Ingrams was forced into a
humiliating climbdown, and de'Ath vanished into the attentions of
Her Majesty's constabulary. He was later prosecuted in a fraud
case, incidentally, by Clive Anderson.

Enter Paul Halloran. Halloran was a New Zealand journalist
living in Oxford, who volunteered to try and repair the damage
for Ingrams. He did not conform to any genteel, dated Kiwi ste-
reotype. He was burly, terse, unfriendly, suspicious, he rarely
used a four-letter word when seven would do, and he had no time
for the niceties of manners and etiquette. In short, he appealed
to Ingrams' sense of theatre. Referring to another figure in the
tale other than Canon Burgess, he assured Ingrams, 'You don't

have to worry at all – this bloke's a piss-artist and a shirt-lifter.'
Ingrams couldn't wait to present him to Wells, Booker and the
rest, and to watch the look of horror on their faces.

Halloran toured Oxford, digging up the university world. He
visited *Cherwell*, the student newspaper, in search of an occasional staffer whose name he had been given by a contact on
the *Telegraph*. She would not be in the office until the weekend,
he was told. The *Cherwell* staff watched astonished, as Halloran,
refusing on principle to believe what he had been told, spent the
entire day hunched silently in the corner of the office, waiting
fruitlessly, regarding all comers with a beady, suspicious eye.
Eventually, some days later, he completed his damage limitation
exercise. 'I must have achieved something,' he growls, ''cos for
all the huff and puff Burgess settled for an apology and two grand
in damages.'

Halloran swiftly moved on to the *Eye* offices in Greek Street.
According to Jane Ellison, who arrived shortly afterwards, 'Halloran was completely illiterate. He couldn't spell anything. His
copy! You couldn't believe that anyone calling themselves a journalist could have done it. No one could believe this creature was
sitting there in the office. One of the things Richard used to do,
which gave him great amusement, was to mimic people's disgust
at Halloran. When people came in – often quite civilised people
– Halloran would shout and swear at them, and Richard would
spend days afterwards mimicking their horror and outrage. He
loved that. At the *Eye* lunches, Halloran used to get drunk and
abusive, and Richard just sat their spectating.' When women
passed his doorway, Halloran was liable to shout 'Come here
darling, would you like to sit on my dick?' The old guard were
horrified. One of them said: 'None of us could understand why
Richard brought in Halloran, he absolutely ruined the *Eye*. There
was no confidentiality any more. Before that, there had been a
real bond between us all.'

Ingrams further attempted to torment his staff in a social
setting, by inviting Halloran – indirectly – to the Aldworth cricket
match. 'He would say to me, "Halloran – the cricket match is on
such and such a day, and I'd regard it as particularly offensive and
306

appalling if you were to turn up. This is where it is – it's at one thirty. I'd be grateful if you'd avoid the area". Of course, that was his way of telling me to turn up. If he didn't want to invite you, you'd hear nothing. I'd say, "Where I come from, only poofs play cricket".'

'Halloran is a rough diamond indeed,' grins Ingrams. 'I always remember a wonderful interview on a Peter Sellers record, where Sellers was playing the part of a buffoon aristocrat who'd opened his country mansion to the public. Anyway, he was being interviewed for the BBC, and whenever he was asked a question, there was a man who would say, "Don't answer that, my Lord. Don't answer that one." And in the end the interviewer said, "My Lord, could you tell me who this man is, who keeps interrupting?", and Sellers said, "One must have such a man". Halloran is such a man. He has done sterling work. I was very impressed when he managed to get the *Eye* offices occupied by the members of a religious cult. Waugh had to come down to them and claim that the article had been written by Wilfred de'Ath, and they traipsed off to find him. Halloran is a sort of rottweiler character, who's extremely useful.' Halloran barks back: 'I'm happy to accept the comparison with a dog in terms of temperament, if Ingrams is happy to accept the comparison of a rottweiler in terms of his looks.'[2]

Halloran, of course, came up with a number of good stories, which he is not slow to claim the credit for: 'We had some outstanding successes – Canary Wharf, Mark Thatcher. The papers used to knock the stories off, but didn't give us any credit for them. In one month six of my *Eye* stories were in the national press as exclusives. Not one bloody word said "First in *Private Eye*". Fuck 'em. Who was telling everyone about Wafic Said (the "businessman") and Mark Thatcher? *Private Eye*. Then it was splashed all over the *Independent*. Bollocks!' What's more, most of the stories cost the *Eye* nothing. 'I don't pay people,' says Halloran. 'I take the view that if you come to me with a story, your reward is having the story told.' The older, more genteel days of journalists like Patrick Marnham and Richard West had come to an end. 'People like West, Marnham and Jeffrey Bernard wrote the most appalling copy,' snorts Halloran. 'The number of writs was becoming unsustainable. Christ knows how many stories Ingrams gave to me and said, "This has come from X, it's probably bullshit, can you check it?" '

Of course, there were also a number of stories that Halloran fed straight to the national press – or so Ingrams believes. Certainly, the New Zealander moves in a devious way. It was Halloran, for instance, who – for whatever reason – effected the first meeting between David Mellor and Antonia de Sancha, whom he sometimes introduced to people, with his tongue in his cheek, as 'my niece'. Aware of this independent activity, Ingrams was keen that his new recruit should not become complacent in his new role. Maggie Lunn, who took over from Liz Elliot, recalls: 'Halloran was always hanging on by a gossamer thread, as McKay called it. Richard and Peter had this joke. Whenever Peter was bitchy about Ian Hislop, Richard used to come in and say "Gossamer thread, McKay". Well, Halloran was *always* on a gossamer thread, because he's the most enormous stirrer.' Given the fierce bulk of Halloran, a gossamer ship's hawser would have been more appropriate.

Underneath the uncouth exterior, Halloran had the vital mischievous streak that appealed to Ingrams. When the *Eye* held a twenty-first anniversary ball, for instance, he sent out bogus invitations to a number of highly inappropriate Tory dignitaries. He enjoyed his shock effect on people as much as his editor did. Interviewed by the BBC about Ingrams' views, he explained delicately: 'I personally had considerable distaste for them, but you know a job is a job. Ingrams had this tremendous antipathy towards homosexuals, whom he thought were unwashed, and to drug addicts, whom he thought should all be shot. As to AIDS, he described it as God's judgement on the homosexualists, and anyone darker than a Portuguese he described as sub-human, or the yellow peril. He thought that Hitler was a good chap and believed that Mother Teresa was a man. All of these things I was required in my capacity as a rather junior journalist in this organisation to address myself to. It's to my eternal shame that I did not stand up for my rights and call the NUJ. I mean, I'm one of the more misunderstood people around here . . .'

In 1982, Paul Halloran went on a short holiday, and returned to find that he had a new colleague. Jane Ellison was a sharp-tongued, intelligent, attractive blonde from the north of England, who had found herself sitting in pole position next to Ingrams at an *Eye* lunch. On the point of leaving the *Evening Standard*, she was invited by Ingrams to deputise for Halloran, and stayed on when he came back. She was put in charge of 'Street of Shame', the *Eye*'s Fleet Street column, and handled much of the Desmond Wilcox and Esther Rantzen material. 'She was very mischievous and satirical,' says Ingrams with admiration, 'the only good woman journalist we had at *Private Eye*. She also wrote a brilliant novel, called *A Fine Excess*.'

Like Halloran, Jane Ellison didn't fit into any of the established *Eye* groupings: the McKay–Dempster journalistic axis had coalesced too firmly to accept newcomers. Sharing an office, Ellison and Halloran quickly forged a friendship. 'I liked Halloran,' she says, 'because the *Eye* was very cliquey and Halloran wasn't part of any clique. Most people regarded him as revolting, but I was very fond of him. I liked him because underneath it all, Halloran had much more humanity about him than many people there.'

Like Peter McKay and Nigel Dempster, neither Ellison nor Halloran cared much for Ian Hislop. The new boy seemed uninterested in their brand of journalism, nor in them. He knew that real power at the *Eye* lay with Ingrams, and that his clearest path to the top lay above the mire of office politics. The journalists looked down on him, and he looked straight through them. Says Maggie Lunn: 'Jane didn't like Ian. Ian never set out to win her over. He is very good at targeting influential people. He makes it terribly obvious. There are some people he will bother with, some he won't. Jane was one of the ones he decided not to bother with, so trouble began to brew.' Halloran would sit in their joint office, making jokes about Ian's feet not touching the ground when he sat in Richard's chair. 'Ian didn't care for that at all,' says Jane, with a trace of satisfaction.

'I think Hislop was obviously groomed – he was obviously grooming *himself* – right from the start,' she adds. 'He was

309

very determined and ambitious. He certainly played the role of novice to Richard straight from the start. I never ever heard Hislop disagree with Richard – he was like a foil, he never had his own opinions. He was also very clever. He never got drunk, or confided in anybody. He was pleasant enough, but shrewd. Richard was always very protective towards Ian. We all had a humorously abusive way of talking – it was just an act. Halloran would shout at Richard, and he would shout back. A lot of quite savage joking went on, but Richard never tolerated it against Hislop. Hislop was sacrosanct. That's why I got into bad odour. I remember Richard saying to me that "Hislop isn't like us, he can't take it". I always remember him saying that.' Richard was protecting Ian, not just because he thought he was personally vulnerable, but because he embodied the future. He needn't have bothered. Beneath the genial façade, Hislop was as hard as any coterie of hacks, and as capable as Ingrams of remembering a slight.

Later that year, Peter McKay, who was by now working for the *Daily Mail*, found himself suddenly posted to America. This time, Ian Hislop himself had a hand in selecting some new blood. An acquaintance of his, Christopher Silvester, had been working at Conservative Central Office in the run-up to the 1983 election. Following Mrs Thatcher's victory, Silvester was taken on to write 'The New Boys', a series of profiles of the new intake of (largely Conservative) MPs. He was the grandson of danceband leader Victor Silvester, and spiritually belonged to an era of slicked-back hair and pencil moustaches. He was a ladies' man, a flatterer and a lounge lizard by nature, who often affected a bow tie, natty waistcoat and spats to offset his inappropriately bouffant blond hair. Alongside his *Eye* work, he attempted to launch a parallel career as a nightclub crooner of 1940s *chansons*, an experiment that was drowned at birth by the enthusiastic boos and catcalls of his new colleagues. He also had a rather unjustified reputation for extracting advances from unsuspecting publishers, for books that never seemed to see the light of day. Silvester quickly became known as 'The Spiv'.

Jubby Ingrams was excited to discover that a new young man

had arrived at the *Eye*. 'Shortly after I joined the magazine,' says
Silvester, 'I was in a little cubby hole at 34 Greek Street, when
I heard a girl's voice coming up the stairs saying, "Where is he,
where is he?" I saw this rather attractive but extremely young
girl of about eighteen, slightly awkward but still ebullient. I went
out on a date with her and Fred and a friend of mine, to see
Nina Simone in concert, and then we went back to Fred's awful
council flat or whatever it was, and spent the night there. Fairly
soon, I was being taken home to Chateau Ingrams for Berkshire
weekends. Richard and Mary's running joke was that I was the
prospective son-in-law, but I had no plans to be married.'

Hislop was not best pleased that Silvester, who was always
intended as a temporary freelance, had established himself in
the Ingrams family nest. 'I gradually sort of wormed my way in,'
admits The Spiv, 'and that annoyed Ian, because he had hitherto
been the only member of the younger generation, and Richard
took a shine to me.' Silvester was, after all, from a family of
entertainers. 'Of course Silvester just worked his passage on
the back of Jubby,' snorts Paul Halloran. 'Although to be fair
that wasn't how it started. She was a terribly unworldly girl
who had just come down from a secretarial college (The Oxford
& County), and she used to come down to the Coach and get
fucking plastered. Many's the time I'd put her in a taxi and give
her the money, 'cos Silvester'd just left her to it.'

This allegedly unsavoury behaviour aside, there is no doubt that
the presence of his daughter's boyfriend lightened up Richard's
weekends. 'I think Richard adored Silvester, because he could
gossip and chatter,' suggests Sheila Molnar. Richard was prepared
to admit cautiously that Silvester 'showed promise'. Mary seemed
to like him too, although he committed a major faux pas one weekend, when he forgot to send her a thank-you note; unwittingly, he
too had stored up a reservoir of future trouble for himself.

The Spiv joined Richard on his regular rambles across the
Berkshire Downs. 'I'm not a country man myself,' he smiles,
'but I did the things one should do in the country. We were
walking one day across the Downs, and coming back round to
approach the house from the village, when we walked through

the churchyard. And Richard just stopped in front of the grave of Arthur, and there was a moment of silence. It was very touching. I'm perfectly relaxed with Richard's silences. I do think a lot of people find that aspect of his character rather disconcerting. If we were at the dinner table, you could be telling an anecdote, and unlike the normal reaction that people would give, Richard would often sit there in silence. The impression you *could* have got is that he was completely bored by the whole story. We have a running joke that he thinks I'm a bore.'

Although he had been introduced originally by Hislop, The Spiv quickly fell into an alliance with Jane Ellison and Paul Halloran. The new party was gaining ground. Like Halloran, Silvester was not averse to selling stories to other newspapers, but Richard was too enthralled by the *Eye*'s shifting allegiances to mind unduly. 'It was good fun when Jane, Silvester and Halloran used to share an office,' he admits. Silvester and Ellison often joined Ingrams for lunch in the Coach, where Hislop did not follow.

In the mid-1980s, as Ingrams prepared to pull his vanishing act, the *Eye*'s outlook was healthier than ever. Sales were approaching a quarter of a million, four times the total sale of *Punch*, W.H. Smith and John Menzies had finally relented after twenty years and agreed to handle the magazine, profits were high and David Cash's company pension scheme had come to fruition. Ingrams had originally mocked this manifestation of bureacracy, but he had quietly signed on. He was now being talked about by the owners of the *Observer* as the paper's next editor; and *Private Eye* had been named Magazine of the Year.

The *Eye* had named Sarah Keays and brought down Cecil Parkinson, on the basis of an anonymous scrap of paper that had passed the 'ring of truth' test; it had exposed a Foreign Office cover-up over the murder of Helen Smith, a British nurse working in Saudi Arabia; it had forced the resignation of Richard Somerset-Ward, the BBC executive who attempted to spank his female staff; and it had broken up a child pornography ring involving the former diplomat Sir Peter Hayman, once again with information provided by the police after the DPP's refusal to take any action. The magazine had found new comic targets, in the shape of loquacious taxi drivers, BBC political correspondent John Cole and the Poet Laureate Ted Hughes, whose attempts to commemorate royal occasions were parodied with blunt Yorkshire verses about dead moles and bloodstained ferrets. It had also targeted a new adversary in the shape of Jeffrey Archer, whose life history had been found to contain a number of remarkable inconsistencies. This was to culminate in 1987 when the prostitute Monica Coughlan's allegations against Archer were brought to the *Eye* and rejected by Ian Hislop on Richard Ingrams' advice; the only supporting witness, unfortunately, was palpably foreign. 'We've got the evidence of an Asian and a tart. Do you think that's going to get us anywhere in an English court?' Ingrams asked him. It was good advice. A national newspaper bit instead, and ended up paying Archer £500,000.

Despite all this success, or perhaps even partly because of it, the *Eye* just didn't seem as much fun any more. Ingrams' friend Graydon Carter, the American humorist, told him about a magazine in Italy that had become so successful it had been forced to close, because success was contrary to its founding principles. 'Richard felt that too,' says Liz Elliot. 'He didn't mind the success, but hated the paraphernalia of it.' There was a limit to the extent that employing humorously ill-assorted staff could compensate for endless legal meetings. 'It was becoming a terrific strain,' he admits.

Success had spoiled the Coach and Horses too. Articles and documentaries about the famous *Private Eye* lunch, together with a series of mentions in Jeffrey Bernard's *Spectator* column, had turned the lovable spit-and-sawdust local into a tourist attraction. Now it was packed every night, as Soho media types gathered in the newly hip watering hole, ponytails jostling for space. In 1984 the lease on the Greek Street office ran out, and David Cash found a larger, smarter, better-appointed office, on Carlisle Street in north Soho, away from the Coach. The *Eye* lunches still take place in Norman's upstairs room, but as an office pub it was gradually abandoned to its own devices.

Carlisle Street just wasn't the same for the old guard either. 'Greek Street was more fun,' reflects Ingrams sadly, partly at

313

his mistake in letting the Chief Boxwallah get the upper hand for once. 'There was a completely different atmosphere in the old days, in the old offices, when we used to go to the Coach and Horses. There was more of a gang.' Sheila Molnar agrees: 'After we moved offices, it just wasn't intimate any more. It all fragmented.' The new recruits, by contrast, were pleased with the switch. 'Carlisle Street was much more civilised,' says Jane Ellison. 'Greek Street had seedy stairs, with just the one lavatory. We used to hate it.' The old days, when the gang laughed together, boozed together, and shivered together on cold mornings as they strove to keep their tiny magazine alive, were a fading memory.

In 1984, Ingrams gave the twenty-four-year-old Hislop his first trial crack of the whip, just for one issue. The announcement met with resentment and astonishment among the hacks, and a virtual all-out strike. Halloran, Ellison and Peter McKay, who'd returned from his American sojourn, refused to deliver any copy at all. Nigel Dempster grudgingly delivered out of respect for Ingrams' wishes. Silvester was too diplomatic to risk antagonising the new boss, but *Private Eye* looked as if it would contain almost no news at all.

'Richard's little holiday was just intended to irritate everybody,' reckons Hislop, 'just his idea of fun. He never went on holiday, at least not in those days. He wanted to see what would happen. Predictably, all the hacks told me they wouldn't work for me. Jane Ellison disappeared, saying she didn't work for the second eleven.' Remarkably, as Jane stalked out à la Antonia Fraser, it occured to no one that Richard was preparing the ground for his resignation. That was unthinkable. Richard Ingrams *was* the *Eye*. Hislop's week in charge was just a joke, in extremely bad taste.

'No one would do anything apart from the comedy people, who all thought it was hysterical,' recalls Hislop. 'They didn't give a monkey's, as long as their stuff got in. They just assumed they'd been left in charge anyway. So I called up Foot and said that I hadn't got anything for that issue. Did he want to write loads? Footy was absolutely brilliant, and essentially he just filled the whole magazine. All his stuff was better than theirs anyway, so the mag came out and it was OK.' Foot had tended to stay away from the magazine more and more during the 1980s, considering it 'Thatcherite' and reflective of the fact that Ingrams had voted for Thatcher rather than Michael Foot at the 1983 election. In fact Ingrams found the Prime Minister power mad and ghastly, but was pleased that she had managed to get rid of Foot's intrusive friends from the print unions. Foot, though, had identified a more sympathetic point of view in Hislop, and forged an alliance which was to see him return to the *Eye* after Ingrams' departure.

Richard's next leave of absence was not voluntary but forced. His health was beginning to deteriorate, and he found himself increasingly plagued by terrible back pains. Depressingly, he had to give up cricket. In 1985, he took three months off for major surgery, which was carried out, coincidentally, by Art Themen. Wells decided to visit his friend at Aldworth. 'It had been an absolutely terrible operation. I turned up at the house, and Mary just said, "He's upstairs". I went up, and Richard pulled the door open, barely able to walk. He seemed near to death. There was something very brave about it. I remember his cousin, Charlie Douglas-Home, dying of bone marrow cancer, and Charlie had just said, "It's a bore". Richard had that same kind of British phlegm.'

This time the hacks had no option but to knuckle under, for they could not afford to go three months without pay, and anyway, Hislop now had Foot on his side. Jane Ellison sent a regular bulletin to Richard in his sick bed: 'To borrow the golden words of a celebrated Australian, Mr A.A. Graham, "It's not been a happy ship, Dick". To put it bluntly, fear and loathing have broken out all over the place. I expect you are wondering how my new and cordial relationship with Mr Hislop is bearing up under the strain of watching him edit the magazine. I am sorry to say that things have cooled. We do not, any longer, exchange friendly greetings. When I passed him on the stairs and merrily cried out "Goodbye, Hislop!" he merely stared at me and laughed in an unpleasant way. I assume it is the strain of office. He has become very remote, occupies your chair with some difficulty (*do* his feet actually touch

315

the ground?) and keeps the door closed most of the time. He has also threatened Silvester most unpleasantly.'

A month later, she wrote: 'It's reassuring to know you are walking and able to write . . . this can only be good news for the languishing hacks, horribly oppressed by the new regime of Hislop (or Himmler as we call him now). Here at Carlisle Street there is a *very great deal* of unpleasantness.' She went on to describe how Hislop had accidentally become locked in the *Eye*'s offices, and had phoned Norman Balon at the Coach and Horses to bring a spare key. Norman had told him to 'fuck off', adding that he didn't have a key, but that if he did have one he wouldn't have brought it over anyway. Hislop had then phoned Tone for help. Tone had told him that he was 'too busy'. Ian Hislop may have been *in situ*, but he was under siege. His enemies, though, had underestimated his will to win.

A few weeks later Ingrams suffered a relapse. 'The news of your delayed return caused immense gloom and despondency among most of us at Carlisle Street; there is an atmosphere of unpleasantness here which is almost impossible to describe. Himmler is now trying to insinuate himself with my boys, behind my back. I believe he is going to some lengths to try and sack me. Well, it will do him no good . . . Incidentally, I switched on the radio one morning last week only to hear the nasal whine of Mr Barry Fantoni explaining all about Chinese horoscopes for the thousandth time. Having said that his own sign (the Dragon) was the best, he then rambled incoherently about buffaloes, pigs, dogs etc. etc. while everyone else in the studio seemed lulled into a state of torpor.'

Finally, Ingrams' enforced stay in Berkshire came to an end. The journalists celebrated. Silvester got drunk on port. 'Himmler has bought a new jacket,' wrote Jane. 'It is very eye-catching (some might say loud) and makes him look like an estate agent. Far be it for me to try and point out that whatever Himmler might report to you about *me* is almost certain to be grossly distorted . . .' Ingrams didn't need to talk to Hislop. *Private Eye* had been fetched to his bedside for the last three months, and he had been quietly impressed with the standard of the magazine.

Before Ingrams could make it back to Carlisle Street, however, the *Eye* was riven by a terrible row; one that in the short term was to see the magazine taken off the street altogether, and in the long term was to change his life. Nigel Dempster had been writing the Grovel column increasingly unwillingly during Ingrams' absence; he had not even come in to meet Hislop, but had merely filed his copy through Tony Rushton in desultory fashion. Finally, he ground to a halt. 'I had been playing squash one day,' recounts Dempster, 'and just as I got out of my game, I got a call from Liz Elliot, who said, "Look, there's a whole page empty for Grovel and we're expecting you to fill it". And I told her, "I'm not doing it. I can't be bothered". She said "We're *relying* on you".' Dempster reluctantly dragged himself over to Carlisle Street, bearing a story about Cecil Parkinson and his new secretary – Sarah Keays' replacement – which was notably unsupported by any evidence at all. 'It was probably injudiciously written,' admits Dempster. Parkinson was tipped off about the story by someone on the *Mail*, obtained an injunction, and *Private Eye* had to be pulled off the streets. Every copy had to be recalled, and Parkinson had to be paid off.

Stories differ as to how the disaster had been allowed to happen. 'I told Hislop to his face that I didn't know anything about the story, that it was anonymous, that I couldn't vouch for it,' insists Dempster. 'Every other Monday for years, the *Eye* lawyer had rung me. This Monday he did not do so, so I thought it was OK.' Paul Halloran, who had no great love for Dempster, tells it differently. 'Hislop did nothing wrong. Dempster came in with this story. Ian mentioned it to me, and I went to Dempster, and asked, "How does this stand up?" He said, "I asked this guy and that in Reuters". On what Dempster said, Ingrams would have run that story. It was nothing to do with [Hislop's] alleged "raw inexperience". Dempster put the boot into Hislop when they were looking for a scapegoat. He said, "I told Hislop it wouldn't work and that he shouldn't put it in", which was a lie, he said quite the reverse. He said it to me, I fuckin' asked him.'

Unfortunately, Dempster's remark that he had advised Hislop

317

not to run the story was made in an interview with the *Sunday Times*. The withdrawal of the *Eye* from the shops had made national news. Dempster had agreed to be interviewed as a gossip expert, not as the author of the piece, a fact he wished to keep secret. 'I was left with egg all over my face and no possible legal defence,' says Hislop. In retaliation, *Private Eye* broke with twenty-four years of tradition and, through the medium of a comic piece, identified Dempster as the author of the Parkinson story.

'The next thing I know,' says Dempster, 'is that Hislop, the so-called editor, and therefore someone who should protect his journalists, is not saying, as Richard would have, "I stand by my story, it came from an anonymous source", but he's saying that it was my story, straight out. I walked in and called him a cunt, and said, "You're not a professional journalist and never have been, you could have destroyed my career, and there's absolutely no point working for you. Go fuck yourself." Hislop was like a man with watchsprings coming out of his ears. After I left, Grovel was done by Halloran. Halloran knows bugger all about society. He's like the supergun, potting away at long range.'

Yet it was not Hislop who had identified Dempster. It was Ingrams. Ingrams, whom Dempster had taken to lunch every Friday for all those years, had now – as he saw it – betrayed him for some kid. He had no idea of the nature of Ingrams' regard for his deputy, and no conception of exactly how much Ingrams had riding on Hislop's success. He could not see how Ingrams could take Hislop's word over his own. Dempster was mortally offended.

Soon, everyone was taking sides, everyone had a conspiracy theory. McKay rallied to Dempster's side, and thought that 'Ian wanted to get rid of Dempster anyway'. Jane Ellison, who like Halloran didn't give two hoots for Dempster, thought that 'he hated Hislop and would have left anyway'. Ingrams thought that the *Eye* had been used by the *Mail* to 'float' an unreliable story in public, that once Dempster had been named by the *Eye* he had been warned off further involvement by his editor at the *Mail*, and that Dempster had consequently 'fabricated a phoney row'. In public, Ingrams stayed cool – 'I was very impressed by Hislop's amazing feat of having a whole issue of *Private Eye* withdrawn,' he said – but he knew that in the wounded Dempster he had made an enemy for life. From now on, Dempster would hound Ingrams at every turn, as Sir James Goldsmith had once promised. Dempster was the most prominent and influential gossip columnist in the country, and Ingrams had become his number one target; only this time, Ingrams' own moral perspective would not be acting as a restraining influence.

Events now began to move quickly. Richard suffered another damaging blow when Liz Elliot announced that she was pregnant, and that she was quitting the *Eye*. The father was Henry Porter, a journalist. Ingrams cooled towards her. Sensing the loss of his affection, Liz cried in her office. Everyone assumed that this was some form of moral censure on his part, but it probably had as much to do with sadness at losing her. 'Every so often, women on *Private Eye* think, "Sod this, I'm off to do something else",' he mused.[3] In fact, he'd had just two secretaries in seventeen years, an incredible degree of loyalty; but the mere fact that Liz was going at all reminded him that she was, in the end, just an employee, and not one of the gang. Gang members did not leave. Even Richard, when he resigned the editorship, wasn't planning to leave entirely.

He was to forge another close relationship with Liz's successor, the irrepressibly cheerful Maggie Lunn, in the last few months of his editorship. 'I went for the interview,' remembers Maggie, 'and I saw him in the street beforehand. So I scampered up to him and said, "You are Richard Ingrams and I claim my five pounds", and offered him a mint. He likes mints. So we were chat, chat, chat in the street and that was that. We just hit it off. Dave Cash didn't want me at all.' Which was, of course, another excellent reason for giving Maggie the job. Maggie soon developed the traditional crush on her new boss. 'He used to come in and do Lord Denning impersonations every morning, and every morning you'd laugh. If it was anyone else you wouldn't have. It was so infectious'.

Relations with Mary were not so relaxed. On Richard's birthday, she was invited to a special lunch at the Coach and Horses. 'They didn't talk at all,' remembers Jane Ellison sadly. 'They just sat at opposite ends of the table and didn't speak to each other. She was very depressed and very lonely. Everybody assumed that she drank a lot. Norman played a joke, and got Richard's birthday cake ready downstairs – because Richard likes puddings – and then served him a big chunk of cheese. Mary shrieked "But Richard doesn't *like* cheese!" in an appalled voice, almost as if he was a child.' The joke hung frozen in the deathly silence of the room.

At the start of 1986 came the clinching blow. Auberon Waugh announced he was leaving, after sixteen years, to edit the *Literary Review*. 'I had rather been looking round for something else,' admits Waugh. 'I was generally feeling that Ingrams was taking less and less interest in *Private Eye*. There were more and more duff issues – he'd been doing it too long and he was fed up. My particular corner of it was slowly dying. There was also a very unpleasant person called Halloran. He had a brooding, toad-like presence. He looked at you as you came in and went out, with this awful red-faced hostility, going on about "bloody public schoolboys". He transformed the atmosphere. Ingrams liked having this universally hated person who was loyal to him and him alone. He could play them off against each other.' Losing Waugh was a bitter pill. Naim Attallah, who was the publisher of the *Literary Review*, believes that 'Richard left *Private Eye* because Bron left *Private Eye*. He felt a kind of loneliness.'

One or two people had begun to smell a rat. Patrick Marnham told the BBC that 'Ingrams put "editing *Private Eye*" down in *Who's Who* as his recreation, but at times he must get awfully bored with it. But at the same time, he wouldn't want anybody else to do it. He wants it to be his own monument, so if he finds he can't bear it to continue . . . he'll be tempted to destroy it, to blow himself up with it.'[4] Still nobody had accurately managed to guess what Ingrams had in mind.

On Friday 14 March 1986, the entire *Eye* staff, together with one or two old friends, assembled at L'Escargot restaurant in Soho for Waugh's retirement lunch. At the end of the meal, Ingrams stood up and gave a gentle and witty speech in tribute to Waugh's work. Then, he quietly mentioned that he, too, had an announcement to make. In September, Ian Hislop would be taking over as the editor. There was a moment of shocked silence, as the news sunk in. Then Liz Elliot and Sheila Molnar burst into tears. Willie Rushton said 'About time too', and stalked out. From that moment on, in the words of Maggie Lunn, 'It was chaos. Halloran and Silvester were rushing for the phone, whacking each other out of the way. The women were all weeping, Bron was sitting there gobsmacked, Ian was in a frenzy of keeping his end up. And I sat back and thought, "Yet again, he's got the whole thing in turmoil".'

Ingrams' sense of theatre had triumphed again; but the battle to secure the succession was by no means over. It had only just begun.

22 The Dogs Turn

Some might say that the chaos surrounding Ian Hislop's succession was a failure on Richard Ingrams' part; but under any circumstances, handing on the editorship of *Private Eye* to a twenty-four-year-old would have caused a furore. As Fred Ingrams pointed out, Hislop's main offence was his youth. At least – the way things turned out – the chaos was of Richard's own choosing, and he could manoeuvre a path through it with all the advantages enjoyed by one who is calling the shots.

Hislop was, after all, the only possible choice. The original gang would have fought like jackals if one of them had been selected, and they largely recognised this. The hacks, for all their squalling, could have handled the funny side of the magazine as easily as they could have climbed Kilimanjaro before breakfast. As Ingrams' hero G.K. Chesterton said, it is easy to be solemn, hard to be frivolous – or at least, successfully frivolous. Hislop was the only candidate who came close to Ingrams' overall vision of a crusading, laughing, mischievous force for good.

Of the old guard, Auberon Waugh was vociferous in his refusal to accept this. After Ingrams had made his resignation announcement, Waugh rose and addressed the ruins of his retirement lunch. Pretending not to know Hislop's name, and referring to him variously as 'Hinton' and 'Driscoll', he described the change of editorship as 'in tune with the *Eye*'s misguided policy of seeking the custom of yobbo readers'. He outlined his nightmare vision of a *Private Eye* full of arcane rock music references, as purchased by youths in backward-facing baseball caps. In the days following the lunch he was to expand on this theme in print, writing in the *Spectator* that the *Eye* would 'degenerate into a teenage comic' and telling another paper that Hislop 'did not have the strength of character for the job'. Auberon Waugh became the latest recruit to Mary Ingrams' little black book.

Within minutes of the lunch ending, there was a crowd of pressmen and TV crews outside the Carlisle Street office. So great was the hubbub, a passer-by might have been forgiven for thinking that it was the Archbishop of Canterbury who had passed his job on to a twenty-four-year-old, not a mere magazine editor. Ingrams came out and confessed that he was no longer able to cope with the strain of going to court. 'I have found myself thinking more and more like Reggie Perrin,' he told the media, 'a strange recklessness creeping in, feeling "What does all this matter? What does Robert Maxwell matter?" '[1] Then Hislop came out and explained that he was going to tighten up on libel actions, 'for reasons of self-respect and necessity'. Goaded into outlining what new targets he would be encouraging his staff to attack, he mentioned advertising and PR, and raised the dread prospect of popular music.

The press reaction to the new editor was largely hostile, led by Nigel Dempster and the *Eye* journalists themselves. 'I don't think people like midgets,' Dempster told the *Sunday Times*, 'especially pushy midgets. I think he is a deeply unpleasant little man. He is the one and only reason that I left the *Eye* . . . He knows nothing about journalism. He is not a journalist in any shape, size or form. And *Private Eye* is essentially about journalism.' This last profound misunderstanding encapsulates why Dempster himself could probably not have edited such a unique institution successfully.

Jane Ellison was quoted, anonymously, as saying that 'Hislop is an absolutely ludicrous figure. I can't tell you how aggressive he is . . . he is very boring'.[2] Peter McKay, meanwhile, concentrated on the legality or otherwise of the appointment. How, he pondered, was a 'tired editor able to choose his successor without consulting anyone?'[3] He wrote a column for the *Standard* suggesting that Peter Cook, as proprietor, could and should give

Ingrams the sack. McKay found an ally in the person of the Chief Boxwallah, David Cash. 'I can dig my heels in if I want to,' said Cash. 'My view is that Hislop should run the funny side of the magazine, but that we need someone with more experience to run the serious side of things. That would alleviate the problem that Hislop does not have the backing of the hacks. The one thing that Hislop could not do as editor is hire and fire staff. He does not have the authority'.[4]

In the main, the press felt free to direct its abuse at Hislop, and not Ingrams, for much the same reason that the old guard did not seem too bothered: which is that most of them erroneously assumed Ingrams would continue to pull the strings. Peter McKay confidently told *Mail on Sunday* readers that the resignation was 'a sham', and David Cash ventured the opinion that Hislop had in reality been appointed as 'an assistant editor'. 'Once Richard leaves, the magazine we know will wither away,' Andrew Osmond was on record as saying.[5] 'It is inconceivable to imagine it operating without him,' Paul Foot had said.[6] Yet neither seemed unduly worried, for everyone assumed that Ingrams would continue to grind the organ while Hislop danced. After all those years, they should surely have remembered that Ingrams was a man of his word. Only Tone had it roughly right: 'Even if you took Richard away it wouldn't matter now. The editor is no longer vital.'[7] As long as the right kind of editor was in charge, he might have added.

Nigel Dempster called a meeting of the anti-Hislop plotters at the Gay Hussar restaurant. A small band assembled for lunch, consisting of Auberon Waugh, Patrick Marnham, David Cash, Richard West and Peter McKay. The guest of honour, whom they hoped to persuade of the illegality of Ingrams' action, was Peter Cook. Waugh told the gathering that *Private Eye* had no need of the type of readers that Hislop would bring. Dempster argued that Hislop was not a journalist, and so should be fired. Cash confirmed that the staff would not stand behind Hislop in the event of a coup. McKay reiterated that Ingrams should not have been allowed to choose his successor without reference to his 'senior colleagues' (in other words, those present at the lunch). Cook sat and listened, and consumed a great many bottles of wine. Eventually, an election was held to appoint the new editor-in-waiting, and Peter McKay was voted in. Peter Cook and David Cash set off up the road for Carlisle Street to confront Ingrams.

Unfortunately for the conspirators, Cook was now blind drunk, a state in which he tends to agree amicably with the last person who has spoken to him. He may well have set off from the Gay Hussar with the best intention in the world to remove Ian Hislop, but by the time he had staggered across Soho Square, into Carlisle Street and up the stairs into Ingrams' office, he had completely forgotten why he had come. Hislop was there too, and Cook recognised him through an alcoholic blur. 'Welcome aboard!' said Cook, clapping him enthusiastically on the back. This left Cash on his own. There'd been this lunch, he stammered, and there'd been a sort of vote, and Peter McKay . . . Like the Mekon, Ingrams turned his piercing blue eyes onto Cash and shrivelled him to a crisp.

Looking back with the hindsight of relative sobriety, Cook laughs uproariously at his actions. 'The idea of having *Private Eye* run by McKay is a joke. If Richard had appointed Christine Keeler I might have intervened, but Ian was the ideal choice. Bron was the only worthwhile person to oppose Ian.' Cash is more embarrassed: 'Of course Richard's choice was right,' he claims, 'it was just how he implemented it. I think the magazine wobbled for a few months before Ian found his feet, but now it's fine.' Even Peter McKay now concedes that Hislop might have been the right choice: 'If Richard had given it to Footy, all the jokes would have been lost. If he'd have given it to me, I'd have extended Grovel across every single page.'

Of course, in reality, there was no hierarchy to invoke against Hislop. Peter Cook would not have been able to exercise any authority over Ingrams, even if he had been capable of it, for the simple reason that he had never once attempted to establish any. The only time he had ever previously been asked what he might do, if, say, Ingrams went mad, he had merely replied, 'Oh, he did that years ago.' The plotters should have realised, anyway, that whereas attacking Ingrams' position usually invokes stubborn immobility, giving him *orders* to change tack, as they

325

had attempted, invariably leads him to head off in the opposite direction.

What they had also failed to appreciate was that however pally they had been with Ingrams, however many lunches they had bought him, they were, ultimately, mere employees. Hacks, who can always be replaced with other hacks. They were not members of the gang. When gang members left the *Eye*, Ingrams could be cast down for months. When a journalist like Dempster swopped sides, it was just part of the wider game. They had failed to realise that *Private Eye* is primarily a humour magazine, and that however keen Ingrams was to hear the latest gossip, he would fight to protect the *Eye*'s humorous core, the tradition that linked it to Oxford and *Parson's Pleasure*, against all-comers. The emotional importance of the magazine to its outgoing editor had eluded them, buried as it was under the layer of squabbling hackery that he had imported for his own entertainment. 'Mr Ingrams sits in a rats' nest, but it is one he created himself,' Peter McKay later observed disdainfully in the *Standard*.[8] Unfortunately for the hacks, Ian Hislop had plans for a rat-hunt.

Jane Ellison was the first reporter to go, before Hislop had even taken over. She wrote a piece for the *Literary Review*, again anonymously, attacking the new regime. A paragraph condemning her own character failed to disguise her authorship of the piece. Ingrams himself delivered the *coup de grâce*. He telephoned her as she was on her way to the *Eye* lunch. 'I don't think you should come, Jane,' he said. She could not believe it: 'I've never been more astonished in my life. I said, "What do you mean?" He said, "I don't want you to come in any more." That was it, total, outer darkness.' Within the confines of the office, her barbs were considered entertaining. Printed with a view to turning the world outside against the new editor, she had committed the fatal sin of disloyalty. Like Dempster, she had failed to grasp the nature of Ingrams' relationship with Hislop and the priority he put on it. Like Dempster, she was left hurt, bewildered and in the cold.

Hislop had vowed privately to his friends that Silvester would be the first to be sacked when he took over in September, leaving The Spiv to fulfil his long-stated ambition of becoming a Tory MP;

but Silvester had six crucial months in which to charm his new boss. 'Let me be the first to toady to you!' were the first words he had cried when Hislop's appointment had been made known. Somehow, Silvester managed to stay on, although Halloran was left alone in the little room where the two of them and Jane had sat. 'Ingrams' resignation hit me like a bolt,' says the New Zealander. 'I've not been invited to any *Eye* lunches since then. You know, when you're out in front of society, as you are when you attend an *Eye* lunch, you are dealing with people with a great deal of sophistication. To tell them that they've dropped a bollock or that they don't know bullshit from music, I mean it's completely out of order.'

McKay was the next to go, largely on account of *Inside Private Eye*, a book hurriedly scrambled together to cash in on the succession saga. Like Jane Ellison, he felt free to sling abuse at Hislop, but he also managed to antagonise a number of his other colleagues. '*Inside Private Eye* was the biggest load of fucking drivel ever put on earth,' reckons Halloran. 'There was a lie on every page.' According to Peter Cook, the book was 'a load of old tosh'. According to Ingrams, it was 'pathetic. He was incredibly rude about Hislop and as a result, Ian made it clear that he wasn't wanted any more.' Another *Eye* journalist had cut his own throat. 'There are only two mistakes in that book,' insists McKay in his defence, 'and I left of my own accord. Ian says I was sacked. I don't remember being sacked.'

The most surprising thing about McKay's book is not the inevitable failings of structure or fact that accompany a rush release, or the strong opinions predictably expressed in it, but – once again – the complete failure to understand what Ingrams had seen in Ian Hislop. 'Unlike Ingrams, Hislop is not a moral crusader,' wrote McKay. 'He will print "legover" stories for amusement.' On the contrary, Hislop's morals are so formidable that he has tried to eliminate 'legover' stories from the *Eye* altogether. 'The image of Ingrams which has generally been accepted,' continued McKay, 'is of a tired crusader handing his sword to a younger man. The reality is different. Ingrams will continue to run *Private Eye*.'[9] The reality was in fact precisely the opposite. Every journalist in town thought that Ingrams would continue to run *Private Eye*, but the tired crusader had had enough.

The dogs turned on the apparently harmless Hislop in a pack. Almost every national paper, it seemed at one stage, was keen to run page after page of witless abuse at his expense. He was, said Tim Willis in *Today*, 'a balding, pug-faced little fogey'. Or, if you believed *Midweek*, 'too cocky by half'. Val Hennessy wrote, somewhat extraordinarily, in the *Mail on Sunday*: 'Hislop. Say it slowly. Roll it round your tongue. *Hiss . . . slop-p-p*. Let the second syllable splash. The name suits him. He is 24. He is going bald.'[10] Only Dempster and McKay dared to attack the seemingly powerful Ingrams as well. Ingrams, wrote Dempster in the *Mail*, was a 'pustulous reformed alcoholic' with a 'Bohemian home life' and a wife who was 'frumpy'. 'I wish him nothing but ill. I shall dance upon his grave,' the diarist told the *Sunday Times* in blind anger.

The *Eye* hit back with parodies of Dempster's *Mail* column. Like Wells, Dempster had recently befriended royalty – in this case Princess Michael – and his attentions on the royal personage were derided as spineless arselicking. One day, Silvester gleefully discovered that according to his entry in *Who's Who*, Dempster was 'the son of Eric Richard Pratt and Angela Grace Dempster'. A nickname was born. Of course Dempster was not called Pratt at all, he had merely saved space by not bothering to write out his surname twice, but it was too late for him to do anything about it. The war spilled over onto the pages of *Ritz* magazine, which ran a feature entitled 'Is Dempster a Pratt?' Dempster telephoned *Ritz*'s editor David Litchfield in a white-hot rage, little realising that Litchfield was recording the conversation in order to publish it in his next issue: 'OK. So how are you going to pay for it? You're going to have to do something, buddy, because I'm going to take you to the fucking cleaners! . . . You are a cunt and you know you are, so I'm warning you that I want some recognition . . .' and so on and so on.[11]

McKay, meanwhile, was busy claiming that the *Eye*'s attacks on any of Ingrams' contemporaries, such as Peter Jay, were motivated by the fact that they had got better degrees than he had. Ingrams was 'functionally mad,' he said. 'If he wasn't editing a magazine he'd just be wandering the streets shouting at people.' McKay also spread the astonishing fairy tale that Ingrams, while searching Aldworth for his escaped Jack Russell, had encountered a prostitute on a street corner, had availed himself of her services, and had not returned home until three days later. Obviously McKay was not entirely familiar with the sleepy Berkshire hamlet. John Wells couldn't resist saying I told you so, pointing out yet again that if you take in dangerous dogs they will invariably end up biting you on the bum.

McKay's attack on Hislop was, if anything, even stronger. An unsigned piece taking up nearly a quarter of a page of 'Mr Pepys' Diary' appeared in the *Standard*, under the headline 'Ian is so simmler to Himmler'. Referring to a TV appearance by Hislop, it said: 'Ian Hislop looked and sounded like the nasty little creep he is. Stick him in a Nazi uniform and you have a Heinrich Himmler lookalike.'[12] Hislop responded with parodies of McKay's column, attributed to 'Peter McLie, the world's worst columnist'.

Despite the apparent ferocity of these articles, McKay is loath to admit that his campaign against Ingrams and Hislop was anything more than just joshing. Dempster, he claims, is the man with the real grudge. 'Once Dempster started churning out stuff about Ingrams' marriage, and I was still friendly with Dempster, then I kind of got grouped with Dempster,' he explains somewhat disingenuously. 'I'm fond of Richard.' So what does Dempster really think of Ingrams? 'I adore Richard,' he says, through clenched teeth.

Initially, the rest of the press were reluctant to join the pair in their attack on Ingrams. Laying into the editor of *Private Eye* had traditionally been a dangerous pastime. 'It is extraordinary how keen people are that someone else should do it,' the *Sunday Times* had reported. 'People were scared of him,' says Jane Ellison. 'He was seen as a powerful figure.' Gradually, though, as the years passed, it began to dawn on Fleet Street that the editor of *Private Eye* was not Richard Ingrams, but Ian Hislop, just like it said on the nameplate. Ingrams was not in fact the puppetmaster after all. Hislop

329

was the powerful one, Ingrams was the one in the vulnerable position.

Most Fleet Street journalists are cowards by nature, particularly feature journalists and reviewers, who like to run with the pack. For all their confidently expressed opinions, they prefer to attack the same celebrities, and defer to the same celebrities, as everybody else. The history of journalism is littered with bewildered public figures, unable to comprehend how they have progressed from being the darling of the press to Public Enemy No.1 almost overnight. They are unaware that the process is probably no more sinister than that which makes the lead buffalo in a stampede aimlessly switch direction, followed by all the others in a blind rush to conform. Whatever one might think of McKay and Dempster's campaigns, at least they had the courage to go against the consensus, in the tradition of their former editor. Now, suddenly, the rest of the pack was running in behind them, falling over themselves to get in a blow against the man over whom they had fawned for so many years.

Ingrams stood up and took the fusillade unflinching, much as he had stood up against Jimmy Goldsmith and Robert Maxwell. Jocelyn Targett in the *Guardian* called him 'a shambles of decrepit jokes and potty, unshakeable prejudices. He has made not laughing but hating his life's achievement. He hates Jews, and he hates "pooves" . . . he hates Nigel Dempster, because he'd rather work for Lord Rothermere than Lord Gnome – in other words, the smalltime, self-interested hatred of a cantankerous nincompoop.'[13] Hunter Davies in the *Independent* spoke of 'a pitiful image – this tired old fart, sitting with his little shopping bag between his feet.'[14] Lynn Barber in the *Independent on Sunday* described his relationship with Hislop as 'nauseating'.[15] The *Sunday Telegraph* called him 'cantankerous, moody, buttoned-up and strange'.[16] Journalist friends, like Sir John Junor of the *Sunday Express*, quietly excused themselves from Ingrams' social life.

A distinct whiff of King Lear spread itself about Ingrams, now shorn of his power and forced to endure this withering onslaught. There was, at least, no shortage of Cordelias, as the young ladies of *Private Eye* and his daughter's friends from the

Groucho Club rallied round affectionately but helplessly. 'Ingrams' male friends are aggrieved by his behaviour in the Groucho Club,' scoffed Jocelyn Targett in the *Guardian*, 'where . . . he paws the waitresses and then passes it off as a joke.'[17] The allegation was palpably ludicrous. 'If Targett had gone into the Groucho Club, he would have been torn limb from limb by hordes of angry waitresses,' pointed out the alleged groper.[18]

A number of people wrote to complain to the *Guardian*, not that any of the letters were printed. Two of the complainers shared the same name: 'A man named Humphrey Phelps wrote to me, saying that he had written to the *Guardian*, and a girl called Catherine Phelps told me that her father Edward Phelps had also written in. I was going to write to the *Guardian* saying, "If two men called Phelps have written in, how many more Phelpses will have to write in before you print a letter?" ' Ingrams creases with laughter at the Beachcomberesque notion of battalions of Phelpses angrily writing to the *Guardian*.

Despite his good cheer, there is something dispiritingly shabby about the wave of press attacks upon him: in part, it is the phoney friendliness with which each journalist in turn obtained and conducted their interview, and in part it is that his attackers seemed primarily to be motivated by the perceived weakness of their target. They no doubt persuaded themselves that they were giving Ingrams a taste of his own medicine, but there was no comparison; he at least had the courage to go for powerful targets and was always motivated by some form of consistent principle. Dangerous dogs indeed.

If the initial point of McKay and Dempster's attacks had been to denigrate Hislop's ability to edit *Private Eye* – Dempster gave the magazine no more than two years – then the result of the publicity was rather the opposite. Readers' attention was drawn to the fact that nothing whatsoever had changed. Auberon Waugh was honourably quick to acknowledge his mistake: 'At the time I thought the change was unnecessary and a great shame, and I thought the magazine would collapse without Ingrams, but in fact it jolly well hasn't, as anybody can see. It's rather good, actually. Young what's-his-name has pulled it together and it's really scarcely distinguishable from what it was.' Paul Halloran concurs: 'Hislop had a winning formula, and an intelligent man knows that.'

The threatened introduction of popular music never took place. Hislop bought a weekend cottage in Somerset in which to shelter his family from the excesses of London life, a purchase faintly reminiscent of Ingrams' own move to rural isolation; today he wouldn't know a pop group if it mugged him in the street. Gradually, though, he has moulded the *Eye* in his own image. The gossip content has decreased dramatically. Christopher Silvester, who took over the Grovel column, explains: 'Ian has a puritanical streak – even more so than Richard . . . Despite my best efforts, the magazine contains less filth now than it used to.' Sniffs Hislop: 'I just don't care who the Marquess of Nobody is getting his leg over.'[19] In 1993, Silvester unwisely confessed to Hislop that he wished 'to distance himself from the magazine', in his search for a safe Tory seat. Fine, said Hislop, no distance could be too great. That year, Hislop finally scrapped the Grovel column, and also sacked Paul Halloran. In 1994 The Spiv resigned of his own accord, to join the *Evening Standard* full-time.

In place of the gossip has come a series of specialised columns, such as 'Rotten Boroughs', 'Doing the Rounds' and 'Media News', designed to appeal directly to specific middle-class professions. Critics complain that the number of big exposés has fallen, but this is hardly surprising. Today every newspaper and news magazine is looking for the big story that will bring down the government. Whereas thirty years ago newspapers often connived in protecting the reputations of those in high office, now they follow the lead set in the 1960s by *Private Eye*, and by Paul Foot in particular. On his own terms, Foot may have failed to bring about the major changes to society that he hoped for, but, on most people's terms, he can be said to have brought about a measurable improvement. Foot is now back in his old berth at *Private Eye*, where the editorial direction has swung to the left to accommodate him.

The comedy side has barely changed at all. Ingrams still comes in three days a fortnight to write the jokes, closeted in an office with Booker, Fantoni, Hislop and sometimes Peter Cook. The room still rocks with mirth and the standard is as high as ever. If there is a difference, it is that Hislop is unwilling to goad his readers in the manner that Ingrams did: Larry Adler's interminable correspondence, for instance, would not survive in the modern *Eye*. Hislop is resistant to old jokes creeping back in. 'I'd have loved to get Barry McKenzie back,' says Peter Cook wistfully. 'I had vague talks with Barry Humphries, but he's a superstar now, and anyway Ian didn't want it.'

Hislop is also more ruthless with contributors: he swiftly killed off 'The Last Chip Shop in England', Bill Tidy's follow-up to 'The Cloggies', then abandoned the aggrieved Tidy's next effort after only a few issues. Despite this decisiveness, if there is one area in which he fails to match up to Ingrams, it is as a cartoon editor. Too many illustrated puns creep into the magazine. For instance: Reporter – 'Mr Zhirinovsky, how do you feel about topping the polls?' Zhirinovsky – 'I don't mind topping the Poles, or the Czechs, Bulgarians or anyone else who stands in my way'. Such jokes are no more worthy of visual illustration than are the comments of two men as they walk past a newsvendor's placard.

Hislop's pledge to bring down libel costs has failed, but not for want of trying. Freely admitting that he possesses no 'ring of truth', he has tried to be more careful; the number of cases has gone down, but, sadly, the size of the damages awarded has gone up. Increasingly stupid British juries, taking their lead from increasingly stupid American juries, have begun to award insane amounts of money at the slightest suggestion of hurt feelings. Most absurd of all was the Sonia Sutcliffe case, a 'libel' dating from Ingrams' editorship in 1981 at which Mrs Sutcliffe suddenly decided to take offence in 1987. *Private Eye* had alleged that she had taken money from a *Mail* journalist for information about her husband, the Yorkshire Ripper. She said she hadn't, and a jury awarded her £600,000, a figure grotesquely in excess of anything ever awarded to the Ripper's victims. 'If this is justice, I am a banana,' exclaimed Hislop famously on the steps of the High Court. Sonia Sutcliffe then enthusiastically sued the *News of the World* for making exactly the same allegation. The *News of the World* was able to produce the *Mail* journalist who had actually paid her – a woman who had pointedly refused to help

Private Eye – and Sutcliffe lost heavily. It was not without a certain glee that the legal establishment refused the *Eye* leave to try and get its money back. Booker, like a familiar and much-loved variety act, trotted out his usual lack of sympathy, but nobody seemed to mind. He was part of the family, was old Booker.

Organisationally, Hislop has tried to dispense with the amateur ethic, and add a touch of efficiency here and there. Maggie Lunn regrets the change: 'With Ian it got a lot less gossipy and naughty. They're trying to get it organised, but the whole point about the *Eye* is that it shouldn't be organised. Ian is keen to have some sort of office system. For example, he made a vague attempt to get some shelves up, which wouldn't have occurred to Richard. They were supposed to be for the *Who's Who*s and other reference works, but when Ian came in, Silvester's shoes were up there. Ian gets driven to distraction.'

Willie Rushton, on his occasional visits, has noticed how the old Ingrams *Eye* has slowly disappeared. 'It's a totally different atmosphere. In the old *Eye*, everyone was much closer to each other, everyone went to the pub, all the decisions were taken there, at our regular table in the Coach. Now Tone goes and eats at that table alone. Everyone has a separate office, Ian doesn't share what he's doing. He's a "get on with your work" type.' Hislop has changed the menu at the *Eye* lunches – the old stodgy food isn't served any more – and has sacked Tony Rushton from one of his two jobs, replacing him as advertising manager with a professional. 'When you get in qualified people – and we have recently got in qualified people – it becomes so boring and staid,' laments Sheila Molnar.

One long-overdue change is that Peter Cook, for the first time in thirty years, has finally been paid. 'I now get wages as a contributor,' says Cook. 'It's only just occurred to me to ask. I've never been paid anything as proprietor either. I've been totally unpaid for a third of a century.' Astonishing. 'Stupid, I'd say.' Wages and other such administrative details have now been put onto computer. *Private Eye* is becoming a smoother-running and perhaps less interesting place, despite the best efforts of Silvester's shoes.

The circulation has slipped – by 40,000 – but it is still extremely healthy. Nigel Dempster puts the decline down to his own absence. 'They were employing me, the best-known columnist in the world, for nothing,' he says.[20] Yet in recent years, Dempster and McKay have attacked Hislop's editorship less and less. 'Hislop isn't a bad editor,' wrote Peter McKay soothingly at the beginning of 1994. 'He's also a nicer man than Richard Ingrams.'[21] 'For a while I even thought McKay would come back,' says Maggie Lunn, 'but Ian's not a great forgiver.' Dempster, meanwhile, was ignoring Hislop for the sake of a more satisfying target. He had set his sights on Ingrams' marriage.

23 Ingrams Alone

By the time he resigned the editorship of *Private Eye*, Richard's relationship with Mary had stumbled through the tangles surrounding the death of Arthur, and had reached a clearing. She now had something to do: she had bought a bookshop in Wallingford with an inheritance from her mother, and the newly-retired editor would come down and help her out when he wasn't working in London. 'I thought that bookshop would be the saving of our marriage,' he says. 'She was very good at doing it, and she seemed much better when she was doing it.' The shop was a commercial success, and Richard was confident enough to tell the press that their marriage was 'very happy'.

There were foreign holidays, to the USA and on a number of occasions to Malta, where the Ingrams family stayed with a former *Eye* correspondent, Godfrey Grima – patricians, of course, preferring to avoid hotels wherever possible. Sadly one Maltese trip was marred by an unfortunate incident that boded ill for the future: Mary drank a glass or two of Pimms, there was a row, orange juice was thrown, she departed for the airport in a rented car, and flew home in a huff. Yet despite such queasy moments, by the end of the 1980s Richard and Mary appeared to have established a *modus vivendi*.

Also present on the trip was Jubby's new husband, David Ford, who had a highly enjoyable time frightening his father-in-law in speedboats. Christopher Silvester had fallen by the wayside some time ago, and his replacement was the epitome of suit-

336

ability: an Old Etonian, whose father Sir Edward Ford had been the Queen's Assistant Private Secretary and had attended West Downs. Not that any of this was at all relevant – 'If I'd brought home a dustman, Dad wouldn't have cared,' stresses Jubby. Asked how he would have reacted if his daughter had indeed turned up with someone totally unsuitable, Richard replied: 'It happened with Silvester.'

Jubby had been introduced to her husband by Naim Attallah, her boss at Quartet, through whose life she had cut a sizeable swathe. 'Jubby is outrageous, a free spirit – in Richard's eyes she can do no wrong,' he smiles affectionately. Still reeling from her demand to be included in *Nude London*, Attallah found himself banned from the Reform Club after he took her there and she used the gents' lavatory to save time. Then there was a Quartet launch party on an Egyptian theme, to which Richard had been invited; Attallah discovered that his female staff, Jubby among them, had decided to paint their bodies gold and wear see-through muslin dresses. Like a man in fear of his life, Attallah quailed at the mere thought of her father's avenging pen. 'I'd been attacked in the *Eye* since I took over Quartet in 1975,' he laments. 'I'd taken Jubby on because I thought to myself, if she can do the job, probably *Private Eye* will look more sympathetically on me because I'm employing the daughter of the editor. And of course when I did employ her, the attacks became more fierce.'

Fred, meanwhile, had obtained work with Alan Coren at *Punch*, prior to making it as a serious painter, mostly of bold, brash, explicit nudes and Berkshire landscapes, sometimes together in the same painting. Francis Bacon purchased his work. Daniel Farson wrote in the *Mail on Sunday* that 'the dullest of spirits will be lifted by the radiance of his colour . . . and his paintings exude a quality rare in British art – they are sexy.' Fred's skill is inherited from his father, as are the bold brushstrokes. Says John Wells: 'I remember painting with Ingrams at Edinburgh, looking up the hill towards the castle. Most watercolourists work in from the dark to the light, and don't really go for the outline. Ingrams actually draws around the outline with a pen, very bold and confident, but very charming. Rather like the rest of his work, it's done with pure instinct.' Fred considers his father's work 'a bit primitive'. As for his father's view of his own efforts, 'He likes the landscapes but he doesn't like the nudes, because they're about sex. Like a typical English male of his generation, he's not comfortable with sex in an open way.'

In 1989 Fred made Richard a grandfather when he and his girlfriend Sarah Jane Lovett produced a son, Otis Arthur. According to Fred, 'Mum and Dad couldn't believe that we'd called him Otis. My mother told me that if my brother hadn't been called Arthur, he would have been called Otis. My dad would have called him that because of Otis P. Driftwood, the Groucho Marx character, whereas we named him after the lifts'. Richard fell hopelessly for his grandson. When Fred, Sarah Jane and Otis came to stay for the weekend, Otis wet his bed, then got so frightened his parents would find out that he took off his pyjamas and hid them. He came down to breakfast crying, to find his grandfather alone. 'What's the matter, Otis?' asked Richard. 'I wet my bed,' replied Otis. Richard told him not to worry, and asked him what he would like for breakfast. 'I'd like some cheese, please,' said Otis, taking a tiny piece of cheese and pushing it into his mouth. After a while, he admitted, 'I'm only eating the cheese to stop me crying', and started weeping again. At this, Richard started to cry too; and there the pair were discovered, sobbing quietly together at the breakfast table.

Otis was followed in due course by Jubby's children Sam and Phoebe, who calls her grandfather Bummer, and by Fred's second child Queenie. Sheila Molnar reflects: 'There was this very hard, aloof man, who just became a piece of jelly when his grandchildren were around.' They made him extremely happy, and slightly sad as well. 'That,' suggests Liz Elliot, 'would be Richard's melancholia on being presented with this innocent being who's come into this corrupt world. Richard did once say to me that he felt extremely guilty about the world in which we live.' Eventually Jubby left her job to become a housewife and to look after her children; which pleased Richard, for he is old-fashioned in that respect.

Parallel with this happy mushrooming family was a sense of new-found freedom at having given all those lawyers the slip. 'It

felt wonderful, to be free of the worry, and the responsibility,'
he admits.[1] There seemed to be enough interesting work on
offer to make his professional existence as quietly satisfying as
life at home. His plan, upon resigning the editorship, had been
to produce updates of the late John Piper's Shell Guides to the
counties. He looked forward to much tramping down meandering
country lanes on sunny summer afternoons; but the project, sadly, fell through. Instead he took to the airwaves and the aural
equivalent of a meandering country lane, BBC Radio 4.

Since the end of 1985 he has been a regular on *The News Quiz*,
under the chairmanship of Barry Took, where he has forged a
highly effective and contrasting rivalry with Alan Coren. Gradually, he has developed a persona based on a deliberate exaggera-
tion of his own innermost conservatism – a grumpy, elderly,
English curmudgeonliness, an amateur to Coren's consummate
and usually victorious professional. Using this comic voice he
pecks away at the absurdities of modern life and politics. 'He's like
a vulture perched on a branch,' observes Barry Took. 'When the
hyenas have had their fill, he swoops.' He is always at his best
when partnered by the free-ranging John Wells. 'He's not a great
verbal humorist, because he can't fantasise,' offers Coren grudgingly. 'He doesn't embellish to a baroque fantasy, like Wells
does.' Or like Coren does, for that matter; but then Coren, conversely, cannot lay claim to a comic persona. Hence the strength
of their pairing. Often, they reduce Took to helplessness. 'Took's
pissed,' said Coren once. 'No,' said Ingrams, recognising the
condition, 'he has the euphoria of sobriety.'

Richard went on to record a number of series of *Beachcomber . . . by the way*, faithful versions of the old Beachcomber
columns adapted by Michael Barfield, in the company of Wells,
John Sessions, Brian Perkins and Patricia Routledge. On the
strength of this, there followed a series of public readings of
Beachcomber at arts festivals around the country. Throughout,
the Ingrams–Wells partnership flared and glittered by turns as
it always had. On the way to the Salisbury Festival, Wells
driving, Ingrams navigating, they took a wrong turning. Wells
objected. 'Nonsense, Wells, I taught map reading in the army,'

339

commanded Ingrams editorially. They arrived half an hour late after completely losing their way amid countless further wrong turnings.

Ingrams' great ambition was to take over as the host of *Desert Island Discs*, a job relinquished by Michael Parkinson in 1987; the programme's producer was keen, but BBC bigwigs vetoed the suggestion, and Sue Lawley was selected instead. Ingrams had not endeared himself by publicly castigating Parkinson, for describing the show as 'a silly little programme' and for selecting Robert Maxwell as a castaway. Instead, Richard had to make do with occasional slots as a celebrity disc jockey on Radio Two, where his musical guest – very much at the listeners' expense – was the former scourge of the *Eye* letters page, Larry Adler.

Ingrams also found work as a journalist, writing a column first for the *Sunday Telegraph*, and latterly for the *Observer*. The views expressed were thought too radical by the *Telegraph*'s editorship, but the *Observer*'s Donald Trelford was kind enough – in the light of all the pastings he had taken in the *Eye* – to allow Ingrams free rein. The result was a column wherein each paragraph was deliberately calculated to annoy anyone who had agreed with the previous one. There wasn't much wit – being essentially a comic collaborator, he was less effective working alone in this regard – rather a solid meat-and-potatoes exposition of his point of view. Again and again he spoke up for the same causes, notably the oppressed Palestinians and the Catholics of Northern Ireland. Of course these are not really radical causes, but orthodox in their way: whereas the British working man admires the Israelis for their pale skin and their efficiency, patrician support for the Arabs is an older collective memory, dating back at least as far as T.E. Lawrence, and still an article of faith in the Foreign Office. Catholic patrician support for Irish republicanism is essentially sectarian, dignified by the sense of virtue that comes from sticking up for the underdog. The liberal readers of the *Observer* were pleased though, at least until he deliberately annoyed them with his views on other subjects.

By the end of 1990, both professionally and personally, things seemed rosier for Richard Ingrams than they had done four years before. Asked about his domestic situation, he ventured: 'My own view is that once you're married, you're married come what may. The whole thing may go wrong, and obviously does from time to time, but to go to the extent of divorcing I find a very objectionable idea. Obviously I can't make predictions for myself. Maybe in ten years time I shall be divorced, but I hope not.'[2] It was a rash promise. The following year, like a dark cloud that seems only to be passing at first then slowly fills the sky until there is no break in sight, Mary's condition took a considerable turn for the worse.

Mary persuaded herself that Richard was having an affair, or several affairs. Photographs of her husband's professional life, at lunches or book launches where he was inevitably surrounded by adoring women, both fuelled the flames and compensated for the lack of any evidence. Maggie Lunn, who had kept in touch with her old boss, remembers that 'he was rather surprised she minded seeing pictures of him surrounded by all these gorgeous girlies. She said, "He's bonking girlies! He's bonking girlies!" But he wasn't. It wouldn't even have occurred to him.' Mary turned detective, combing Richard's address book and desk drawers for proof of extramarital liaisons. The best she could find was a mildly affectionate letter – unsent – to Julia Reed, an American journalist friend of his pal Graydon Carter's, who lived in New York. Mary announced that their marriage was over: she was leaving. Or rather, *he* was leaving, as he was to get out of their house forthwith.

Rejected and dejected, Richard divided his time between Fred's house, *Private Eye* and a tiny holiday cottage near Rye that the family had recently bought. Mary pursued him with a string of enraged faxes, transmitted to offices where he was working all over London. Several turned up at the *Eye*, where they were seized upon by the journalists with great glee, and by the other staff with some sorrow. 'Her faxes were obscenities,' says David Cash, 'incoherent ramblings really. She had a total fixation that Ingrams was having legovers, which of course he wasn't.' It was rather akin to suggesting that Mother Teresa was running a brothel in her spare time. 'I think she was a very, very disturbed, unhappy lady,' says Tony Rushton.

Several women were named in the faxes. One of the earlier, cleaner specimens starts with a trawl through the 'R' section of Richard's address book: 'As you do Julia Reed under Rushbridger (*sic*) – I'm not very keen coming back from work to hear Julia Reed sqwaking (*sic*) away "You write such wonderful letters I can't wait to see you" You must think me very guillable (*sic*) if you think you can fob me off by saying "it was Graydon Carter" Ha! By the way Polly's surname is Sampson that you record you can't remember in your filthy little notebook but you can be bothered to write down her address and telephone number.' (Polly Sampson being another journalist, a friend of Richard's daughter with whom he had no relationship of any kind.)

Mary also faxed through the original letter to Julia Reed; according to a disappointed Christopher Silvester it 'seemed fairly innocuous, I must say'. Adds The Spiv: 'Mary could easily have contacted Richard by post or by phone, but using the fax meant that whoever happened to be standing by the machine at the time picked it up and thought, "Ooh, this looks interesting". I picked up a couple myself, actually. Richard got most of them last, of course. The girls in the office didn't want him to see them at all.' By faxing a copy of one of his own letters to him, Mary had at least proved that the transmissions were primarily intended for public consumption. It was cruel of her, knowing her husband's professional reticence about his marital difficulties, to publish them so spectacularly. Silvester telephoned Jubby to warn her of her mother's activities, and to see if she could do anything to stop it. A few hours later Mary was on the phone to Silvester herself, spilling out the grievances of many years, shrieking that he was a 'pathetic shirtlifter' and a 'cocksucking little shit'. He burst out laughing. She never spoke to him again. He later claimed to the press that 'I was so dumbfounded I immediately went and told everyone.'[3] Mary then telephoned Hislop on the editor's personal line over and over again, shouting 'You shit, you fucking arsehole'. Hislop had the number changed.

Mary now turned to the tactic that she knew would hurt her husband more than any other, that would pierce him to the core. She telephoned Nigel Dempster at the *Daily Mail* and poured out her incoherent heart. Dempster gave her free rein. 'My husband is a hypocrite,' he quoted her as saying. 'For years he was this high moralist, but the truth is I left him because he is the prototype dirty old man.'[4] 'Dempster ran whatever Mary told him,' says Ian Hislop scornfully. 'Mary would ring up, and Dempster would just put it all in, every bloody time – all about Richard having the affair with the American woman [Julia Reed], which he hadn't. I wish he had. Might have made him a bit happier. But Richard would never say a thing against Mary, so you never got the other side – rather like Charles and Di. Then Mary would say that Dempster had betrayed her! As though Dempster wasn't going to put it all in the paper!'

Time and time again Mary's crazy accusations would appear in the *Mail*. Reflects Richard: 'It was a sign of very great madness that she started talking to Dempster, because she hates him. He's written very nasty things about her over the years, in cold blood.' Indeed, that same year, Dempster informed London Weekend Television that Mary Ingrams was 'an enormous snob'. Yet their uneasy alliance continues to operate to this day. 'Mary spends half the time telling Dempster stories, and the other half of the time screaming down the phone telling him he's a cunt,' chuckles Peter McKay. One senses that McKay is enjoying the game, but that Dempster – although he is the one vigorously pursuing it – is not. The *Mail* diarist still feels hurt, even if it is his pride that has suffered most. The rejection of 1985 still rankles.

Dempster defends himself: 'Why she started calling me, I've got no idea. The whole saga of Richard and his marriage break-up reflects badly on him and not her. If you've got a wife who's got a problem, it's better to protect her than to deride her.' In fact, Ingrams has never derided his wife – quite the reverse – but Dempster continues: 'It may be her fault, who knows. He never spoke about it. She's in many ways a good egg under it all. OK, so clearly he didn't humiliate her by running off with other women, but you can humiliate a woman in many other ways.' Dempster told the *Independent on Sunday* that Mary 'needed help'.

Richard's mother Victoria, by now eighty-three, wrote anonymously to Dempster to remonstrate with him. 'I said that he didn't seem to know that Mary had been a manic depressive for twenty years, that her family had suffered greatly, and that he should consider this when he wrote his next "nasty". I went through agonies having posted that, thinking that he would know who it was, that Ditch would be angry.' Of course, Dempster was already well aware of Mary's mental state, and the unlikelihood of her allegations, but he was not to be deterred from publishing them. Interviewed by BBC Radio, Richard had once rationalised the recruitment of Nigel Dempster to *Private Eye* by describing him as 'a very moral type of writer, who often in his gossip columns seems to be taking the side of wives who have been abandoned, and attacking miscreant men and women from a moral point of view, not from the point of view of pure muck-raker.'[5] Now he was being made to eat his words by the dozen.

Richard exacted his revenge in the way that he has always exacted his revenge – in the form of a joke. In the old days, he would simply have used the columns of *Private Eye* for the purpose, but he no longer had free access to them. He could have asked Hislop, but preferred not to. 'I've been quite careful not to put pressure on Hislop,' he stresses. Instead, he devised a scam to make Dempster's campaign look idiotic. It had long been thought that Paul Halloran was in the habit of telephoning Dempster whenever anything newsworthy happened at the *Eye*; so to catch his attention, Pamella Bordes was invited by Silvester to the next *Eye* lunch. 'Why's that Indian tart been invited?' inquired the New Zealander suspiciously. Hilary, the *Eye*'s receptionist, who had been primed beforehand, dropped hints that there were 'special reasons' behind Pamella's invitation. Pamella, after all, had a record of courting middle-aged editors. The bait was taken. Next, Ingrams set about composing an anonymous letter to the *Mail*:

> Nige. Keep after that organ-playing humbug Ingrams. Who should be seen arm in arm with the old hypocrite walking through Hastings today, but Pamella BORDS. I knew it was her because my mate asked for her autograph. Much to the embarrassment of her pock-marked companion. Fact: Ingrams

is living near Hastings because his wife has thrown him out
because of his womanising.

Go for it. *Private Eye* has never been any good since
you left and that little pigface Hislop makes me sick.

Signed Mail Reader.

Ian Hislop, who was in on the joke, recalls: 'Richard said to me,
"Do you think it will work?" And I said, "It will never work, no
one is that stupid". But Richard said that the last paragraph was
why it would get in, the appeal to Dempster's vanity, and he was
right.' Dempster was totally convinced: the *Mail* diary splashed
with news of the Ingrams–Bordes relationship. The matter did
not end there: poor A.N. Wilson of the *Evening Standard* went
on to write a hurried full-page article identifying the relationship
as part of a major social trend. The following day's papers were
full of crowing revelations about how Dempster and Wilson had
been taken for a ride, including a full page of ridicule in the *Mirror*
at Dempster's expense.

The backlash came the day after that: another full page
in the *Standard*, this time written by Peter McKay, laying
into Ingrams for being 'mad'. A large photograph of Ingrams
appeared with the bubble caption, 'Has anybody seen my mar-
bles?'. Dempster continued to maintain stoutly that the story was
true, and that the anonymous letter was an ingenious double bluff
intended to conceal the fact that the affair had really happened.
Pamella Bordes was not amused. A disgruntled A.N. Wilson
complained that 'Richard is a solipsist who lives entirely within
his own world, more than anyone I know. He's almost like an
autistic child in that respect. He just doesn't realise the effect
his words or actions will have on other people. So he didn't for
a minute think about how the Pamella Bordes hoax would affect
Pamella.'[6] Or, he might have added, how it would affect A.N.
Wilson.

The prevailing conclusion of the national press, torn between
their rivalry with the *Mail* and their desire to put the boot into
Ingrams, was that the whole affair made its originator look foolish.
It didn't particularly, but they certainly hoped that it had. Given
that Richard's marriage was already being pulled to shreds in

345

public, there was some virtue in highlighting the nonsensical nature of Mary's allegations and reducing the whole thing to farce, and something brave in trying to laugh about it. What was odd about the joke, for a man who had always adhered so stolidly to a particular set of moral values, was that he did not seem unhappy for the world to believe him a hypocrite, even in the cause of humour. 'Be true to yourself' was the only philosophy he seemed to care about.

'Unhappiness comes from breaking your principles, not sticking to them,' says Richard's son Fred stoutly. 'My dad's always been utterly consistent. She left him, not the other way around. He wanted to go back, he tried so hard. Anybody else but my father would have left my mother a long time ago, except that he loved her so much.' Former victims of the Ingrams *Eye* felt that he had been gloriously hoist by his own petard, exposed by the press as he had exposed others in the past; but there was no such trite symmetry. His behaviour was indeed utterly consistent and well-meant. The trouble was that even if sticking to his principles had brought Richard personal moral satisfaction, it did not – despite Fred's loyal support – appear to have made him a happy man. Principles don't keep marriages together; indeed they provide little more than comfort, in the face of irrationality. The truth is that Richard couldn't win, he was just lightening the misery of inevitable defeat.

Although she was a Catholic, Mary now requested a divorce, the one thing he had promised himself would never happen. 'I gather I haven't much choice, but I don't want it,' he told the *Independent*. 'It's all taken some getting used to after more than thirty years of marriage.'[7] He tried hard to dissuade her, but her mind was made up. She felt unable to stay at Aldworth even though the house, put in her name to avoid its being sequestrated by the libel courts, was officially hers. 'Their house always felt like *his* house,' says Christopher Silvester. 'All the papers everywhere, the wonderful books, the paintings, the cartoons, the homeliness of it was Richard's.' So the bookshop was sold, and Mary sloped off to the tiny cottage at Rye, while he stayed at Aldworth. There he would grow apple trees, read Dickens, listen to Horowitz records and play the piano to himself. A minor consolation was that he could play the piano whenever he wanted, sometimes even at 3.30 in the morning. Word soon got about that the house was often unoccupied during the day, and it was repeatedly burgled. Many of his valuables were taken. In a very masculine way, Ingrams did not care about his missing camera, but he mourned the undeveloped film within it; the invasion of his personal space meant little. He did not even bother to get the broken windows fixed.

Back in the mid-1970s, Richard had been commissioned to write the biography of Malcolm Muggeridge; in all the intervening years, he had never yet found time to begin unravelling Muggeridge's diaries. Now that he had all the time in the world, his mind was too troubled to begin. 'Since my wife left me I've just found it impossible to sit at home on my own writing a book,' he admitted. 'I need eight hours' sleep, a clear mind, nothing worrying me. I can't manage that because of what happened. I just can't sit on my own all day. I can't do it.'[8]

Sartorially, his appearance deteriorated. 'Mary used to do *everything* for him,' explains Maggie Lunn, who observed the change. 'She used to lay his mints out, and his change and his hankie for him, on the table the night before. It was like Jeeves and Wooster.' Now he was forced to grapple with the mysteries of the washing machine and negotiate supermarkets unaided. 'He's totally useless and impractical,' observes Ian Hislop. 'When his marriage fell apart he would just wear the same old jumper time after time. Sometimes Jubby would get hold of him for a week, and suddenly he'd come into the office wearing a suit, and he'd have had his hair done, and you'd think "Oh! I remember you from ten years ago". I think he let himself go because he was unhappy. There was always an air of sadness about Richard, and I think it got worse.'

Jubby and her family would go down for the weekend to organise the clean-up sessions. 'We would always take our own food with us, because he didn't buy any. I'd have to send him off with shopping lists. And when we came back three weeks later, the food bought that weekend would still be in the fridge and there'd be a terrible smell. Hundreds of carrots fermenting in a bag. Still, women were all over him because he looked so scruffy and helpless.' Mavis Nicholson, Liz Calder, Carmen Callil, Beryl Bainbridge, and Germaine Greer, feminists all, were among those fussing over him. In 1992 they held a birthday party for him; Beryl Bainbridge sang 'Lili Marlene' in German and Germaine Greer sang Schubert. 'They even got a bit catty among each other,' marvels Jubby's husband David. They could not, however, make the old man happy for very long.

Maggie Lunn took Richard out to the theatre, and chattered at him to help him forget. 'He was so sad,' she remembers, 'so bemused by it all and so out of control of it all. He could hardly bear to speak about it. Sometimes he'd be keen to see me, but wouldn't say anything all evening. Then there were a couple of occasions when he couldn't stop talking about it. Once, when he was talking about Mary, he gave himself away by clutching his head. He was really concerned about her. He felt she was really going off the rails. Richard doesn't mind that sort of thing – he's not the sort of person who's unable to cope with someone behaving erratically. But with Mary he was just not able to cope with this incredible bitterness she had for him.' Still he clung to the hope that it would all come right in the end. 'It would demand a great effort to pick up the pieces,' he said, 'and I wouldn't be averse to it. The trouble is, I don't think she does want to come back. I think she's frightened, because she's broken up with so many of her friends. It's not just me.'

All the attention he was getting from members of the public, all the well-meaning questions, just drove him further into himself. Says Maggie Lunn: 'My reigning vision of Richard is of him wandering down the street to *The News Quiz* wearing this bright orange kagoule, with this plastic bag full of newspapers, saying, "I don't want to be bothered by bores". And me saying, "But you *are* attracting attention, Richard". He said, "No I'm not, they can't see me, I've got my hood up". He's always convinced that bores are going to start accosting him. There's this brilliant manner he's got when he's not interested in what someone's saying. We went to the King's Head and someone came up to the bar and was going on and on about "I always thought you were bald when I heard you on the radio". And Richard was staring at me and would not even acknowledge this man. It was real tunnel vision.' When bored, Ingrams could turn silence into an art form.

His only true remaining consolation was his grandchildren. Phoebe was his favourite. 'He likes girls. They get extra special treatment,' says Jubby. Richard asked, hopefully, if his daughter and her family would come and live at Aldworth, but of course they already had a house of their own. 'He did sweet little things to entice us down,' recalls Jubby, 'like framing a picture and putting it up in Phoebe's room to make things more homely. Tears came into his eyes when we had to leave at the end of the weekend. It was quite heart-wrenching to drive off into the night and leave this old man standing at the end of his drive, crying in the headlights.' Richard had reached a point so melancholy that he was capable of feeling nostalgic for the happiness he had experienced that same afternoon; standing there, in his drive, with only Berkshire for company.

24 The Melancholy Heart of England

When a mood of clogging sadness envelops Richard Ingrams, where does his melancholy take him? Always to the past, and always to England. Ingrams yearns for England. Not a flag-waving, morris-dancing, biscuit-tin England, but the big, messy whole, with all its contradictions and disappointments; an England with its ancient heart somewhere up on the Downs, but its sinews stretching into every council estate and seedy pub, exerting its mysterious pull of loyalty. The vast majority of Englishmen may not give two hoots for old churches and country lanes, preferring to make do with videos and lager, but they will fight to the death to defend their inheritance like no other race.

In 1989 Ingrams published *England – An Anthology*, a collection which together with its introductory essay is one of his most revealing works. In it he confesses that his – and *Private Eye*'s – lifetime of railing against motorways, tower blocks and pylons is itself part of an English tradition, the 'triumphant pessimism' of Ruskin: 'Running through the whole of our literature, especially that of the Romantic era and beyond, is a deeply held conviction on the part of the nobler spirits that the country is irrevocably doomed.' Ingrams gives this example, from the index to the 1892 edition of Dr Johnson's letters:

ENGLAND, all trade dead, 120; poverty and degradation, 150; sinking, 264; fear of a civil war, 286; times dismal and gloomy, 370; see also INVASIONS.

'So while on the surface everything has changed', he concludes, 'nothing has really changed at all.'[1]

The book's epigraph – Ruskin's phrase 'Blind, tormented, unwearied, marvellous England' – encapsulates this tradition of damning and loving England in the same breath. It is this duality that lies at the core of Ingrams' feelings for his country, that has enabled him to satirise it so affectionately in the person of such characters as Sir Herbert Gussett. *Private Eye* has always loved England, which is why it attacks her and all her foibles so mercilessly. The butts of the magazine's jokes have often failed to appreciate the affection that their admission to the *Eye*'s comic cast denotes. Genuine dislike was always reserved for the Maxwells and the Goldsmiths, who never understood England, and tried to make her do their bidding.

Ingrams himself is instantly recognisable in some of the pieces he has anthologised. Maurois, for instance, complains that 'In France it is rude to let a conversation drop; in England it is rash to keep it up. No one there will blame you for silence. When you have not opened your mouth for three years, they will think, "This Frenchman is a nice quiet fellow".'[2] Nowhere is Ingrams' true nature more accurately captured, though, than in his own definition of melancholy and nostalgia as the abiding characteristics of the English. 'Cricket is our national game,' he observes, 'but the most famous line of cricketing literature (unintelligible to any foreigner) – "Oh my Hornby and my Barlow long ago" – typically harks back to the cricket matches of the past and the very English names of two totally forgotten men. It strikes a chord. Dickens strikes a chord arguably more than anyone because he describes . . . an England just out of reach which we all long to recapture, like a fading dream, but which we know never existed in reality.'[3] Ingrams is a true nostalgist, one of those people who suffers from a wistful, aching nostalgia for times past, even those he has never experienced. It is for this reason that he will never be truly happy. Even not particularly happy memories are made heartbreaking by the fact that they can never be recaptured. The idealised past populated by the happiest memories is thus the most heartbreaking of all.

Richard Ingrams

Fittingly, Ingrams' favourite cartoonist (for a collection of whose work he provided an introduction) is English and long dead. Pont, the brilliant pre-war *Punch* artist who died so very young, drew a world of social rituals and nuances scarcely penetrable to the foreigner, for Englishmen proud to recognise themselves as obsessive, taciturn, phlegmatic, traditionalist, pragmatic, insular, impassive, rather proper and slightly mad. One drawing, entitled 'Disinclination to go anywhere', shows a man slumped in a comfortable armchair while his wife, who has got someone on the phone asking them to dinner or drinks, gazes at him with a look of desperation in her eyes. 'That man is me,' admits Ingrams. Pont said of his work: 'I do not try to draw funny people. I try hard to draw people exactly as they are.'[4] Meaning that the accurate observation of his countrymen was funnier, and less liable to date, than trying to 'tickle the fancy' of the Englishman; which is perhaps where *Private Eye* got it right and where *Punch* went wrong in its dying years.

The novelist Sebastian Faulks suggests that 'the most successful expressions of Englishness have been indirect. They have come when the writer has been describing something else, usually a known and loved part of the English landscape. Hardy's Dorset, Ted Hughes' Yorkshire and Devon have the quality, as do Housman's hills in a more sentimental way. There is something mysterious even in the words Wenlock Edge.'[5] It would be pleasing to say the same about Richard Ingrams' Berkshire, but sadly it remains more evocative in his emotions than it does on paper.

Ingrams' illustrated book on the Berkshire Ridgeway, published in 1988, derives from his love for the ancient track and those luminaries such as Betjeman and Kenneth Grahame that settled there, but it is a love that tends to resist explanation. Referring to the Wansdyke, we are told merely that it is 'one of the many wonders of Wiltshire'. The general reader seems to be held at arm's length. Like being a member of a club, one has to belong already to share his sense of affection, and Ingrams is not interested in any recruiting drive.

The same restraint characterises *Piper's Places*, Ingrams' 1983

352

record of the work of John Piper, and the English and Welsh counties that he painted. Piper found nondescript Britain in the rain a source of beauty; there is a priceless anecdote recording George VI's struggle to find something to say after perusing his work. 'You've been pretty unlucky with the weather, Mr Piper,' he eventually managed. One can just imagine those words in the voice of Edward Fox. Piper's own descriptions, as quoted by Ingrams, are evocative and knowledgeable, for instance this passage concerning a group of unfashionable mid-Victorian villas near Reading:

'It is their uselessness I like, and their over-richness and their proportion all their own. These illustrate Sherlock Holmes, for it was in a house like these that the Norwood builder lived. Verandahs which are never sat in; gas light in stained glass halls; under-servants; murders in the basement; death on the first floor; plaster ceilings that the uninitiated might think were seventeenth century, and a great plaster chrysanthemum for the gasolier. Geraniums in urns in the garden. "In" and "Out" on the front door and a gravel sweep for the brougham and a hot house for the orchids. Sunday dinner and a well-established firm in the town. Tea and croquet.'

That elusive Englishness that Faulks referred to, of an enthusiast at home in familiar surroundings, radiates from every line; by contrast, Ingrams' own description of the fens in the same book seems – to use an appropriate adjective – rather flat. 'Richard doesn't really care about writing at all, in the way that some writers slave for the perfect words,' suggests Andrew Osmond. 'He is an editor and a parodist.' His great strengths are clarity and humour rather than description. Journalists don't paint landscapes, they merely tell you what there is to see.

When he deals with people, Ingrams is transformed. The strongest passages in *Piper's Places* concern John Piper's friendships with Betjeman, J.M. Richards and Geoffrey Grigson. The comradeship and companionship of bygone Englishmen stirs Ingrams' sense of melancholy and nostalgia to its depths. His closest male friends have always been of profound importance to him – as Andrew Osmond said, take them away and the night would close in – but almost as if none of those friendships have quite fulfilled their idealised promise, Ingrams has a curious habit of appropriating the friendships of other men. Perfect friendships, in which he can wallow without ever leaving his fireside, with friends he will never meet.

Malcolm Muggeridge introduced Ingrams to his two closest friends, Hugh Kingsmill and Hesketh Pearson. They in turn became Ingrams' friends, even though both had been dead for many years. He read their letters to each other, and in due course wrote up the story of their friendship in *God's Apology*, the book taking its title from Kingsmill's remark that 'Friends are God's apology for relations'. According to Andrew Osmond, '*God's Apology* is the key to Richard Ingrams. In as far as he's ever put his own creed on paper, it's that – indirectly, of course. The book stands for England, for male friendship, shared laughter, literary pursuit, and there's a religious element throughout.' It is also about unsuccessful marriage, a problem that seems to have bedevilled many of his heroes. Ingrams had initially cultivated Muggeridge as one of his 'old men', but ultimately the book is nostalgic for the friendship of three young men, a friendship which, as he had never directly shared it, could never be brought back or tarnished.

Although undemonstrative, Kingsmill was the dominant figure in the trio, an iconoclastic and much underrated author in the tradition of Chesterton and Belloc, with an Ingrams-like eye for spotting humbug in men of power. It was he who brought the other two together. Pearson, jollier and more secular than Kingsmill, was a biographer and writer of great wit: in the 1930s he sat through a tiresome dinner with a man who expounded the benefits of Nazism at great length, concluding with the remark, 'Makes yer think, eh?' to which Pearson replied, 'Nothing could make *you* think'. Muggeridge, the junior member of the trio, was to Ingrams 'the one person I know in whose company I never experienced one moment of boredom'. This was a rare tribute indeed. Like Ingrams, Muggeridge was extremely easily bored. Pearson used to speak of his 'N.A. (standing for Next Appointment) look'. Acerbic and pessimistic, Muggeridge instilled in

354

Ingrams many of the values that the trio held dear: 'A love of England and English literature; a dislike of intellectuals; a deep suspicion of all institutions and any form of collective activity and a shared sense of humour with no traces in it of snobbery . . . or class consciousness.'[6]

Their lack of respect for authority and their sense of humour led them into ventures not dissimilar from *Private Eye*. At one stage Pearson faced jail for writing a bogus diplomat's memoirs that lampooned the publisher of the *Daily Mail*. He survived by being 'classically defiant' – although, as he admitted, 'I shall not pretend for a moment I didn't piss myself pretty frequently during the process of being classical'. In 1936 Muggeridge and Kingsmill tried unsuccessfully to start their own humour magazine, after attacking *Punch* because 'its ultra-respectable prosperous atmosphere no longer corresponds to the temper of the age'. Instead they joined *Night and Day*, a humour magazine started by Graham Greene, that was finished off after just one year by a libel writ from Shirley Temple.

The three shared an Ingrams-like disregard for men of influence and systems of power: 'Systems, whatever the philosophy out of which they have grown, necessarily value truth less than victory over rival systems,' wrote Hugh Kingsmill. Both he and Muggeridge recognised that power needs something to feed on, an acquiescent hoi polloi: 'People believe lies not because they are plausibly presented but because they want to believe them,' observed Muggeridge. The less politically conscious Pearson merely expressed the view that 'I love people who blow respectability and the establishment to bits'.

Ingrams was most crucially influenced by a guiding philosophy of Kingsmill's that divided the human race into those who live by the will and those who live by the imagination. 'Richard sets a lot of store by this division,' confirms Andrew Osmond. Into the former category went the power-seekers, the men of action; into the latter group went the creative, the poetic, the artistic, and of course the humorous. 'The will draws a man towards the collective, the imagination towards himself,' concluded Ingrams. 'The pursuit of power is barren, the life of the man of action –

Napoleon or Caesar – boring.'[7] This last is a fairly substantial paradox to swallow: it would perhaps be more accurate to suggest that the likes of Ingrams and Kingsmill would not have enjoyed the administration of a mighty empire for the sake of power. 'The distinction has always seemed pure bollocks to me,' says Osmond. 'Ingrams imposed his will on people and events, very much so.'

Humour, especially at the expense of those who seek to rule over us, was for Ingrams a sign of the imagination at work. 'Laughter dissolved the absurd solemnities of the will, of power, of the world of action . . . [pomposity was] for Kingsmill not a cause of anger or indignation – "To be angry is to be wrong", he once said – but of mirth.'[8] This, according to Osmond, is how Ingrams has lived his life and directed the efforts of *Private Eye*: 'It's not so much that he hates authority – he finds it ridiculous. Most human endeavour is absurd in his eyes.'

Kingsmill was also keen to stress that no man's professional life can be judged in isolation from his personal life: 'To dismiss the poet and concern oneself only with the poetry has a specious air of dignity and superiority to personal gossip . . . No man can put more virtue into his words than he practises in his life.'[9] It might have been a manifesto for *Private Eye*. Ironically, Kingsmill too liked to keep his own professional and private lives separate: 'Keep things in their frame, old man, keep things in their frame,' he said when Alec Waugh expressed a desire to meet his wife.

All three men were of course linked by a love of England, a nation of individualists where the imagination ultimately tended to triumph over the will. Said Pearson: 'I love a nation that does not go off the deep end on the slightest provocation. We are a balanced race. Our main virtue is that we never feel enthusiasm for abstract ideals. Humour is our greatest gift, our divinely rational merit. Kings may come and kings may go, but we scarcely trouble to notice.'[10] Kingsmill, Pearson and Muggeridge loved the landscape and the literature of England, the England of Sussex and the Cotswolds, of Shakespeare and Dr Johnson. Like Ingrams they looked back with melancholy nostalgia to a day-dream England; as Kingsmill described it (with reference to

356

the illustrations of Hugh Thomson), 'people and houses just far enough away, diminished but distinct, a little Eden of jollity and content, far more appealing . . . than any heaven one must work to get into.'[11]

Dr Johnson, naturally, being a stout and comforting figure, was one of Ingrams' heroes as well. Christopher Logue recalls: 'Ingrams is difficult to flatter, but I flattered him by accident when I told him that if I was doing a film about Johnson, I'd cast him as Johnson. His face lit up.' In 1984 Ingrams edited a memoir of Dr Johnson by Mrs Thrale (not in fact a creation of J.B. Morton, but the wife of one of the Doctor's close friends). Mrs Thrale saw Johnson as 'more of a man of Imagination than Passion',[12] a description that fitted Kingsmill's division perfectly. Appropriately, Johnson had 'a Contempt for small matters . . . Politics not excepted',[13] and fashioned a measured world where *bons mots* and insults were a civilised corrective to those who attempted to rise above their station in life. There were other obvious parallels with Ingrams. In his introduction to *England – An Anthology*, Ingrams wrote: 'How appropriate it should be that Dr Johnson is still regarded as the quintessential Englishman, a man whose popular image is that of a convivial old party seated in a tavern surrounded by cronies, but who was in private a deeply melancholy man troubled by all kinds of doubts and feelings of guilt.'[14]

Ingrams has always felt obliged to collate, edit and disseminate the work of his literary heroes; much of the task has been under-taken since he resigned the *Eye*'s editorship. The greatest hero of all was William Cobbett, who was first on the list with *Cobbett's Country Book*, an anthology of his writings on rural matters. The pamphleteer was truly a man after Ingrams' own heart: 'With his nostalgia, his love of the countryside, his philistinism and strong views, his sympathy with working men and hatred of parsons and politicians he represents the stubborn spirit of the best kind of Englishman more closely than any other character in history.'[15] Like Ingrams, Cobbett's view of England was coloured by the past. He too looked backward rather than forward; each parish church was to him a melancholy reminder that things had once been otherwise.

Cobbett labelled the powers-that-be THE THING, 'by which he meant the network of MPs, stockbrokers, money-lenders, placemen and hacks bound together by mutual interests, who were running the country.'[16] THE THING viciously persecuted Cobbett for his boat-rocking activities. He had to flee abroad after he tried unsuccessfully to expose a military fiddle. He spent two years in Newgate following a charge of criminal libel, when he attacked the flogging of mutinous soldiers. He was acquitted when the government tried to make him personally responsible for an outbreak of agricultural rioting. As Ingrams notes, Cobbett's 'ripest abuse was reserved for those whose conduct was at odds with their stated principles . . . Humbug of any kind Cobbett had an eye for. Once he spotted it, his abuse was merciless.'[17] In defence of *Private Eye*'s investigations into the private lives of the famous, Ingrams would frequently quote Cobbett: 'Amongst the persons whom I have heard express a wish to see the press what they call free, and at the same time to extend their restraints on it with regard to persons in their private lives . . . I have never, that I know of, met with one who had not some powerful motive of his own for the wish, and who did not feel that he had some vulnerable part about himself.'

Richard Ingrams' life and work must be seen in the context of this great English radical tradition, and the men who upheld it. Critics will say that he stands in line self-consciously, wanting to belong; but of course he does, how could it be otherwise if he wishes to fight the same causes as they? The test is to ask whether he would have lived the same life if Johnson, Cobbett, Kingsmill and others had never existed, and the answer is indubitably yes.

If such men influenced Ingrams' secular life, one who influenced his religious thoughts – and whose sayings he has more recently anthologised – is G.K. Chesterton. Again, the parallels are striking: Chesterton edited his own magazine and enjoyed having his own platform; he too was a mixture of sage and joker; he was a consummate professional writer able to turn out articles to order; he took risks with facts where he sensed

358

authenticity; and his work was suffused with his own brand of moral orthodoxy. Chesterton's orthodoxy was Roman Catholic, making it both an appeal to older, deeper-rooted values, truer and nobler, and at the same time a minority viewpoint that would strike the Establishment as alien, disloyal or even dangerous. It finds its echo in Ingrams' own almost Catholic morality.

Chesterton's arguments for Catholicism strike Ingrams as especially persuasive: 'First of all, his general attitude towards religion, which is to say that it is natural for people to believe in God, and that the people who don't believe in God are the freaks. Then, in a more specific Catholic way, he describes how he's very attracted by the idea of the Virgin Mary – whom the Protestants elbowed out, hence the ridiculous "God is a woman" attitude caused by her absence. I feel inclined towards Catholicism partly because it's become impossible to hold the Church of England in the kind of romantic affection that someone like John Betjeman stood for . . . very possibly I might convert to Roman Catholicism in old age.' More specifically, Ingrams believes that the Church of England has abdicated the clear moral lead that still emanates from Rome, and has lost the Catholic Church's sense of discipline.

Chesterton's arguments, of course, have fallen on fertile ground. Ingrams has felt drawn to Catholicism since childhood on account of his upbringing. His sense of guilt has a strong whiff of Catholicism about it. Yet something has always held him back from embracing Catholicism wholeheartedly. It is difficult to iden-tify the source of this ambivalence, as Ingrams himself seems to have trouble doing so. Perhaps it is twofold. On the one hand, it may be a simple matter of divided loyalties. Ingrams believes in loyalty, and to leave the Church of England would be disloyal, even if he feels that the Church has gradually abandoned him over the years. On the other hand, it may also find its roots in the debate as to whether Catholicism really does represent a purer and nobler faith than that which replaced it, as Catholics such as Auberon Waugh insist. Catholicism was thrown out of England by Englishmen, notwithstanding the Welshman Henry VIII's help, because it was foreign and corrupt, riddled with abuses of power and bogus saintly ritual intended to fleece its adherents. If Richard Ingrams had been alive in the sixteenth century he would have railed against its excesses. However irrelevant a 450-year-old description of the Catholic Church may be today, the Church of England still boasts the magic word 'England'.

Now that the importance of religion in our political lives has receded so dramatically, the most important contradiction in Ingrams' powerful array of views is unlikely ever to be seriously challenged; for the discipline and the centrally imposed moral code that Ingrams so admires in Catholicism is directly at odds with the individualism and the imagination he urges upon the secular world. The organised church, especially the Roman church, promotes collectivism and is packed to the fan-vaulting with power-seekers. It is hierarchical, authoritarian and centralist. Chesterton, of course, would counter that the chief aim of such order is 'to give room for good things to run wild'; but this is a specious argument applied by powerful hierarchies throughout history.

This contradiction emerges strongly in Ingrams' memoir of John Stewart Collis, the much-neglected writer on matters rural whom he befriended in the last years of his life. Although an admirer of Collis, Ingrams clearly dislikes what he sees as Collis' 'nature worship' – making a personal approach to God outside the official channels. The likes of D.H. Lawrence, Edward Carpenter, Walt Whitman, Wordsworth and Havelock Ellis are similarly criticised for their 'pseudo-religious writings'. Ingrams quotes St Clement of Alexandria (from the second century AD), to the effect that 'the beginning of truth is to wonder at things' – and not the ultimate revelation, when the wondering must stop. He concludes: 'Men who create their own private religions, as Collis's heroes did, do so because they cannot humble themselves before God . . . God is replaced by an "inner voice" which is another word for self.' Theologically, at least, this is what the Reformation was all about; Ingrams speaks here with the authentic voice of Rome.

Ingrams' own sense of wonder about the unknown is carefully bottled under 'mysticism' as opposed to 'spiritualism'. Mysticism, in the words of Hugh Kingsmill, 'is the intuition of a harmony which envelops but does not penetrate this life, and which can be apprehended but not completely possessed'.[18] Spiritualism, conversely, is fanciful nonsense for the unimaginative. In other words, does it conform with religious orthodoxy or not? This division enables Ingrams to be fascinated by corn circles, and he will happily spend hours standing in a field surrounded by hippies holding dowsing rods, their faces painted with CND symbols. The photograph which has pride of place in his family album shows his grandson Otis sitting in a corn circle in a rasta hat. Corn circles are mystical puzzles of Christian rural England; they are exclusive. There aren't any rice circles in Burma, for instance.

When Ingrams steps into better understood territory, such as the history of the Berkshire Ridgeway, the need to stay on orthodox religious ground leads him into difficulties. 'Nobody knows for certain what the Ridgeway's purpose is, what it commemorates (if anything) or even who put it there,' he says. 'Such lack of information is reassuring.'[19] Comforting, rather, as the reality is almost certainly pagan. Referring to the White Horse of Uffington, he quotes Paul Nash's description of it as 'more of a dragon than a horse', but ignores this important pointer to pre-Christian origin. This is the area where Arthur and Alfred beat back heathen invaders, he points out (very, *very* approximately), so 'whatever the truth of these matters it cannot be perverse or inappropriate if we insist on regarding the White Horse of Uffington as a symbol of Christian England victorious over invading pagans.'[20]

Well, yes it can. The White Horse is probably pre-Christian, Arthur was a Briton who defeated the English, and Dark Age kings felt quite able to pick up and drop Christianity – about which they knew little – as it suited them, depending upon how the military campaign of the day was doing. The paths, standing stones, tumuli, forts, holy sites and festival days of England are far, far older than the church established here by St Augustine. Where possible, later clergymen endeavoured to make this jumbled reality conform to orthodox Christian organisation, and where they could not, they let the grass grow long. After all, is not the New Testament itself a retrospective fourth-century cobbling-together of various confused second-hand accounts? As Richard Ingrams should know, not all the facts ever quite fit the official version.

Richard Ingrams

By the second half of the 1980s, when Ingrams sat down to anthologise and annotate the work of his various heroes, all the old men he had cultivated were dead or about to die. Piper, Cockburn, Muggeridge, Collis, A.J.P. Taylor, Betjeman ('another very English Englishman who, behind his jolly, avuncular façade, was inwardly tormented'[21]), all the woolly, reassuring blankets of Englishness he had wrapped himself in were gone. One of the inevitable sadnesses involved in replacing your father with older friends is that his death must eventually be revisited time and time again. Ingrams now felt that he had emerged alone from the ranks of these men, to take on the mantle of seniority himself; a little early perhaps – as his *News Quiz* persona bore witness, there was an element of comic self-parody involved – but behind the jokes lay a genuine desire to welcome the embrace of old age, with an enthusiasm that most people reserve for resisting it.

When Beachcomber died in 1979, alone and forgotten, Ingrams was horrified to discover that all his effects, his unpublished writings, had been bundled together and thrown away. Obsessed with finding and discussing the latest thing, the media – and society in its wake – seemed to be callously ignoring all these wise and wonderful old men that Ingrams had known and loved. What price the words of G.K. Chesterton, when George Michael had something important to say about world peace? 'I sometimes feel there aren't any great men any more,' lamented Ingrams.[22] What too of the wise old heads still alive, the ones about to slip from our grasp? He felt, even more strongly than he had thirty years before, that society was too wrapped up with the fashion of the moment, that it had no time for the wisdom of experience. Now that he had time that needed killing, he resolved to do something to rectify matters.

25 Older Than Thou

Naim Attallah, the butt of so many *Eye* jokes, had finally become friends with Richard Ingrams when Jubby had invited her father over to the Quartet offices for lunch. 'I saw him in a different light then,' explains Attallah. 'I got to like him. I discovered that Richard is marvellous as a friend, terrible as a foe. He became my champion.' Ingrams allowed himself to be interviewed by Attallah for his book *Singular Encounters*, and persuaded Yehudi Menuhin to do likewise. A staunch Palestinian, a Catholic and a long-time friend of Auberon Waugh's, Attallah slotted neatly into the Ingrams pattern of friendships. He was not intimidated by Ingrams, a prerequisite for any sort of mutual regard. As well as being the owner of Quartet books and the *Literary Review*, Attallah was also chief executive of Asprey the jewellers, which made him staggeringly rich; but this made no difference. 'Naim is the first rich person I've met whom I like,' said Ingrams.[1] In fact, it was to become a very useful attribute indeed.

The idea of a magazine that would entertain the old at heart began life unseriously. 'He probably felt it was his turn to start a magazine,' joked Willie Rushton, in reference to Ingrams' absence from *Private Eye*'s founding fellowship. Hislop suggested *The Old Bore* as a title. Ingrams thought it a funny idea, and the title mutated into *The Oldie*. Soon all the talking became serious. 'The idea may have started as a joke, but now he cares very passionately about it,' said Fred Ingrams. Unfortunately, the days when you could start a successful magazine from your mother's bedroom

363

with just £450 and a tin of Cow gum were long past. Feasibility studies suggested that such a magazine would need £230,000 to get off the ground. Ingrams' friend Stephen Glover, one of the founders of the *Independent*, set about looking for backers; the most obvious candidate was not hard to find.

Naim Attallah eventually put in £70,000. 'I'd do anything to help Richard,' he says with the same gleam of helpless devotion in his eye that has infected so many of Ingrams' staff over the years. In fact Attallah had to be actively restrained from funding the whole project, a slight which annoyed Auberon Waugh. 'Waugh has no commercial sense – which I do,' growled Ingrams in reply,[2] stressing the need for independence from any proprietor, however benevolent. Eventually Ingrams put up £20,000 of his own money – the first time he had dared to invest in anything since Tomorrow's Audience thirty years before; £12,000 each came from Waugh, Glover, Alexander Chancellor, John McEwen and Patrick Marnham, now apparently recovered from the dis-agreements of 1982.

There was a lot of money at stake. *The Oldie* would have to sell 30,000 copies a fortnight to survive; but accounting, marketing and other such financial disciplines had the same effect on Ingrams as the law, sending his attention drifting off out of the window and away to pastures green. 'At the board meetings of *The Oldie* he just sits there like a mouse,' says Auberon Waugh. 'All the running is made by me, Naim, Stephen Glover, or Johnny McEwen.' On a humbler administrative level, Ingrams found himself making rueful telephone calls to Tony Rushton, David Cash and Sheila Molnar, the *Eye* boxwallahs, to ask what to do. One obvious concession to economy he made without ceremony: before long he waived his right to an editorial salary.

Ingrams had once outlined to a journalist how old age had changed his point of view: 'When I was young I fell in love with women, recited poetry, drank too much, and had ideals – all of them time-consuming and debilitating traits. When you are young you believe the world can be changed and this is a danger-ous illusion.' This accorded with Hesketh Pearson's observation that 'The youth of twenty who does not think the world can be improved is a cad; the man of forty who still thinks it can is a fool.'

The point of *The Oldie* was precisely to celebrate old age as a point of view; it was never intended as special-interest reading for pensioners. 'The men in suits say, "Who are you targeting? Who is it aimed at?", but I don't have an audience in view,' complained Ingrams. 'In fact, I am rather distressed at all these letters coming in from oldies who assume it's their magazine. I think this should be discouraged. I don't *want* all the readers to be oldies.'[3] The financial press envisaged articles about hip replacement and advertisements for Sanatogen, and reacted cautiously. The media page of *The Times* warned that 'Media-buying decisions are so often made by smart young things for whom anyone over 40 has dropped off the demographic map'. Indeed Ingrams couldn't resist one joke which inadvertently played into the smart young things' preconceptions, by offering free subscriptions to anyone over the age of 100. Mr J.W. Beard of Warsop, Mansfield, aged 102, was the first to take advantage of the offer.

On account of this mistaken perception, the magazine was careful to avoid the complaining tone of the pensioner at the bus stop, adopting instead a more positive view than that of the *Eye*. Says Ingrams: 'When I was talking to Candida about doing a thing on heritage and architecture, I thought we ought to have something knocking the mess that people have made. And then I thought, well that's what she and her father did in *Private Eye* with 'Nooks and Corners'. Why don't we have articles about how nice certain places are? In a certain sense you could say that *The Oldie* became the positive side of *Private Eye*.' Candida Lycett Green was commissioned to write a series called 'Unwrecked England', which could equally well have served as a title for the magazine itself.

A four-page *Oldie* prospectus sent out early in 1992, and designed in such a way as to make Tone look professional, encapsulated the Ingrams creed in every item. There was 'Voice from the Grave', a memorable quotation from a dead Englishman, in this instance G.K. Chesterton: 'Christmas is a contradiction of modern thought. Christmas is an obstacle to modern progress

. . . Born among miracles reported from two thousand years ago, it cannot expect to impress that sturdy common sense which can withstand the plainest and most palpable evidence for miracles happening at this moment . . . Christmas is a superstition, Christmas is a survival of the past. But why go on piling up the praises of Christmas?' (Actually 25 December was a long-standing pagan festival to which the celebration of the birth of Christ was retrospectively applied, but one takes Chesterton's point.)

In similar vein the prospectus included a cartoon of a bearded C of E vicar, intoning 'Give us this day our daily high-fibre loaf with added B-vitamins, iron, calcium . . .' There was an excerpt from a forthcoming Naim Attallah interview with Bill Deedes, who had clearly forgotten or forgiven the 'Dear Bill' letters, in which Deedes warned, 'The great risk of old age, unless you exercise your mind, is that you become a tremendous bore.' There was also a column entitled Youthspeak, first of a series of incoherent youthful ramblings, in which the lead singer of the Happy Mondays, Shaun Ryder, explained to NME readers that 'I had to show me head, there's no point going to a pub where people don't know me and cause a scene, I had to go where there was heads that knew me. I got narked and smashed some mirror in the Dry Bar, I just wanted people to see that I was annoyed. Some people from the bar said "Why pick on us?" But I wasn't picking on anybody. I don't give a f***, though, they can't say anything, they [Factory] owe me a hundred grand. I'm paying for nish.' The TV critic of the new magazine was to be none other than Ingrams himself, highly inappropriately as his television had been burgled. Not that he enjoyed television anyway – at the *Eye* he had had a sign printed saying 'I did not watch telly last night'.

In keeping with these familiar opinions was a list of very familiar prospective contributors indeed. Apart from Waugh, Marnham, Attallah and Candida Lycett Green, there were A.N. Wilson, Germaine Greer, Henry Porter, Graydon Carter, Christopher Booker and the *Eye*'s latest recruit Francis Wheen. Jubby was signed up to cook the regular *Oldie* lunch, and her husband David Ford was taken on as business manager. Mere nepotism? 'Certainly not,' barks Auberon Waugh, 'giving his family a lot of dud jobs.'

Lord Soames' daughter Emma was hired as deputy editor, and the girls in the office were to be Sloanier than ever before. There was to be a nice, easy-going, well-bred atmosphere. Halloran was not invited. 'Nobody wants to join Ingrams' club anyway,' retorted the New Zealander. 'Who's there? Journalism's fuck-ups. Marnham. Porter. Waugh. A. N. Fucking Wilson,' he added, referring with characteristic delicacy to Wilson's previously unpublished middle name.

Premises were hired at the top of several flights of rickety stairs in Charlotte Street, and Ingrams ferried over all his favourite *Eye* souvenirs and paraphernalia to create a womb-like air of instant mess. Maggie Lunn and Jubby went to help set up the new office. 'There were all these terrifying Sloanes in leopardskin trousers,' remembers Maggie. 'I had to buy the office chairs. Me and Jubby, who was quite pregnant at the time, were wheeling these chairs up Charlotte Street, and then sweating up the stairs with them. He can get people to do the most extraordinary things. He was completely charming. "These chairs are marvellous. What wonderful chairs". I've adored him for years,' she sighs. 'I'm just another one of the girl fan club that got chucked over.' Her eyes go all misty.

'I never understand how he does it,' says David Ford. 'It's a complete mystery to me, because you think nothing is going to happen, but it always does. There doesn't appear to be a great deal of organisation, but quietly it all materialises. For a magazine launch, he was the most unflappable editor. It was complete chaos at the launch of *The Oldie*. We had one month to set everything up, but throughout it all he was completely serene. He's got an incredibly light touch.'

The magazine's launch took place at The Academy, a literary club founded by Auberon Waugh in Beak Street. John Wells happened to drop in to see Ingrams at the *Eye* that day: 'He wasn't there, but they said he was down at The Academy, so I went down there and pushed the doorbell and went downstairs, and there were the remains of this very large lunch. It turned out to have been the launch of *The Oldie*. I said, "I think you might have asked me", and he avoided my eyes and mumbled

"Oh, invitations go astray". He's so insensitive to other people's feelings. I was terribly upset and irrationally offended – like a real husband-and-wife relationship.'

In February 1992, the first issue of *The Oldie* was published. Fleet Street's response to the new magazine was, predictably, a critical onslaught, led by Dempster and McKay. '*The Oldie* is the ultimate conceit and folly of Richard Ingrams,' wrote Dempster in a full-page *Mail* attack. 'But his day, as proved by this silly venture, is over . . . Auberon Waugh, probably the most prolific journalist of our time, fails to deliver . . . Even the reporting content is unsound: an attempt at a gossip column – called 'Outed' – tries to make a mystery out of the age of Lord King, the British Airways Chairman. Turn to the reference book I published a year ago for his birthdate and the answer is: August 29, 1916.'[4]

'*The Oldie* is a joke. It'll go down with all hands,' says Peter McKay with some scorn, describing Ingrams as 'Peter Pan in reverse.' Hearing a rumour, not in fact correct, that the magazine was an illegal tenant at Charlotte Street, the *Standard* sent a reporter to check on the lease in the hope of having the staff evicted. The paper also more or less accused a male relative of Ingrams – unnamed – of sexually harassing editorial assistant Lucy Blackburn, although no such complaint had been made. This could only have been a reference either to Fred or to David Ford. 'McKay was just throwing a stone in the water to see where the ripples went,' offers Ford. Whatever the reason, Fleet Street's treatment of the gentle new magazine seemed to be going well beyond the normal bounds of a reviewer's criticism.

'*The Oldie* is sure to be a lot of fun,' joined in the *Guardian*, 'full of poisonous carping about the young and thinly concealed jealousy of their fast, bright lives. It will prove that this satirist of a certain age, this doyen of the dinosaur hacks, this gerontosaurus rex, is committed only to the cares of his class, sex and generation. Sod the rest.' Of particular worry to the hysterical hacks were the editor's attempts to publicise his creation. Continued the *Guardian* apoplectically: 'Every half-baked afternoon chat show or early evening quiz, there's Ingrams, peeking over the top of his half-moon specs and picking his nose.'[5] Peter McKay had informed

London Weekend Television that 'Richard is a grotesque self-publicist. He's like a page three girl. I mean, he would have gone on a coach to the Orkneys to take part in a radio phone-in show.'[6]

It is true that Ingrams is an enthusiastic promoter of whatever publication he may be working on at the time, but no more so than many other editors or authors. He had frequently mentioned his own books in his *Observer* column, he had consented to appear on radio's *In the Psychiatrist's Chair*, and as far back as 1966 he and Willie Rushton had agreed to pose for a fashion shoot in *She* magazine. Now he agreed to pose for the fashion pages again, appearing in the *Observer* in the self-consciously anti-*Oldie* garb of a leather jacket and jeans. Lynn Barber in the *Independent on Sunday* sneered that he looked 'like a middle-aged queen trying to pass himself off as a bit of rough trade.'[7] *Private Eye*, slightly more mischievously, published an 'Ena B. Rushton' lookalike letter – of the sort that had made Robert Maxwell sob – comparing Ingrams' photograph to that of a leather-clad gay dancer in *City Limits* magazine. Ingrams retreated ruefully to lick his wounds. 'It might have been a mistake,' he admitted.[8]

Voices of support were few and far between. Old friends such as Christopher Logue and Noel Picarda surfaced to offer their congratulations – and with reason, too, for despite the early loss of Emma Soames to the *Standard*, *The Oldie* quickly established itself as an excellent general interest magazine. Ingrams' natural talent as an editor imposed a cohesive, conversational style that has not diminished the magazine's intelligent voice. Again, he has demonstrated his remarkable talent for commanding the loyalty of first-rate contributors: William Trevor, Patricia Highsmith, Beryl Bainbridge, Ruth Rendell, Eric Newby, Harry Enfield, Barry Humphries, even Barbara Cartland, all have contributed work in return for the traditional Ingrams microscopic fee. As with the *Eye*, outspokenness has been encouraged – by Auberon Waugh and by *The Oldie*'s own discovery, Harry Enfield's father Edward – without seeming to pull the whole in any discernible political direction. 'Richard never commissions a piece for or against anything,' explains Naim Attallah. 'He always leaves the opinion up to the journalist.'

Richard Ingrams

All the fatuous predictions about thinly concealed jealousy of fast, bright young lives, and the threatened obsession with the cares of Ingrams' sex and class, have failed to materialise. The magazine is indeed about the cares of his generation, but then that is what it is supposed to be about; some of the articles are submitted by the readers themselves. Ironically, with its roster of well-known contributors, its witty illustrated pieces and its gentle tone, *The Oldie* resembles nothing so much as a high-class *Punch*. Indeed, it has now been in touch with all the old *Punch* subscribers, hoping to secure their custom. The wheel has turned full circle since 1961. 'There's some incredible oldies sitting around with nothing to do,' says Ingrams excitedly about his search for new contributors. 'Men from *Punch* in 1950!'

Whether *The Oldie* will survive in the long term is difficult to predict. By the end of 1993 it had become locked into a Catch-22, needing to advertise to increase sales to a profitable level, but unable until sales became profitable to afford advertising in the first place. The sales figures were bumping along just under the break-even point. It had taken *Private Eye* almost a decade to reach permanent financial security, but its overheads had been lower, and the whole enterprise for many had been a labour of love. *The Oldie*, by comparison, was a fully staffed and equipped magazine, with computers programmed to growl 'Bollocks!' in the recorded voice of the editor, whenever a typing error was made.

It was clear that, despite Ingrams' initial remarks about business sense, Naim Attallah would have to be approached again. Another £300,000 was needed, but this time Attallah balked. He did not have that kind of ready cash, he complained. Tiny Rowland of Lonrho was approached instead, but he too pulled back at the last minute. Things looked bleak, and *The Oldie* seemed set to close. Then Attallah relented. He could not, he explained, bear the thought of Dempster and McKay crowing over the magazine's closure. For their sakes alone, he would save it. Ingrams' old muckers had indirectly done him a huge favour.

Six months later, a similar crisis occurred. This time, Attallah decided to pull all his money out – ironically at a time when the magazine was in credit – and the closure of *The Oldie* was

370

announced in the national press in July 1994. The magazine's small but loyal readership wrote to complain in droves, and once again its publisher relented. As of August 1994, *The Oldie* re-appeared as a monthly.

On the same day that *The Oldie*'s closure had been announced, Richard had received a communication from BBC Radio 4. In search of a new, go-ahead, youthful identity, the station would be dropping him from his regular captaincy on *The News Quiz*; in the Autumn series, he would be appearing just four times, on the grounds that he was 'too old'. Ingrams had been hoist by his own comic persona. In the same post he received a letter from the programme's producer, unaware of the managerial decision. 'I hope you are having a relaxing summer,' it said.

Richard seemed untroubled by the news. 'Perhaps I am too old for it,' he mused. 'I can see why they want someone else. These days the questions are no longer aimed at the individual panellists like me – they're all about vicars travelling the wrong way up the motorway. It's not what it was. In the whole of 1994, for instance, there hasn't been one question about the Child Support Agency. If you only cover funny vicars, the thing loses its satirical bite.' The old Ingrams would have exacted a terrible revenge at this slight. The new-look Ingrams simply shrugged his shoulders and moved on.

In 1994, a grand 'Oldie of the Year' lunch was held at the Dorchester. If the patching up of any previous differences with Patrick Marnham and Bill Deedes had been surprising, then the cast of elderly celebrities that joined Ingrams at the top table was positively eyecatching. Denis Thatcher, Lord Longford, the Duke of Devonshire . . . former *Eye* targets all, the subjects of relentless merriment and scorn; Nigel Dempster had once nominated the Duke as *Private Eye*'s 'Shit of the Year'. Clearly, an atmosphere of reconciliation was in the air. Ingrams was becoming more relaxed and forgiving in his old age.

Yet this generosity was not, for the most part, born merely of indulgent seniority; far from it. For in the absence of Mary, one of those fast, bright young lives had passed into and softened Ingrams' own.

26 Big Debbie

The Groucho Club, for those unfamiliar with this Soho landmark, is an *ersatz* London club established with members of the media in mind, rather as the Garrick was once set up for actors. The armchairs are convincingly deep but the atmosphere is fashionably informal. Simply to be seen there is one of the most important professional advantages that membership can confer. The fast, the bright and the young are much in evidence. Sawdust and old men in cloth caps there are none. Back in the late 1980s, it was probably the last place on earth in which you'd expect to find Richard Ingrams.

'One night Dad and I were sitting in the Coach and Horses,' relates Fred Ingrams, 'and Jeffrey Bernard was pissed and shouting at him, and there were millions of trendies and it was packed, and he said, "I can't stand this pub any more". I said to him, "Why don't you come to the Groucho?" And he said, "I can't possibly. It's full of dreadful advertising people". And I said, "No it's not, come along". So I took him there, and in walked Liz Calder and a dozen other people that he knew, and we ended up with a table of about ten people, who were all totally gobsmacked to see him in there, and he had a blinding evening. He became a member on the spot. Now he's got somewhere to go, that's really brought him out of himself.'

Norm down at the Coach was scornful. 'He said he didn't want to go there. Now he's completely changed his whole outlook on life,' muttered the deserted landlord. Nigel Dempster in the

Mail was equally surprised, as he described how Ingrams had become the instant focus of youthful attention at the Groucho: 'His grizzled head remains smiling and, yes, gnomic as gales of twentysomething laughter and bright-eyed chatter swirl around him.'[1] The Ingrams mixture of avuncular charm and scruffy helplessness had earned him a new female fan club, with his own daughter at its centre. 'I do enjoy the company of women,' admitted Ingrams, 'and now I'm very old and grey I like the company of young girls – Jubby and her friends, for instance. I love being with them and I suppose they make me feel younger.'[2] By which he meant that he could combine the social enjoyments of youth with the undue respect accorded to one of his advancing years.

Deborah Bosley managed the members' accommodation at the Groucho Club. A working-class girl from a Brixton council estate, she was in her late twenties, tall and blonde (in a Mediterranean-looking rather than a Germanic way), chatty, independent and self-assured. Her father was a builder and her two brothers professional footballers; one of them had kept goal for Wimbledon. Deborah too was athletic, and had once represented Surrey as a swimmer. Some years before, while on a hitch-hiking holiday in North America, she had met and fallen in love with Brett Bennett, a smart, dazzlingly good-looking architect from Michigan. She had abandoned a place at the London School of Economics and taken a job researching the *Rough Guide to California,* in order to return to America to be with him. There, on her second visit in 1988, they married. Before the wedding, he confessed to her that he was homosexual, and announced that he had been diagnosed HIV positive. They married anyway, for love. In 1990 he left her, to spare her the pain of watching him die, and she returned heartbroken to England.

In the summer of 1992, while she was working at the Groucho Club, her husband's mother contacted her, to tell her that Brett had reached the end, and was on his deathbed. She resigned her job to go and be with him as he died, and thereafter to make a new life in America. Richard Ingrams – no more than a nodding acquaintance – sympathetically wished her well, gave her a copy of *England – An Anthology* as a memento of her former home and told her to send him a postcard. From such unlikely beginnings, a romance flowered.

On her first night in Michigan, Deborah had a vivid dream of Richard, standing by the railway track beside her home. 'I thought, "Why am I dreaming about Richard Ingrams? This is mad". Because I certainly wasn't attracted to him, he was far too old, he was about the same age as my dad, probably older. I thought, "Old git". But he kept coming into my mind.' So she wrote to him, and he wrote back to her, and a regular correspondence of increasingly heartfelt and intimate detail developed. 'We gradually revealed more and more to each other,' she says, 'so I suppose I felt I knew him quite well.'

For Richard to discuss his personal life with his close friends was almost unheard of, let alone with a complete stranger; but the fact that Deborah was thousands of miles away and not coming back made her a safe and sympathetic ear for a man who longed to confide in somebody. When she wrote to him, suggesting that she change her plans and return to England, he wrote back advising her to be resolute, and to stay in the States. It was too late: his letter crossed the Atlantic at the same time as she did, travelling in the opposite direction.

Upon returning to London, she deliberately did not get in touch; she does not know why. Then the Groucho Club inadvertently put its oar in. Jubby Ingrams was organising a fortieth birthday party for her husband, and the cook who had been hired had let them down. Would Deborah come in and help out? Short of ready cash, she agreed; and there she was, arranging the food, when Richard came in and saw her. 'He walked in, and I looked at him, and I just felt *incredibly* embarrassed. I thought, *Oh my God, I fancy him, I can't stand it.* I was busying myself at the oven, and tossing salads, and mixing drinks, and I just couldn't look at him, couldn't talk to him, couldn't say hello to him.'

Unaware of this internal melodrama, Richard invited her down to Aldworth for the weekend, with David and Jubby. Dry-mouthed with embarrassment, she accepted. 'I don't think I'd have gone if David and Jubby weren't there. But then I didn't think anything was going to happen. I was just nervous because I knew the way I felt.' In due course, the inevitable did happen. 'I suppose I felt that it would last a month. And here we are, years later. In many ways it's the nicest relationship I've ever had. It's certainly the least complicated – although we never talk about the future. He's just a joy to be with – he's so *easy* to be with. It's certainly not what I had in mind for myself at all.'

In the spring of 1993, soon after Deborah had moved into Aldworth, the press found out. According to Ingrams, he let the secret slip at an *Eye* lunch, and Silvester was out of the doorway to the public telephone faster than the Flying Scotsman. Silvester denies this, and claims that the journalist Michael Bywater discovered the story by himself. Certainly it was Bywater who devised the nickname 'Big Debbie'; although, apart from the fact that she is 5 foot 10 inches tall, it's not easy to see why. 'That was made up because it fits the newspapers' idea of this fantastic busty Scandinavian-type blonde,' she suggests.

For days, tabloid journalists camped outside the house. When Deborah drove into Goring, two cars of *Mail* reporters and photographers pursued her across the Downs. A troublesome Ingrams cartilage was transformed at the stroke of a pen into a recurrence of the old back injury, with the clear implication that it had been triggered off swinging upside down from the chandeliers. The *Mail* also revealed that another elderly journalist, the sixty-year-old Jeffrey Bernard, harboured an unrequited passion for 'the statuesque blonde', and quoted Bernard likening Ingrams to Hitler. That well-known fount of reliable gossip *The Times* reported eagerly on how the 'flashing-eyed party in her late twenties' had been 'unable to resist the call of the corduroy'.[3] Mary, of course, was canvassed for her views. 'I think it's pathetic,' she told the *Mail*, 'ending up with a girl younger than his daughter.'

The further discovery, a fortnight later, that Deborah's husband had died of AIDS was a source of barely repressed journalistic glee. 'Will this put years on the Oldie . . . ?' asked Nigel Dempster in his lead story, going on to describe Ingrams as 'scrofulous', his estranged wife as 'long-suffering' and his girlfriend

375

as 'strapping'. 'Says Debbie reassuringly: "I haven't got AIDS",'
quoted the diarist in conclusion.[4] Other, later stories returned
to the AIDS theme, and claimed (wrongly) that Deborah 'likes
the idea of having children and is off the Pill'.[5] The *Mail* offered
cash for her exclusive story, but she dismissively turned the
money down. The demise of the relationship has since been reported (entirely eroneously) in various newspapers.

Concentrated press attention notwithstanding, the change of
partner from Mary to Deborah has undoubtedly had a beneficial
effect on the man at the centre of it all. 'Richard's more relaxed
now, more laid back,' remarks a surprised David Cash. 'He's a
much easier person to get on with these days.' Richard's garden-
er told Jubby Ingrams that her father 'goes about his day like
he hasn't got a care in the world'. According to Naim Attallah,
'Lately, Richard is much more relaxed than I've ever seen him. I
think perhaps he's discovered that to enjoy yourself doesn't make
you immoral. Morality doesn't necessarily make you happy, or
sustain your family life.' It cannot have been a coincidence that
Richard Ingrams, a man trying to preserve moral standards in an
often unhappy marriage, always reserved his sternest disapproval
for those whose immoral behaviour undermined their otherwise
happy marriages.

'Perhaps in my time I have been too censorious,' admits a
chastened Ingrams. 'When you're young and have a secure married life, you tend to be critical of people with chaotic lives. I was
genuinely appalled by Profumo's behaviour all those years ago.
Now I would be more tolerant. I would have mocked and attacked
the Bishop of Gloucester [accused of homosexual offences] in the
past, but now I feel very sorry for him. I believe he succumbed
to a mad urge which he now regrets. I think his case is tragic.'[6]
Sitting on *The News Quiz* next to Ian Hislop, as Hislop laid into
Sir Allan Green, the hypocritical kerb-crawling Director of Public
Prosecutions, all Ingrams found himself thinking was 'Poor Old Sir
Allan Green'. Reflects Hislop: 'I think Richard might be less cruel
now in some of his humour, because he's got older, and he's got
hurt more.'

Ingrams' former staff on *Private Eye* couldn't believe the

way their old boss was mellowing. 'He's changed his mind so much,' marvels Maggie Lunn. 'He was against people living together until his son Fred started living with Sarah Jane, then he realised it was all right. He didn't approve of Foot or McKay or A.N. Wilson splitting with their wives, then when Mary left him, suddenly it was fine.' Sheila Molnar agrees: 'Until something directly happens to him he's too single-minded to see others' points of view. We all wanted Fred to turn out gay, so he'd know what that was like too.'

The accusation of hypocrisy, historically the most damaging on the Ingrams charge-sheet, hangs unspoken in the air; but that would not be fair. For Ingrams has stuck to his principles as always, and has done his damnedest to avoid these fates befalling him. He did not ask for a divorce, or to be left, or to be the grandfather of an illegitimate child. The difference now is not that he has changed his view, but that he has become tolerant, through experience, of those who have such situations thrust upon them – whether by others, or, in the case of the Bishop of Gloucester, by their own private urges. One hesitates to suggest it, but there is a degree of tolerance here worthy of the most bearded Church of England vicar. The foot that Ingrams had planted on the road towards puritanism was now being firmly withdrawn. Lord Lambton, who had once resigned from a Conservative government over his affair with a prostitute, was gratefully embraced as a backer for *The Oldie*. Ingrams even agreed to present a television programme, in praise of the older man, whose executive producer was none other than Jocelyn Targett. Dempster and McKay excepted, Ingrams had declared a general amnesty.

One possible reason that the Ingrams moral grip has relaxed lies in the different kind of relationship he enjoys with his new partner. Whereas Mary was happy to back him up in any argument but ready to fight him over matters marital and domestic, with Deborah it is rather the reverse. Any Catholic moral attitudes that cautiously poke their heads above the parapet are liable to be scythed down by a hail of twenty-nine-year-old opinions. 'Don't be ridiculous,' she will exclaim peremptorily. Not that it is easy

377

to square up to anyone as unconfrontational as Richard Ingrams. 'It's almost impossible to have an argument with him,' she says. 'I have the argument, and he takes it manfully, that's it. Whenever I get into a temper I think, "This is no good, I should just meet someone my own age, I mean this is ridiculous, I can't live with someone the same age as my dad, I want to do things, have a good time, live in London" . . . except I don't, really. I just say it. I am actually really happy with him. I sometimes think, "I must need more than this. Our life together is so *dreary*, it's so *boring*". But that's what makes me so happy.' Richard has even learnt to cook and wash up – as long as he's not ordered to do it, of course.

The age gap has not been a problem for Jubby, who has become one of Deborah's best friends. Fred, who once said, 'It wouldn't bother me if he got a girlfriend', found it harder to adjust initially, but is coming to terms with the idea that he is older than his father's girlfriend. The content of Mary's phone calls to Deborah is not difficult to guess.

Mary finally got her divorce in 1994; Richard was allowed to keep the house, but had to find half its £300,000 value in cash in addition to alimony payments. Once again, there were lawyers to be listened to at length, and to be paid at fantastic expense. 'A nightmare,' says Richard.

'He would have stuck by Mary if she'd have had him,' says Deborah. 'He'd have done it to the death, that's the amazing thing about him. He would have sacrificed his personal happiness to have stuck by her. He shows absolutely no signs of bitterness towards her. It's almost like he's striving to be good. He doesn't want to lower himself into the fray of personal malice and nastiness. He wants to be a good man. He *is* a good man. There's no question about it, he's a really good man. He's generous, he's kind, he's loving. Maybe he used his professional life as an outlet for all the anger that he refused to spray around in his personal life. I don't know.'

Richard's divorce will cost him a huge amount of money, but it's money he probably possesses. There's the *Eye* pension, there are shares in the *Eye*'s distribution company and in Private Eye

Productions Limited (which produces the *Eye* books), and there's probably still some family money somewhere, lying around at the bottom of the vaults. Certainly, he felt sufficiently comfortably off to turn down £150,000 to write his autobiography. His finances remain an utter mystery to everyone, himself included. The *Eye*'s accountant Sheila Molnar reckons that 'he probably doesn't know what his income is, until he goes to see his own accountant once a year.'

In 1994 he even took three months off work, and handed the editorship of *The Oldie* over to Donald Trelford, formerly of the *Observer*, formerly the butt of several 'pixie' jokes in the *Eye*, a journalist, no less, who had once sued Richard Ingrams. Truly it was the season of forgiveness. The reason for this departure from his beloved magazine was to write, after twenty years, his long-awaited biography of Malcolm Muggeridge. Deborah typed it, grudgingly, because Richard only possessed a manual typewriter that predated Harold Macmillan. To undertake a task like that, she had to be happy; and so did he.

'I *am* a lot happier,' he smiles grudgingly.

27

'Richard is like looking at something through a prism,' concludes
Barry Fantoni. 'You think you've got it all sorted out and then
suddenly the light shifts, and you see a whole area that you
haven't seen before, that's not been examined, and you suspect
that he hasn't been there very often himself. It does make him
one of the most interesting men. If not a great man, certainly an
original man.' Richard Ingrams is indeed a complex character, full
of contrasts that verge on the contradictory: he is an elitist, but not
a snob; he is a moralist, but not a puritan; he is brave, but unable
to face a fuss; he detests power-seekers, but he is the autocratic
leader of the gang; he is a teetotaller, who loves to be with his
friends in the bar; he adores women, but is prepared to let them
run around after him; he is a self-publicist, who likes to keep his
cards close to his chest; and – not such an uncommon paradox,
this – he makes people laugh despite having led a largely unhappy
life. He used to list his chief faults as intolerance, and a refusal to
admit errors; but in recent years, he has even begun to display
tolerance and flexibility.

Much of the perceived enigma of Richard Ingrams derives
from these and other contrasts, which give so much ammunition
both to the friend and to the foe in any argument regarding
his character. Harnessed to them are a number of memorable
attributes: an obsessive need to fight hypocrisy, an inspirational
capacity for leadership and an admirable refusal to buckle under
when bullied. The whole is framed by an air of mystery created
380

by nothing more sinister than a love of domestic privacy and a vivid horror of meeting new people, lest they bore him. As Peter McKay said so memorably, 'Ingrams would justify the Second World War by saying it repelled bores.'[1]

At the heart of all Ingrams' attitudes lie three fundamental influences. The first is his fellow-travelling Catholicism, with its attendant feelings of guilt and inner melancholy. Personal tragedies, of the sort that he has suffered so repeatedly, tend to inspire their victims either to reject God utterly, or to be drawn more closely to him; Ingrams falls into the latter category. 'That sort of unhappiness makes someone closer to God and makes them a better person,' reckons Candida Lycett Green. The truths for which Ingrams' *Private Eye* always strove sprung indirectly from these religious beliefs: 'In making certain kinds of judgement, that certain things that people did were reprehensible and were not to be trusted,' explains Christopher Logue, 'there was an idea of truth to which Ingrams responded, and that truth was a rationlisation of faith.'

Also strongly influential is Ingrams' patrician background, and the love for England he holds, suffused with his innate capacity for nostalgia. *Private Eye* was not a force for revolution, despite Foot's fantasies, but a conservative force, intended to keep England on the rails. In many ways it was, as Ingrams admitted, 'an ultra-respectable publication – one of the few left, along with the *Daily Telegraph*.'[2] Its amateur appearance was deliberate, but not, as its enemies protested, intended to conceal a professional capacity for subversion; rather, it was the traditional cultivated amateurism of patrician England. Historically, many successful satirists have tended towards conservatism: revolutionaries usually employ hatred and resentment rather than wit or mockery. Ian Hislop likens Ingrams to Juvenal – 'Upper middle class, old Roman money, displaced and wandering the streets, looking at ghastly Egyptians who had made lots of money and useless poets who weren't any good; and so he retreated to the country.' Eventually, Juvenal's Rome was destroyed by the barbarians. One hopes that Ingrams' England will prove more enduring.

Thirdly, there is Ingrams' vital sense of humour, and above

all his sense of mischief, partly inherited from his father and partly born of misery, like that of so many comedians. 'You must never forget with Ingrams that he is a performer,' Willie Rushton reminds us, 'and that sometimes he is howling with laughter behind that face; for instance when people think, "Oh Jesus Christ, I've obviously upset the old man". I mean this old man thing, he's been putting that on for years.'

The sheer pervasiveness of Ingrams' sense of humour has led to accusations that it is nothing more than a defence against emotional involvement, like his fear of being bored. Lynn Barber wrote that 'Ingrams – and also Auberon Waugh – use the word "bore" in a very distinctive way. They don't really mean someone who bores you by talking about knitting or how to get on to the M11: they mean someone who threatens you with moral reproach. Bores are people who have convictions, who passionately believe in something, and try to persuade you to their viewpoint . . . They cannot be deflected with a joke – hence their alarmingness. But I believe that, deep down, both Waugh and Ingrams admire such people and feel guilty at their own comparative frivolity.'[3]

Wrong. Hopelessly, utterly wrong. People whose opinions are so important to them that they cannot be deflected with a joke *are* boring, or worse than that, dangerous. They are extremists, whether they be tiresome and unimportant or powerful and frightening. In that sense, yes, the Second World War did repel a bore, the most terrifying, humourless bore that ever passionately believed in his own convictions. Of course Ingrams and Waugh do not admire such people, they have spent their lives fighting such people. Frivolity – and in particular the capacity to make jokes at those whose passionate beliefs have carried them into authority – has been one of the most powerful stabilising forces in English society. Ingrams and Waugh have harnessed frivolity brilliantly; of course their choice of targets is entirely open to debate, but they have chosen the noblest weapon available to them. To suggest that their very calling might inspire guilt is laughable.

Private Eye's enemies have always accused it, and Ingrams, of using 'schoolboy humour'; the charge has been levelled time and time again. This too is nonsense. Children laugh principally at parts of the body and at broad slapstick, not at satire. Children's humour finds its adult parallel in the *Carry On* films and their like, not in the pages of *Private Eye*, which have been notably free of naughty words and *double entendres*. As Ian Hislop complained, 'All humour is described as schoolboy unless it's Jimmy Tarbuck and Molly Sugden, and somehow that's "adult". I've never quite understood why that constitutes "adult" humour.'[4]

Humour is of course hugely subjective. When somebody does not laugh at something that many others find funny, it often means that their sense of humour is either more sophisticated or less sophisticated than the level of the humour on offer; but of course, nobody can understand or accept that they have a less sophisticated sense of humour than their peers. So they deride the humorist from a position of superiority, often with the accusation that he purveys 'schoolboy' or 'undergraduate' humour. Comedians and comic writers are relentlessly pilloried by dim-witted reviewers in this fashion, and suffer abuse on a level that no other entertainers, broadcasters or writers have to experience. To suggest, however, that an inability to take things seriously in itself betokens immaturity is nonsense. Children take the slightest of matters seriously; the ability to undercut this with humour is one of the very last attributes that they develop. Humour is the most sophisticated quality in the animal kingdom, the one that above all else marks man out from his fellow creatures. The person who does not have the capacity to laugh at anybody or anything if they so choose is the one who has not developed; not the other way around.

Of course Shrewsbury School did play a large part in fashioning Richard Ingrams and his colleagues, as most schools do to their pupils. His dislike of pretension and pseudo-intellectualism and his contempt for grey conformity were both formed there; but the early and confident formation of adult points of view is a sign of maturity, not of immaturity. On the negative side, Ingrams' relentless capacity for revenge is perhaps a reaction to the bullying of West Downs, the army and Shrewsbury's early years, while the emotional reticence of his family and of his class was undoubtedly exacerbated by the English public school system and the military.

383

'You're sent away to school when you're seven and you crawl into a shell from which you never quite come out,' he admits.[5]

Most people tend to react to their schooling either by becoming liberated ('When I'm grown up I'll do all the wonderful things I'm prevented from doing now') or empowered ('When I grow up I'll be able to push people around just like the teacher/prefect/school bully'). The eccentric lives of Richard Ingrams and his friends were a classic reaction in the former manner, to the regimented nature of their schooling and their military service. Their enemies were those who followed the latter course. *Private Eye* lay in direct line of succession from *The Salopian, The Wollopian, Parson's Pleasure* and *Mesopotamia*. Although Ingrams may not have known it, he was a natural satirist from an early age; for if we are to believe Fowler, the aim of humour is discovery, that of wit is to throw light, of sarcasm is to inflict pain, of invective is to discredit, and of irony is to exclude; but the aim of satire is to amend, in the province of morals and manners.

Private Eye was Richard Ingrams' 'astonishing accomplishment' and 'amazing achievement', to use the words of Paul Foot. The magazine's founding fathers have probably had a more profound effect on post-war British journalism than anybody else except Rupert Murdoch (a man who, unlike Robert Maxwell, had the good sense to keep his head down, and who has suffered remarkably little at the *Eye*'s hands as a result). *Private Eye*'s reportage influenced and educated the intelligent British middle class in a manner that had the rest of the quality press scurrying to catch up. More than that, it was the only humour magazine of consistent quality available in this country throughout the Sixties, Seventies and Eighties.

The Fleet Street gossip network that once sustained the news side of *Private Eye* has broken up now, scattered to the suburbs and to the grubby Docklands by the breeze of new technology that blew away the old print unions; but Ian Hislop has subtly altered the magazine's nature, specialising the news side in such a way that the industrial changes have not done any damage. Nor will libel ever finish off the *Eye*'s satirists: if a really monstrous, gigantic sum is ever awarded against them, they'll simply set up another company, flog the title to themselves for 5p and leave Peter Cook with debts of several million pounds, in revenge for naming the Krays all those years ago. No, the principal danger facing the *Eye* is simply that, as Tony Rushton says, 'We'll all fall off our perches soon.' When that happens, then Hislop will have a task on his hands. 'I hope he does stay,' says Ingrams, 'because I don't know who else could take over.' For the time being at least, though, the old Oxford gang still meets three days a fortnight at Carlisle Street, to bicker affectionately and make each other laugh.

Today, Ingrams' past is crumbling away to nothing. Ellon Castle has been sold, as has the Chesnuts, which has been made into flats. The wall that enclosed the garden in which he and his brothers used to play as children has been demolished. West Downs has closed for good. The house in Cheyne Row was sold many years ago, and the King's Head and Eight Bells is unrecognisable from what it once was. Peter John and Rupert are dead, all the old men are dead, and Mary has gone. Still, Richard Ingrams seems happier now than he has been for a long time. He even has a relevant Kek 'spell' to answer any nosy questions about his state of mind:

'Was he free? Was he happy? The question's absurd.
Had anything been wrong we should certainly have heard.'

Notes

Chapter 1

1. Sefton Delmer/*Black Boomerang*
2. Ellic Howe/*The Black Game*
3. Ibid.

Chapter 2

1. Michaela Reid/*Ask Sir James*

Chapter 3

1. Mark Hichens/*West Downs*
2. Ibid.
3. Ibid.
4. Willans & Searle/*How To Be Topp*

Chapter 5

1. Richard Ingrams/*The Life and Times of Private Eye*
2. Ibid.
3. Ibid.

Chapter 6

1. Richard Ingrams/Foreword to *England – An Anthology*
2. *Observer*, 28 October 1990
3. Ibid.
4. *Vogue*, 1971 and *Daily Telegraph Magazine*, 1993

Chapter 7

1. *Independent on Sunday*, 16 February 1992
2. Ibid.

Chapter 8

1. *Oxford Opinion*, 1959
2. Edward Whitley/*The Graduates*
3. Ibid.
4. Ibid.
5. Ibid.
6. Ibid.
7. Patrick Marnham/*The Private Eye Story*
8. Ibid.
9. Edward Whitley/*The Graduates*

Chapter 9

1. *Observer*, 28 October 1990

2. *Vogue*, 1971
3. Ibid.

Chapter 10

1. Patrick Marnham/*The Private Eye Story*
2. *Private Eye – Public Interest?* BBC Radio 4, 16 October 1978
3. Patrick Marnham/*The Private Eye Story*
4. Richard Ingrams/*The Life and Times of Private Eye*
5. Ibid.

Chapter 11

1. BBC Radio 4, 1991
2. The *New Daily*
3. BBC Home Service, 1962
4. *Q* magazine, 1991
5. Patrick Marnham/*The Private Eye Story*
6. Ibid.
7. Ibid.
8. Richard Ingrams/*The Life and Times of Private Eye*
9. Ibid.
10. Ibid.
11. Ibid.
12. Ibid.
13. Ibid.
14. BBC Radio 4, 1991
15. Patrick Marnham/*The Private Eye Story*

Chapter 12

1. Patrick Marnham/*The Private Eye Story*

2. Richard Ingrams/*The Life and Times of Private Eye*
3. BBC Radio 4 *Woman's Hour*, 1977
4. Richard Ingrams/*The Life and Times of Private Eye*
5. Edward Whitley/*The Graduates*
6. Patrick Marnham/*The Private Eye Story*
7. Richard Ingrams/*The Life and Times of Private Eye*
8. Ibid.
9. Patrick Marnham/*The Private Eye Story*
10. Ibid.
11. Richard Ingrams/*The Life and Times of Private Eye*
12. Patrick Marnham/*The Private Eye Story*
13. Ibid.
14. LWT/*South Bank Show*, 1991

Chapter 13

1. Richard Ingrams/*The Life and Times of Private Eye*
2. Ibid.
3. Ibid.
4. Patrick Marnham/*The Private Eye Story*
5. Richard Ingrams/*The Life and Times of Private Eye*
6. Ibid.
7. Ibid.
8. Richard Ingrams/*Goldenballs*
9. *Sunday Times*, 1967
10. *Woman's Own*, 1967
11. Richard Ingrams/*The Life and Times of Private Eye*
12. Ibid.
13. Ibid.
14. Patrick Marnham/*The Private*

Eye Story
15. *Independent,* 30 March 1993
16. *Observer,* 28 October 1990
17. *Sunday Telegraph*
18. *Private Eye – Public Interest?*
    BBC Radio 4, 16 October 1978

Chapter 14

1. *Sunday Telegraph,* 9 May 1993
2. *Campaign,* 30 April 1976
3. *Ibid.*
4. Patrick Marnham/*The Private
   Eye Story*
5. *Observer,* 28 October 1990
6. Patrick Marnham/*The Private
   Eye Story*
7. *Observer,* 28 October 1990
8. Edward Whitley/*The Graduates*
9. Richard Ingrams/*Goldenballs*
10. *Campaign,* 30 April 1976
11. Richard Ingrams/*Goldenballs*
12. BBC Radio 4, 1983
13. Edward Whitley/*The Graduates*
14. Patrick Marnham/*The Private
    Eye Story*
15. BBC Radio 4, 1991
16. Patrick Marnham/*The Private
    Eye Story*

Chapter 15

1. Edward Whitley/*The Graduates*
2. *Observer,* 28 October 1990
3. Ibid.
4. Patrick Marnham/*The Private
   Eye Story*
5. Ibid.
6. Ibid.
7. *Observer,* 28 October 1990
8. Ibid.

9. *Private Eye – Public Interest?*
   BBC Radio 4, 16 October 1978
10. Patrick Marnham/*The Private
    Eye Story*
11. LWT/*South Bank Show,* 1991
12. Patrick Marnham/*The Private
    Eye Story*
13. Ibid.

Chapter 16

1. Edward Whitley/*The Graduates*
2. *Campaign,* 30 April 1976
3. Patrick Marnham/*The Private
   Eye Story*
4. Ibid.
5. *Spectator,* 1976
6. Patrick Marnham/*The Private
   Eye Story*
7. Ibid.
8. BBC Radio 4, 1983
9. Patrick Marnham/*The Private
   Eye Story*
10. Ibid.
11. *Private Eye – Public Interest?*
    BBC Radio 4, 16 October 1978
12. Ibid.
13. LWT/*South Bank Show,* 1991

Chapter 17

1. *Vogue,* 1971
2. *Private Eye,* 12 May 1978
3. *Private Eye – Public Interest?*
   BBC Radio 4, 16 October 1978
4. LWT/*South Bank Show,* 1991
5. *Private Eye – Public Interest?*
   BBC Radio 4, 16 October
   1978
6. *Observer,* 28 October 1990
7. Ibid.

8. *Sunday Telegraph,* 9 May 1993
9. Ibid.
10. *Cream* magazine
11. *TLS,* November 1972
12. *Observer,* 28 October 1990
13. Edward Whitley/*The Graduates*
14. LWT/*South Bank Show,* 1991
15. Patrick Marnham/*The Private Eye Story*
16. *Media Week,* 26 July 1985
17. Edward Whitley/*The Graduates*
18. *Observer,* 28 October 1990
19. Ibid.
20. BBC Radio 4, 1991
21. *Sunday Telegraph,* 9 May 1993
22. Patrick Marnham/*The Private Eye Story*
23. *Observer,* 28 October 1990
24. BBC Radio 4, 1991
25. BBC Radio 4, 1991
26. BBC Radio 4, 1991
27. LWT/*South Bank Show,* 1991
28. *Observer,* 28 October 1990
29. BBC Radio 4, 1983

Chapter 18

1. Richard Ingrams/*Goldenballs*
2. Ivan Fallon/*Billionaire*
3. *Campaign,* 30 April 1976
4. Richard Ingrams/*Goldenballs*
5. Ivan Fallon/*Billionaire*
6. Patrick Marnham/*The Private Eye Story*
7. Richard Ingrams/*Goldenballs*
8. Ibid.
9. Ibid.
10. Patrick Marnham/*The Private Eye Story*
11. Ibid.
12. Ivan Fallon/*Billionaire*

Chapter 19

1. *Observer,* 28 October 1990
2. *Independent on Sunday,* 16 February 1992
3. *Evening Standard,* 1981
4. *Independent on Sunday,* 16 February 1992
5. *Country Homes and Interiors,* August 1992
6. Patrick Marnham/*The Private Eye Story*
7. *Independent on Sunday,* 16 February 1992
8. Ibid

Chapter 20

1. BBC Radio 4, 1983
2. Edward Whitley/*The Graduates*
3. BBC Radio 4, *PM,* 1982
4. BBC Radio 2, *John Dunn Show*
5. Patrick Marnham/*The Private Eye Story*
6. Ibid.
7. *Harpers & Queen,* 1991
8. Patrick Marnham/*The Private Eye Story*
9. Ibid.
10. *The Listener,* November 1982
11. *Spectator,* 1992
12. London Weekend Television
13. *Spectator,* 1991
14. *Independent on Sunday,* 1992
15. *Observer,* 28 October 1990
16. *Q Magazine,* 1992
17. LWT/*South Bank Show,* 1991

Chapter 21

1. LWT/*South Bank Show*, 1991
2. BBC Radio 4, 1991
3. *Observer*, 28 October 1990
4. BBC Radio 4, 1983

Chapter 22

1. BBC Radio 4, 14 March 1986
2. *Sunday Times*, March 1986
3. Peter McKay/*Inside Private Eye*
4. *Sunday Times*, March 1986
5. Patrick Marnham/*The Private Eye Story*
6. Ibid.
7. Ibid.
8. *Evening Standard*, 20 September 1991
9. Peter McKay/*Inside Private Eye*
10. *Mail on Sunday*, 1986
11. *Ritz*, 1986
12. *Evening Standard*, 17 September 1991
13. *Guardian*, 17 February 1992
14. *Independent*, 30 March 1993
15. *Independent on Sunday*, 16 February 1992
16. *Sunday Telegraph*, 9 May 1993
17. *Guardian*, 17 February 1992
18. *Q Magazine*, 1992
19. *Sunday Times*, 1993
20. Ibid.
21. *Night & Day*, 30 January 1994

Chapter 23

1. *Independent on Sunday*, 16 February 1992
2. *Observer*, 28 October 1990
3. *Independent on Sunday*, 16 February 1992

4. *Daily Mail*, 1 May 1993
5. BBC Radio 4, 1983
6. *Independent on Sunday*, 16 February 1992
7. *Independent*, 30 March 1993
8. *Independent on Sunday*, 16 February 1992, and *Independent*, 30 March 1993

Chapter 24

1. Richard Ingrams/*England – An Anthology*
2. André Maurois/*Three Letters on the English*
3. Richard Ingrams/*England – An Anthology*
4. Graham Laidler/*The World of Pont*
5. *Guardian*, 12 September 1992
6. Richard Ingrams/*God's Apology*
7. Ibid.
8. Ibid.
9. Ibid.
10. Ibid.
11. Ibid.
12. *Dr Johnson* by Mrs Thrale/(ed. Richard Ingrams)
13. Ibid.
14. Richard Ingrams/*England – An Anthology*
15. Richard Ingrams/*Cobbett's Country Book*
16. Ibid.
17. Ibid.
18. Richard Ingrams/*God's Apology*
19. Richard Ingrams/*The Ridgeway*
20. Ibid.
21. Richard Ingrams/*England – An Anthology*
22. *Observer*, 28 October 1990

Richard Ingrams

Chapter 25

1. *Independent on Sunday*, 28 February 1993
2. *Independent on Sunday*, 16 February 1992
3. *Q Magazine*, 1992
4. *Daily Mail*, 20 February 1992
5. *Guardian*, 17 February 1992
6. LWT/*South Bank Show*, 1991
7. *Independent on Sunday*, 16 February 1992
8. Ibid.

Chapter 26

1. *Daily Mail*, 20 February 1992
2. *Observer*, 28 October 1990
3. *The Times*, 17 April 1993
4. *Daily Mail*, 1 May 1993
5. *Daily Mail*, 27 February 1994
6. *Independent*, 30 March 1993

Chapter 27

1. Peter McKay/*Inside Private Eye*
2. BBC Radio 4, 1983
3. *Independent on Sunday*, 16 February 1992
4. Peter McKay/*Inside Private Eye*
5. *The Independent on Sunday*, 16 February 1992

Index

393

Vaughan Williams, Ralph, 21
Victoria, Queen, 9–10, 11, 17
VIIe Bodies society, 305
Viz, 196
Vorster, John, 206

Walden, Brian, 81, 85, 88, 259
Wallace, Colin, 285
Ward, Stephen, 153, 154, 227
Wardrop, Dr, 16
Warren, Master, 264
Watkins, Alan, 185
Watson, Colin, 157
Waugh, Alec, 356
Waugh, Auberon ('Bron'), 81, 87–8,
194, 196, 200, 212, 219, 227, 231,
232, 237, 254, 262, 272, 273, 286,
292, 299, 300, 307, 325, 359, 363,
364, 382; joins *Private Eye* (1970),
217–18, 283, 290; leaves the *Eye* to
edit *Literary Review*, 320–1; criticism
of *Private Eye* and Hislop, 322–3,
324, 331–2; and *Oldie* magazine,
364, 366, 367, 368, 369
Waugh, Evelyn, 87, 215
Webster, David, 93
The Week, 153
Weekending, 188
Weidenfeld, George, 262
Wells, John, 56, 74, 94, 98, 99, 106,
116, 118, 119, 121, 137, 138, 139,
150, 199, 203, 216, 217, 272, 273,
275, 294, 306, 328, 329; National
Service in Korea, 58, 61–2, 64; and
Mesopotamia, 90–2, 95; at Oxford,
81, 96, 97, 101, 108–9; Richard's
friendship with, 108–11, 198, 226,
283, 289–90, 315, 339–40, 367–8;
schoolmaster at Eton, 120, 137; and
Private Eye, 121, 122, 129, 137, 143,
161, 165–6, 173, 176, 177, 180, 184,
193, 195, 196, 197, 210, 213, 226,
229, 231, 237, 242, 244, 245, 248,
258, 292, 337, 339; leaves job at
Eton, 138; 'Dear Bill' letters written
by Richard and, 288–9; *Anyone for
Denis?* by, 288, 289; Princess
Margaret's friendship with, 289–90;
Lionel: The Musical by, 292
Wesker, Arnold, 117, 156
West, Richard, 185, 307, 324; *Victory in*

Vietnam, 292
West Downs prep school, 30, 337, 385;
Richard at, 22–9, 101, 194, 383
What The Papers Never Meant To Say,
209
What The Papers Say, 146
What The Papers Say, awards, 211
Wheen, Francis, 366
Wheldon, Sir Huw, 116
Which? magazine, 161
White, Sir Dick, 154
White, Sam, 262
Whitley, Edward, 197, 209
Whitman, Walt, 360
Widgery, Lord Chief Justice Lord, 264
Wien, Mr Justice, 259
Wigg, George, 153, 176–7, 224
Wilcox, Desmond, 3, 235, 240–1, 309
Williams, Geoffrey, 27
Williams, J.P.R., 279
Williams, Shirley, 216
Williamson, Professor, 103
Willis, Tim, 328
Wilson, A.N., 345, 366, 367, 377
Wilson, Harold, 128, 170, 185, 210,
211, 213, 219, 241, 255, 256, 267,
268, 287, 299; *Private Eye*'s attacks
on, 176, 177–8, 180, 210, 253–4,
268; alleged MI5 plot against, 254,
285; resignation as PM (1976),
261–2; and Honours List of, 262, 263
Wilson, Mary, 177–8, 210
Windsor, Barbara, 137
Wodehouse, P.G., 90, 169
Wogan, Terry, 241
Wolfenden, Sir John, 47
The Wollopian, school magazine, 46,
384
A Woman Killed With Kindness, 113
Woodstock Gallery, 144
Wordsworth, William, 51, 360
Worker's Press, 211
World's Press News, 122–3
Worsnip, Glyn, 81, 97, 116
Wright, Peter, 254
Wynne-Morgan, David, 205

Yeats, W.B., 52, 53

Zhivkov, Todor, 295
Zulueta, Father de, 20, 37